ANG NIMA SHERPA

पेनुरी शेर्पा खुम्जुङ
तेम्बा तेन्जी शेर्पा
कामी नोर्बु शेर्पा
पासङ तेन्जी शेर्पा
पीठ दफ्तरि

SIRDAR
PASSANG KAMI
SHERPA

THE SHERPAS OF NEPAL

By the same author

THE NAKED NAGAS (*Thacker, Spink*)
THE CHANDUS (*Macmillan*)
THE REDDIS OF THE BISON HILLS (*Macmillan*)
THE RAJ GONDS (*Macmillan*)
HIMALAYAN BARBARY (*John Murray*)
THE APA TANIS AND THEIR NEIGHBOURS (*Routledge*)

THE SHERPAS OF NEPAL

Buddhist Highlanders

Christoph von Fürer-Haimendorf
*Professor of Asian Anthropology
in the University of London*

OXFORD BOOK CO.
Park Street, Calcutta
& Scindia House, New Delhi

© *Christoph von Fürer-Haimendorf 1964*

*Printed in Great Britain
by Butler and Tanner Ltd, Frome
and London*

To
BETTY
my constant companion
on many
Himalayan journeys

Contents

	Preface	xiii
	Introduction	xvii
1	Environment and Economy	1
2	An Open Society	18
3	The Pattern of Family Life	39
4	Village Organization	100
5	Monastic Institutions and Priesthood	126
6	The Practice of Religion	175
7	The Control of Invisible Forces	251
8	Values and Moral Concepts	271
	Appendix	289
	Bibliography	292
	Index	295

Illustrations

Summer settlement at Gokyo, a typical high-altitude *yersa* with stone huts and walled-in meadows	xvi
Gelung Ngawang, the hermit of Nagarjung, in his meditation seat above Dingboche	xvii
Monks at the gate of Tengboche monastery; Mount Everest is visible in the background	xvii
The Monastery of Thami, consisting of small houses owned by individual monks	12
House and private chapel (*lha-kang*) in Khumjung	13
The temple and houses of Pangboche	13
Houses and fields of Khumjung; in the background a *chörten* and *mani*-wall	28
The central part of Khumjung; the village temple and sacred juniper grove are in the right hand background	28
Ploughing with *zopkio*; the woman walking behind the ploughman broadcasts buckwheat	29
Plough drawn by a team of men	29
Harvesting potatoes in Khumjung	44
Women of Khumjung preparing a field for the planting of potatoes	44
Yak on a high pasture above Gokyo	45
Harvesting barley at Dingboche	45
Sherpa girl of Namche Bazar	60
Young Sherpa couple of Khumjung	61
Women of Khumjung; the older holding a prayer-wheel, the younger offering liquor in a silver cup	61

Ngawang Ritu, a monk of Tengboche	76
A-Tutu, the spirit-medium (*lhawa*) of Khumjung	76
Pemba Kitar of Khumjung	77
A polyandrous wedding in Namche Bazar; the weeping bride sits between the two bridegrooms	92
Welcoming the bridegroom's party at a wedding in Khumjung. Pasang Sona Mendoa wields a whisk as he sprinkles a libation of beer	93
Wedding dance in the house of the bride	93
Participants in a meeting of the village-assembly (*yül-thim*) of Khumjung	108
Members of the village-assembly of Khumjung scrutinize the text of a resolution	108
The abbess of Devuche and Ang Nima, a layman of Khumjung living in retirement at Devuche	109
Nima Teshi, the guardian (*chorpen*) of the Khumjung temple, and his wife turning prayer-wheels during the Niungne celebrations	109
Monks and novices in the courtyard of Tengboche monastery	124
Chörten and *gomba* at Tengboche	125
The houses of monks surrounding the *gomba* of Tengboche monastery	125
The young reincarnate abbot of Tengboche monastery	140
Altar with sacrificial dough and butter figures (*torma*) at a mortuary rite held in a house of Khumjung	141
Chapel in the temple of Tengboche monastery with a statue of Gulu Lama, the founder of the monastery in the central niche and books in the racks to both sides	141
Novices in Tengboche monastery; the boy to the right is believed to be the reincarnation of a Tibetan lama	156
Frescoes in the private chapel of Kapa Kalden, the painter of Khumjung. The central figure represents Guru Rimpoche (Padmasambhava); to the extreme right is Opame (Amithaba)	157

Illustrations xi

Frescoes in the temple of Pangboche representing Chana-Dorje, the Wielder of the Thunderbolt (left) and one of the Guardians of the Four Quarters (right)   157

Procession encircling the village land of Khumjung during the Osho rite   172

Sprinkling libations at one of the corner stones of Khumjung during the Osho rite; a *torma* has been placed on the top of the corner stone   172

Procession during the Niungne rite. Penitents circumambulate a *mani*-wall and *chörten* outside Khumjung   173

A lama reads a legend to participants in the Niungne rite of Khumjung   173

Burning the Lokpar *torma* representing demonic fiends at the Dumje rite   188

A festive crowd during the Dumje celebrations in Khumjung   188

Weighing butter for the Yer-chang offerings   189

Dorje Ngungdu re-dedicating a yak to Khumbu-yülha at the Yer-chang rite   189

Dance of the heralds (*rul-tsam*) during the Mani-rimdu celebrations at Thami   204

Monks playing flageolets   205

Monks blowing conch-shells   205

The abbot and senior monks of Thami preside over the Mani-rimdu celebrations   220

Dance of the skeletons (*rurang*) at the Mani-rimdu   220

Dancer representing Raja Dorje Tolo at the Mani-rimdu in Thami   221

Dorje Ngundu reciting an invocation to the mountain-gods at the Yer-chang rite   221

Lamas before an altar with offerings and ritual objects at a cremation rite in Khumjung   236

Lamas reciting the prayers for the departed at a funeral in Khumjung   236

The distribution of money at a memorial rite (*gyewa*)	237
Guests at a memorial rite in Kunde awaiting the distribution of rice-balls and salt	237

MAPS (*between pp. 284/5*)

The regions of Khumbu, Pharak and Solu

The distribution of Sherpa and Bhotia Settlements in Eastern Nepal

Preface

In 1953 Nepal was a country virtually unknown to anthropologists, and when I set out for Khumbu, the region of high altitude at the foot of Mount Everest, I had only the vaguest idea of the people I would encounter. On that occasion I stayed for two months in the village of Khumjung and made a rapid survey of the other main settlements of Khumbu. Travelling on foot from Kathmandu to Khumbu I passed through Solu, and on the way back I spent some time there as well as in Pharak, while later that year I paid a brief visit to the Sherpas of the Yelmu region. These journeys were in the nature of a reconnaissance. In April 1957 I returned to Khumbu for a more intensive study of the Sherpas. Based on the twin villages of Khumjung and Kunde, I visited all their main villages and followed several groups of families to their summer settlements among the high pastures. In the late autumn of that year I moved from Khumbu south-eastwards, visiting Sherpa settlements in the area of the Hongu and Inukhu rivers, and undertook a brief survey of the Bhotia populations in the upper Arun valley and the Walungchung region.

My information on the scattered Sherpa groups in Western Nepal was gathered during a tour of the hills north-east of Pokhara in early 1958, and in 1962 I learnt about recent developments in Khumbu from Dorje Ngungdu and other Sherpas who accompanied me on a tour to Thak Khola, Dolpo, and Lo (Mustangbhot). The data on the Bhotias of Western Nepal included in this book for purposes of comparison were also obtained on that occasion.

All my work in Nepal was shared by my wife, who collected the greater part of the statistical data presented in the following chapters. On our journey in 1953 we were accompanied by Mr. Upendra Man Malla, and in the years 1957, 1958 and 1962 we benefited by the assistance of Mr. Dor Bahadur Bista. To both of these Nepalese scholars I am greatly indebted for their co-operation, given in a spirit of unflagging enthusiasm for the work we were doing.

For permission to work in Nepal and for many facilities provided I am deeply grateful to the Government of His Majesty the King of Nepal, and to the staff of the Royal Nepalese Embassy in London. Among the officials who gave me help and advice I should like to mention specifically my old friend Mr. Kaisher Bahadur, K.C., the late Mr. Nara Pratap Thapa, Professor Yadunath Khanal and Mr. P. C. Thakur. During our stay in Kathmandu we enjoyed on various occasions the hospitality of Sir Christopher and Lady Summerhayes, of Lt.-Col. and Mrs. Proud and Mr. and Mrs. Peter Wilde of the British Embassy. It was due to their unfailing helpfulness that mail and essential supplies reached us from time to time while we were in Khumbu and Thak Khola. For hospitality and much assistance we are indebted also to Dr. Toni and Mrs. Hagen, and to Mr. and Mrs. Werner Schulthess of F.A.O. Our special thanks are due to Dr. Charles Evans for introducing us to many of his Sherpa friends when, in 1953, we travelled together to Khumbu. I also wish to thank Mr. Pasang Khambache, a Sherpa well-known to students of Buddhist Nepal as Dr. Snellgrove's companion on many memorable journeys, for helping me to check the vernacular terms used in this book.

We shall always think with gratitude of the Sherpas of Khumbu, whose generous hospitality, friendship and good humour made the time spent in Khumbu a pleasurable and often moving experience. The completeness of the *rapport* we soon established seemed all the more gratifying as long years of anthropological work have taught us that comparatively advanced populations are frequently more resistant to the inquisitiveness of outsiders than primitive tribal societies. But among the Sherpas there was never any difficulty over personal relations. Farmers, merchants and learned lamas welcomed us in their houses in the same open-hearted way. They shared with us whatever they had, and allowed us to participate without restraint in every social and religious event. Once we had set up house in Khumjung, people of the village and from neighbouring settlements would drop in as frequently and as casually as in other houses, and this gave us an opportunity of repaying some of the hospitality we were continuously being offered.

Dorje Ngungdu of Khumjung, whose name figures in many of the subsequent chapters, was our constant companion first in 1953, then in 1957 and, outside his own home ground, again in 1962.

Preface

Outstanding in intelligence and character he proved an invaluable informant and helped us greatly in establishing good relations with the people of villages where we were not yet known. Among our many other friends and helpers only a few can here be mentioned by name: Sonam of Chaurikharka, who looked after our material comforts and, together with Dorje Ngungdu and Sun Tenzing of Phortse, accompanied us in 1953 to Kathmandu and Yelmu, and in 1957 on a long trek to Darjeeling; Konje Chunbi of Khumjung, who in 1960 visited us in London; Kapa Kalden, the famous painter, and the late Sharap Lama, one of the most striking and amiable personalities of Khumjung. I am also deeply appreciative of the kindness shown to us by the reincarnate abbot of Tengboche and many of the other inmates of his monastery. The material advantages our Sherpa friends derived from our association were not very considerable, and the few donations we offered at the times of religious rites were more than balanced by all the entertainment and other tangible and intangible benefits we enjoyed while living in Khumbu.

The research on which this book is based has been sponsored and generously supported by the School of Oriental and African Studies, University of London, as well as by the Wenner-Gren Foundation for Anthropological Research. For my tour in 1957 I also had a grant from the Mount Everest Fund, and the fieldwork in 1962, which provided data incorporated in the first two chapters, was financed by the National Science Foundation. My sincere thanks are due to all these institutions.

The plan of this book has undergone certain changes since it was first written. The original draft contained four chapters on Sherpa economics, but as their inclusion would have made the volume unduly bulky they have been condensed into a single introductory chapter. The full data on Seasonal Nomadism, Agriculture, Animal Husbandry, Trade and Crafts will be published at a later date, together with comparable material collected in 1962 among Bhotia communities of Western Nepal.

This book is dedicated to my wife whose delight in the company of the Sherpas was as great as my own. Her friendly feelings were fully reciprocated, for, themselves warm-hearted and spontaneous, the people of Khumbu have a sharp eye for genuine affection. To many she endeared herself also by ministering to their medical needs, and their faith in her remedies enabled her to achieve several notable cures, not the least acclaimed of which was the successful mending of the broken leg of a yak.

C. VON FÜRER-HAIMENDORF

School of Oriental and African Studies,
  University of London
    June 1963

Summer settlement at Gokyo

The hermit of Nagarjung

Monks at the gate of Tengboche monastery

Introduction

The hermit of Nagarjung had no men above him. From his rocky seat of meditation he looked up at the dazzling peaks of Lhotse and Ama Dablam, thrones of mountain gods revered by the Sherpas of Khumbu whose homesteads lay in valleys far below him. At 15,397 feet above sea level his hermitage was one of the highest permanently inhabited dwellings in Asia, though of this fact he was not conscious. The snow-mountains surrounding him, and even Mount Everest, hidden from his view by the Lhotse wall, had been familiar sights for close on eighty years, the greater part of which he had spent at the monastery of Tengboche, a day's walk from the retreat of his old age. But here in the untrodden wilderness of mountains and glaciers, he was closer to the gods and a state of bliss than he had ever been in a monastery cell. His present life might be drawing to an end, but he was certain that death meant only a transition from one form of existence to another and that in his next reincarnation he might well live again in this land of Khumbu, wiser by the knowledge now gained and better equipped to serve his fellow men. Though he had deliberately withdrawn from their company, those who sought him out found him always ready to listen to their problems, and to help them with advice, spiritual guidance and prayers.

The conviction that this life is only one link in a chain of existences colours the Sherpas' outlook on many aspects of life. The basic unity of all sentient beings is obvious to those who consider animals as sharing the human fate of rebirth and man's involvement in his society is accentuated by the possibility of successive reincarnations within the same environment. Individual actions, on the other hand, lose their irrevocability when judged against the background of a belief in eternally recurring opportunities. If this life is not the only one on earth, there is no finality in any fate, and no permanence in either fortune or misfortune.

The Sherpas' tolerance of unconventional conduct is consistent with their belief in an impersonal and inexorable rule of moral law, operating throughout the chain of rebirths. In a world where every action creates its own reward or retribution men need not feel emotionally involved in the rights and wrongs of their fellow men's doings. For the expectation that any balance of merit or demerit is carried over into the next life mitigates the desire to impose sanctions on offenders against the society's accepted standards. Man's morals are considered his own affair, and the Sherpa is more inclined to smile at his neighbour's shortcomings than to condemn him publicly.

It could be argued, however, that the belief in rebirth can hardly be the reason for the Sherpas' humane and tolerant spirit, for this belief is shared by the majority of Hindus, and yet there is no social order less tolerant of individual deviations than Hindu caste society. This objection would be valid if the ideas of reincarnation and the continuity of personal responsibility through consecutive lives were as vital a part of the thinking of the average Hindu as they are of that of the Sherpas. But in my experience Hindus hardly ever talk of reincarnation and though the concept is known to the educated it does not form a main spring of action in social conduct. While all Sherpas have personal experience of reincarnate lamas, there are no such tangible manifestations of the Hindu belief in rebirth.

Among the Sherpas, moreover, Buddhist concepts have been interwoven with attitudes common to many small-scale societies of a tribal character. A sentiment of equality and general brotherhood is one of the characteristic attitudes of many such societies, and the Sherpas' comparative isolation and long maintained self-sufficiency has favoured the persistence of this attitude. The spirit of amiability so striking in Sherpa social relations grows naturally in an environment where man is a lonely figure in the vastness of uninhabited mountains. Unrelieved solitude is here a far greater problem than social strains and stresses, for a man may spend days and weeks without more than an occasional chance encounter with other herdsmen. With so much opportunity for privacy it is easy for the Sherpa to be tolerant of his fellow men and rejoice in their company whenever work or celebrations bring larger groups together. The exuberant enjoyment of festive gatherings is one of the notable features of Sherpa society, and one of which even outsiders easily gain first-hand experience. Life is not exclusive, and strangers, be they mountaineers or anthropologists, are easily drawn into the prevailing atmosphere of conviviality and mutual good will.

Another factor contributing to the formation of Sherpa character is the traditional freedom from outside interference in the community's affairs. Living in a remote and inaccessible mountain region, the Sherpas have never been subject to the dominance of oppressive local chieftains or officials, or to the control of Tibetan ecclesiastical authorities. In this respect their fate differs from that of many Bhotia groups in other parts of the Himalayas.

Not until I had gained experience of conditions in the highlands of Western Nepal did I see the special character of the Sherpas' social order in its perspective. Although the Tibetan-speaking people of the western border regions also practise Buddhism and live in the seclusion of remote and sparsely populated Himalayan valleys, one does not encounter there a basic outlook comparable in humanity and breadth with that prevailing in Khumbu. Thus we would err if we ascribed the general ethos of Sherpa society solely to the effect of Buddhist ideology. Its influence has certainly been profound but environment, historic accident and contacts with other populations have all contributed to the development and growth of the Sherpas' world-view and way of life. Though linked with the people of Tibet and the other Bhotia groups of Nepal by manifold racial, cultural and economic ties, the highlanders of Khumbu stand out as a people distinctive in their character, their civic sense and the mode of their adaptation to life in extreme altitudes.

This book does not provide all the answers to the problem of the Sherpas' unique place among the Buddhist peoples of Nepal, and it is indeed doubtful whether so elusive a phenomenon as the national character of any ethnic group can ever be satisfactorily explained. What I have set out to do is to describe and analyse the type of society in which the Sherpas have developed their spirit of independence, their ability to co-operate smoothly for the common good, their courtesy and gentleness of manner and their values which are productive of an admirable balance between this-worldly and other-worldly aims.

I
Environment and Economy

Along the world's highest mountain range extends a belt of country inhabited by Mongoloid populations of Buddhist faith and Tibetan speech. Part of this area lies within the border of the kingdom of Nepal, for the traditional political frontier between Tibet and Nepal[1] does not coincide with the southern limits of the sphere of Tibetan culture, and many communities whose religious affiliation, have always lain with the great centres of Tibetan Buddhism owe political allegiance to the royal house of Gorkha. The average Nepali of the Kathmandu valley and the middle ranges refers to all these populations of Tibetan culture and language indiscriminately as Bhotes or Bhotias, generic terms derived from 'Bhot' the Nepali name for Tibet.

Bhotias dwell in the highlands close to the Nepal-Tibet borders but their penetration southwards is normally confined to regions above the 8,000-feet line. In areas of great altitude, particularly in the parts of Nepal which lie north of the Annapurna and Dhaulagiri ranges, they occupy more or less compact tracts, but further south Bhotias settled on the crest of ridges dovetail with other ethnic groups occupying the lower slopes and valleys.

From among the variety of Bhotia populations extending from the borders of Kumaon in the west to those of Sikkim in the east, the people of one tribe stand out by virtue of their fame and prowess in the field of mountaineering and their highly specialized adaptation to a habitat of extreme elevation. These are the Sherpas, whose homeland consists of a number of narrow valleys surmounted by some of the world's highest snow-capped peaks, including Mount Everest and Lhotse. The name Sherpa is derived from the Tibetan word *shar-pa*, which means 'easterner', but it is not clear in what manner this term came to be associated with this particular group.

[1] In 1962 the frontier was formally reaffirmed and a joint Sino-Nepalese boundary commission demarcated the border in those places where doubt about its course had arisen.

From the Tibetan point of view Sherpas are southerners rather than easterners, and even within a purely Nepalese setting the term has no real justification for other Bhotia groups dwell to the east as well as to the west of the Sherpa country. Yet, the term has gained wide currency and must be accepted as the name of an ethnic group with a pronounced sense of separateness from other Bhotia groups.

When travelling along the northern border of Nepal, I often wondered how one could explain the distinctive character of the Sherpas and their pattern of life, a pattern confined to one particular section of the vast Himalayan region. Neither among the Tibetan-speaking people on the upper course of the Arun and Tamar rivers in Eastern Nepal, nor among the Bhotias of such areas in Western Nepal as Thak Khola, Lo (Mustangbhot) or Dolpo does one encounter people comparable with the Sherpas in the combination of a high standard of living, spirit of enterprise, sense of civic responsibility, social polish and general devotion to the practice of Buddhism. It is not accidental that Sherpas have become the trusted guides and companions of innumerable foreign mountaineers, and that no year passes without numerous Sherpas travelling with large and small expeditions over the length and breadth of Nepal. The physical prowess of these sturdy mountain people is matched by that of other Bhotias used to a hard life in inhospitable Himalayan valleys, but the Sherpas' moral fibre, reliability and charm of manner are qualities one does not meet to the same degree among any of the other Tibetan-speaking communities on Nepal's northern borders.

The three regions which contain the main concentration of Sherpas are Khumbu, Pharak and Solu. The former extends between the Tingri District of Tibet and the confluence of Dudh Kosi and Bhote Kosi. The main villages here lie at an average altitude of 12,000 to 13,000 feet, and summer settlements and pastures extend above the 15,000-feet line. Pharak is the strip of country flanking the Dudh Kosi gorge, and in this area the villages lie partly on the banks of the river, and partly on broad, slightly sloping terraces high above the deep and narrow gorge. Their average elevation is 8,000 to 9,000 feet, and at the southern end of Pharak Sherpa villages occupy the higher ridges, whereas the lower slopes are inhabited by a population of Rais. Solu, known in Sherpa as Sha-rang, which extends south-west of Pharak, is a region of broad

Environment and Economy

valleys and great rhododendron and pine forests. Its gentle hill slopes offer much better prospects for agriculture than the rugged landscape of Khumbu and Pharak, and the Solu Sherpas, the richest of whom live in great mansions, have attained a standard of living markedly higher than that of their kinsmen in Khumbu.

The collective terms Solu-Khumbu or Shar-Khumbu are sometimes used for the entire area consisting of the three regions of Khumbu, Pharak and Solu. But though the Sherpas of these regions constitute in some respects a single society, freely intermarrying and occasionally engaging in joint trading enterprises, the use of these collective terms is nevertheless inadvisable. Environmental conditions in Khumbu differ greatly from those of Solu, and have given rise to the development of a highly specialized economy which has little in common with the farming economy of the climatically much more favoured Solu region.

While Khumbu, Pharak and Solu form the solid core of Sherpa settlement, numerous Sherpa villages are scattered over a very much wider area, extending both to the east and the west. In the latter direction Sherpa settlements are found in the valleys of the Likhu Khola, the Khimti Khola and even further west to both sides of the upper course of the Sun Kosi. The inhabitants of several villages of the Yelmu region, three days' walk north-east of Kathmandu, also describe themselves as Sherpas and, though their dialect and many features of their material culture differ from those of the Sherpas of eastern Nepal, these differences do not stand in the way of occasional alliances with Sherpas of Solu. A group of some 300 Sherpa families in the hills of the Pokhara district trace their descent to Yelmu, but it is not known under what circumstances their ancestors left that area.

East of Pharak the distribution of Sherpas extends across the valley of the Inukhu Khola into the hills flanking the Hongu Khola, and more or less isolated villages of Sherpas, whose ancestors emigrated some three to four generations ago from Pharak and Solu, are found on both sides of the Arun river. Other emigrants from the traditional Sherpa homeland live today in the area of Taplejung, their small settlements being interspersed between the indigenous Limbu population of the area. The eastward movement of Sherpas did not come to a halt at the border between Nepal and the Darjeeling District of Bengal. In 1947 the strength of the Sherpa community in the Darjeeling district had already reached 6,929, and this figure included the numerous residents of the Sherpa quarter of the town of Darjeeling as well as the inhabitants of several Sherpa villages in the hills along the Indo-Nepalese border. In the years before 1951, when Nepal was closed to foreign travellers, it was in Darjeeling that Sherpas were recruited as high altitude porters, and to many a poor but enterprising Sherpa of Khumbu the prospect of well-paid work in the service of mountaineers offered an attractive alternative to remaining at Khumbu and working perhaps for a more prosperous fellow-villager. Over the past thirty to forty years the Sherpa community lost numerous able-bodied young men to Darjeeling, but at the same time it was relieved of many a misfit or offender against tribal custom, for a rapid departure to Darjeeling became recognized as an easy way out of disputes and marital tangles.

Unlike the Sherpa settlers in the region of the Arun river and other eastern areas of Nepal, the Sherpas of Darjeeling seldom lose touch with their parent villages. There are frequent occasions for contact between the emigrants and those who remained in Khumbu. Many Khumbu men have gone to Darjeeling for purposes of trade, or with the idea of earning wages without intending to settle there permanently, and mountaineering expeditions in the Khumbu region have brought many Darjeeling Sherpas back to the scene of their childhood. Even second generation Darjeeling Sherpas often meet kinsmen from Khumbu, and thus remain conscious of a link with the ancestral land.

TYPES OF SETTLEMENT

The pattern of Sherpa settlements in the Khumbu area has been shaped by a climate and an environment which precludes the possibility of combining mixed farming with a sedentary way of life. There is no single locality where even a few families could maintain themselves and their livestock throughout the year. The owners of yak have to move with their herds to pastures lying at different levels, and those without cattle undertake extensive trading excursions in order to supplement their income from the tillage of land. Neither can afford to spend the whole year in one place, but only the cattle-owner is in need of houses and hay stores on several widely dispersed sites.

Environment and Economy

It is the herdsmen's habitations on different levels of altitude which lend the settlement of Khumbu its distinctive character. While in other Himalayan regions, such as Dolpo or Thak, the owners of yak herds have solid houses only in one settlement, and live in tents when grazing their animals on the higher pastures, the Sherpas build houses of stone and timber even in places where they spend only three or four weeks a year. However, there is a difference between such subsidiary settlements and the main villages, where the Sherpas have the greater part of their immovable possessions.

The number of these main villages is strictly limited. In the triangle enclosed by them are Namche Bazar (73 houses), Khumjung (93 houses) and Kunde (45 houses), in the upper Dudh Kosi valley there is Phortse (63 houses), and in the valley of the Imja Khola lie the ancient village of Pangboche (58 houses) and the small and comparatively recent villages of Milingbo and Changmitang (18 houses). The main villages in the valley of Bhote Kosi are Thamo, Thami and Thamote, which are collectively known as Thamichok (192 houses).

Most of these villages lie in localities where there is sufficient level space for fairly extensive cultivation; the only exception is Namche Bazar, known in Sherpa as Nauje, which has so small a cultivated area that only a few of its 73 households can support themselves by the pursuit of agriculture. It is primarily a settlement of traders and, as such, the newest of the main villages of Khumbu.

Despite the differences in the natural features of the various village sites, there is a common pattern in the arrangement of houses. They invariably stand scattered over a considerable area, with fields and kitchen gardens separating individual homesteads or groups of houses. Nowhere do we find a configuration even vaguely reminiscent of a village street.

Most of the houses in the main villages are substantial and often even spacious buildings, consisting of a framework of wooden posts and walls of crudely cut stones smeared with mortar and whitewashed. While the poorer people live in single-storeyed houses, most Sherpas of Khumbu own double-storeyed houses constructed on a pattern which allows of few variations. The ground floor of such a house serves partly as a shelter for calves, goats and cows, which unlike yak cannot be left in the open during the height of the winter. Entering a Sherpa house one has to pass through this dark storeroom and grope at the back for the wooden stairs which lead up into the main room of the house. In the average home this room, well lit by two or three windows on the front side of the house, is about 30 to 36 feet long and 12 to 16 feet broad.

Next to the entrance there is invariably an open hearth where all the family's meals are cooked. A long, low window-bench runs along the front wall, and the traditional seat of the head of the household is the one nearest to the fireplace. Low tables stand in front of this window-bench, and all food and drink served to the men of the house and male guests is placed on these tables, while the women eat squatting on the floor, next to the hearth.

Chests for stores stand along the walls and in the houses of the wealthy there are rows of shining copper and brass vessels arranged on richly carved wooden shelves. While the householder and his wife sleep on a bedstead standing in an alcove behind the hearth, other members of the family spread their bedding on the floor-boards of this main room.

Some of the larger houses contain a private chapel, accessible only through the main room. Here an altar with one or more statues of Buddhas or Boddhisatvas faces the window, and the wood panelling of the walls is covered with religious frescoes.

All Sherpa houses have moderately inclined gable roofs covered with broad pine planks which are weighed down by large stones in a manner reminiscent of houses in the Swiss Alps.

Many of the Sherpas of Khumbu spend only six or seven months in their comfortable main houses and live during the rest of the year in subsidiary settlements. These fall into two distinctive categories, the winter settlements (*gunsa*) and the summer hamlets (*yersa*).

The winter settlements where the Sherpas shelter with their herds from the icy storms of the winter, lie in protected places at altitudes lower than the average elevation of the main villages. There may be only three or four houses built on the narrow bank of a river, or as many as thirty houses may occupy a broad ledge at some height above a gorge. Around the houses there are usually a number of fields and potato plots, and the crops grown and stored on the spot are used to feed the householders during the winter, while hay, stored in the houses, serves as fodder for the cattle.

The summer hamlets lie among the high pastures far above the tree-line. Ownership of houses and meadows in several of these

Environment and Economy

settlements is an indispensable concomitant of yak-breeding, for no one without such property can maintain even a moderately sized herd of yak. Many *yersa* lie at distances of two to three days' walk from the main villages, and it is not unusual for men of different villages to own houses and land in one summer settlement. The families congregated in such a settlement at any one time are thus not a section of a village community but belong to several main villages, and disperse again when they have to move their cattle to other pastures. The highest of these *yersa* lie at altitudes between 15,000 and 16,000 feet and here the dwellings are small huts roofed with slabs of stone, containing only a minimum of woodwork, rafters and beams having to be brought from great distances.

Similar in purpose but very different in form are primitive encampments known as *resa*. These structures, consisting of a permanent though crudely built stone wall and a temporary roof of bamboo mats or yak-hair blankets, serve the herdsmen as shelters on pastures where they graze their cattle only for a few days. They are found on very high pastures, beyond the highest *yersa*, and at fairly low levels in the vicinity of the main villages. Here young boys look after the cattle during the day, and the *resa* serve as shelters for the adults who spend only the nights near the herds and return in the morning to their houses in the village.

AGRICULTURE

For six months of the year the soil of Khumbu is normally frozen and all agricultural operations are at a standstill. While the Sherpas of Solu and Pharak are able to grow winter crops of wheat and barley in addition to the summer crops of buckwheat, maize and potatoes, the people of Khumbu depend on a single cultivation period lasting from the middle of April until early October. In most villages only bitter buckwheat, potatoes, turnips and some coarse greens are grown, but in the high valley of Dingboche a bearded, short-stemmed barley is raised on irrigated fields.

Most of the agricultural work is done by hand. It begins with the digging over of the potato fields in the lowest lying of the *gunsa* settlements. This is women's work, while the ploughing of fields in preparation for the sowing of buckwheat is invariably done by men. The Sherpas' light wooden plough with its narrow, iron-tipped share is drawn either by a team of three or four men, or by a pair of yak or *zopkio*, cross-breeds between yak and oxen. Ploughing with yoked animals, though universal in Tibet and common among most Bhotia populations in Western Nepal, is an innovation in Khumbu. As recently as thirty years ago all ploughing was done by teams of men, and even in 1957 this method was still the more widely practised. By that time only four of the ninety-three households of Khumjung had adopted ploughing with draught animals. While the plough is invariably led by a man, the sower walking a few steps behind and broadcasting buckwheat or barley is always a woman.

Fields to be planted with potatoes have to be dug over with hoes, for the light Sherpa plough only scratches the surface of the soil, and this is inadequate preparation for the planting of potatoes. The weeding is done by groups of women, and so is most of the work of harvesting potatoes. By the middle of August the potatoes in the lower subsidiary settlements are ready to be dug up, and the potato harvest starts in the main villages early in September. It is soon followed by the reaping of barley and buckwheat, and by the beginning of October agricultural work comes to an end.

As many families own fields in various settlements outside the main villages, there is a continuous shifting of labour from one locality to another, for not only the herding of cattle but also tillage of the soil at different levels of altitude necessitates a high degree of mobility. While burdening landowners and labourers with the extra effort of long journeys from one settlement to another the system of dispersed holdings has the advantage that a family's limited labour force can be employed to the best effect. In the village of Khumjung, for instance, the planting of potatoes cannot be begun before the middle of April, when the soil has thawed, but in the lower-lying *gunsa* settlements agricultural work can start two to three weeks earlier and for those owning fields at different levels the slack time of the year is thus appreciably reduced.

THE INTRODUCTION OF THE POTATO

Potatoes form the mainstay of Sherpa diet and the economy of the villages of Khumbu depends to so great an extent on the cultivation of this one crop that it is difficult to imagine conditions before potatoes found their way into Khumbu. Yet, it is certain that the potato was not known in the Himalayas until comparatively recently and the two most likely sources of its spread into Eastern Nepal are the gardens of European settlers in Darjeeling and the garden of the British residency in Kathmandu. Sir Joseph D. Hooker[1] found potatoes in the region of Yangma, on the western approaches of Kanchenjunga, as early as 1848, and he remarked that those had been only recently introduced. His surmise was that they had come from 'the English garden at the Nepalese capital' and that at that time potatoes had not spread further east than the Sikkim border. If this assumption was correct, potatoes may have reached Solu and Khumbu a few years earlier, but if Sir Joseph Hooker was mistaken and the source of the Yangma potatoes was Darjeeling, their introduction into Khumbu may have occurred several years later. No documentary evidence regarding the arrival of potatoes in Khumbu exists, and most Sherpas are ignorant of the fact that there was ever a time when no potatoes were grown in Khumbu. In 1953 Sun Tensing of Phortse, then a man in his middle forties, told me that as a young boy he knew an old man of over ninety of whom it was said that he had first planted potatoes on Phortse land and I was shown the plots of land on the right bank of the Imja Khola, roughly opposite Milingbo, where these first potato fields were supposed to have been. If we assume that the owner of those fields died in, say, 1925, it would be possible that as a young man he experimented with planting potatoes soon after 1860, and this would bring us near to Hooker's dates for the presence of potatoes in the Yangma area. Moreover, Phortse is the most conservative of all villages of Khumbu and the one where even today cattle-breeding receives more emphasis than either agriculture or trade. It is not unlikely therefore that in other parts of Khumbu potato cultivation began about the middle of the nineteenth century. This tallies with the statement of an 83-year-old woman of Thami who told me in 1953 that potatoes were brought to her village by people of her father's generation.

Compared with buckwheat, potatoes have obvious advantages. In the light, sandy soil of Khumbu they thrive so well that a field in which potatoes are planted yields very much more food than the same acreage sown with buckwheat can yield even in a good year. Particularly on the marginal land taken under cultivation by many of the more recent Khamba immigrants, potatoes are the only economic crop, and it is unimaginable that villages such as Khumjung and

[1] *Himalayan Journals*, p. 167, London, 1905.

Kunde could have supported their present population in the absence of the ample and dependable basic food-supply provided by the potato.

The population of Khumbu was a fraction of its present size until the middle of the nineteenth century and there can be no doubt that the great increase of the last hundred years coincided with the introduction and spread of the potato. In 1836 there were in the whole of Khumbu only 169 households, compared with the 596 households in 1957. No great imagination is required to realize that the introduction of a new crop and the spectacular increase in population must have been connected. The improved food-supply is likely to have reduced mortality among the Sherpas themselves, and the availability of a surplus may have attracted immigrants from Tibet. The usual explanation Khamba settlers give for their move from the neighbouring regions of Tibet to Khumbu is the ampler food and easier life which they found in the Sherpa country. Nowadays even beggars can collect sufficient potatoes to keep themselves alive and most Sherpa landowners have enough potatoes to feed not only the members of their own family but also casual Khamba workers, who help at harvest time or offer their services as tailors, shoemakers or weavers.

But even the natural growth of population and the influx of new settlers did not absorb the increased supply of basic food. For the first time in the history of Khumbu an average family of farmers could produce more food than its members required for their day-to-day needs. The scope for export was limited, and thus arose the possibility of maintaining, in addition to the farming population, a small number of people not engaged in the production of food. It is in conformity with the basic trends in Sherpa culture that the energies of those freed from the necessity to provide for their needs by farming was devoted almost entirely to the practice of religion and of the arts, linked with Buddhist ritual and worship.

Although Buddhism has been well established in Khumbu for at least 300 years, the foundation of monasteries and nunneries as well as the construction of new village temples and many religious monuments have taken place within the last fifty to eighty years. This points to economic events which favoured a sudden spurt of non-productive activities and in my opinion there can be little doubt that these events were brought about by the introduction of the potato and the resulting increase in agricultural production. Obviously the sudden development of a surplus in food supplies must be regarded as permissive and not as causative of the flowering of the religious life. Among the Sherpas, as among Tibetan Buddhists, the religious impulse is so strong that any margin of resources left after essential needs have been met is largely devoted to religious purposes. This seems to have happened not only in Khumbu, but also in Solu where no less than five monastic establishments—Chiwong, Trakshindo, Gole, Tolaka and Thodung—have sprung up during the past forty years when the development of potato cultivation not only improved the local food supplies but provided a commodity for a profitable export trade to India.

Thus the potato has revolutionized Sherpa economics. At a time when the old-established trade with Tibet is threatened by a new orientation in that country's economy and relations with its neighbours, the existence of this crop will at least prevent the Khumbu Sherpas from starving while they adjust themselves to the new conditions, and may cushion the blow which any reduction or rerouting of the Tibetan trade with Nepal would inevitably deal to their economy.

ANIMAL HUSBANDRY

Though agriculture provides the Sherpas with the bulk of their food-supply, they regard the breeding of yak and other cattle as a far nobler occupation. No other form of property has quite the same prestige value as a herd of yak, and rich men, who would never put their hand to a hoe or sickle, unhesitatingly undergo the hardships of grazing their herds for weeks and months on high pastures. Yet, it would be misleading to think of the Sherpas foremost as a pastoral people. Whereas every Sherpa family engages to some extent in agriculture, yak breeding is one of several economic choices, and there are numerous wealthy men who apply their energy to trade rather than to animal husbandry.

Among the 596 householders of Khumbu there were in 1957 only 254 owners of cattle, and the total number of yak and cows in their possession was 2,894. The greater part of the livestock was in the hands of a few wealthy families. While even families of modest means owned one or two cows, yak were kept only in herds of at least six or seven animals. Thus in Khumjung 347 yak were owned by 17 householders, whereas 16 families kept a few cows; only 17 of the 108 households of Khumjung were engaged in the type of cattle-economy which involved seasonal migrations from one high-altitude settlement to the other.

The Sherpas of Khumbu breed cattle not only for their own use as dairy animals but also for sale. The greatest profits are derived from the sale of calves bred from Tibetan bulls (*lhang*) and female yak (*nak*), for, both in Solu and in Tibet, there is a great and constant demand for such hybrids, which combine the desirable qualities of both yak and oxen. Female cross-breeds (*zhum*) give more milk than yak-cows (*nak*) and the male cross-breeds (*zopkio*) are more manageable pack- and draught-animals than pure yak.

While the sale of *zhum* and *zopkio* calves results nowadays in the most spectacular return for the labour expended on looking after a herd of yak, the cash earned in this way is by no means the only benefit a Sherpa derives from the ownership of cattle. Fresh milk is not consumed in large quantities, but curd is highly valued food and butter-milk remaining after the churning of butter is regularly drunk. Great quantities of butter are needed for domestic as well as for ritual use. Butter is eaten with or as part of all the more highly valued food; it is used as fuel in the butter-lamps lit in the course of Buddhist ceremonies and is moulded into various shapes for the decoration of sacrificial dough figures (*torma*).[1] Butter is used also as a medium for the payment of wages, and it forms an important article of trade eagerly sought in the Tibetan market.

Yak are regularly shorn and their long coarse hair, as well as the soft wool, is used for weaving blankets. Though, as devout Buddhists, Sherpas are not supposed to kill any animal, they are not averse to eating the meat of yak which are killed accidentally or slaughtered by others. Professional butchers of *hyawo* class[2] used to come once a year from Tibet and there are also some *hyawo* living in Namche Bazar. In the late autumn, when the pastures dry up and the cattle must be fed on hay, old yak are slaughtered and the meat partly eaten fresh and partly hung up to dry.

Besides contributing milk and meat to the Sherpas' diet, and providing hair and wool for blankets, yak and cross-breeds serve as the principal means of transport in the trade with Tibet and are used in the seasonal migrations between main villages and subsidiary set-

---

[1] Cf. pp. 176, 190, 191.   [2] This class is *khamendeu*, cf. p. 34.

The Monastery of Thami

House and private chapel in Khumjung

The temple and houses of Pangboche

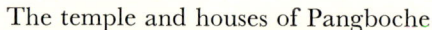

tlements. They are the only pack-animals available in Khumbu for, unlike the Bhotias of such areas of Western Nepal as Thak Khola, Lo and Dolpo, the Sherpas do not use ponies, mules, donkeys, sheep or goats for the carriage of goods. There are no mules or donkeys and only a very few ponies in Khumbu and the number of sheep and goats is exceedingly small. Sheep do not seem to thrive in the climate of Khumbu, and most of the sheep brought in 1959 by Tibetan refugees had died by 1962, largely no doubt because there were not sufficient stores of hay to feed them during the winter.

TRADE

Agriculture and animal husbandry could never have enabled the Sherpas of Khumbu to attain a standard of living far superior to that of the Rais, Tamangs, Gurungs and Magars inhabiting the middle ranges of Eastern Nepal. It was the trade with Tibet which gave the Sherpas the chance of acquiring valuable jewellery, clothing, household goods and ritual objects of Tibetan and Chinese origin, while the many journeys connected with this trade kept them in touch with the aesthetic and intellectual interests of their Tibetan neighbours.

The trade route which links Khumbu with the Tibetan province of Tingri leads across the Nangpa La, a pass close on 18,000 feet high, and it is symptomatic of the Sherpas' energy and enterprise that they could develop this route as a channel for substantial commercial exchanges between the fertile grain producing areas of the Dudh Kosi basin and the Tibetan plateau. The inhabitants of Khumbu did not produce many goods marketable in Tibet but their geographical situation and their ability to carry merchandise over glaciers and snow-bound passes have gained them a position as middlemen. This position was further strengthened by an order of the Nepalese government forbidding the Sherpas of Solu to trade direct with Tibet and Tibetan traders to carry goods further south than Namche Bazar. These regulations gave the Khumbu people a virtual monopoly of trade along the Nangpa La route.

Salt and wool have always been the most important commodities purchased from Tibet. In exchange the Sherpas exported grain, butter, cattle, paper, hides, sugar and various commodities of Indian origin. Until half a century ago Khumbu was also a centre for the export of Nepalese iron to Tibet, but this trade declined when the development of an easier trade route via Kalimpong led to the competition of the cheaper Indian iron in the Tibetan markets.

Though no longer as important as in previous times, when no Indian salt penetrated into the middle ranges of Nepal, the Tibetan salt is still widely used throughout the hills south of the Sherpa area, and the entire population of Khumbu, Pharak and Solu utilizes only Tibetan salt. The Sherpa traders' profits are based on the great difference between the rates of salt-grain exchange in Tibet and in Nepal. In Tibet one measure of rice has always bought several measures of salt while conversely in the villages of the Sherpas' southern neighbours one measure of salt is exchanged for several measures of rice.

The barter of salt for grain lies mainly in the hands of small traders, whereas the big traders of Namche Bazar are accustomed to trade primarily in such commodities as butter, sugar, hides, paper, dyes, cotton goods and, above all, in cattle. Before the events of 1959 they used to buy young female yak from Tibetans and exported large numbers of cross-breeds, both male and female. Much of this trade involved cash transactions in either Nepali, Indian or Tibetan currency, but the Chinese régime in Tibet does not favour cash deals and such trade as continues to flow over the Nangpa La is now mainly on a barter basis.

Next to the salt trade the import of Tibetan wool is of vital importance to the Sherpas. Virtually all the wool used by Sherpa women in weaving cloth for their own use, as well as for sale, has always been bought in Tibet and carried across the Nangpa La. Every autumn most Sherpa families used to organize at least one trip to Tingri or Kyabrak, the first village on the Tibetan side of the border, and there bought raw wool as well as, occasionally, woven woollen material.

It is too early to say whether the political changes in Tibet will permanently affect the Sherpas' trade, but there are indications that for some years to come at least the barter trade will continue along traditional lines. The prospects of the big merchants of Khumbu and Solu, on the other hand, appear at present very uncertain. The network of long-standing personal contacts has been disrupted and can hardly be restored under present circumstances. Many of the trade deals used to involve a long-term credit and the personal prestige and trust-worthiness of a trader were often the only security offered. A system of 'ceremonial friends' (*thowu*) enabled the traders to operate safely in distant areas, and several of the Khumbu Sherpas had relatives in Tingri, Shigatse and Lhasa.

The share of trade in the Sherpas' income has always varied from village to village. Two thirds of the population of Namche Bazar which in 1957 numbered 296, then lived almost exclusively on the income from commerce; in Khumjung and Kunde there were several men who devoted the greater part of their energy to trade, but in the villages of Pangboche and Phortse few people undertook trade journeys and many households obtained Tibetan salt and wool from the small traders of Khumjung and Kunde.

Considering all these factors one may venture the estimate that until the Chinese intervention in Tibet, external trade, i.e. trade with areas outside Khumbu, accounted for between one third and one quarter of the Sherpas' total income from all branches of their economy.

CRAFTS

Few of the Khumbu Sherpas can be regarded as professional artisans. Most men and women are experienced in the one or other craft, but practise it only for their own domestic purposes. Both know how to spin and it is not unusual even for rich men to walk about the village holding a piece of sheep's fleece in their left hand and turning a spindle with their right hand while gossiping with friends. Weaving is exclusively women's work, and though many women have never attained any proficiency in the craft, others, and particularly poor women, have made weaving their main profession, either working for wages or buying their own wool and selling their products for cash.

The Sherpas use two types of loom. The one employed for weaving yak-hair blankets is a simple loom of the so-called Indonesian type. The other is a treadle-loom, reputedly introduced from Tibet as recently as the beginning of this century. Today it is used universally for weaving woollen cloth.

In many households men's as well as women's clothes are made by members of the family, but there are also some professional tailors who come for a few days to the house and receive food in addition to their wage. Though most Sherpas know how to re-sole their high boots, not many men are expert in making new boots.

These are manufactured by professional boot-makers, who either produce boots for sale or work in their clients' houses for a daily wage.

The majority of the tailors and boot-makers are immigrants from Tibet and their craft is not very highly esteemed. Carpentry on the other hand is considered an art worthy of a Sherpa and the carpenters employed on house-building are relatively well paid. No Sherpa, however, is completely specialized in carpentry. House-building is confined to the summer months, and carpenters do not find employment throughout the year. The rôle of a carpenter resembles in many ways that of a village lama; he is called in when his special skill is in demand, while at other times he pursues the occupation of an ordinary farmer.

Totally different is the position of the blacksmiths. Sherpas do not work at the forge and the whole of Khumbu is served by a few Nepali-speaking blacksmiths who came some generations ago from the lower regions and settled in Namche Bazar. These blacksmiths, known as Kami, belong to one of the untouchable castes of Nepalese Hindu society and the Sherpas, though normally not pollution-conscious, imitate the higher Hindu castes in their attitude to the Kami blacksmiths. The latter are not admitted to Sherpa houses and stand in every respect outside Sherpa society.

With the exception of metal-work there is little specialization according to crafts. The Sherpas of Khumbu do not share the Hindu attitude to certain types of manual work. Prosperous men of good social status will on occasions do their own carpentry work, tailor their own clothes, tan yak hides and repair their own boots. Only in those fields, where special skills have to be acquired by a great deal of practice, is there some scope for professional craftsmen. Thus the boot-maker or expert carpenter provides services which are beyond the ability of the ordinary householder and in this respect his rôle is not different from that of the painter commissioned to paint the frescoes in a temple or private chapel. Neither is the boot-maker despised nor the painter particularly honoured, except for his knowledge of Buddhist scriptures which usually goes with the practice of an art devoted entirely to religious purposes.

The Sherpas' attitude to occupational specialization resembles more the attitude of their tribal neighbours than that of the Hindu castes of Nepal. A man's work is evaluated according to its usefulness and the profits he derives from it. There is no gradation of activities based on a distinction between pure and polluting occupations and no Sherpa endangers his social status by undertaking any specific task.

2
An Open Society

All Sherpas share the tradition of having immigrated from Tibet, but the circumstances and time of this migration are obscure. While the subsequent arrival and miraculous feats of various lamas are the subject of numerous legends, traditions and myths relating to the Sherpas' migration to the regions of Khumbu and Solu and to the establishment of the present villages are almost completely lacking. This lack of legendary, as well as historical, accounts of their ancestors' arrival in their present habitat is all the more surprising as many Sherpas are literate and well acquainted with myths and traditions regarding the establishment of Buddhism in Tibet and the fates of such historical figures as the 'lotus-born' saint, Padmasambhava, known to Tibetans and Sherpas as Guru Rimpoche ('Precious Master'). There is no agreement even about the route of migration from Tibet to Khumbu and Solu. Most Sherpas of this area believe that their ancestors migrated south along the Rongshar Chu—west of the Rolwaling Himal—and then, turning east, settled first in Solu, where they ousted an earlier Kiranti population. From Solu they moved—according to this tradition—northwards into Khumbu, but a contradictory belief is expressed in the view that the ancestors of some clans came to Khumbu straight from Tibet across the Nangpa La, the present main trade-route between Khumbu and the Tingri region. Thus it is said that the forefathers of the Mende clan came from the vicinity of Karte in Tibet and that, after crossing the Nangpa La, they first lived in a cave above a place called Mende, between the present villages of Thami and Khumjung.

There is fairly general agreement, however, that the ancestors of all Sherpa clans (*ru*) arrived in the area at approximately the same time and that ever since the number of major clans has remained constant. None of these clans lays any claim to seniority or higher status on the grounds of prior arrival in Solu and Khumbu, nor is the numerical predominance of the one or other clan in any specific area considered a significant indication that its members were the first settlers.

In some villages there is a vague tradition that the members of certain clans were the first to settle in the locality, but this belief does not find expression in ritual or social behaviour. Thus it is believed that Khumjung and Kunde were first inhabited by people of Paldorje, Chusherwa and Jongdomba clan. The latter clan is now nearly extinct, and there is no suggestion that either Paldorje or Chusherwa people should be accorded any special privileges as the members of 'founder-clans'. Indeed, the idea that historical claims should be reflected in present-day rights is foreign to the Sherpas, and this attitude accounts perhaps for their scant interest in the past.

There is nevertheless a widespread notion that the number of clans or *ru* constituting the Sherpa society in Khumbu, Pharak and Solu is eighteen. Not all Sherpas are able to enumerate off-hand as many as eighteen clans, while a list comprising all the clans represented in the various villages of this region runs to the following twenty-one names, arranged here in alphabetical order: Chiawa, Chusherwa, Gardza, Gole, Goparma, Jongdomba, Khambadze, Lakshindu, Lama, Lhukpa, Mende, Munming, Nawa, Paldorje, Pankarma, Pinasa, Salaka, Shangup, Sherwa, Shire, Thaktu.

Some Sherpas explain the discrepancy between the traditional figure of eighteen and the actual number of clans found at present by pointing out that several clans, though known by different names in different regions, are in fact identical. Thus the Paldorje and Salaka people are said to constitute one single clan, known as Paldorje in Khumbu and as Salaka in Solu. Others explain the special relations between such clans, whose members are debarred from intermarriage, by saying that they are brother clans. The view that every group of 'brother clans' should be counted only as *one* clan would reduce the number of basic clans to seventeen, a not unlikely figure considering that one of the original eighteen clans may have died out, just as the Jongdomba clan, once well represented in Khumjung, is near extinction, the only male member living at present in Darjeeling. Three recognized groups of 'brother clans', whose members do not inter-marry, are Gole, Pinasa and Thaktu; Paldorje and Salaka; and Nawa and Lhukpa.

Apart from these comparatively few groupings of clans on the basis of a traditional brother relationship, there is no principle according to which the various Sherpa clans can be brought into any specific order. No clan claims seniority or privileges, and there is no significant territorial distribution of clans. True, certain clans, such as Gole, Pinasa and Lama, are found mainly in Solu, whereas the clans of Mende, Shangup, Sherwa and Shire are concentrated in Khumbu. But a man of Gole clan who settles in Khumbu labours under no disadvantage compared to the people of locally predominant clans and, if he happens to have several sons, his clan may, within two or three generations, be numerically strong in the village of his adoption. One of the headmen (*pembu*) of Khumjung, for instance, is a man of Gole clan from Solu, who married into the house of a rich man of Khumjung and inherited his father-in-law's position together with the property to which he was entitled in his capacity of *maksu* or resident son-in-law.

In the absence of any socially relevant order among the Sherpa clans occurring in Khumbu, Pharak and Solu, we may now consider the nature of the individual Sherpa clan in its social and ritual aspects.

The Sherpa term for 'clan' is *ru*,[1] which means literally 'bone'. The idea is that children inherit their father's bones, and that all descendants of one ancestor in the male line are hence of 'one bone'. This belief has practical implications similar to those of the widespread belief in the ties of 'blood'. The essential feature of the Sherpa clan is its rôle as the basic exogamous unit. All Sherpas of the same *ru*, irrespective of the distance which may separate their villages and the impossibility of tracing genealogical links, consider themselves as agnatic kin and debarred from marriage. Sexual relations between clan members are regarded as incest, and are virtually unheard of. Though there is a great tolerance of casual sex relations, both premarital and extra-marital, I have failed to discover a single case of even a fleeting amorous attachment between members of the same clan, and all my informants were emphatic in expressing the view that dire punishments would be meted out to anyone offending against the rules of clan exogamy.

Similar restrictions apply to members of such brother clans as

[1] The Tibetan term for the patrilineal clan is *rus* ('bone'), while the kinship link based on descent in the female line is called *sha* ('flesh'). Cf. R. A. Stein, *La civilisation tibétaine*, Paris, 1962, p. 70.

An Open Society

Paldorje and Salaka, Thaktu and Gole, or Nawa and Lhukpa. But the reaction to a breach of the rules of exogamy involving members of two brother clans seems to be far less violent. Some years ago a man of Paldorje clan of Phortse village had an affair with an unmarried girl of Salaka clan of Kunde, as a result of which a child was born. Whereas otherwise the birth of an illegitimate child causes no adverse comment, there was a great deal of indignation on account of the brother relationship of the two clans. The *pembu*, as leaders of public opinion, went out of their way to oppose the possibility of a marriage, but one or two men took the opposite view, and maintained that there had been a precedent for a marriage between people of Paldorje and Salaka clans in Namche Bazar. Yet popular feeling seems to have run high enough to induce the offending man to leave for Darjeeling, where he subsequently died, and the offspring of the controversial union also happened to die. The girl, however, subsequently married the son of one of the wealthiest men of Kunde, and is now a respected woman with several legitimate children.

Among the 567 marriages recorded in the house lists which I compiled in the villages of Khumjung, Kunde, Namche Bazar and Phortse, there occurs no union between members of brother clans. This confirms that the pairs and groups of clans believed to stand in a brother relationship constitute effective exogamous units even though casual sexual relations between members of such clans do not evoke the same feeling of horror as those between a man and a woman of the same clan.

THE CLAN AS RITUAL UNIT

While Sherpa clans have no corporate existence in either the economic or the political field, they do appear as distinct units in a limited number of ritual matters. Thus the members of every clan recognize certain mountain gods as their specific protective deities, and on some occasions clan members resident in the same village may combine for the worship of such clan deities. Among the gods associated with localities in Khumbu and worshipped by Sherpa clans not only in Khumbu but also in Solu are the following:

Pari-lha-tsen karbu, associated with a mountain in Khumbu, worshipped by the Paldorje clan.
Tonak-lha-tsen karbu, associated with an area north of Gokyo,

and Long-gyo, associated with a dried-up lake close to Gokyo, worshipped by the Thaktu clan.

Tawoche-lha-tsen, associated with the mountain Tawoche above Pangboche, worshipped by the Nawa clan.

Loudze-lha-tsen, associated with the mountain Loudze (Lhotse) near Mt. Everest, worshipped by the Chusherwa clan.

Arkamtse-lha-tsen karbu, associated with a locality above Tangnak, worshipped by the Sherwa clan.

Chiawitsa-kyung karbu, associated with a locality above Maralung, worshipped by the Chiawa clan.

Karte Gyelbu, ('King of Karte'), associated with the village of Karte in Tibet, worshipped by the Mende clan.

All these deities worshipped by specific clans fall into the category of *zidag* (Tibetan: *gze-bdag*) or 'Lords of the Soil', and as such they occupy an inferior position in the Buddhist hierarchy of deities. Their status is lower too than that of Khumbu-yülha, the principal *kyela-yülha* or locality god of the whole of Khumbu. They are his attendants and on all important occasions when Khumbu-yülha is invoked, the lamas invoke also twelve of his attendants, and among them the deities of the principal clans of Khumbu.

The main occasions for the worship of the clan deities are the three *lhachetu*,[1] namely the So-lha in the month of May, the Yer-chang ('Summer-beer') in the month of August, and the Ten-lha in the month of October. As the Yer-chang is performed when yak-owning families live in the various summer settlements (*yersa*) there is at that festival no occasion for a gathering of clan members. But at the two other *lhachetu* the members of a clan resident in a village may gather in the house of a senior clan member and co-operate in the act of worship. Thus in 1953 all the Thaktu people of Khumjung assembled for the Ten-lha in the house of Nima Teshi, a rich and prominent man of Thaktu clan, who incidentally held the position of *chorpen*[2] of the village temple, but two years later there was a quarrel, and subsequently the rite took place in the house of Kushang (Thaktu) while some of the Thaktu families split off and held separate celebrations.

The significance of a joint performance of a *lhachetu* by the

[1] *Lha* = god; *chetu* = ceremony.
[2] *Chorpen* is the guardian of the village temple (cf. p. 113).

An Open Society

members of a clan resident in a village should not be overrated, however. There is no firm organization concerned with the holding of clan rites and it must not be assumed that a clan acts as a corporate body with all clan members combining for the worship of their ancestral deities. Sherpa clans have neither officials nor clan priests who could organize the co-operation of clan members on a permanent basis. The joint celebration of a *lhachetu* rite by several families belonging to the same clan is a convenience and a way to invest the rite with additional solemnity. It is not prescribed by tradition and hence entirely optional. Whereas the Thaktu people of Khumjung were in the habit of gathering for the *lhachetu* rites in one house, the members of other clans also well represented in the village did not follow this practice. Neither the Paldorje nor the Mende people gathered for the performance of the *lhachetu* in the house of one of their clan members but each family, or perhaps two closely related families, performed the rites separately.

Yet, there remains the link of the common recognition and worship of one and the same deity, and hence a vague feeling of solidarity between members of the same clan. This feeling of solidarity does not find expression at any of the major village festivals, such as the Dumje, but it may be responsible for a slight preference to celebrate the Yer-chang, the *lhachetu* rite in August, in a locality where other members of the same clan stay at the time with their cattle. But neither at this nor at any other *lhachetu* rite need the ministering lama be of the same clan as the other worshippers.

Whereas membership of a Sherpa clan does not involve any definite obligations other than the observance of the rules of exogamy and the worship of the clan deities three times a year, it is of supreme importance as being the indispensable symbol of a person's status within the core of Sherpa society. For in Khumbu, Pharak and Solu only members of the twenty-one clans listed on p. 19 are considered as true Sherpas, and only they have a clear place in the exogamous system. Numerous other inhabitants of the region, closely akin to the Sherpas in language and customs, and largely indistinguishable in appearance, are known as Khambas and regarded as slightly inferior to the original Sherpas.

Most of these Khambas are recent immigrants from Tibet, and it is somewhat illogical that the Sherpas, who themselves claim descent from similar immigrants of past ages, have nevertheless the tendency to look down upon those who have been settled south of the Great Himalayan Range only for the last one or two generations.

Yet, for all practical purposes the Khambas form part of Sherpa society. They can acquire land and houses, marry into Sherpa families, be elected as village officials, function as lamas and attain even the highest positions in any of the local monasteries. But despite all these facilities Khambas can never become part of what is traditionally the core of Sherpa society. They can neither acquire membership of Sherpa clans nor do they have comparable exogamous units of their own which could be added to the list of Sherpa clans and thus lead to a gradual expansion of the Sherpa clan system.

As a rule no distinction is made between different types of Khambas, this 'blanket term' being applied to anyone who either came from Tibet or is descended in the male line from such immigrants. Strictly speaking Khambas are only those who hail from the Tibetan province of Kham, while those from the nearby frontier regions of Tibet should be described as Pheipa. But in practice the term Pheipa is rarely used, and everyone who is not a member of one of the recognized Sherpa clans is labelled 'Khamba'. When asked the name of their *ru* most Khambas describe themselves simply as Khambas, though in rare cases they give the name of their village of origin in place of a clan name. Thus several Khamba families in Phortse are known as 'Nedzunga' and others as 'Penakpa' after two villages in the Tingri region whence their ancestors came. But these pseudo clan names of Khambas are in no way equivalent to the clan names of Sherpas. They are not indicative of exogamous units, for people stemming from the same Tibetan village may freely inter-marry.

The one distinctive name frequently given to a section of Khambas is that of Rongsherwa. The ancestors of these people lived in the villages of the valley of the Rongshar Chu, just north of the Nepal-Tibet border, and many settled in the area of the Rolwaling Himāl. From there some came across the Teshi Lapcha Pass into the Khumbu region, and there are now several families of Rongsherwa Khambas in Namche Bazar and in Phortse. These families like to be distinguished from the mass of Khambas who reached Khumbu by the usual Nangpa La route, for they consider themselves more fully assimilated to the old Sherpa clans, and hence superior to the 'newcomers' of whom every year brings a fresh contingent across the short Nangpa La track. Some of my Sherpa informants suggested that the Rongsherwa Khambas are more like Sherpas than other Khambas because their homeland is climatically more like northern Nepal than like the rest of Tibet, and they breed *zhum* and *zopkio* as the Sherpas do. This similarity in environment and cattle economy may have been productive of other affinities which facilitated rapid assimilation to the Sherpa way of life.

The practice of referring to anyone who is not the member of a Sherpa clan as 'Khamba' extends even to certain persons believed to be of Gurung and Newar origin. Some of these reached Khumbu by the way of Tibet, and Sherpas say that in their eyes anyone coming from Tibet is a 'Khamba'. The large number of people claiming Gurung ancestry puzzled me throughout my stay in Khumbu, but I failed then to discover a satisfactory explanation for the presence of so strong a 'Gurung' element in Sherpa society. The main location of the Gurung tribe lies in central Nepal, and though scattered Gurung colonies extend as far east as Okhaldhunga, none of them has any links with Khumbu. The solution of the puzzle became obvious, however, when travelling in Thak Khola and the Mustang region of western Nepal. I found that many of the local Bhotias described themselves as 'Gurung' though they had clearly no close affinities with the true Gurung clans occupying the southern slopes of the Annapurna range. These Bhotias claiming the caste status of 'Gurung' maintain regular contacts with Solu and Khumbu from where they obtain most of their cross-breeds (*zopkio*) used as pack-animals and for ploughing. A 'Gurung' of this type would be completely at home in Khumbu; speaking a Tibetan dialect and dressing in Tibetan style he would appear to the Sherpas in no way different from any Tibetan of the border regions. My immediate conclusion that the Khumbu familes described as 'Gurung' must be descended from Bhotias of such areas as Mustang and Thak Khola and not from Gurungs in the normal sense of the term, was confirmed by the discovery that the father of the 'Gurung' Kapa Kalden, the most prominent painter of Khumbu, had lived as a young man in a small monastery at Sauru, a village in Thak Khola. He too had been a well-known painter, and an old lama remembered that after studying at Sauru he had gone to practise his art in Tibet and finally in Khumbu. There he had married a Sherpa girl, and the people of Khumjung referred to his son Kalden as 'Khamba' although most of them were well aware of his claim to 'Gurung' ancestry. Somewhat similar was the case of a Newar believed to have had a Tibetan mother who came to Namche Bazar as the assistant of a Tibetan lama. Despite the fact that his father's original home was at Patan, a town near Kathmandu, he was described as a 'Khamba' because he had reached Khumbu by way of Tibet.

While the core of Sherpa society, consisting of a limited number of exogamous agnatic clans, shows a high degree of constancy, the total society demonstrates a remarkable power of absorption and assimilation. Round the permanent core are arranged numerous accretions, which in some villages account for as much as half the population. The influx from Tibet, which seems to have greatly increased within the last two generations, is responsible for the greater part of these accretions, and in the villages of Khumjung, Kunde, Phortse and Pangboche the percentage of Khamba households was 49, 33, 37·5 and 39 per cent respectively in 1957. Diagrammatically these accretions to Sherpa society can be represented by concentric rings surrounding the original core. Those Khambas who have been settled in Khumbu for several generations are represented by the ring closest to the core, and each successive ring represents a new wave of immigrants. Minor sections of these rings correspond not to Tibetan immigrants, but to Gurungs, Newars and the descendants of other non-Sherpa settlers in Khumbu.

The sections of this diagram do not represent water-tight compartments comparable to the strata of a caste society. Though no new agnatic clan can be added to the central core, fresh blood is continuously being introduced into it by marriages between men of the old Sherpa clans and women of immigrant families. Similarly daughters of Sherpa families may marry into the one or other of the marginal rings. As a rule inter-marriage is more frequent between elements of the society represented in the diagram by immediately adjoining sections than, say, between families of the core and very recent arrivals represented by the outermost ring. The strict adherence to the patrilineal principle in determining a person's position in this system prevents the addition of new lineages to the core, but inter-marriage between different sections has had the effect of gradually blurring the social distinctions between the old families of true Sherpa stock and the descendants of Khambas and other newcomers.

An Open Society

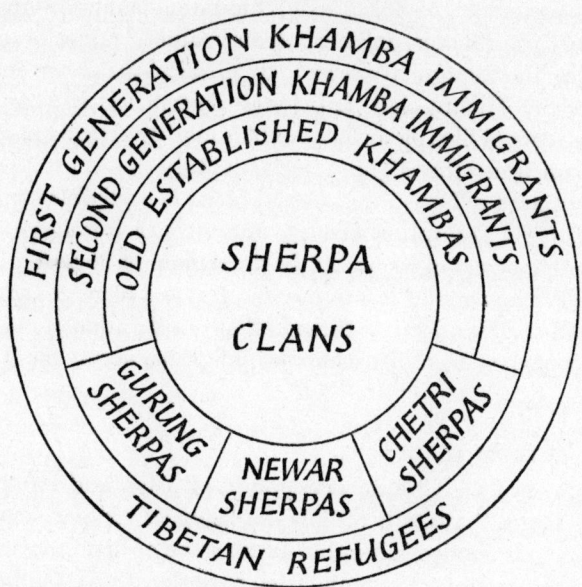

In villages such as Khumjung and Kunde no Khamba family has as yet risen to a position of wealth and influence equalling that of the more prominent families of old standing. In the trading community of Namche Bazar, on the other hand, where social status is directly correlated with wealth there are several Khambas among the leading men of the village, and prejudice against Khambas seems to be very much less pronounced than in a village like Khumjung.

The influx of Newar and Chetri blood into Sherpa society is almost entirely due to marriages or casual intercourse between men of these communities and Sherpa women. Within the last two or three generations there seems to have been no case of a Sherpa marrying a girl of any such community, but several Sherpa women have lived with non-Sherpa men, either in permanent unions or for short periods. Their children and grandchildren are the Newar- or Chetri-Sherpas we find today in several villages. Culturally and linguistically they are indistinguishable from other Sherpas, but in some cases their mixed parentage is reflected in their appearance.

Thus Dorje Ngungdu of Thaktu clan, one of the most respected and most knowledgeable Sherpas of Khumjung, had on his mother's side a Chetri grandfather, and his and his brothers' rather prominent noses betray the foreign strain in their physical make-up, but as a member of the Thaktu clan he belongs nevertheless in every sense to the inner core of Sherpa society, and his mother's mixed parentage does not constitute the slightest social handicap.

The admixture of Newar and Chetri blood is negligible compared to the recurrent absorption of large numbers of immigrants from Tibet into the society of Khumbu. In the regions of Pharak and Solu Khamba elements are far less numerous, but as I have no figures for these areas I shall not include them in the consideration of the causes and effects of the constant trickle of immigrants across the Tibetan frontier.

IMMIGRANTS FROM TIBET

At the time of the Chinese occupation of Tibet and the flight of the Dalai Lama thousands of Tibetan refugees escaped across the Nangpa La and flooded Khumbu. Later some of them moved on to Solu and lower regions, but many tried to settle, at least temporarily, in Khumbu where conditions are closest to those of their Tibetan homeland. At one time over 6,000 of these refugees were camping in Khumbu, an area with a normal population of just over 2,200, and many of them had brought large herds of cattle. There was too little pasture and hardly any surplus winter fodder, and thousands of yak, sheep and goats died within a year of their arrival. Among the refugees themselves there was much distress but no actual famine, for the Sherpas lived up to their best traditions in aiding those in need and offering shelter to as many families as could be accommodated in their houses. The story of this great invasion of Tibetan refugees has still to be told, and its long-term effects on Sherpa society may well warrant a separate study. For although many Tibetans have moved on and some returned to Tibet, others have stayed in Khumbu and are likely to be absorbed within the local society. Yet to consider in this context the large and sudden population influx of 1959 would obscure the process of the slow infiltration of Tibetans into Khumbu which has been going on for several generations. The following analysis of the condition of the Khambas in Khumbu relates to the time previous to the recent upheavals in Tibet, a time when the route across the Nangpa La was

Houses and fields of Khumjung

The central part of Khumjung

Ploughing with *zopkio*

Plough drawn by a team of men

still open in both directions and neither Sherpas nor Tibetans thought of the pass as a politcal and economic barrier.

Throughout the spring, summer and early autumn of every year there was continuous traffic of men and animals along the route which leads from Namche Bazar past the village of Thami to Kyabrak in Tibet, and thence to Tingri. Along this route travelled not only Sherpa and Tibetan traders with their merchandise, but also small bands of Tibetan families, often consisting of a couple and their young children, carrying—as some Sherpas contemptuously said —nothing but 'a basket and a stick'. These migrants were almost invariably poor people who had been attracted by stories of ample employment for seasonal labourers, plenty of food and, on the whole, a higher standard of living. Sometimes they might carry with them a few pieces of woollen material or some dried meat which during the first days in Khumbu they might barter for food and shelter. But hardy and resourceful as the poorer Tibetans are, they usually had little anxiety as to the manner of supporting themselves, nor were they too proud to go with their basket from house to house, begging a few handfuls of potatoes from every Sherpa family. The avowed intention of most of these immigrants was to find work, and if possible a new home, in one of the Sherpa villages. Many Tibetan families succeeded in this aim, and the numerous first, second and third generation Khambas in villages such as Khumjung and Kunde are evidence of the continuity of this process of gradual infiltration.

With hundreds of Khamba families already established in Khumbu, the new arrivals often had kinsmen or friends who would help to smooth their first steps in a new environment. The problem of shelter was in most cases easily solved. In many Sherpa houses there are unused ground-floor rooms, and a Khamba could obtain permission to occupy such a windowless store-room in return for some help with the work on the fields or the cutting and bringing in of firewood. During the time of planting and sowing, and again during harvest, many Sherpa families are short of hands, and Khambas had usually no difficulty in finding employment as agricultural labourers. Many Khamba men, moreover, are skilled in boot-making and tailoring, and the women know how to spin and weave. The wealthier Sherpas are often in need of helpers possessing these skills, and it was not unusual to see newly arrived

Khambas busily sewing boots and clothes in a Sherpa house where they were fed in addition to receiving a daily wage.

In 1957 there were in the village of Khumjung thirteen Khamba families and single individuals, who had no property, lived in the houses of others, and made their living by casual labour and petty trade. Among the men, six did only unskilled work, such as farm-labour, wood-cutting and load-carrying, three did tailoring and boot-making, two worked as spirit media and soothsayers, and one was a house-servant. Four of the women were expert weavers and only occasionally did work other than weaving, while six of the women of these Khamba families did general unskilled work, such as spinning, farm work, dyeing, any odd household task and load-carrying.

One may ask why Khambas preferred a hand-to-mouth existence as daily labourers, dependent on the good will of the wealthier Sherpas, to the life they led in their home villages in Tibet. From all accounts it appears that for the poor life in the neighbouring areas in Tibet was harder than in Khumbu. Village headmen and others in authority demanded a great deal of unpaid labour, and it was extremely difficult for a poor man to raise his economic status. Moreover food was more plentiful in Khumbu, where even the poorest family was seldom short of potatoes, and anyone prepared to work hard could keep himself and his family free from want and reasonably clothed.

It goes without saying that not all Tibetans who came to Khumbu succeeded in establishing themselves in a Sherpa community and many were those who returned to their homes after having worked for a few weeks or months as seasonal farmhands. Yet, the number of those who made good and remained in Khumbu was appreciable. In Khumjung and Kunde alone there were thirty-four Khambas who had arrived in their own lifetime, and were more or less permanently settled. No less than twenty-one of them owned houses and plots of land, and some of the second generation Khambas had acquired considerable wealth or had married into some of the old-established Sherpa families. There were among the 137 families, in Khumjung and Kunde numerous marriages between first- and second-generation Khambas and members of Sherpa families.

Every Khamba settling in a village of Khumbu expects to acquire sooner or later a house and some land of his own. The time it takes to achieve this aim is usually not less than ten to fifteen years, but many Khambas have succeeded in this aim and there are some who have attained considerable prosperity. As a rule families with small children can only just maintain themselves, but as soon as some of the children are old enough to add to the parents' earnings the position changes. Once there is a son capable of carrying loads the father may forgo now and then the wages he might earn and undertake trading journeys on his own account, buying salt in Tibet and exchanging it for grain in the south, or carrying such comparatively cheap commodities as dried potatoes, madder or hides to Tibet, exchanging them for wool, which might be spun and woven into cloth by the women of the family, and then sold at a considerable profit. It is usually by such petty trade that a Khamba begins to gain economic independence, and those men whose wives are skilled weavers have a better chance of rising quickly than those who have no regular additional source of income, because their wives' earnings are only those from casual unskilled labour. In 1957 there were in Khumjung and Kunde alone twenty-one immigrants from Tibet who had succeeded in establishing themselves as independent householders. All but two of them owned the houses in which they lived, they all owned some fields, and nine of them had also acquired livestock.

The fate of a single Khamba family may demonstrate the rapidity with which such immigrants can be absorbed into Sherpa society. Some twenty-five years ago a Tibetan couple came with seven children to Khumbu and settled at Kunde. In 1957 only the wife was alive, but her four sons were all established as independent householders, and of her three daughters two were married to well-to-do men and one to a Khamba of moderate means. Two of the sons had married into families long settled in Kunde and Khumjung while the other two, who had started life as herd-boys in the service of a wealthy Sherpa, had made their own fortune, gradually acquiring houses, land and even a herd of yak. The least prosperous of the four brothers has achieved distinction in another field: as a successful high-altitude porter he was taken on a visit to England as a sequel to the British Kanchenjunga expedition of 1955. At the time of my inquiry the descendants of the original immigrant couple numbered thirty-three, including young children; five of them were married to other Khambas, while four had married members of Sherpa clans.

In Khumjung and Kunde, where there is still scope for a modest expansion of the cultivated area, and in Namche Bazar, where trade is the main economic activity, the influx and absorption of Khambas showed in 1957 no signs of abating. In the village of Phortse, with its strictly limited arable land and the almost exclusive emphasis on agriculture and animal husbandry, this process had by that time come to an end. There, too, fifteen of the fifty-five householders were of Khamba descent, but none of them had immigrated in their own lifetime, and most of the Khamba families had been settled in Phortse for as many as three generations. In Pangboche the position was very similar and only in Milingbo, the village most closely linked with the monastic settlements of Tengboche and Devuche (cf. pp. 131–4), were there any first-generation immigrants from Tibet.

The Sherpas' attitude to the Khambas who have settled among them is of considerable complexity. On the one hand, there is the widespread feeling that Khambas are basically inferior to Sherpas, and this sentiment finds expression in many a loose generalization on Khamba character and behaviour. As most Khambas arrive in Khumbu as paupers their standards of honesty are as a rule much lower than those of the comfortably settled Sherpas. Such petty thefts as occur in Khumbu are usually committed by Khambas, and Sherpas are no doubt justified in doubting the trustworthiness of seasonal workers and new arrivals who live from hand to mouth and have very little to lose. Similarly there is the belief that Khambas are particularly prone to promiscuity, and that men and women of Tibetan origin are more likely to live together in a common household without having gone through any marriage ceremony than the old inhabitants of Khumbu. This idea too seems to be based on fact. First generation immigrants often do not bother to incur the expense of formal wedding ceremonies, and both men and women are inclined to change their partners without much ado. The Sherpas themselves are extremely free and tolerant in sexual matters, but their marriages are not as easily dissolved as those of immigrant Khambas, who have neither family connections nor property claims to consider.

When talking among themselves, Sherpas will often refer to Khambas in derogatory terms and, in the course of a quarrel, even the most respectable Khamba may be told to his face that he or his

An Open Society

father arrived in Khumbu as a pauper, carrying nothing but a stick and a begging basket. When discussing any less commendable behaviour of recent immigrants, Sherpas will often shrug their shoulders with the remark: 'What, after all, can you expect of Khambas?'

Yet, there is another side to the Sherpa-Khamba relationship. Newly arrived Khambas are useful as farm-workers and load-carriers, tailors and boot-makers, and their women as weavers and casual domestic helps. Many a rich Sherpa could neither cultivate all his land, or carry on his trading business, were it not for these hard-working immigrants from beyond the Nangpa La. However much scorn some Sherpas may occasionally heap on Khamba habits there are few who would like to see even the first-generation immigrants depart in a body from Khumbu. The realization of the Khambas' usefulness was reflected in many of the villagers' reactions to the departure from Khumjung in 1956 of A-Rinsing, a Khamba from Karte, who had lived there for fifteen years, but left abruptly in order to escape the responsibility of acting as *lawa*[1] and entertaining his fellow-villagers at the principal seasonal festival, the Dumje. Like any other resident he had been asked to take his turn in contributing provisions for this festival, but although he was no longer poor and had ever since his arrival enjoyed the hospitality of other Dumje *lawa*, he returned to Tibet rather than undertake the obligations of this appointment. The Khumjung people might well have been enraged by this lack of civic sense, but even though no one could question the reasonableness of the demand made on the new resident, there were some who blamed the *gomba* officials for having caused the flight of such a useful man by asking him to incur the expenditure incumbent on a Dumje *lawa*.

Another check on the Sherpas' somewhat contemptuous attitude to the more recent immigrants from Tibet, is the frequency of inter-marriage between Sherpas and Khambas. There are many Sherpas who have the one or other Khamba among their close relatives, and the consciousness of these ties of consanguinity and marriage prevents such men from giving vent to expressions of any general prejudice against Khambas. Yet, the feeling of the inherent superiority of Sherpas vis-à-vis new as well as even old Khamba families is never very far from the surface, and the Khambas are

[1] Cf. p. 186.

fully conscious of this valuation. This became very obvious when at a seance of A-Tutu, a Khamba spirit-medium (*lhawa*), the spirit of a deceased Sherpa spoke through the medium's mouth. The Sherpa's spirit demanded that the offerings he was to get must not be given by so low a person as a Khamba, from whose hands he would not accept them, but that a Sherpa of one of the old clans must offer the gifts of food and diink. Though himself a Khamba, A-Tutu pronounced these stipulations while in trance, and discussed them later, when he had regained full consciousness, without any sign of surprise at the spirit's capricious wishes.

While a feeling of slight superiority colours most Sherpas' attitudes towards the first- and second-generation immigrants from Tibet, there are a few wealthy Khamba families settled for several generations in Khumbu which for all practical purposes are considered the equals of Sherpas, though in the heat of a dispute the word 'Khamba' may be used as a term of abuse even in relation to such people.

Under the influence of drink or the passion of a violent quarrel, the reproach of being a newcomer who airived with empty hands and made his fortune by the grace of the local Sherpas may be levelled even against a Khamba who in his capacity of lama is normally treated with the same respect as any lama of old Sherpa stock. There are several lamas of Tibetan origin who have married Sherpa girls and made their home in the one or other village of Khumbu. Kusho Kapkye, for instance, a Khamba, who came as an adult from Tibet, was for many years the senior lama of Khumjung, and Sharap Lama, who was born in western China, studied in Lhasa, and finally settled in Khumjung, played an important rôle in the ritual life of the village. Of even less relevance is the natal status of those recognized as the reincarnations of famous lamas. Thus the young abbot of Tengboche is the son of undistinguished Khamba parents of Namche Bazar, but as a reincarnation of the founder of Tengboche and present head of the monastery, he is treated with a veneration such as only the greatest of lamas are ever accorded.

AN UNDERPRIVILEGED CLASS

Unlike the caste societies of the Hindu populations of Nepal, Sherpa society is for the greater part unstratified. The distinction between two castes, and even outsiders who are not of Bhotia origin, such as Newars, can be absorbed into the main body of Khumbu society. There are, however, two exceptions to this potential social equality of all residents in a Sherpa village. While there are no status differences between any of the old Sherpa clans, there is among the immigrants from Tibet a class of people considered inferior by other Khambas and, no doubt in consequence of this discrimination, also by the Sherpas. People of this inferior class are referred to as *khamendeu*, an expression which means literally 'mouth-bad' and is associated with the refusal of people of superior class to drink from a vessel touched by the mouth of any person of *khamendeu* status. The opposite of *khamendeu* is *khadeu* or 'mouth-good', and other Khambas and all Sherpas are thus described in relation to the people of *khamendeu* status. The discrimination against the latter does not go as far, however, as the ban on inter-dining between Hindu castes, for persons of *khadeu* status may freely eat the food cooked and served by members of *khamendeu* class, and the only restriction on commensality is the rule that those of *khamendeu* class may not drink from a cup which passes in usual Sherpa fashion from mouth to mouth. Nor does their touch pollute a vessel permanently; when it has been washed it can be used again by people of superior class. But the sharing of the same cup is so important a feature of Sherpa festivals and entertainment that a *khamendeu* person's exclusion from this type of conviviality is a more irksome disability than it may seem at first sight.

There is, moreover, a ban on inter-marriage between persons of *khadeu* and *khamendeu* status, and anyone of superior status who entertains permanent sexual relations with a person of *khamendeu* class loses his or her *khadeu* status and is henceforth treated as *khamendeu*. A casual breach of this rule can be expiated, however, and it is only a lasting association with a person of inferior class which leads to a permanent loss of *khadeu* status. The children from any mixed union rank as *khamendeu*.

Apart from the Khambas of *khamendeu* status, there is another category of people subject to a similar social disability. They are known as Yemba, a Sherpa term synonymous with the Nepali term Gharti. Yembas or Ghartis are released slaves or persons of slave descent. Throughout Nepal slavery was officially abolished in 1926, but the freed slaves and their children are still considered of very low status, and the same restrictions apply to them as to the Khambas of *khamendeu* class. Though Yembas rank according to general belief even lower than *khamendeu* Khambas, there is no restriction on commensality and inter-marriage between these two categories of low-status people. Indeed there are so few Yemba families in Khumbu that they would experience great difficulties in finding mates were it not for the possibility of marrying *khamendeu* Khambas.

Both *khamendeu* Khambas and Yembas are debarred from becoming lamas. While there is no objection against their studying the sacred scriptures, a person the touch of whose lips pollutes a drinking vessel could not fulfil priestly functions, and there is, to my knowledge, no case of a person of *khamendeu* status having entered any religious institution or receiving training as a lama.

The percentage of *khamendeu* families among the immigrants from Tibet is not very high. In 1957 there were among the Khamba families of Khumjung six of *khamendeu* status. There was, in addition, one Yemba family and one single woman, who many years ago came to Khumjung as a slave, being part of the dowry of a girl from Solu, and after the emancipation of slaves stayed on as a servant in the house of her previous masters until finally she acquired a house of her own.

Though *khamendeu* Khambas and Yembas are clearly inferior to *khadeu* Khambas and Sherpas, and there is no machinery by which they could improve their status, they are not excluded from the social and ritual life of a Sherpa village. In Khumjung, for instance, one of the organizers (*lawa*) of the Dumje festival of 1957 was a Khamba of *khamendeu* status. He entertained the villagers in his house, like any other of the nine *lawa*, and fully participated in the rites performed in the *gomba*.

Similarly a Khamba woman who had been born *khadeu*, but lost her status by living as the wife of a *khamendeu* man, commissioned an elaborate *tsho* rite in the village *gomba* for the benefit of her deceased husband. On this occasion she entertained with food and drink not only the officiating lamas, but also many of the villagers, and even the most prominent men had no compunction in accepting the hospitality of a *khamendeu* woman. Nor did I hear any adverse comment on her action of having voluntarily relinquished her *khadeu* status by living with a man of inferior class. In any caste society such a step would undoubtedly have been condemned by the members of her own class, but the Sherpas, though accepting a discrimination imported from Tibet, are not caste conscious and consider such an action entirely the affair of the persons directly concerned.

ALIEN ELEMENTS IN SHERPA SOCIETY

The absence of any sentiment comparable with the caste consciousness of Hindu society and even the present-day Buddhist society of the Nepal valley, has facilitated the absorption of various alien ethnic elements into the body of Sherpa society. We have seen that men of such non-Bhotia groups as Newars and Chetris experience no difficulty in entering temporary or permanent unions with Sherpa women. Their presence in a Sherpa village produces no problem, for Sherpas will admit members of other societies to commensality and normal social intercourse. There is no prejudice against the children from such mixed marriages, and unlike the offspring from *khamendeu* Khambas the descendants of Newars, Chetris, Gurungs and Tamangs are accepted as the social equals of pure Sherpas. This attitude towards the issue from short-lived unions between Sherpa girls and men of other communities springs partly from the general tolerance vis-à-vis children born outside wedlock (cf. p. 88). Such children are accepted and cared for by the mother's family, whether the father is a Sherpa or an outsider, and a good many people of Khumbu have among their ancestors men from other parts of Nepal who had lived only for a short time with a Sherpa girl. Thus in Khumjung and Kunde there are four brothers whose mother had a Chetri father and who have Chetri relations in the vicinity of Aisyalukharka. In the Pharak village of Chaurikharka there are several descendants of non-Sherpa men and all of them are fully privileged members of the village community and socially indistinguishable from pure Sherpas, except for the fact that they have no Sherpa clan name. Several of these men, known as Newar-Sherpa, are the sons and grandsons of a Newar trader who settled in Chaurikharka, and lived for about twelve years in a large house with two Sherpa wives, both of Pankarma clan, but not closely related. A wealthy man described as Chetri-Sherpa, is the son of a poor Sherpa woman who, during the winter when employment and food were scarce, used to go and work in the Chetri village of Dumre near Aisyalukharka. There she entered into an association with a Chetri, and later gave birth to a son who grew up in Chaurikharka and married a Sherpa girl. Another case of a man of mixed ancestry was Puroa Lama of Lukla, a village adjoining Chaurikharka. He passed as a Sherpa but his paternal grandfather was a Tamang and, as one of his sons married a great grand-daughter of a Newar trader settled in Chaurikharka, there are now Sherpa children with both Newar and Tamang blood.

One could continue this list of mixed marriages almost indefinitely. An analysis of the alliances concluded by men and women with a strain of non-Sherpa blood tends to show that there is no prejudice against the issue from such unions. Men and women of Gurung origin have inter-married with some of the most prominent families of Khumbu and Solu, and I have never found that people who to all appearances are Sherpas make any attempt to disguise their non-Sherpa ancestry. Nor does it seem that even in the excitement of a quarrel are Sherpas liable to refer to the descendants of Gurungs, Newars or Chetris contemptuously as 'newcomers'.

Indeed the Sherpas of Khumbu, Pharak and Solu constitute a basically open society which stands in pronounced contrast to the closed caste societies of other parts of Nepal. The comparative ease with which members of neighbouring populations can be absorbed and assimilated recalls a similar flexibility of certain tribal societies which have remained untouched by the influence of Indian ideas of caste. Buddhism in its Tibetan form has allowed such tribal characteristics to persist, and it would seem that the Sherpas combine the basic features of a tribal society with the consciousness of actively sharing in the great civilization of Tibetan Buddhism. This participation in the civilization of a wider society found expression above all in the close links between Sherpa and Tibetan monasteries and the great number of Sherpas who went for training and study to Tibetan centres of learning. Sherpa lamas and monks felt at home not only in Rongphu, but even in such distant places as Shigatse and Lhasa, and the frequent contacts between Tibetan and Sherpa lama, were a continuous source of inspiration to the religious institutions of Khumbu and Solu. When the Chinese communists destroyed monastic life in Tibet numerous Tibetan lamas fled to Khumbu, where the Sherpa clergy and laiety gave them shelter and generous support.

3
The Pattern of Family Life

The Sherpa family consisting of husband, wife and their unmarried children or, in some cases, of two husbands and one wife or one husband and two wives, constitutes a social and economic unit of great independence. Inherent in the settlement pattern and the system of seasonal transhumance is the need for the individual family's self-reliance and divorce from the support as well as from the fetters of kinship ties over prolonged periods. Unlike a primary family among such sedentary populations as Chetris, Newars or Rais, the Sherpa family is not permanently embedded in a web of close kinsfolk. From the moment of its establishment as a separate unit, a moment which coincides usually not with the inception of the husband-wife relationship but with the husband's separation from the parental household, a married couple stands by itself, responsible to no one and relying on no one's support.

There is among the Sherpas no joint-family system, and a general principle, modified only in such cases as that of an only or youngest son staying on in the parental home, demands that every married couple should set up an independent household, even if at first this aim can only be achieved by partitioning the house of the husband's parents. The emphasis laid on the self-sufficiency of the primary family stems partly from the very nature of the marital relationship, which is a freely entered and terminable association between two equal partners, each of whom retains the right over the property he or she contributed to this association. The independent position of a Sherpa wife would be incompatible with the subservient rôle of a daughter-in-law in a Hindu joint-family and, though in the case of youngest sons co-residence of mother-in-law and daughter-in-law is sometimes inevitable, there are various devices designed to shorten this period as far as possible.

As a rule each primary family lives in a separate household, and it is a peculiarity of Sherpa society that the formal establishment of such a family is often postponed until after the birth of one or two children.

PRE-MARITAL RELATIONS

Barring those young people who choose a religious life as monks or nuns, all Sherpas expect to marry and to found in due time a family of their own, but there is no urge to precipitate marriage. Many young people of both sexes defer even a firm betrothal until they are in their middle twenties without meeting with either surprise or disapproval on the part of their parents and kinsfolk. Such a delay in binding themselves to a permanent partner does not involve, however, long periods of sexual abstinence, for the unmarried Sherpa is free to enter into casual sex relations with any unmarried person not excluded from the range of potential mates by the rules of clan exogamy or the prohibition of sexual intercourse between persons of *khadeu* and *khamendeu* status. Such pre-marital love-affairs, even if not in the nature of a prelude to a permanent union, do not arouse adverse comment, for sexual intercourse between those neither bound by the ties of marriage nor by vows of celibacy is not regarded as sinful or socially reprehensible.

This attitude of indifference to the sexual behaviour of unmarried youths and girls is shared by the parents of adolescent and grown-up daughters. Girls are free to receive at night the visits of young men, and considering the fact that all the members of a Sherpa family sleep in the one large living-room, parents must purposely turn a blind eye to their daughters' amorous adventures. Young men will find out the place where a girl usually sleeps and, having silently entered the house, creep up to her without attracting anyone else's attention. Before going so far, a boy has usually made sure that his advances will be well received, and he may have paved the way for the final step, by coming frequently to the girl's house and gossiping with her and any other young people present. Work in forest and fields, and journeys to subsidiary settlements, to the lower country and to Tibet offer numerous occasions for contacts between young boys and girls, and at feasts and dances there is very little restraint on courtship and a peculiar kind of rather rough horseplay. Even on ordinary evenings groups of young people of both sexes may be seen chasing one another through the narrow lanes between fields and houses, wrestling with each other and rolling in heaps of three and four on the ground. There will be shrieks and laughter, and the older people watch this play with amusement and obvious approval.

The jokes bandied between the young people at the least provocation are very direct and hearing them one might well conclude that Sherpa girls are almost indiscriminate in granting sexual favours. Such a conclusion, however, would be erroneous. While in general no 'shame' is attached to sexual matters, and no girl resents a man's open request to let him sleep with her, there are only a few women who are frankly promiscuous. The average Sherpa girl has probably not more than one or two lovers before she formally accepts a young man as her betrothed. A child born to a girl not yet engaged may be considered an inconvenience, hampering the mother's freedom to go on trading expeditions, but no disgrace is attached to having such a *themba* child, nor does it materially affect a girl's chances of a satisfactory marriage. The parents of a girl who has given birth to a child whose father she is not going to marry, either because he is already married or because a brief mutual attraction did not lead to a lasting attachment, usually accept the situation with equanimity and raise no objection to bringing up the child in their own house. With the freedom of the unmarried in sexual matters the birth of children before marriage is inevitable and, as contraceptive practices are unknown, it is somewhat surprising that the number of *themba* children is not greater. Their comparative infrequency is due partly no doubt to the relatively infertile period following the menarche, and the ease with which in the case of a pregnancy the situation may be regularized by a formal proposal (*sodene*) followed by a firm betrothal (*dem-chang*).

AVENUES TO MARRIAGE: *SODENE*

The freedom enjoyed by boys and girls to form attachments and become lovers naturally results in many marriages which are entirely of the making of the two partners. The parents, who are usually aware of the young people's doings, will in such cases endorse the decision made by the couple itself, unless there are grave reasons of family prestige or an obvious unsuitability of the proposed match. Yet, there are also cases of parents forestalling any decision on their children's part and arranging a betrothal which links two important families or is otherwise economically advantageous.

Such a betrothal concluded when both or either of the prospective partners are too young to have very definite ideas of their own is nevertheless unlikely to force an unwilling bride into the arms of a man favoured by her parents, for between the first proposal and the final wedding there are several stages during which an engagement can be broken off without much loss of face to either side.

The first formal step in the conclusion of any alliance is a proposal made by the father or a senior kinsman of the prospective bridegroom to the girl's parents. This proposal is called *sodene*,[1] and it may be made at a time when both bridegroom and bride are still adolescents, or when the young people to be betrothed have already been lovers for some time and the girl might even already be pregnant. In the former case and if no informal understanding has been reached it is usually not the young man's father but some other kinsman or even a trusted friend who takes a wooden flask of beer to the bride's parents and asks for the girl's hand. If there is, however, a practical certainty that the proposal will be accepted, the young man's father supported by several kinsmen will make the formal request. The boy in whose name the proposal is made never accompanies the party, even if he has been a frequent visitor in the girl's house.

The girl's parents have three choices. They may refuse to accept the beer and indicate their opposition to the proposal, a course usually taken only if the request is unexpected and the girl herself is disinclined to accept the proposal. Alternatively her parents may accept the beer, and tell the visitors that they will think about the proposal and consult their daughter. The third possibility is the acceptance of both the beer and the proposal, and this happens in cases when informal agreement has already been reached or the young people have been lovers for some time. In this case the ceremonial proposal only regularizes an existing situation.

An accepted *sodene* gives the young man the right to visit his

---

[1] The word *sodene* is derived from the Nepali word 'to ask', but is in general use among Sherpas. Some of my informants maintained that the proper Sherpa term for this proposal was *ti-chang* ('asking-beer') but others were of the opinion that *ti-chang* referred to a subsequent visit during the marriage negotiations. The term *ti-chang* corresponds obviously to the Tibetan *dri-čan* ('asking-beer') and in Ladakh this word is used for the first proposal made to the bride's parents. Cf. S. R. Ribbach, *Drogpa Namgyal. Ein Tibeterleben*, München-Planegg, 1940, p. 242.

betrothed at night, and unless the girl is very young, it is taken for granted that an engaged couple will have sexual relations. If they get on well and both live in the same village, a young man will spend every third or fourth night with his betrothed, but trading trips and the movements of families to different subsidiary settlements may involve fairly long periods of separation. The time between the acceptance of a *sodene* proposal and the next formal stage in the conclusion of a marriage may nevertheless extend to several years, though on an average it is not more than about one year. A child born to a couple betrothed by *sodene* is normally not considered legitimate, and in the case of a pregnancy the second major step, known as *dem-chang*, is therefore usually speeded up. If, however, a girl is already pregnant at the time of *sodene*, a somewhat extended betrothal ceremony, including the offering of ritual scarves to the bride's parents, saves the child from being born as *themba* and anticipates the social and legal effects of the *dem-chang*.

Betrothal by *sodene* does not give the partners exclusive sexual rights to each other. While a married man can claim compensation (*phijal*) from anyone who has had sexual relations with his wife, and a wife has the corresponding right in the case of her husband's unfaithfulness, a man whose betrothed sleeps with other men has no legal redress. All he can do is to break off the engagement, but few young men take so serious a view of what is little more than an extension of the period of pre-marital sexual freedom into the time of betrothal. Often the acts of unfaithfulness of engaged partners cancel each other out, and no one thinks worse of a man who shuts his eyes to casual amorous adventures of his betrothed.

The relationship created by a betrothal does not involve economic obligations. Neither is the young man expected to render his parents-in-law any help, nor will a girl normally work in her future husband's home. This does not exclude casual assistance at the time of feasts or in the preparations for religious ceremonies, but even such assistance cannot be asked for as a right.

Both sides are free to break off an engagement without having to pay any compensation. Even if a child has been born during the period of betrothal, the girl who had been asked in marriage by the child's father has no claim to any special damages if her betrothed decides to break off relations. In such a case the rules regarding the contribution payable by the father of any *themba* child come into operation, and the decision whether the child should remain with the mother or be taken to the father's house is left to mutual agreement.

The breaking off of a betrothal is not unusual, and my records of the ninety-one households of Khumjung contained twenty-three cases of formal engagements which did not end in marriage. It is obvious that reliable statistical data on the broken engagements of older people, who have long been living in successful unions with other partners, are not easily obtainable, but from the case histories I could follow up from 1953 until 1957 it would appear that about 30 per cent of the engagements formally initiated by *sodene* proposals do not lead to permanent unions.

The comparatively high percentage of broken engagements must not be attributed to a frequency of *sodene* proposals put forward and accepted against the will of the young people. A boy's parents do not usually make such a proposal without their son's previous agreement, and one hears often of *sodene* requests refused by the girl asked in marriage, even though her parents would have been prepared to accept the proposal.

The young people, moreover, are not only free to express their own views and, if necessary, oppose a parental choice, but they can even take the initiative. There are many who become lovers without giving much thought to their parents' wishes and only subsequently ask for a formal engagement to be arranged by their elders. Such requests may run counter to the parents' ideas of a suitable match for their son or daughter, and in 1957 there were in Khumjung and Kunde alone several cases of young men of respectable and well-situated Sherpa families who had married Khamba girls of a social and economic status clearly inferior to their own. But I recall only one instance of Sherpa parents refusing to help regularize their son's union with a Khamba woman. In everyone's but the young man's opinion, this woman was a most unsuitable choice, but even in this case the parents could not prevent their son from continuing his relations with a girl whom they would not accept as their daughter-in-law. As all the formalities leading up to a wedding as well as the wedding rite itself require the active participation of the men's closest kinsmen, determined opposition on the part of a young man's parents is an effective bar to the conclusion of a lawful marriage.

But Sherpa parents are, on the whole, exceedingly accommodat-

Harvesting potatoes in Khumjung

Preparing a field for the planting of potatoes

Yak on a high pasture above Gokyo

Harvesting barley at Dingboche

ing, and young people will seldom pit themselves against their parents' strongly held views. The cases of violent disagreement between parents and children are therefore few, and I have never heard of any tragic outcome of parental opposition to a passionate attachment.

Even though parents do not ignore their children's wishes in the selection of a husband or a wife, they often guide them in their choice, and many alliances between families of equal status or wealth are no doubt the result of a combination of parental suggestions and youthful common sense. This becomes obvious when we scrutinize the marriages concluded within the last two generations by members of the six most prominent families of Khumjung, families which belong to the three dominant clans of Thaktu, Mende and Paldorje. Among 34 marriages 28 were with members of other old Sherpa clans, and only six with members of Khamba families. But even these Khamba families were among those long settled in Khumbu; most of them were of Namche Bazar and so wealthy that at least economically they were not inferior to the prominent Khumjung families with which we are concerned. Not one of the 34 marriages could be considered a definite mésalliance.

At the other end of the social scale we find the same tendency to marry within one's own class. Khambas of *khamendeu* class have normally no alternative to seeking their mates from among those of equally low status. But if we consider those nineteen families of first-generation immigrants from Tibet who have succeeded in acquiring property in Khumjung and Kunde, we find that of 41 marriages 31 are among Khambas and only 10 between Khambas and members of Sherpa families. This ratio does not greatly change if Khamba families settled in Khumbu for two or three generations are included, and it is only the wealthiest Khambas who freely intermarry with Sherpas of good status. In Khumjung there is only one family of this type, but among the Khambas of Namche Bazar there are several rich traders who have inter-married with some of the most respectable Sherpa families.

Proximity of residence plays a considerable rôle in determining the choice of spouses. If we consider the twin settlements of Khumjung and Kunde as a single village, as they are indeed for ritual purposes, we find that of 174 marriages concluded within the last two generations 98 were between people of the same village and only 55 involved men and women of other villages, while the remaining unions were among recently immigrated Khambas. The ratio among the householders in Namche Bazar was 29 marriages between co-villagers, against 16 marriages with people of other villages, but these figures do not include the many couples who came as husband and wife from Tibet and settled in Namche Bazar. In Phortse the ratio in 1957 was 50 marriages within the village against 12 marriages with people from neighbouring villages.

While some of the leading Khumbu families have concluded alliances with members of a prominent family of Solu, there has been very little inter-marriage with Sherpas of Pharak. Neither in Khumjung and Kunde nor in Phortse did I find a single person married to a man or woman of one of the Pharak villages, and this is all the more remarkable as young people from Khumbu regularly visit Pharak for purposes of trade and when they are on their way to the Terai and India.

On the whole we find that spatial distance of residence is a strong counter-indication against the likelihood of marriage alliances, and in this respect the Sherpas greatly differ from such populations as Chetris and Brahmans, who for all practical purposes practise village exogamy. The infrequency of marriages with Sherpas from distant villages, though at first sight surprising in a society with a wide range of trading connections and an unusual experience of distant areas, is probably explicable by the long period of separate residence during a stage in the husband-wife relationship which although termed here 'betrothal' corresponds to the first years of marriage in other societies. Only if the parental houses of the betrothed young people are reasonably near to each other, is the system of nightly visits and the deferment of the final wedding rites until after the birth of a child or children a practicable proposition. Distance makes such contacts difficult or even impossible, and prevents the young people from reaching at an early stage in their relationship that intimacy which Sherpas consider a valuable safeguard against ill-considered matches and a likelihood of divorce owing to incompatibility.

The analysis of the marriages recorded in the house lists of the four villages Khumjung, Kunde, Namche Bazar and Phortse has shown that in the choice of marriage partners the majority of Sherpas follow two preferences: the preference for persons of similar social and economic status, and the preference for those living within the same village.

Consanguineous kinship is as a general rule considered a strong counter-indication to the desirability of a marriage. The rigid rules of clan exogamy preclude any union with a person of one's own patrilineage, and there is also the feeling that it is not advisable to marry a member of one's mother's lineage (*kalak*). There is no objection to marrying a person of one's mother's clan, as long as he or she is of another lineage, i.e. common descent cannot be definitely traced.

Sherpas of Khumjung say that to marry one's mother's brother's or father's sister's daughter used to be strictly forbidden but that the recent marriage of Tsiring Tenzing Lama, the most important man of Solu and self-styled political leader of the Sherpas, with his father's father's brother's daughter's daughter, who stood to him in a relationship equal to that of a cross-cousin, has weakened this prohibition. I nevertheless have not come across any marriage between the children of brother and sister, but among the maternal kinsmen of the same Tsiring Tensing Lama there was a case of a man marrying his father's sister's son's daughter.

Both these cases are exceptions, however, and whereas Tibetans are said to practise cross-cousin marriage, even Khambas recently arrived from Tibet conform to the Sherpas' dislike of such unions.

The children of two sisters, who are described as *mawin*, should not marry either, even though they may be of different clans. The reason given for this prohibition is that as a man addresses his mother's sister as *ama* (mother) such a union would involve marrying the child of a woman whom he calls 'mother'. Grandchildren of sisters may marry, however, and in that case the relationship term for the grandmother's sister will be changed from *ama gaka* (grandmother) to *iwi* (female relation-in-law).

There is no preferred type of marriage except for a man's marriage with his real or classifactory elder brother's widow or his deceased wife's younger sister. Marriages of this type, however, do not involve the establishment of a new relationship between two families, and hence they do not necessitate the ceremonial which normally follows the acceptance of a *sodene* proposal and leads up to the entry of the bride into the husband's house.

The practice of sister-exchange marriage is known to the Sherpas who refer to it as *ngien-dzi-geu*.[1] It is not a frequent practice, however, and several of my informants thought it rather unlucky and quoted the cases of men whose sisters had married their wives' brothers, and had died after only a brief spell of married life. There is no prejudice against two brothers marrying two sisters, and in Thamote there was a family of four brothers, two of whom had married one sister, and two the other. For many years all six lived in a common household, but later they separated and each polyandrous ménage had a house of its own.

Apart from the degrees of kinship or affinity which render a marital union between two persons unlawful or undesirable, there is also the artificial link of ritual friendship, which can be a bar to the marriage of two people otherwise not related. Ceremonial friends (*thowu*)[2] regard each other as brothers, and their children are forbidden to marry.

AVENUES TO MARRIAGE: *DEM-CHANG*

The relations established by the acceptance of a *sodene* proposal are neither inherently permanent nor of legal effectiveness. They can be broken off at any time by either side without incurring a liability to compensation and a child born to a couple linked only by an engagement based on such a proposal is no less illegitimate than any other *themba* child. To put these relations on a more solid basis and give children the status of legitimate offspring it is necessary to endorse the provisional agreement reached between the two families at the time of the *sodene* by a far more elaborate ceremony which requires the active co-operation of a large number of kinsmen on both sides. This ceremony, which resembles and indeed anticipates in several features the final wedding rite, is known as *dem-chang* ('beer of tying'). Its performance does not involve the transfer of the bride from her parents' to her husband's house, and it can therefore be held even when the couple is very young, and there is no intention to precipitate the girl's separation from her natal home or the setting up of a new household. Some parents, anxious to cement a betrothal of young children by endowing it with legal force, may arrange for the *dem-chang* long before the young couple

[1] Lit.: 'marrying one changing'; *geu* is the Sherpa pronunciation of the Tibetan *giurwa*.
[2] Tibetan: *thokpo*.

is likely to take up sexual relations but, in general, *dem-chang* is performed only when it has become apparent that the young people are suited to each other and there is a strong likelihood that the engagement will result in a permanent union.

The performance of a *dem-chang* necessitates lengthy preparations and involves the parents of the girl as well as those of the young man in considerable expenditure. Consultation regarding a convenient date for the ceremony is therefore essential. Such consultation may take place informally, or the boy's father may go with a bottle of beer to the house of the girl's father, and inquire what specific date would be acceptable. Once the date is fixed both families can proceed with the preparations. The most important part of these preparations is the brewing of large quantities of beer and the distilling of liquor, and—on the part of the girl's family—also the procurement of rice and other eatables for the entertainment of the guests. In the case of wealthy people, expecting to entertain a large number of guests, the resources of a single household may not suffice and close relatives and friends may be given the necessary raw materials and be asked to lend a hand with the making of beer and liquor.

On the appointed day the bride's parents prepare their house for the reception of the bridegroom's party. To speak of 'bride' and 'bridegroom' seems justified as the *dem-chang* is an obligatory prelude to the final wedding rites and the Sherpas themselves often refer to the *dem-chang* loosely as *zendi*[1] (wedding) and to the bridegroom's party as the *zendi*-party. The preparations for the guests' reception include almost invariably the borrowing from friends or relatives of numerous low tables and mats and a great deal of crockery. The tables and mats are so arranged as to provide as many places facing the window-bench as possible in the main room of the bride's house The members of the groom's party assemble in the meanwhile in his parents' house, where they are lavishly entertained before setting out for the bride's house.

The groom's party consists of his parents and kinsmen and such villagers as may have been specifically invited to join it. The bridegroom himself, however, is never a member of this party, though if he is already on familiar terms with the bride and her parents he may join the festivities and the dancing once the ritual part of the

[1] *Zendi* is a Nepali word, cf. p. 57.

proceedings has been concluded. All the members of the groom's party are dressed in their best; the men in brocade hats, white shirts, dark blue or brown coats, and colourful boots, and the women in silk blouses of bright colours, long silk or wool dresses of darker colours, broad silk cummerbunds, often matching the blouse, and multi-coloured aprons of Tibetan manufacture, either of heavy silk or the finest of wool, with gold and silver embroidered corners. For this occasion the women usually wear broad gold head-bands and embossed gold ear-plaques as well as large collars made of gold discs, and whatever necklaces of coral, *zhi*-beads and turquoise they possess or are able to borrow.

It is significant that the members of the bride's family and their friends are not as gorgeously attired, and they usually do not participate in the entertainment provided in the houses of the bride's kinsmen, which follows the proceedings in the bride's house.

If both partners in the proposed marriage live in the same village, the groom's party has only a short way to its destination. But in the case of inter-village matches, there will be a lengthy procession to the bride's village and wealthy men or women may ride on a pony, both for their convenience and to add splendour to the party's appearance. When the groom's party arriving from a neighbouring village reaches the village boundary the men fire one or two shots from a muzzle-loader, and this is a sign for the bride's people to make ready for their formal reception, and to await them with bottles of beer at a central place of the village.

The groom's party then files into the village; in front are the men, including a young man carrying a barrel of beer, which is called *yangdzi*.[1] Another man carries a large bottle of beer known as *kyekal*,[2] which is a special gift for the bride's father and mother. The women in their gorgeous attire form the second part of the procession, and as a great deal of drink has already been consumed, the members of such a procession are usually in high spirits.

At a central place of the village, the bride's mother and another woman of the bride's side, both dressed in a special kind of sleeveless multi-coloured Tibetan cloak (*angi-tang-za*),[3] await the procession

---

[1] Any alcoholic drink brought as a gift with a view to gaining a person's good will is known as *yangdzi*.
[2] *Kyekal:* bottle containing beer or spirits presented as a gift on any occasion.   [3] *Angi:* woman's garment; *tang-za:* ornament, tassels.

with large wooden bottles of beer and there follows a rite known as *sur-chang*.[1] Incense is burnt and a prominent member of the bride's kin, who need not be of her own clan, then dips a grass-whisk into this beer and sprinkles some offerings (*sirkim*, Tibetan *gser-skyems* 'libation') while he recites a blessing according to a standard formula, which most older men know by heart.

When this prayer has been said the beer is offered to the guests, and several other women, related to the bride, who also carry bottles of beer, serve similar refreshments without the recital of any prayer or blessing.

The groom's party then moves to the bride's house and, in the courtyard or at the door, there are again women with beer, who offer drinks to all the guests before they are allowed to enter.

Inside the bride's house men of her father's clan and a few affinal kinsmen and friends have occupied the window-bench. The guests then enter without further ceremony and occupy the prepared places facing over their low tables the host's kinsmen. The women sit in the first row, while the men occupy the seats behind them and along the wall. If both families are wealthy there may be as many as sixty people in the groom's party, and a slightly smaller number of relatives and guests invited by the bride's parents.

As soon as all are seated the women of the house serve beer, liquor and tea, and shortly afterwards a meal of boiled rice and some kind of meat or vegetable stew, followed by another round of beer. Next, a brass plate containing rice-grains and salt is put before a lama sitting on the window-bench among the host's kinsmen. Putting a whisk into the barrel of beer brought by the groom's party, which has been placed near him, the lama pronounces the same blessing as recited before, sprinkles some drops of beer and scatters rice-grains.

Thereupon follows the most vital part of the entire ceremony: the presentation of scarves by members of the groom's party to the parents and relatives of the bride. Two young men, whose parents must be alive but who need not be close kinsmen of the groom, first drape a white scarf round the centre post of the house, and then place a large dough-figure (*torma*) before the bride's father. They then proceed to put scarves (*kata*, Tibetan *k'a-btags*) round the neck of the bride's father, any of the bride's grandparents, the bride's

[1] *Sur:* a mixture of flour, butter, sugar and juniper burnt as incense.

elder brothers if she has any, the bride's mother, and then in a rough sequence of seniority to the other clansmen and relatives of the bride. While presenting a scarf they also offer a drink of the beer brought by the groom's party. This phase of the ceremony may take a considerable time.

So great is the significance of this presentation of ceremonial scarves that in the event of a *sodene* proposal made for a girl already pregnant scarves may be offered to her parents together with the *sodene* beer in order to confer legitimacy on the unborn child. If this is done the *dem-chang* may be deferred until after the birth of the child, who otherwise would be considered a *themba*. Although such a presentation of scarves at the time of the *sodene* does not absolve the parties from performing a *dem-chang* ceremony in due course, all its legal consequences are anticipated by the simple giving and acceptance of two scarves.

All those offered scarves at the *dem-chang*, even if only friends and not kin of the bride's family, are placed under the obligation of giving the bride a present at the time of the wedding. If people are poor and cannot provide enough scarves, they put roasted barley flour (*tsampa*) on the shoulders of those to be honoured and this creates the same obligation as the giving of scarves.

As soon as the presentation of scarves has been completed, the bride's father, or another spokesman of the bride's family, rises from his seat, and makes a short speech. This begins invariably with an announcement on the following lines: 'Today, on the 5th day of the month of Dawa . . . , my daughter X has been given to Y, the son of Z of that and that village. From now on she is Z's daughter-in-law.' The rest of the speech may be in a jocular vein, and after every sentence there are calls of '*tutse, tutse*' (thank you, thank you) on the part of the groom's party.

Immediately after this short speech the groom's father, who until then has not taken any active part in the proceedings, goes up to the bride's father, offers him a bowl of beer and drapes a second scarf round his shoulders. This completes the ceremonial part of the *dem-chang*, in which neither the bride nor the groom figures in any way. The latter is never present, and the bride remains inconspicuous among the women of the house, engaged in the preparation and serving of food.

Shortly after the bride's father has received the second scarf, tables and mats are removed, and the members of the groom's party form a semi-circle and begin to dance. The rhythm of the first song is usually slow and solemn, and the dance accordingly sedate. But it is soon followed by livelier singing and dancing, and many of the dancers are by that time extremely merry. More and more beer is served, and some of the host's kinsmen are drawn—sometimes dragged—into the circle of dancers. At that stage the bridegroom may join the gathering and even take part in the dance but it seems that the bride, though present, never dances at her own *dem-chang*.

The dance in the bride's house rarely lasts long, for members of the groom's party—but not necessarily the other guests—have invariably been invited to the houses of several of the bride's nearest relatives, such as her father's brothers, married brothers and sisters established in separate houses, father's brother's sons, mother's brothers and sisters, and even married cross-cousins. In each of these houses the same procedure is followed. The guests enter and are invited to be seated in much the same order as in the bride's house. They are then served tea, beer and also distilled liquor. During this time the guests laugh and joke among themselves and with their hosts, and individual men and women will shout across the room remarks and suggestions to each other which in most other societies would be considered exceedingly risqué, if not altogether too forthright even for a joke. This general conversation is soon interrupted by the serving of a meal which consists invariably of boiled rice with some stew or vegetable sauce. By the time the guests have been entertained in several houses they cannot eat very much, and it is the accepted custom to take the rice with them in bags specially brought along for this purpose.

As soon as the meal is over, tables and mats are removed, and singing and dancing is resumed. If the night is far advanced, any one of the guests may be too drunk or too tired to join in the dance, and no one minds if he snatches half an hour of sleep on a bench or in a corner but when the party moves to the next house, he will usually be woken up and dragged along by his friends.

This succession of entertainment in the houses of the bride's kinsmen may last into the early hours of the morning, and when the last house expecting the party for that night has been visited the individual guests go to sleep wherever friends or kinsmen offer them a convenient place. If the families involved in the *dem-chang* are wealthy, and many kinsmen have offered to entertain the groom's party, the visiting, drinking and dancing may be resumed the next day and extend even into the following night. The formal farewell from the bride's parents will then be on the third day, when the guests may be once more entertained to a meal. But normally the celebrations end on the second day, and the members of the bridegroom's party return to their houses or set out for their village during the morning of that day.

The costs of the entertainment during a *dem-chang* vary greatly according to the economic status of the two families. A rich man of Khumjung spent at the time of his daughter's *dem-chang* approximately Rs.180 on the food and drink offered to the guests on the first day, and about Rs.30 on the meal on the third day. These sums did not include the produce from his own fields and herds which he used for feeding the guests. The expenditure of the groom's parents is much less, as they have to provide only beer for the entertainment of the guests when they assemble before setting out for the bride's house. The beer is carried there as a gift, and the scarves are for presentation to the bride's kinsmen. There is, however, some deferred payment for the hospitality received in the houses of the bride's relatives and friends. At the time of the wedding, when the groom's party once more visits those same houses, the bridegroom as well as each member of his party has to give to each host a cash gift commensurate with the entertainment received.

The performance of the *dem-chang* has an important effect on the legal aspects of the relationship between the prospective spouses, but it makes for little change in their day-to-day behaviour. Both continue to live in their parents' houses and remain full members of their parental economic unit. If they have been in the habit of sleeping together they will go on doing so, but if the young man has not yet begun to visit his betrothed at night, the *dem-chang* celebration will not necessarily mark the commencement of sexual relations. A very young boy may still be too shy to approach his betrothed, and the young girl may refuse to yield to his advances even though she knows that any child conceived would be legitimate.

In some respects the legal relationship of those united by the *dem-chang* rite is identical to that of husband and wife. Their children are legitimate, neither partner can break off the engagement without paying fees equal to those due in the case of divorce, and if either of the partners dies the rights created by the performance of the *dem-chang* are inherited by the nearest kinsmen of the same sex junior in age to the deceased. Thus a man's younger brother is entitled to marry his late brother's betrothed without having to repeat *sodene* and *dem-chang*, and if she is unwilling to do so he can claim the same compensation as his deceased brother might have done in the event of a rupture of the betrothal. Similarly the younger sister of a girl who dies after the celebration of the *dem-chang* assumes all her elder sister's rights though she is not under an obligation to marry the latter's betrothed.

The fees payable by those who break off an engagement solemnly endorsed by the *dem-chang* ceremonial are the same as in the case of the dissolution of a marriage by divorce (cf. p. 74). There is, however, one important difference between the rights bestowed upon the partners by the *dem-chang* and those resulting from the final wedding rites. While the latter include the right of a husband or a wife to levy a fee known as *phijal*[1] from any person committing adultery with the other partner, no such right results from the *dem-chang* procedure. A man has no legal redress if his betrothed has sexual relations with other men, nor can a girl claim *phijal* from women who had such relations with the man to whom she is bound by the tie created by her parent's acceptance of scarves from his kinsmen.

Thus we find the unusual position that a betrothal ceremony creates far-reaching mutual rights to a permanent partnership, dissoluble only by the payment of compensation without, however, giving either side exclusive sexual rights.

Nor does the *dem-chang* give the man any right to his future wife's labour. In the rare case when a girl enters her betrothed's house before the performance of the wedding rite—such as may happen in the event of her parents' sudden death or any other unforseen circumstances—he has to pay her 'wages', known as *kissin*[2], for the work she does in his household or fields. These 'wages' are usually paid at the time of the wedding, and as a rule they are given not in cash but in the form of clothes or jewels. The amount payable

---

[1] *Phi* = to remove, *jal* = payment; *phijal* = a payment to remove the guilt of adultery.
[2] *Ki* = manual work.

depends on the economic status of the parties and also on the type of work a man's betrothed has been doing. The traditional minimum figure for this *kissin* payment is Rs.15 per year, but the devaluation of the currency has necessitated a radical adjustment of all such rates, and even poor people would today pay not less than Rs.50 while in the case of a rich man the *kissin* paid for a year may amount to Rs.200.

The payment of *kissin* is customary only if for one reason or the other there has been a delay in the performance of the regular wedding rite. In the irregular unions of couples living together without any intention of going through a formal marriage ceremony, such as are not uncommon in the cases of widowed and divorced persons as well as among certain recently immigrated Khambas, the question of *kissin* never arises.

In the present context the practice of paying *kissin* is significant mainly as an indication that even after the *dem-chang*, which confers full rights of legitimacy on a couple's children, the woman remains a member of her parental economic unit, and is entitled to wages for any service she may render to the man with whom she is regularly sleeping.

After the performance of the *dem-chang* several years may elapse before the parents of bridegroom and bride agree to hold the final wedding rite. More often than not the first child of a couple is born in the girl's parents' house, and in some cases there may be even two children before the wedding is held and the young people set up a household of their own or the bride moves into the house of her husband's parents. Such a delay may occur for various reasons. The girl's parents may be in need of their daughter's labour and hence unwilling to dispense with her any earlier than necessary. Conversely the young man may for some time not be in a position to set up a household of his own; and unless he is a youngest or only son it is not customary to introduce his bride into his parents' home. The wedding may therefore have to be postponed until he has been able to acquire a house or a separate part of a house. Khambas newly arrived from Tibet or setting up a new household are prepared to live in a single, windowless ground-floor room of someone else's house but no Sherpa is normally willing to accept such conditions; and if a father wishes to accommodate a married elder son in his own house, he must divide it vertically and provide at least one room on the upper floor with a separate entrance and staircase for the new family.

To the Sherpa a delay in the performance of the wedding rites does not appear irksome or embarrassing, and it is only in the case of couples living in different villages that a bride's prolonged residence in her natal home is prejudicial to the development of normal relations between the spouses. In these cases there is usually no long interval between the commencement of sexual relations and the performance of the final wedding rite. In Khumjung and Kunde there were, in 1957, altogether twenty-seven girls whose *dem-chang* had been performed and who lived with their parents. All except three of these girls were betrothed to men of Khumjung and Kunde; eleven had given birth to children and the fathers of these children all resided in the twin villages of Khumjung and Kunde.

The final wedding rites, known as *zendi* or *gyen-kutop*[1], either follows upon the *dem-chang* without further intervening ceremonies, or the groom's parents and kinsmen may pay two more ceremonial visits to the bride's parents. These are called *ti-chang*[2] and *pe-chang*[3]. Neither of them is obligatory, but wealthy people sometimes surround the *ti-chang* with nearly as great a show of hospitality as that offered during the *dem-chang*. It is considered desirable that on this visit too the groom's father should be accompanied by as many kinsmen as possible. The ostensible purpose of the *ti-chang* is to obtain the bride's parents' consent to an early celebration of the wedding, and in the formulation of his proposal the groom's father may point out that it is troublesome for his son to come night after night to his betrothed's house and that the wedding should therefore take place soon. When the approximate time for the wedding has been decided upon—and it is usual to allow two or three months for the preparations and the collection of the dowry—there is drinking and dancing as at the *dem-chang*.

The next optional ceremonial visit, the *pe-chang*, takes place a

---

[1] *Zendi* is a Nepali word, but in frequent use among Sherpas; *gyen* = 'ornamental mark on forehead'; *kutop* = 'to put on'. I was told that *gyen* means literally a mark of vermilion, but in Khumbu the marks put on the foreheads of the bridal couple are of butter.
[2] *Ti-chang* = 'question beer'; the 'question' relates to the time of the wedding.
[3] *Pe-chang* = 'meeting beer'; the 'meeting' relates to the discussion of the auspicious date for the wedding.

short time before the wedding with the purpose of fixing an auspicious day for the *gyen-kutop*. The number of kinsmen who accompany the groom's father need not be large on this occasion but a lama must be called in to discover an auspicious day.

Both *ti-chang* and *pe-chang* may be replaced by informal consultations, and it is only rich people who use these negotiations as occasions for a display of wealth and hospitality. Unlike the *dem-chang* neither of these ceremonial visits has any effect on the legal position of the betrothed, and their only positive function is to increase, through their participation in feasting and dancing, the familiarity between the kinsmen of the future spouses.

THE WEDDING RITE: *ZENDI* OR *GYEN-KUTOP*

The culmination of negotiations and ceremonial visits which usually have extended over several years is the rite by which a man and a young woman, who may or may not have had sexual relations but often have already one or two children, are finally recognized as husband and wife. This rite terminates the girl's membership of her parental economic unit, and it is at the time of the wedding that she is given a share of the family property in the form of a dowry (*nor*).[1] This dowry remains her personal property for the rest of her life, irrespective of the success or failure of the marriage, and the wedding rite has thus the subsidiary effect of establishing a woman as an independent legal person in possession of individual property. Though at the wedding there are several brief religious ceremonies, the emphasis of the whole procedure is not on the ritual but on the economic aspects of the change in relationships. Much of the preparations is concerned with the collection of the dowry which consists not only of the property the parents give to their daughter but also of the gifts of kinsmen, friends and co-villagers invited to the wedding. It is usual for the bride's parents to ask kinsmen and friends on the eve of the wedding to an informal party, known as *nor-lung*, which means literally 'dowry-asking'. Those who accept the invitation give on that occasion a wedding gift (*nor*) or promise it for a later day. All such gifts and promises of gifts are recorded in a document which contains also all the items of the dowry given by the bride's parents. Indeed, no distinction is made between the dowry and the gifts of kinsmen and friends;

[1] *Nor*—also a general term for 'property'.

both are known as *nor*. The gifts remain the bride's property, and are not considered presents given to both bridegroom and bride.

Persons who contribute in this way to the dowry can expect a gift of approximately equal value from the bride's parents or nearest kinsmen when one of their own daughters marry. In this way a chain of obligations is created, and the parents of the bride invite on this occasion mainly the members of those families with whom such a relationship of mutual assistance is already established, as well as new friends whom they wish to draw into the net of reciprocal support.

The record of gifts and dowry, which is retained by the bride's parents, may be required for the settlement of disputes arising from either a divorce, when the wife is entitled to retain all the property she received as wedding gifts and dowry, or from the division of property among the heirs of husband and wife. It is also available for reference when at a future wedding the reciprocal obligations of gift-giving come into operation. I have already mentioned that anyone presented with a scarf at the time of the *dem-chang* is expected to give the bride a wedding gift, and such gifts vary according to the closeness of relationship and the economic status of the persons concerned. A wealthy man may give the daughter of a close relation a wedding gift worth about Rs.100, while a distant kinsman of modest means need not give more than two or three rupees.

There is neither an upper nor a lower limit to the dowry (*nor*) parents give their daughter on the occasion of her wedding, neither does the dowry represent the bride's final share of her parents' property. She may subsequently receive further gifts, or be given a share (*norkal*) on the occasion of any division of the parents' property in their lifetime.

The dowry may consist of land, houses, cattle, jewellery, clothes and household utensils. Although cash is seldom given, the items are recorded with their estimated money value. Wealthy people with moderately large holdings of immovable property usually include in a daughter's dowry at least one field. Houses and land in subsidiary settlements are also often disposed of in this way. The trading families of Namche, for the most part, own little land, and in their case dowries consist of jewels, household goods and clothes. At a wedding of Namche people of average economic status which I attended in 1957 the parents' gifts to the bride were evaluated—

and probably somewhat over-evaluated—at Rs.3,500, and among the gifts contributed by kinsmen there were ten yak-hair blankets each worth Rs.100 or more. At a wedding of the daughter of a rather poor Khamba widow of Khumjung to a newly immigrated and even poorer Tibetan the dowry given by the mother consisted of one field worth Rs.200 and clothes and jewels worth about Rs.360. Though most of the family's relatives and friends were by no means affluent, their gifts totalled an estimated value of Rs.292.

The receipt of a dowry by the bride is one of the distinctive marks of a union legalized by the full wedding rites. A girl who lives with a man in a common household without having gone through the marriage ceremonial hardly suffers any social disabilities, but does not receive a dowry. Thus the elder sister of the Khamba girl who had received a dowry and gifts to the value of Rs.752, had set up a household with another immigrant Tibetan, but as in her case there was no wedding, she had received no dowry and no gifts whatsoever. She nevertheless contributed to her sister's dowry.

Whereas the bride's parents have to provide a dowry, the groom's parents have to give their son a share of their property if he is setting up a separate establishment. In the case of a youngest or only son, however, no such share is given for such a son rarely separates from the parental household and he ultimately inherits the house as well as the entire property, remaining after elder sons, as well as daughters, have received their shares. Kinsmen and friends do not give any wedding-presents to the bridegroom, though they usually contribute beer and even food to the celebrations in his house.

The obligations of the bridegroom's parents at the time of the wedding consist mainly of contributions to the food and drink served in the bride's house and of cash payments to the relatives and friends of the bride, who entertained the *zendi*-party at the time of the *dem-chang* as well as during the wedding. The minimum contribution to the entertainment in the bride's house is laid down by tradition and amounts to Rs.2 for 80 lb. of grain for making beer, Rs.2 for 40 lb. of rice, Rs.1 for the presentation of beer when the bride leaves the parental house, and Rs.1 for the presentation of beer at other phases of the ceremonies. The amounts set against the quantities of grain required are nowadays entirely unrealistic and have to be multiplied by at least ten. It has therefore become usual to give the quantities of grain required in kind, or to adjust

Sherpa girl of Namche Bazar

Young Sherpa couple of Khumjung

Women of Khumjung

the cash contributions to the drastic drop in the value of the rupee.

The ceremonies and the feasting surrounding the rite of *gyen-kutop*, which is the vital part of a wedding, extend usually over two days. These celebrations are in many respects almost identical with those connected with the *dem-chang*. It will suffice therefore to sketch the procedure in outline and to describe only the essential features of the wedding rite in greater detail.

On the first day of the wedding celebrations the members of the bridegroom's party, often referred to as the *zendi*-party, assemble in the groom's parental house, or—if he already lives in a house of his own, as may happen in the case of an eldest son or of a widower remarrying—in the house which will be the couple's matrimonial home. The guests are all in their best clothes, and the bridegroom himself is as festively dressed as possible. Wealthy people on this occasion may wear Tibetan or Chinese ceremonial silk gowns and hats with silken tassels such as are worn by Chinese officials.

A painting on cloth representing calendrical and other symbols, known as *sipa-kolu*[1] and used for warding off evil spirits, is brought by a lama, who may possess one of his own or borrow it for the occasion from the local temple, and is tied to a pole in front of the groom's house. When the groom's party finally emerges a blessing is recited by the officiating lama and the women of the groom's family offer drinks of beer in ceremonial manner.

The *sipa-kolu* is then untied and carried by the lama like a banner at the head of a procession consisting of the bridegroom and the members of the *zendi*-party. In the bride's house kinsmen and friends have meanwhile also gathered but, unlike the bridegroom, the bride is not dressed in festive clothes and wears as a rule her very oldest clothes, which she will not take with her to her new home.

As the procession approaches the bride's house shots are fired and crackers let off. A fire of juniper branches is lit in front of the house, and women of the bride's family, dressed as at the *dem-chang* in sleeveless, patterned Tibetan cloaks, offer the guests drinks of beer from large wooden flasks. There is a repetition of the *sirkim* and the recitation of a blessing and the party then enters the house.

The seating resembles that at the *dem-chang*, except that the

---

[1] *Sipa* = 'whole world'; *kolu* = wheel; cf. Waddell, *The Buddhism of Tibet*, London, 1895, *sipa korlo (srid-pa k'or-lo)*.

bridegroom occupies a prominent place next to the lama. The latter brings in the *sipa-kolu* and hangs it up above his own seat. After tea and beer have been served a spokesman of the bride's party, who is not necessarily one of the senior men, welcomes the groom's party, expressing the bride's family's pleasure at their arrival, and refers in traditional phraseology to the hardships they had undergone on their way across the hills, even if they only came from another house of the same village. Considering that the majority of marriages are within one and the same village, this reference to a long and tiring way would seem to reflect the memory of a time when inter-village marriages were more frequent, possibly because the clans were more localized than they are at present.

A member of the groom's party, chosen for his skill in oratory rather than for the closeness of kinship ties, replies to this speech and thanks the hosts for the cordial reception. In these speeches there is usually no direct reference to the forthcoming wedding rite, and they are not in the nature of a marriage sermon. The speeches are followed by a general exchange of drinks, and next formal *yangdzi* drinks are offered to the guests by the women of the household, beginning with the lama and the bridegroom. While goodwill and sentiments of friendship are expressed in this traditional manner, the guests begin to sing, interweaving their voices skilfully in a complicated chorale. When the offering of *yangdzi* drinks has been completed, the room is cleared and men and women of the *zendi*-party form a semi-circle and dance to the rhythm of their own singing. The dancing does not usually last long and at the end young men of the bride's party distribute small strips of white cloth to the dancers which represent scarves and are known as *yangdzi kata*. They are given as a reward for the singing and dancing and not as a symbol of the establishment of a new relationship, such as the scarves offered at the *dem-chang*.

After the receipt of the *yangdzi kata* the groom's party leaves the bride's house, and there follows the same visiting of the houses of the bride's kinsmen which takes up most of the time at the celebration of the *dem-chang*. Except for the obligatory presence of the bridegroom at each of these entertainments there is no difference between the procedure at the *dem-chang* and that at the wedding. There is drinking, eating and dancing in each house visited, and most of the night is usually spent in this way.

The Pattern of Family Life

If many of the bride's kinsmen have invited the *zendi*-party, the greater part of the following day may be required to complete the round of hospitable houses, and the climax of the marriage ceremonies, consisting of the *gyen-kutop*, may be deferred until the late afternoon. During all that time there is little activity in the bride's house and the bride takes no part in the celebrations. The auspicious time for the bride's departure from her parental house, which has been selected by the lama, often does not coincide with the termination of the entertainments in other houses. The device of a token departure is therefore employed in order to comply with the lama's advice without having to hurry up or delay the proceedings. At the time of this token exit the *sipa-kolu* is taken from the bride's house and tied to the flag-pole in front. Once this has been done the actual 'going away' can be postponed until any later time.

When the members of the groom's party have at last completed the visits to all the houses where they had been invited, they return to the bride's house and once more take their seats according to precedence. This time several ritual objects and bowls with the usual offerings are arranged on the table in front of the lama's seat. The lama then recites an auspicious text from a book and scatters offerings of rice-grains.

Next, a low table is placed opposite the lama's table and behind it a mat is spread out as a seat for the bridal couple. On this mat a pattern of two swastikas, one of them inverted, has to be drawn with rice-grains, before the couple sits down. A young man of the groom's party then leads the bride and bridegroom to this mat, and they sit down facing the lama. Shortly before this the bride has been dressed in new clothes and when she has sat down a ceremonial cloak (*angi-tang-za*) is draped round her shoulders. It is customary for brides to weep at this stage, and this they do even if they have lived with the bridegroom for years and have already borne him children. Tea is then served to the bridal couple and they sip from the cups while the lama recites a blessing.

The stage is now set for the most essential part of the wedding ritual, the *gyen-kutop*. The groom's father, or another prominent man of the groom's party, anoints the bride's head with butter, and a kinsmen of the bride does the same to the bridegroom. The former says that from that day on the bride will be given the status of a daughter-in-law, and he admonishes her with words such as these:

'From now on you must always sleep with my son; if you sleep with any other man you will be fined. May you both live to be a hundred years. May not even a mouse obstruct your path, may not even the birds be higher than you, may not even the air come between you. There may be much wealthier men than your husband, but you should not go with them, even if they show you all their wealth. There may be stronger and healthier men than your husband, and they may try to seduce you, but you should not yield to them. There may be men more handsome than your husband, and they may try to persuade you to go with them, but you should not let yourself be persuaded.'

Corresponding admonitions are given to the bridegroom by the father or a kinsman of the bride, and he too is told that if from now onwards he sleeps with other women, he will be fined 'according to the law'.

As soon as the anointing and the speeches are over, and sometimes while they are still in progress, the men of the groom's party blow conch-shells and break into a wild dance known as *silu-chumbu*, in which each dancer turns and swirls round his own axis, and several dancers swing white yak-tails. I have been at a wedding where everyone jumped from his seat as soon as the lama had finished reciting the *sirkim*, and there was such noise and confusion that one could neither see nor here the vital rite of the anointing of bride and bridegroom. But even under normal circumstances there is a great deal of noise and excitement as the dancers swing yak-tails and others play heavy brass cymbals.

In the midst of this din the bridal couple, followed by members of the groom's party leave the house, only to be stopped outside by women of the bride's family, each of whom carries a flask of beer, from which she offers drinks to the groom and his kinsfolk. These women are the hostesses of the houses visited by the groom's party during *dem-chang* and the wedding, and this is the moment of reckoning when the bridegroom and his kinsmen must pay for the hospitality received. The bridegroom may pay as much as Rs.15 to Rs.25 to each hostess and if ten houses have been visited these payments amount to an appreciable part of the wedding expense. His kinsmen and friends give one or two rupees to each hostess, and it is said that in some cases a family entertaining a *zendi*-party gain rather than lose by offering their hospitality.

These proceedings in front of the bride's house may take a considerable time, and I have seen wedding parties getting soaked in a heavy downpour while innumerable drinks of beer were offered and accepted and the bridegroom paid his dues from a thick wadge of rupee notes. When both the drinking and the doling out of cash gifts are finished, a procession forms, headed again by the lama carrying the *sipa-kolu* like a banner. The bride is followed by a number of unmarried girls, known as *kel-mi* ('companions'), who carry the movable parts of the dowry. These bridesmaids must neither have had any *themba* children, nor must they have taken the vows of a nun; they must be unmarried but of marriageable age and status. For three days they remain with the bride in her husband's house, and at the end of that period the bride gives them presents.

At the bridegroom's house the procession is welcomed by women of the groom's family. They serve drinks of beer, and put into the hands of each person entering spoonfuls of curd, butter, *tsampa*, sugar and *thoma*, a kind of small root obtained from Tibet. If the bride has already a child or children by the bridegroom, she must carry them herself over the threshold.

In the bridegroom's house there is more drinking and dancing, and this feast as well as the beer brought by kinsmen and neighbours is known as *dong-chang*.[1]

The next day, and sometimes also on the third day, the bridal couple and the groom's parents are invited to the houses of the groom's kinsmen, and the bridesmaids are included in these invitations, which constitute the final phase of the wedding celebrations.

SUBSTITUTES FOR THE WEDDING RITE

After *sodene* and *dem-chang* have been performed in the customary way there is the possibility of a short cut to a valid marriage, by which the expenditure inevitably connected with a wedding-ceremony can be almost entirely avoided. This short cut is known as *rit*—a term derived from the Nepali word *riti* ('custom')—and consists in the prospective husband paying to the bride's parents the paltry sum of Rs.6 and taking her into his house without any ceremony or ritual accompaniment. By making this payment the

[1] *Dong-chang* is the beer served on any occasion when a person returns to his house, e.g. at the home-coming of a trader after a long journey.

husband establishes exactly the same rights as a man married by *gyen-kutop*, and neither the couple nor their children suffer under any legal disability. The only consideration which makes even poor people hesitate before they take this step is a certain loss of prestige, inevitably connected with such admission of their inability to afford a wedding and the greatly diminished prospects of any kind of dowry.

The device of *rit* is employed not only in cases of poverty, however, but also as an answer to an undue delay of the wedding ceremonies caused by the bride's parents. Thus there was the case of a fairly affluent man of Khumjung who, exasperated by the subterfuges used by his betrothed and her parents to delay the wedding, deposited six rupees with his *pembu* because the girl's parents did not want to accept the *rit* payment and forcibly dragged his bride to his house. This resort to violent means did not lead to a successful marriage, however, and when he found that he could not get on with his wife he let her return to her parents, and she subsequently married another man.

In the case of second marriages even wealthy people sometimes resort to the custom of *rit* and, if both bride and bridegroom had previously been married by *gyen-kutop*, this simplified way of concluding a valid union involves no loss of prestige.

While marriages concluded by *rit* are legally equal to those celebrated with full rites in every respect, there is another type of union which, though permitted by Sherpa custom, has few of the legal consequences of a formal marriage. Such unions, lacking any ritual sanction, are known as *tso-ni-dekino*, which means literally 'two people staying together'. They are formed by a man and a woman setting up house together and pooling their economic assets. People who have been married before often conclude such unions and, though their children are strictly speaking *themba*, no disability is connected with this fact as long as parents and children live together in one household like the members of any other family. Young unmarried Sherpas are unlikely to enter such a union, but poor Khambas, lacking kinsmen, who would co-operate in the celebration of *dem-chang* and wedding, sometimes enter a marital partnership in this informal manner, and if their union lasts there is little to distinguish it from other marriages. It is mainly the absence of any legal safeguards against a dissolution and the interference of

The Pattern of Family Life

other men and women with either of their partners which distinguishes a *tso-ni-dekino* union from a legal marriage. For either partner can terminate the association any moment at will without being liable to the payment of compensation, and no one can be fined for having sexual relations with a woman or a man living in such an unsanctioned union.

Surprisingly enough even fairly affluent Sherpas of good status often do not take the trouble to regularize a second or third marriage by the device of *rit*, but live together in unions devoid of legal validity. Thus Ongcho Lama of Khumjung, who owned a large house and carried on successful petty trade, went to live with his late wife's father's younger brother's widow, who had a house and property in Kunde. The couple continued to run both houses. keeping in each the children from the owner's previous marriage, The young child from their unsanctioned union had the status of a *themba*, but there was no unfavourable comment on their life together and Ongcho Lama continued to play his normal part in the ritual life of the two villages.

THE RIGHTS AND OBLIGATIONS OF SPOUSES

The performance of the wedding rite, or its substitute known as *rit*, adds to the partners' mutual obligations resulting from the *dem-chang* and creates a new position in so far as property rights are concerned. The new obligations entered into by husband and wife can be summarized under the following points:

1. The husband has exclusive sexual rights to his wife, unless the marriage is polyandrous, and the wife has exclusive sexual rights to the husband except in the rare case of a polygynous marriage.
2. Husband and wife share for the duration of the marriage all their economic assets. The husband is under an obligation to maintain his wife, and the wife must devote her energies exclusively to the work of the common household.
3. While each spouse retains a latent right to the property contributed by him or her to the common assets at the time of the wedding, any addition to these assets, be it in the shape of land or livestock, is deemed to have been produced by the joint labours of husband and wife, and is hence equally divided between them in the event of a dissolution of the marriage,

or for purposes of determining the property of one of the spouses at the time of death.

The obligation to compensate the other spouse for a unilateral termination of the partnership is only a continuation of the mutual rights established by the betrothal ceremony performed at the time of the *dem-chang*. This obligation is expressed in a fixed tariff of payments to be made by the defaulting partner irrespective of the couple's economic status (cf. p. 74). Either spouse is free to terminate the matrimonial association, but each has the identical claim to compensation. There is no such concept as the 'guilty party' in the break-up of a marriage, and the husband of an unfaithful wife prepared to remain in the matrimonial home cannot divorce her without paying compensation. However, he can claim a fine of Rs.30 from any man caught in adultery with his wife and this fine is known as *phijal*. The wife has a similar right to fine any woman known to have had sexual relations with her husband, but in this case the *phijal* is only Rs.15, perhaps in recognition of the fact that women usually have less cash at their disposal than men.

The amounts of all these payments appear today rather low. They have remained at the level fixed by custom many years ago, and one of the results of the drop in the value of the rupee is that adultery has become a comparatively cheap pastime.

POLYANDROUS AND POLYGYNOUS MARRIAGES

The Sherpas' basic attitudes to the husband-wife relationship find a particularly plastic expression in the two types of multiple marriages: polyandry and polygyny. Of these polyandry is the by far more frequent marriage type. Thus among 236 marriages recorded in Khumjung, Kunde and Phortse, there were 19 polyandrous and only 5 polygynous unions. This is in accordance with the Sherpa belief that polyandrous marriages are a time-honoured and highly respectable device to prevent the fragmentation of property and foster the solidarity of brothers, whereas a man's marriage with more than one wife at a time is more in the nature of an emergency measure resorted to, if the first wife has remained childless, but neither of the spouses desires a divorce.

Polyandrous marriages are more frequently the result of parental arrangements than any other type of union. They involve, with the rarest of exceptions, pairs of brothers to be married to one wife, and at least one of the brothers is at the time of *sodene* and *dem-chang* in most cases so young that the proposed match can hardly be of his own choice. Any active rôle in the arrangement of a polyandrous marriage is usually taken by the elder brother, and as a rule it is he who first initiated sexual relations with the joint betrothed.

In the arrangement of a polyandrous match it is general practice to propose already at the time of the *sodene* that the girl asked for in marriage should be the joint wife of two brothers. If this request is agreed to both brothers are entitled to pay henceforth nightly visits to their betrothed, but in most cases only the elder brother avails himself of this right. At the *dem-chang* the younger brother's inclusion in the marriage must be formally confirmed, but it is only at the wedding that both brothers appear in the rôle of bridegroom. Throughout the proceedings they remain next to each other, and at the *gyen-kutop* rite the bride sits in between the two bridegrooms, and all three are anointed with butter.

If there are three brothers in a family it is not uncommon for the eldest and youngest to marry one wife with the idea of jointly taking over the parental property and house in due course, while the middle brother enters a monastery as a novice. Many girls prefer to marry two brothers. Such a marriage improves a woman's economic prospects, and assures that in later years she will enjoy the advantages of a comparatively young husband. I have known a girl who refused to marry her betrothed, even though she had already born him a child, unless his younger brother, perhaps eight years her junior, were to be included in the marriage. However, there have also been cases of girls accepting an older brother, but declining marriage with his very much younger brother on the plea that when he grew up they would be middle-aged and there would be family dissensions if he wanted to break away from the joint household and marry a young wife of his own.

This realistic attitude is based on experience, for it happens quite often that a younger brother, who had joined in a polyandrous marriage, later establishes a separate household and takes another wife. This can be done amicably by mutual agreement, or he may have to pay *phorjal* to the joint wife and thereby regain his freedom. Judging from the comparatively large number of young girls engaged by *dem-chang* to two brothers, and the few cases of older people living in polyandrous unions one might come to the conclusion that the durability of polyandrous marriages is not very great. It has to be considered, however, that owing to the high death rate the chances for the survival of three persons involved in such a marriage into late middle-age are not very great and that the stability of Sherpa marriages is in general not impressive.

While the desire to preserve the inheritance of two brothers in a single economic unit is no doubt foremost in the thought of parents arranging polyandrous matches, it would be erroneous to assume that polyandry is an outcome of economic stringency, and that only those brothers 'who cannot afford separate wives' resort to this form of marriage. Far from being most frequent among the poorer strata of society, polyandry is practised by some of the richest Sherpa families and, in a society acutely sensitive to the social implications of both lavish expenditure and the necessity for economy, there is no suggestion that the conclusion of a polyandrous marriage is in any way detrimental to a family's prestige. It is, on the contrary, considered a laudable sign of fraternal solidarity, and I have heard older people complain about the 'selfishness' of present-day young men, who will break up a parental estate because each wants a wife to himself. If there is in fact a decline in the number of polyandrous marriages—and the absence of data on past generations makes it difficult to trace any such tendency—it must be due to the return to Khumbu of young men who have spent some time in Darjeeling and other places where polyandry is frowned upon.

Jealousy between the joint husbands seems to be rarely the cause for the dissolution of a polyandrous union. A more frequent reason for separation is disagreement over economic matters such as the feeling of one brother that the other does not pull his weight in his efforts for the joint household or that he uses cash earnings—such as earnings as an expedition porter—to satisfy personal wants rather than contributing them to the common pool. In the event of separation, which always involves the division of property, the joint wife usually remains with the elder brother, but there are also cases where she decides to live with the younger brother, even if this means leaving the matrimonial home.

Sherpa men do not find it difficult to manage the sexual side of a polyandrous union. Usually the wife sleeps on the only large bedstead of the house and the two husbands, each of whom has a separate sleeping place, consult as to who should join her there. I have also heard of a different arrangement by which the choice lies with the wife, who joins alternately the one or other husband in his sleeping place. This does not seem the usual custom, however, and some older men, who doubted the accuracy of my information, appeared somewhat shocked by the idea that the initiative should be left to the wife.

In the rare case of a polyandrous union resulting from a younger brother's pre-marital sexual relations with a girl, difficulties are more likely to arise than in marriages initiated by the parents or the elder brother. Such a case occurred in Khumjung, where an elder brother whose first wife had left him after several years of marriage and the birth of three children, joined in the marriage of his younger brother. The wife, who before marriage had had sexual relations with the younger brother only, preferred him at first to the older husband, and it took some years before a modus vivendi was reached.

The women's attitude to polyandry is largely coloured by the consideration that a wife of two brothers in possession of a joint property can expect a higher standard of living than the wife of a man with only one share of his parental property. As every year Sherpa men spend many months away from home, the wife of two brothers is moreover less often left alone, and enjoys therefore a more regular sexual life. There is certainly no prejudice against having sexual relations with two men, and there have been cases of women leaving a single husband in order to conclude a marriage with two brothers.

However, once a girl has gone through the *gyen-kutop* rite with only one bridegroom, a younger brother of the husband cannot subsequently be admitted to marriage. In this respect Sherpa custom differs from Tibetan practice, which permits any number of younger brothers to share an elder brother's wife and countenances even the marriage of a woman with a father and his sons.

The normal type of polyandrous marriage among Sherpas is that of one woman with two brothers. The sons of two brothers may also conclude a marriage with one girl, for they correspond, for all legal purposes, closely to a pair of brothers, but among the hundreds of marriages recorded in house-lists and genealogies I have found only one union of this type. Polyandrous marriages in which the two husbands are not of the same clan are disapproved of, mainly because such a marriage must inevitably lead to a doubtful clan membership of the children. Within present memory there has been only one such marriage. A woman of Pangboche married first a Khamba, and many years later, when she was past child-bearing age, a Sherpa several years her junior. The woman and her two husbands lived for some years in a common household, but as there were no children from either husband no difficulties arose, and the other villagers voiced no disapproval.

Another unusual type of marriage is the marriage of two brothers with two sisters. Such a union is never concluded formally at the time of the wedding, but in rare cases two brothers married to a joint wife may take her younger sister into their house and live with both in a kind of four-cornered marriage. The only case of this type which occurred in recent years was that of two wealthy brothers of Khumjung. They first married a joint wife, who left them after giving birth to a daughter and became a nun in Devuche. Their second joint marriage lasted only for six months, but they were not discouraged and married for the third time a wife in common. Some years later their wife's father died, and both their mother-in-law and the wife's younger sister came to stay in their house. From that time onwards both brothers lived with both sisters, but only the elder sister had children. When the younger brother died, the elder continued to keep both wives. In this case there was some adverse comment among the villagers, who considered the promiscuity of this arrangement unseemly. But the four people concerned took no notice of this criticism, and continued happily in their unconventional family life.

I have mentioned already the marriage to two pairs of brothers with two sisters, but as in this case the two older brothers lived with the elder sister, and the younger brothers with her younger sister, the unusual aspect of the arrangement was only that all six lived for a long time in a common household.

An analysis of genealogies covering three to four generations—the furthest most Sherpas can trace their ancestry—reveals the tendency of sons of polyandrous marriages to marry a joint wife, and thus continue the family tradition of polyandry. Perhaps we may conclude from this practice that the family life in polyandrous households is no less harmonious than that of other families, since were it otherwise the sons would hardly feel inclined to follow their fathers' example.

Polygynous marriages are less frequent than polyandrous unions, and I know of no instance of a man marrying two wives at the same wedding ceremony. Yet, a wife's younger sister, who is unmarried, divorced or widowed, may join her brother-in-law's household as a junior wife, and if her parents are still alive there may even be a performance of *dem-chang* and *gyen-kutop* but these ceremonies are usually dispensed with under such circumstances. The wives in a polygynous household need not necessarily be sisters, but in about half of the polygynous marriages they are either sisters or first parallel cousins. While Sherpa custom does not permit marriages of more than two husbands with one wife, there is no limit to the number of wives a man may have at the same time. Yet, in 1957 there was in the whole of Khumbu only one man who had three wives. Two of them were sisters and lived in the husband's house in Namche, whereas the eldest wife, who was of different clan, lived in a house of her own in a village of Pharak; the husband, an affluent trader, divided his time between the two households.

I have heard young Sherpa girls say that they would rather be one of several wives than marry two brothers, as in a polygynous household there would be less work to do. Though such views, expressed in a flippant way by girls not really faced by such an unusual choice, need not be taken seriously, they nevertheless suggest that sexual jealousy is a sentiment strangely foreign to Sherpa mentality. Used to complete freedom in the choice of lovers before marriage, Sherpas have never developed the feeling that there is any inherent merit in sexual exclusiveness. Just as husbands do not mind sharing their wife with a brother—or a wife sharing her husband with a co-wife—so they do not look upon extra-marital sex relations with the horror other societies have of adultery.

The relations between the men of a polyandrous marriage and the children by the joint wife does not lead to any emotional strain either. Unless one husband has been away for several months, and there is hence no doubt about any particular child's biological father, there is no speculation regarding the paternity of the various children, and both husbands treat them as their own sons and daughters. The children address both men as 'father', and I have never heard of conflict arising from a competition for the children's affection. Since, as long as a polyandrous marriage lasts, both husbands hold all their property in common, the question of inheritance is also no source of conflict because every child, whichever of the two husbands may be the father, is entitled to a share of the joint property.

THE DISSOLUTION OF A MARRIAGE BY DIVORCE OR DEATH

Sherpa marriages are free associations between individuals who have the right to dissolve them when they fail to serve the purpose of giving mutual comfort and happiness. There is no need to argue a case for the termination of the marriage tie before a judicial body nor of convincing co-villagers or kinsmen of the desirability of a divorce. Many marriages are dissolved by mutual consent, and if both partners agree to separate a simple ceremony, known as *niatongu*,[1] is performed. The husband invites the wife's parents, brothers or other close kinsmen to his house, entertains them with liquor and beer worth at least one rupee, and declares that he and his wife have separated and that from now on he is no longer their son- or brother-in-law, as the case may be. A thread, held by the husband and one of his wife's kinsmen, is then broken as a symbol of the breaking off of the relationship established by the marriage. The wife finally gives her husband one rupee in repayment of the beer brought by his kinsmen at the time of the *sodene*.

If either husband or wife is not agreeable to a divorce, the other partner is still free to insist on the dissolution of the marriage. There is no need to prove any guilt on the part of the other spouse, but a compensation of Rs.35 has to be paid by the partner who wishes to terminate the marriage. This payment, known as *phorjal*,[2] releases a husband or wife of all further obligations arising from the marriage-bond.

Yet, a different position arises if a man abducts or wishes to marry another man's wife. If the wife is a party to this plan the aggrieved husband has no means of holding her but he can claim damages of Rs.105, known as *thojal*,[3] from the wife's new husband. The opposite case of a wife claiming *thojal* from another woman who wants to

---

[1] *nia* = difficulty experienced in an unsuccessful marriage; *tongu* = to get rid of.
[2] *phor* = to sever, *jal* = payment.
[3] *tho* = higher more.

marry her husband does not arise, as a man has the right to introduce a second wife into his house.

The amicable way in which a man may take over another man's wife is demonstrated by a case which involved people of Phortse and Khumjung. Ani Droma, a young woman of Chusherwa clan from Kunde, was married to a man of Shire clan of Phortse. One day Pemba Kitar of Paldorje clan, a rich man of Khumjung, whose first wife had left him but who had a *themba* son from a maid-servant, appeared with a *zendi*-party in the house of Ani Droma's husband, and declared that he wanted to marry Ani Droma and was prepared to compensate her husband. A *pembu* and other prominent men then asked Ani Droma whom she wanted for husband and she chose Pemba Kitar. The latter immediately paid Rs.105 to her husband, and the party took Ani Droma to his house, where the usual wedding rites, including *gyen-kutop* and the presentation of scarves to the bride's kinsmen were forthwith performed.

Yet not all cases of alienation of another man's wife or betrothed run so smooth a course. A case where the break-up of a betrothal led to violence and heated quarrelling occurred in 1954 in Khumjung. Kami Droma of Thaktu clan was betrothed by *dem-chang* to two Khamba brothers of Tharo, but when her half-sister, who had been married to Anulu of Paldorje clan, died, Anulu turned to Kami Droma. He later explained this move by saying that he thought his wife's half-sister would be a better mother for his small children than any unrelated girl. Whatever his motives may have been, he succeeded in winning Kami Droma's affections and when she became pregnant he deposited Rs.105, the usual amount for *thojal*, with his *pembu* Ang Chunbi and asked him to act as mediator in the negotiations with Kami Droma's betrothed. But on hearing of the latter's intention to bring Kami Droma to his house the two Khambas of Tharo collected half a dozen friends and went with them to Khumjung with the intention of beating up Anulu. There was a violent quarrel outside Anulu's house, and several of his kinsmen and friends came to his assistance. The shouting of threats and abuse was followed by the throwing of stones and Sharap Lama, Anulu's sister's husband, got hurt while fighting on Anulu's side. The latter finally took refuge in Kami Droma's house, several of Khumjung's prominent men separated the combatants, and tried to initiate negotiations.

The talks were held in the house of Anulu's eldest brother, and the mediators spent some money on providing beer. The Tharo men insisted that in this case the *thojal* must be Rs.210 for, as Kami Droma was betrothed to two brothers, each would have to be compensated by the usual payment of Rs.105. This was finally accepted and Anulu's eldest brother lent him the money, which he immediately paid to Kami Droma's previous betrothed.

Shortly afterwards Kami Droma came to Anulu's house, and he entertained his kinsmen at the *dong-chang* feast which always follows a bride's entry into her husband's house. As Kami Droma was Anulu's late wife's younger half-sister there was no need to perform the rites of *dem-chang* and *zendi*. For the younger sister of a deceased wife automatically assumes her eldest sister's rights to the latter's husband and, had Kami Droma not been already engaged elsewhere by *dem-chang*, she could have entered Anulu's house without further ado.

In the case of a married man's death, the obligations and rights created by *dem-chang* and *gyen-kutop* do not come to an end, but pass on to the deceased's younger brother, or failing a younger brother, to those of his father's brother's sons who were his juniors and thus stand to the widow in the relationship of husband's younger brother. If any of these is still unmarried and willing to accept the widow as his wife, and she agrees to this arrangement, there is no need to hold *sodene*, *dem-chang* and *zendi*, for any of the deceased junior kinsmen can take over his part as a husband.

However, if there is no such person, or the widow wants to be free of all obligations towards her husband's kinsmen, she can approach any of his younger brothers or cousins with the request to accept one rupee, known as *chang-ring-lho-wu*[1] and to perform a rite of disassociation, known as *ankan pankan*.[2] If he agrees, two pieces of wood, each incised in such a way that it can easily be broken, are given to the widow and her late husband's kinsman. The man and the woman first exchange the pieces of wood and then, stepping a few feet back, break the pieces in two and throw them on the ground. The widow then shakes and brushes her aprons and de-

---

[1] *chang* = 'beer', *ring* = 'price', *lho-wu* = 'return'; i.e. the repayment of beer given by the husband at *sodene*, *dem-chang*, and wedding.

[2] A term of unknown derivation, the literal meaning of which is unknown to the Sherpas.

Ngawang Ritu of Tengboche

A-Tutu, the spirit-medium of Khumjung

Pemba Kitar of Khumjung

clares that she is now free from any control on the part of her late husband's family.

The kinsmen of the deceased need not accept the *chang-ring-lho-wu* payment of one rupee, however, and in the case of their refusal, the widow can only regain her freedom by paying *phorjal* to the extent of Rs.35. This payment must be accepted by the husband's kinsmen provided the widow has not entered, or is about to enter, into relations with any other man. If, on the other hand, she wants to remarry immediately outside her deceased husband's lineage (*kalak*), she or her new husband must pay the full *thojal* of Rs.105 to her late spouse's kinsmen.

As long as a widow has not freed herself from the control of her late husband's patri-clan, the latter can demand *phijal* of Rs.30 from any other man with whom she has had sexual relations, and similarly the younger sister of a man's late wife has the right to claim *phijal* from any woman with whom he has slept after his wife's death. She has this right, even if she herself is married and cannot take her sister's place as a wife. In that case she has no claim to *phorjal* and *thojal*, however, while an unmarried sister of the deceased wife has the right to demand *phorjal* and *thojal* from her late sister's husband in exactly the same way as a man's brothers or father's brother's sons can demand these fees from the widow of their late kinsman. As an elder brother cannot under any circumstances marry his younger brother's widow he has no claim to any of these fees. He can, however, marry a girl to whom his elder brother was engaged by *sodene* provided no scarves were given, even if a *themba* child has been the fruit of this union. The prohibition of a man's marriage with his late wife's elder sister is not as strict as the bar against marriage with a younger brother's widow; such a marriage can take place on payment of a nominal fine of one rupee to the man's *pembu*.

The fees which a man's kinsmen can claim from his widow, and the corresponding claims a woman's sisters have on her husband, are a clear indication that however individualistic Sherpas may otherwise be, Sherpa marriage is not merely an association of two individuals. The rights and obligations engendered by *dem-chang* and wedding rite extend to a circle of kinsmen and outlast the span of life of any one of the spouses.

THE RÔLE OF A MARRIED-IN SON-IN-LAW (*MAKSU*)

Normally a girl leaves her parental house on marriage and becomes economically and ritually a member of her husband's family. But in some cases this position is reversed, and a man enters the household of his parents-in-law and resides with them until their death. Such a resident son-in-law is called *maksu*,[1] and only couples without sons will arrange for one of their daughters to marry a *maksu* and to remain with him and her children in the parental home. Usually it is the youngest daughter who is married in this way, because she—like a youngest son—has inherently a greater right to her father's house than any older sister. There are cases, however, when —with the genuine or assumed agreement of any younger sister—a *maksu* is introduced into a house as the husband of an older daughter. The position of a *maksu* is not merely the reversal of that of a wife entering the house of her parents-in-law, but he is given rights not enjoyed by a wife. Before the formal wedding an agreement is drawn up by which the girl's father appoints the *maksu* as his heir and specifies in detail the property he will inherit. This written document must be endorsed by the donor's nearest kinsmen on the father's side, such as his brothers or brothers' sons, for it is they who would normally inherit part of the property were it not made over to the *maksu*. In return for their consent they usually are given some gifts or a small part of the estate. The document handed to the *maksu* is known as *tsi-tetup* ('list of gifts'), and it usually reads approximately as follows:

'You, Dawa Tenzing (or whatever the *maksu's* name may be), have been taken as our *maksu*. You must live in our house, look after us and work for the good of our family. If you do not do so, and do not take proper care of your wife, we shall resume our property. You must perform our funeral rites. The property which will be made over to you consists of one house in Khumjung, three fields in Khumjung, one house in Teshinga, two fields and one meadow in Teshinga, three cows, etc.'

Unlike the bride in a normal marriage, a *maksu* may move into the house of his parents-in-law immediately after the celebration of the *dem-chang*. At the time of the *zendi* the groom's party with the *maksu* bridegroom nevertheless sets out from his father's house. But after

[1] The position of a *maksu* is similar to that of a *ghar-juwain* in Hindu society, and of a *lamsena* in Middle Indian tribal societies.

the *gyen-kutop* the *maksu* and his bride remain in her parents' house, and the *dong-chang* party is held there. The *zendi*-party finally leaves the house without the bridal couple, but after a few days the *maksu* and his new wife pay a formal visit to his parents.

The position of a *maksu* in the house of his parents-in-law depends largely on the personalities of the people concerned. Under a domineering father-in-law a *maksu* may have to work very much like a servant, fetching wood and working as a porter on trading trips, but if the girl's parents are old and the *maksu* is a man of initiative he may soon be the leading figure in the household. His legal position is a strong one. The property enumerated in the *tsi-tetup* document belongs, unlike a dowry, to him and not to his wife. If the wife wishes to dissolve the marriage and marry another husband, she must leave the house and the second husband must pay Rs.105 *thojal* to the *maksu*, who remains in possession of the property. Only if the *maksu* wishes to terminate the marriage or if a divorce is arranged by mutual consent must he withdraw from the house and relinquish the property received in his capacity as *maksu*. What he cannot do is to drive out his wife and remain in enjoyment of the house and land as this would be contradictory to the terms of the written agreement.

But if his wife dies a *maksu* remains, during his lifetime, in possession of the house and property and can even marry another wife. If there are children from the first wife only they are entitled to inherit the property, but if the wife dies without issue and the *maksu* does not marry a sister or other kinswoman of his late wife, the property reverts after his death to the original owner's kinsmen, for property made over to a *maksu* does not become his absolute property. The agreement provides only for its unrestricted usufruct during the *maksu's* lifetime and for its inheritance by the *maksu's* bodily male heirs from the donor's daughter. Thus a *maksu*, who has only daughters, may not in turn take a *maksu* for one of his daughters without obtaining the agreement of his father-in-law's kinsmen, who have a residual right to the property.

By marrying one of his daughters to a *maksu* a man can assure himself of support in his old age and of the proper performance of the funeral rites. But he cannot, by this device, prevent the extinction of his lineage, for a *maksu* remains a member of his own clan, and this clan membership is passed on to his children according to the rules of the usual patrilineal succession. The only concession to his father-in-law's lineage is the inclusion of the latter's clan gods in the worship on such occasions as a *lhachetu*-rite. Thus Chopali of Khumjung, the *maksu* of a man of Mende clan and himself of Gole clan, worshipped the Mende clan god as well as that of the Gole clan. In this particular case the *maksu* inherited from his father-in-law not only a large house and considerable wealth, but also the office of *pembu*, which he was able to retain even though as a man from Solu he was a newcomer without kinship ties in Khumjung.

While the Hindus of Nepal look upon the rôle of a *ghar-juwain* with a measure of contempt, there is no such feeling among the Sherpas. Even sons of rich men may accept the position of *maksu* in the house of an equally wealthy father-in-law. Thus the eldest son of Kushang (Thaktu), the head of the most prominent—and at one time also the richest—family of Khumjung, became a *maksu* in the house of an affluent trader of Namche, and continued to develop an already successful business.

By accepting the position of *maksu* a Sherpa does not forego his share in his paternal property, though his father is likely to give him slightly less than to those sons who have to struggle hard in establishing themselves in houses of their own. If there has been no distribution of property in the father's lifetime and there is no will defining the sons' shares, a *maksu* son will get as much as other sons with the exception of the youngest son, who, remaining in the house and responsible for the performance of the mortuary rites, receives under all circumstances the largest share.

THE HUSBAND-WIFE RELATIONSHIP

A Sherpa marriage is basically a partnership between two equals. Nothing in Sherpa tradition and ritual suggests that a Sherpa wife should regard her husband as her lord and master to whom she owes obedience and respect. The admonitions given to the bridal couple at the time of the wedding rite do not distinguish between the duties and responsibilities of a husband and those of a wife, and the rules relating to a dissolution of a marriage also bear out the equal rights of both partners. The fact that neither of them can permanently dominate the other—a fact distinguishing Sherpa marriage radically from the marriage of all Hindu populations of Nepal —does not imply, however, that husband and wife have identical rôles. There is, on the contrary, a very clear demarcation between their respective spheres of activities, but this distinction between their tasks and interests does not involve any valuation. Sherpas do not consider a man's work of greater value or merit than that of a woman or vice versa. In certain respects, moreover, men and women do the same work; both carry loads on trading journeys and devote themselves to the care of their cattle.

Just as both partners in a marriage have an equal share in the economic activities which keep a household free from want, so they share also in the control over their assets. While major transactions, such as the sale and purchase of livestock, are mainly the responsibility of the husband, much of the petty trade and of the disposal and allocation of agricultural and dairy produce lies in the hands of the wife. A man's long periods of absence from home necessitate, moreover, the wife's effective control over the organization of the farm work, as well as over mercantile transactions and household finance. Many women are experienced in trade and money-lending, and will take on considerable commitments even when unable to consult their husbands.

The independence of a Sherpa wife in the handling of economic matters is reflected in a sense of self-reliance and assurance which cannot fail to colour her attitude to her husband. This we find strikingly different from the traditional docility and meekness of a Hindu wife, but most Sherpa wives evince, on the other hand, a cheerful willingness to work hard and unrelentingly in the interest of the family's prosperity.

A Sherpa woman appears as the equal partner of her husband not only in the privacy of the family circle but also in front of outsiders. She joins freely in the conversations of men, responds with gusto to their jokes however broad and personal, and does not hesitate to rebuke and restrain her husband in public should hot temper or intoxication land him in trouble. I have seen a wife actually slap the face of her husband, an otherwise dignified lama, when in the course of a drunken quarrel he seemed in danger of resorting to blows.

The cheerfulness and sense of humour, which are the Sherpas' most endearing qualities reign, on the whole, also between husbands and wives, and in most households the visitor senses a pleasant and relaxed atmosphere. Quarrels occur among Sherpa couples as among married people of any society, but they are usually short-lived, and if a husband and wife frequently quarrel they are likely to part company without retaining any rancour towards each other. This can be seen from the behaviour of men and women who were once married but later separated and found other partners. Life in a Sherpa village inevitably brings them together sometimes and at such encounters they seem to be neither embarrassed nor anxious to avoid each other's company. When, in 1957, one of the Dumje *lawa* of Kunde and his wife had to entertain the villagers in a borrowed house in Khumjung they chose that of the wife's previous husband, from whom she had separated and who since had married another wife. Both couples stayed throughout the six days of the festival under one roof without, as it seemed, feeling the slightest embarrassment. Similarly men and women, who were once lovers and betrothed by *sodene* or even *dem-chang*, meet afterwards freely and without any show of self-consciousness, both alone and in front of their subsequent partners.

All this points to the fact that sexual relations are emotionally not highly charged. In a society where the young people of both sexes are practically unrestricted in the pursuit of casual as well as prolonged love-affairs, such an attitude to sex is perhaps not surprising. It must be remembered, however, that among peoples enjoying a similar pre-marital freedom, such as the Murias of Bastar, the Konyak Nagas and the Apa Tanis of the Assam Himalayas, the absence of sexual jealousy is not equally marked, particularly in so far as married couples are concerned.

Sherpa husbands and wives show on the whole remarkable tolerance towards their spouses' digressions from the path of marital fidelity. Temporary lapses are hardly ever considered sufficient reason for the break-up of a marriage, and even those who were their partners in illicit adventures are let off lightly and—apparently—with a minimum of ill-feeling. Though a husband has the right to claim from his wife's lover a fine (*phijal*) of Rs.30, there are many cases of husbands not exercising this right, but accepting an apology and a bottle of beer bought as *yangdzi*. Particularly if the offender is a lama or monk an aggrieved husband may be reluctant to impose on him the indignity of paying *phijal* and be content to accept the offer of a drink, by which the other man publicly admits his guilt. But the claim of *phijal* may be dropped also for other reasons. Thus a rich man of Khumjung whose wife was caught twice in succession with the same lover did not insist on the payment of *phijal* the second time. The astonishing reason for this leniency was that the luckless lover had only recently paid Rs.30 and that a second payment so shortly afterwards would have been too great a hardship.

Some of the most respectable men of Khumjung, including a famous and recently deceased lama and the heads of the two leading houses are known to have paid *phijal* to the one or other of their equally respectable co-villagers. But, seeing these men drinking and joking with the husbands they had wronged and the wives involved in their adventures, one would never have suspected that any serious quarrel had ever marred their friendship or disturbed for long the harmony of village life.

The claim to *phijal* is not a right vested in men only; a wife can also claim damages from any woman known to have had sexual relations with her husband. These damages are traditionally fixed at Rs.15, half the amount of *phijal* payable by a man to an aggrieved husband. It would seem, however, that on the whole Sherpa wives are even more indulgent than husbands, and that they exercise their right to *phijal* only if angered by their husband's persistent unfaithfulness with one particular woman.

With the offering of *yangdzi* beer or the payment of *phijal* a case of adultery is considered closed, and it does not seem that the guilty wife or husband is made to suffer a great deal under the aggrieved spouse's recriminations. In view of the ease with which a marriage can be dissolved, a husband or wife knows only too well that a spirit of forgive and forget is the only alternative to a break-up of the matrimonial home.

The ease with which cases of adultery are settled must not mislead us into believing that the Sherpas' attitude to extra-marital sex relations is one of complete amorality or indifference. As devout Buddhists they know very well that sexual intercourse with another man's wife is sinful, and that a married man commits a sin (*dikba*) even if he sleeps with an unmarried girl. The payment of *phijal* and the offering of *yangdzi* remove the sin to some extent, but there is in the Sherpas' minds no doubt at all that any act of adultery diminishes the *sönam* (merit) of those involved, and that many deeds of merit are required to expiate the sin and make up for the loss of *sönam*. Sexual intercourse is morally neutral only between unmarried persons; for them it is not sin, provided neither of the partners has taken vows of celibacy.

Like elsewhere, there is a difference between moral principles and actual conduct, but a feature not met with in many societies is the generous tolerance shown by individual Sherpas towards the failings and weaknesses of their fellow men, and the ease with which a lapse in marital fidelity is forgiven.

PARENT-CHILD RELATIONSHIP

The relationship between parents and children in a Sherpa family is one of warmth and informality. Children of all ages are treated with great gentleness and consideration, and their uninhibited and fearless behaviour vis-à-vis strangers is indicative of the sense of security and self-assurance which the atmosphere within the family gives them. From an early age children are looked upon as responsible persons and as soon as a child is firmly on its feet it is left very much to itself. In any Sherpa village one finds groups of children of varying ages, playing on their own while the parents are busy in house and field, and it is not unusual for a woman to spend, if necessary, the whole day away from the village, perhaps weeding or digging up potatoes in a subsidiary settlement, while her children between the ages of four and eight remain behind alone, the older ones looking as well as they can after the younger ones.

From the age of eight onwards many children spend much of their time in herding cattle. Sheep and goats are invariably driven out to graze by young boys and girls, but during the middle of the day even yak are often watched by children under twelve; but once a boy reaches the age of twelve or thirteen his father will train him to take a more responsible part in the herding of yak. He may then be in charge of a small herd throughout the day. During the months when the animals are kept on pastures within walking distance of the village an adult member of the family will join the boy for the night to help guard the animals tethered near the *resa*-shelter inside which the herdsmen sleep (cf. p. 7). At such a time a boy of twelve may be in charge of the animals, constituting his parents' total cattle-wealth, throughout the hours of daylight and the evenings and nights spent by father and son in the solitude of a small shelter no doubt create a sense of comradeship not as easily engendered by the style of life in many other societies. Such herdsboys, who may have to stay away from their houses for several days at a time, cook most of their own food, and learn two lessons of great importance to the Sherpa: self-sufficiency and the ability to spend long periods in comparative solitude.

Girls of that age usually help their mothers in the house and with the farm work. If they have brothers, there will usually be no need to employ them for looking after yak, but in families without sons the daughters too have to take their share in the herding of cattle. Girls, more than boys, spend much of their time in the company of friends of their own age, for much of the spinning and fieldwork is done in gangs (*ngalok*) on a basis of reciprocity. Thus a girl may on twenty evenings go to help with the spinning in the houses of friends and relatives, while on the twenty-first evening the twenty girls will come to her parents' house to repay the help they have received.

Adolescents who take their full share in the work which keeps the family's economy going, are naturally treated very much like adults. Their relations with their parents are coloured by constant co-operation in activities the results of which affect the welfare of the whole family. While the final authority of the parents is unchallenged, children expect to be allowed a great deal of latitude in arranging the details of their work. It is by their example rather than by frequent instruction and criticism that parents pass on their knowledge and skill, and the children speak to their elders in a tone of relaxed familiarity completely free of any shyness or inhibitions.

Between parents and children there is no feeling of 'shame' in regard to matters of sex. The sleeping arrangements in a Sherpa house are such that there is next to no privacy for the daughters receiving their male friends and lovers, or for a married youngest son sleeping with his young wife. Thus parents cannot help knowing a great deal about their children's most intimate life, but this is no cause of embarrassment on either part, and parents are not in the habit of interfering with their daughters' amorous experiences.

Yet Sherpas often take a hand in arranging their children's betrothal and marriage, and it seems that many young people, not greatly swayed by passion, are on the whole well content to let their parents negotiate suitable matches. With a son's or daughter's betrothal begins one of the most significant phases in the parent-child relationship. It is in a father's power to delay or speed up a daughter's wedding and departure from the parental home, and his co-operation is usually needed when an elder son wants to establish himself in a house of his own. Self-interest might suggest a delay of either separation, for grown-up children are economic assets, and the marriage of a daughter no less than the separation of a son may mean the loss of a worker not easily spared. The separation of an elder son, moreover, necessitates a division of the parental property, for it is customary though not legally enforceable, that such a son should receive his share of the family property as soon as he sets up a household of his own.

Many Sherpa fathers make real sacrifices in order to enable their sons to become independent. There are even cases of men who moved out of their houses, and built or bought a smaller house for themselves and the younger children so that the eldest son should have undisturbed possession of the old family home. Though exceptional, such cases demonstrate the strength of the feeling that a father is under an inescapable obligation to assist his sons in the setting up of separate establishments.

Once separated a son is under no further economic obligations to his father. A co-operation which has lasted ever since the son began, as a young boy, to help herding his father's cattle comes abruptly to an end, and in many cases this involves also a loosening of emotional ties. It is the youngest son remaining in the parents' house on whom a father depends for continued support, and such a youngest son is therefore usually most closely attached to his father. Elder sons and married daughters may visit the parents off and on, and bring gifts of food and beer on feast days, but only in exceptional circumstances will they work for their parents without receiving the usual wage. Such exceptional circumstances may arise if the youngest son living with his aged parents should die prematurely. In that case the elder children, even though long separated, may take turns in assisting their parents with the work in their fields. Such casual assistance is insufficient, however, to enable a man too old for the strenuous work of herding yak to care effectively for his livestock, and it is not unusual for an old man to sell his animals because he can no longer cope with the work and does not find it economical to employ a paid herdsman.

Widows usually stay on in the house taken over by the youngest son, but it seems that the bond between son and mother is not always strong enough to withstand serious misunderstandings between a mother and her daughter-in-law. There are cases of women who live alone, or with a young daughter in a hired ground-floor room, because they could not get on with their only son's wife, and had to leave their marital house in which they had lived for decades and raised their family.

An occasional casualness towards aged parents, though by no means frequent, mars to some extent the otherwise pleasant picture of Sherpa family life. The most shocking instance of really callous treatment of an old father occurred a generation ago in Khumjung. A once exceedingly rich but spendthrift man, who in his old age became somewhat eccentric and was dispossessed of his house by a ruthless *pembu*, for failure to pay the revenue lived the last year of his life in a cave above the village temple and died destitute, though a son of his lived in reasonably comfortable circumstances in Kunde, and his sister's son was one of the two richest men of Khumjung. This was no doubt a very exceptional case, but there are nevertheless societies in which such indifference to the plight of an aged father would be considered so disgraceful that, if nothing else, the fear of public condemnation would induce the sons to adopt a more charitable attitude.

Wealthy old people sometimes avoid the possibility of friction with grown-up sons and daughters-in-law by leaving their home and spending the last years of their life in a religious retreat such as the nuns' settlement of Devuche. In 1957 two old couples of Khumjung were living thus in the houses which many years previously they had built for their nun-daughters, and the *pembu* and richest man of Kunde had just then purchased a house in the monastic settlement of Tengboche with the idea of retiring there in his old age.

Unlike the Hindu mother, who expects to be served by her daughters-in-law, the average Sherpa woman accepts the fact that in a society which stresses the virtues of self-reliance and independence rather than those of obedience and conformity two married couples cannot easily live for long in a single household. It is in recognition of this fact that the wedding of elder sons is delayed until they have houses of their own to which they can take their brides, even if this delay involves the birth of several children in the house of the girl's parents. The aversion against the co-residence of two married couples has to be set aside, however, in the case of a youngest, or an only son, who ultimately will inherit the parental house, but by putting off the wedding as long as possible the period when his wife will have to share the house with both her husband's parents can be somewhat shortened and the parents' retirement to a place of religious retreat can further ease the situation. As the expectation of life is not high in Khumbu, there is no great likelihood that both parents of a youngest son will live for many years after he has brought his bride to their house. The prejudice against the co-residence of two married couples in one household does not extend to a widow's or a widower's staying with married children. In such a case the house is clearly run by the young people, and the widowed parent remains sufficiently in the background as to be of no embarrassment to the younger generation.

There is one major exception to the principle that two married couples should, if at all possible, not live permanently in the same household. This exception is the incorporation of a *maksu* into the household of his parents-in-law. But as in this case the two women engaged in the work of the household are mother and daughter quarrels are not as frequent or bitter as those between a middle-aged woman and her young daughter-in-law. And as men usually spend much of their time away from home, be it in the pursuit of trade or in caring for their cattle, a *maksu* is not likely to have to put up continuously with his father-in-law's presence.

Yet, in 1957, even including households with a *maksu*, the number of households containing two married couples was only 6 among the 138 households of Khumjung and Kunde, and 4 among the 61 households of Phortse.

THE ILLEGITIMATE CHILD (*THEMBA*)

The sexual freedom of Sherpa girls before marriage and the lenient attitude taken towards extra-marital adventures of married women, coupled with the ignorance of contraceptive practices, makes the birth of numerous illegitimate children inevitable. The Sherpa term for an illegitimate son is *na-ngun*, and for a daughter *na-ngungma*, but as Sherpas themselves often use the Nepali loan-word *themba*, which covers illegitimate children of both sexes, I shall here use this simpler term.[1] The Sherpas describe as *themba* any child

[1] There is no English word with the same connotation as the word *themba*, which lacks most of the derogatory undertone of the term 'illegitimate'; 'bastard' in its mediaeval usage might come closest to the connotation of *themba*.

in respect of whose parents no *dem-chang* or *sodene* with the presentation of scarves had been performed.[1] Not only the child of an unmarried girl, but also any child of a married woman conceived during a prolonged absence of her husband, and therefore obviously not his offspring, has the status of a *themba*.

The Sherpas make no distinction between a *themba* child born to a girl who had been asked in marriage by *sodene* and that of a girl who had only casual relations with the child's father. If, for the one or other reason, no *dem-chang* follows the betrothal by *sodene* before the child's birth it will always be regarded as a *themba*. Similarly the lifelong co-habitation of a couple never sanctioned by the rite of scarf-presentation does not prevent their children from being *themba*.

In all cases where the parents of a *themba* child live in a common household, the child's legal and social position is indistinguishable from that of any legitimate child, and the term *themba*, though undoubtedly fully applicable, will be rarely used in respect of any of the couple's children. Most *themba*, however, are the children of a man and a woman whose relations were of an impermanent nature, and who perhaps had never had the intention of getting married.

If an unmarried girl not betrothed by *sodene* finds herself pregnant, she will normally name the man whom she knows or—if she had intercourse with more than one man—suspects to be the child's father. As the man in question is likely to have visited the girl in her parents' house, he will usually not be in a position to refute the allegation, and unless he intends to ask for the girl in marriage, he will prepare himself to pay to her parents the customary fee of Rs.70, known as *na-ngun-tipsil*[2] as well as a certain sum ranging from Rs.20 to Rs.200 as compensation for the mother's loss of working capacity before and after the child's birth.

Only rarely does a man pointed out as the father of a *themba* child deny his paternity, and the customary law favours in such cases the child's mother, whose word is normally considered sufficient proof. A case which occurred in Khumjung a few years ago demonstrates this position: Chamji, the daughter of Yemba Lhakpa, a Gharti of *khamendeu* status, gave birth to a child and, as by

---

[1] We have seen that the *gyen-kutop* rite at the final wedding ceremony, though an essential part in establishing other matrimonial rights, is not required to legitimize a child.   [2] *tip* = sin, offence; *sil* = to clear.

that time no one had admitted the paternity, one of the *pembu* and two respected men, who often acted as mediators, formally asked the girl who the child's father was. She named Pasang Chiri, a young Khamba of *khamendeu* status, and said that she had slept with him during the last Dumje festival. Pasang Chiri was called, but at first denied the paternity and asked Chamji what proof she could produce. Was there any witness of their alleged relations? But Dorje Ngungdu, one of the mediators, said: 'How can there be a witness? Who can ever witness such a thing? It is enough that the girl says so.' Then the time between the Dumje and the birth of the child was calculated and, as exactly nine months had elapsed, everyone was convinced of the truth of Chamji's story and Pasang Chiri was asked to pay a fee of Rs.70 to Yemba Lhakpa. He was also liable to pay damages for loss of earnings, but the mediators persuaded him to admit the paternity and to ask Lhakpa to remit the fine and compensation. On this basis a compromise was reached. Pasang Chiri admitted to be the child's father, and Lhakpa dropped his claim. Chamji was willing to keep the child and to seal the agreement each party bought one rupee's worth of beer, Pasang Chiri offered *yangdzi* to her father and Chamji formally asked to be allowed to keep the child. She subsequently married another man, who had recently come from Tibet.

The father of many a *themba* not only admits his paternity freely but insists on taking charge of the child as soon as it can be separated from the mother, i.e. at an age of between two and four years. In such a case the *themba* child is brought up in the father's house, and has the same rights as his legitimate children, including the right to an equal share of the father's property. A *themba* is a member of his father's clan, even if brought up by the mother's family.

On the basis of the situation in Khumjung in 1957 it would seem that approximately two-thirds of all *themba* children remain with their mothers, while one-third are brought up in their father's house. But this ratio does not reflect correctly the attitude of men of Sherpa clans to their *themba* children, for many of the *themba* are the children of Khamba girls who associated with Tibetans and other men not permanently resident in Khumjung. Among Sherpa families of good status more than half of all *themba* children are claimed by their fathers and grow up in their houses.

Very little shame is attached either to having a *themba* child or to

The Pattern of Family Life

being a *themba*. One of the richest men in Khumjung was a *themba*, and had been brought up in the house of his father, Pemba Kitar of Thaktu clan, who had no children from his two legitimate wives. Pemba Kitar himself was a *themba*, and his mother was a sister of the head of the important Mendoa house. Yet, Pemba Kitar, too, was raised in his father's house and inherited his entire property. Both Pemba Kitar and his son as well as the latter's children married into some of the most prominent families of Khumjung, Kunde and Namche Bazar, and their status in the community was in no way affected by their illegitimate birth. Similarly there were many *themba* girls who had married men of wealthy families and enjoyed all the respect due to the wives of prominent men.

There are certain exceptional cases, however, when even men of good status have to disown their *themba* children. This happens almost invariably if a Sherpa had secretly relations with a Khamba girl of *khamendeu* class. As sexual intercourse with a woman of such class pollutes a Sherpa, and if made public deprives him of his *khadeu* status, such cases are usually hushed up, and if the girl is with child it is as a rule not difficult to find an impecunious *khamendeu* man who, for a consideration, will take the paternity upon himself. The villagers often suspect who the real father is, but as they have no interest in raising a scandal they ostensibly accept the story told by the child's mother and corroborated by the man bribed into acknowledging the child.

A problem of a different nature is created if a girl of *khadeu* status becomes pregnant after having had intercourse with two men of different Sherpa clans. The biological paternity then determines the child's clan membership and position in the system of exogamous groups, but as the mother herself may be in doubt as to the child's father an allocation of the child to the wrong man cannot be always avoided. Such a case occurred a generation ago in Phortse. A Khamba girl had two lovers: Lama Tarkia of Sherwa clan, and Pasang Tenzing of Paldorje clan. When she became pregnant Lama Tarkia showed no willingness to recognize the child, but Pasang Tenzing gladly continued his association with the girl and subsequently married her. The daughter she gave birth to was hence regarded as Pasang Tenzing's child and was, as such, of Paldorje clan. But as the child grew up she showed an unmistakable likeness to Lama Tarkia, and even Pasang Tenzing often jokingly said that she was obviously Lama Tarkia's daughter. No one paid much attention to this situation, but when a young man of Sherwa clan fell in love with the girl, and started to go and sleep with her, his father put him wise, pointing out that though nominally of Paldorje clan she was really the daughter of a Sherwa father. As any breach of the rules of clan exogamy is a serious matter the boy withdrew, and Lama Tarkia's natural daughter subsequently married a man of Mende clan of Khumjung.

Only rarely will a child of a married woman be identified as a *themba*. Yet there are cases when the husband's long absence on a trading journey leaves no room for doubt as to the illegitimacy of a child born after his return. In such an event the woman is expected to disclose her lover's name, and the husband will demand from him both *phijal* and the usual fee of Rs.70 as compensation for loss of his wife's working capacity. In the last generation such a case occurred in Namche Bazar. Nima, a rich trader of Gurung descent, left his wife in Namche Bazar while he went for over a year to Tibet. In his absence she had relations with Rinsing Lhakpa, a member of the important Phaphlu Lama family, and by the time Nima returned she was in an advanced stage of pregnancy. Nima had no intention of divorcing his wife on account of her indiscretion, and Rinsing Lhakpa readily paid the customary fines and damages. A boy born shortly afterwards stayed for about seven years with his mother and Nima, whom he called father. Later on he went to live with Lhakpa in Phaphlu, and there grew up as the son of a rich and highly respected man. He ultimately married a girl from one of the two leading houses of Khumjung, and to all appearances he never suffered under any disability springing from the circumstances of his birth.

Cases like those of Rinsing Lhakpa's *themba* son are unusual, however, and among the twenty-six *themba* occurring in the village census of Khumjung based on my records of 1953 and 1957 none was the child of a married woman conceived during her husband's absence. This does not mean that all the children born after their mother's *dem-chang* are necessarily the offspring of their legal fathers. But as long as there is any possibility of a woman's husband being the father of her child, no one raises the question of paternity even in cases when extra-marital intercourse had been admitted and the woman's lover had paid *phijal*.

A polyandrous wedding in Namche Bazar

Welcoming the bridegroom's party

Wedding dance in the house of the bride

An unusual case of a child born to a married woman being expressly claimed by a man other than her husband occurred, however, some years ago in Milingbo. Kungshi, a poor man of Nawa clan, lived there with his wife, Ai-Lhamu, when Tsamba of Thaktu clan, a member of one of the richest families of Khumjung, began to take an interest in Kungshi's wife. Tsamba, who had once been a monk in Tengboche, had later been married, but his wife had died without offspring. While living in Milingbo, Tsamba had for many years regularly had relations with Ai-Lhamu, and as he was extremely wealthy her husband found it advantageous to tolerate this situation. Though the children born to Ai-Lhamu during this period might have been Kunshi's as well as Tsamba's it was mutually agreed that Tsamba should claim one daughter as his child, and this girl, about seventeen in 1957, was hence recognized as being of Thaktu clan. Before he died Tsamba left her in his will money, jewels and other movable possessions, and she was considered a *themba* daughter of Tsamba, while all her brothers and sisters were of Nawa clan and held to be the legitimate children of Kungshi. My informants were of the opinion that, even though at the time of her birth her mother was legally married to Kungshi, this *themba* girl would be allowed to marry a man of Nawa clan.

Disputes over the paternity of *themba* children are rare and this suggests that most Sherpas have too great an integrity to evade their obligations towards the women with whom they sleep. Even when there is genuine cause for doubt as to the paternity of a child, one of the girl's lovers usually agrees to recognize it as his own. I have been told that Khamba boys who have taken turns in spending the night with an unmarried girl may play dice in order to decide who should accept responsibility for a child. The boy who loses in such a game must profess to be the child's father. Sherpas say that in a similar situation they will not leave the decision to a game of chance, but allow the girl to point out whom she believes to be her child's father.

At the name-giving ceremony, performed several days after birth, there is little difference in the ritual treatment of a *themba* and the offspring of a sanctioned union. In the case of a first child the name-giving usually takes place in the house of the mother's parents where the confinement occurred. The child's father and some of his kinsmen bring a prayer-flag to be erected in front of the house as well as beer and the materials for a large sacrificial cake (*torma*) to be cut up and divided among those present, the first pieces going to the new-born child and its mother. A kinsman or friend of the father, chosen from among the young men whose parents are both alive, gives the child its name while smearing butter on its head and mouth, and later affixes a white scarf to the central post of the house.

In the case of a *themba* child the father will perform this ritual, even if he has no intention of marrying the mother or subsequently taking the child to his house. If he has quarrelled with the girl or her family, he might feel awkward about coming to her house, and in such a case he delegates one of his kinsmen to act in his place. But even then he will provide the necessary materials for the ceremony, and thereby accept the paternity of the child. He is also under an obligation to present the child's mother with a blanket and a basket-work cradle, such as Sherpa children are carried about in on their mother's back.

The man recognized as a child's father acts at the name-giving in this way even if the mother is married to another man and the ceremony takes place in her husband's house. The payment of *phijal* and *nga-ngun-tipsil* will by that time have been made, but if relations between the two men are still strained, the child's father is likely to ask one of his kinsmen to represent him at the name-giving.

RELATIONS BETWEEN KINSFOLK

A Sherpa's relations with his kinsmen and kinswomen of various degrees are of an entirely different order from those welding the members of a Hindu kin-group into a tightly integrated community. The Sherpas, unlike most other populations of Nepal, have no joint family system, and there are few of the reciprocal rights and obligations which among populations such as Parbatias or Newars clearly prescribe the behaviour of kinsmen at all such occasions as weddings and funerals. There is, above all, an almost complete absence of differentiation in the everyday behaviour towards kinsmen of distinct categories.

This lack of differentiation does not extend to the terms by which a Sherpa refers to his various kinsmen and kinswomen, however, and a glance at the table of kinship terms on p. 289 will show that the terminology at his disposal enables a Sherpa to distinguish very well between different degrees of consanguinity and affinity. His brothers and his father's brother's sons, who are all included in the comprehensive term *pin*, remain throughout his life the kinsmen with whom he is linked by the closest economic and ritual ties. If he dies childless his brothers—or failing brothers his father's brother's sons—will inherit his property, and he has a similar latent right to all they possess. Any of them can take his place in any ceremonial performance and in the event of his death the rights he has acquired by *dem-chang* and *gyen-kutop* automatically pass on to those among his *pin* who are his juniors in age. A younger brother or parallel cousin thus takes his place beside his wife without having to repeat any of the betrothal and wedding ceremonies, and he himself has a similar right to the widow of any of his older brothers or father's brothers.

If he wishes to alienate any of his property to a *maksu* he has to obtain his brothers' or father's brothers' sons' agreement, and even a wife can remain in enjoyment of her late husband's property only by the grace of the closest of his *pin*.

No comparable community of rights and interests links a man with the sons of his father's sister or his mother's brother. These men are not of his own clan and consequently not his *pin*. They cannot represent him on any formal occasion nor can he take their place, either at the side of a wife nor in the ownership of property.

Yet, in daily life as well as on many ceremonial occasions, a Sherpa behaves in very much the same way towards the sons of his father's brothers and those of his father's sisters or mother's brothers. If there is a wedding in their house he will invite the *zendi*-party to a meal and contribute a gift to the bride's dowry, and if there has been a death he will offer *kem-chang*[1] and later, at the time of the final funeral feast (*gyewa*), give a gift known as *larkia*.

In this respect there is no distinction in his behaviour towards close kinsmen of the different categories. Unlike a Newar or a Chetri a Sherpa has no specific ritual obligations towards his sisters and their children, and if they happen to live in another village he may not see them for long periods. Nor does custom demand that he should treat a mother's brother with greater formality than any other man of his parents' generation. While Sherpas are in general

[1] *kem* = thirst; *kem-chang* = the beer to still the thirst.

extremely courteous, there are few rules of etiquette which prescribe distinct patterns of behaviour in the presence of kinsmen of various degrees. It is true that direct sexual jokes should be avoided between father-in-law and daughter-in-law, brothers and sisters, a man and his younger brother's wife, and between cross-cousins of different sex, but persons standing in any of these relationships behave to each other in all other respects with perfect naturalness and feel no embarrassment if others joke in their presence in the very frank manner usual among Sherpas.

The only verbal avoidance relates to the names of dead persons. Such names should never be uttered, though there are occasions when it is impracticable to observe this rule. The names of all living persons, in whatever way related to each other, can be freely mentioned, and even husband and wife address each other by name. When addressing, or even when referring to their seniors, Sherpas usually prefix the name with the appropriate relationship term. Thus, a man called Dorje will be addressed as Au Dorje by persons of the descending generation unless he stands to them in the relationship of mother's brother, as which he would be addressed as Ajang Dorje, or is related to them by marriage and hence called Mem Dorje.

The custom of teknonymy, according to which a person is addressed as 'father of so-and-so', is not current among the Sherpas of Khumbu. Those of Solu and Pharak, however, who have much closer relations with other populations, often follow this custom, widely practised among Hindu communities, where the mentioning of a person's name is severely restricted by rigid avoidance rules.

Sherpas have few formal salutations and etiquette does not prescribe how a father, grandparent, mother's brother or other relative should be greeted after a long absence. There is consequently no outward index to different degrees of respect or familiarity between kinsmen. The deferential form of greeting which consists in bowing low and offering one's head to be touched by the other person's hands is reserved for the approach to particularly respected lamas, and I have never seen it used as a way of saluting senior relatives.

We would be mistaken if we interpreted the paucity of formal salutations as proof of an indifference to distinctions in seniority or different degrees of social status. The Sherpas are, on the contrary,

The Pattern of Family Life

very sensitive to the necessity of showing respect to those entitled to such treatment, and there is, as we shall see, in every village an accepted order of precedence, according to which people are served and seated on formal occasions. What is absent, however, is an expression of relationships of consanguinity and affinity in terms of superiority and precedence. The very idea, so highly developed among the Hindus of Nepal, that one category of kinsmen, such as those who have married one's sisters or daughters, is inherently of superior status and thus entitled to different treatment than another category is foreign to the Sherpa. The principle of strict reciprocity in all social relations is basic to Sherpa society, and there is no room for any relationship involving a predominance of obligations for the one party, and a predominance of rights for the other. Even close kin retain their right to assistance at the time of weddings and similar occasions only as long as they give equal assistance when the opportunity arises, and the Sherpas rationalize the motivation for rendering such mutual services not by pointing to the ties of consanguinity or affinity but by emphasizing that the families concerned have for a long time maintained an exchange of hospitality and gifts. Just as unrelated persons can establish such a system of exchanges if brought close to each other by friendship or spatial vicinity, a quarrel can cause families of close kinship ties to contract out of the system, and no one can claim the ceremonial assistance of kinsmen as an absolute right, independent of the vagaries of individual personal relationships.

PROPERTY RIGHTS AND INHERITANCE

The Sherpas place great emphasis on the sanctity of individual property, and even children are allowed to dispose freely of any small sum they may have earned or received as a present. Young boys and girls are encouraged to try their hand in small trade deals on their own account, and by the time a young Sherpa woman gets married she may already have considerable commerical experience. The dowry which a bride was given remains her private property just as a man's share of his paternal property, which he received when setting up an independent household, belongs to him personally and does not become the joint property of husband and wife. As long as a marriage lasts both spouses share equally in the enjoyment of each other's property, but if the marriage breaks up each spouse may take what he or she contributed at the time of the wedding, while whatever they earned during their married life is divided equally.

The right of a divorced woman to resume the property which she brought with her as a dowry is limited, however, if there are children. In that case she cannot take possession of any part of this property if she either goes to live with another man or retires to a nunnery unless her first husband, who has to safeguard the claims of the children, gives his consent, for the property a woman receives from her natal family at the time of marriage is considered the potential inheritance of her children. This restriction, however, applies only to immovable property and cattle, and not to personal ornaments, which remain at all times a woman's absolute property.

Corresponding limitations on a man's right to dispose of his personal estate come into operation when a man, who has sons from a first marriage, marries again after being widowed or divorced. In such an event the sons from the first marriage are entitled to equal shares with the father and, if they are grown-up, he should divide his property before he sets up a household with a new wife.

The rules of inheritance are based on the principle that all sons, irrespective of their age, have equal claims to their parents' property, whereas daughters are entitled to a dowry. A father of three sons, for instance, will divide his property into four parts, and as his sons get married and set up their own households he will give to each one share, keeping the last quarter for his own use until his death. If he also has a daughter he will set aside a share for her dowry before he divides the property. After the father's death the share remaining with him will be distributed among all the sons, provided that they contributed equally to the costs of the cremation and the subsequent mortuary rites. It often happens, however, that the youngest son, who lived in the father's house, bears the entire expenditure connected with the funeral. In that case he is entitled to the remaining share of his father's property. Sons who have remained in the father's house are responsible for his debts and creditors who have written bonds can claim payment even after many years. A daughter is not liable to pay her father's debts, however much of his property she received as a dowry, but a *maksu* son-in-law living in the father-in-law's house is in the same position as a son.

The normal rules of inheritance can be modified by a written will, and the popular view of the authority of such a will is reflected in the proverb 'A dying man's will is like a royal command'. Yet there are limits to the modifications in the rules of succession which can be effected by a will.

If a man tries to leave his property to a childless wife, his paternal kinsmen entitled to his property according to customary law may refuse to carry out his wishes even though they are embodied in a written will.

The Sherpa attitude to the disposal and inheritance of property is determined by two principles which sometimes seem to be in conflict. There is firstly the idea of the individual's unrestricted ownership of all property he has inherited or acquired, and this principle allows for the free transformation of one type of property into the other, e.g. land into cattle, and for the donation of property for religious purposes. On the other hand there is the principle of the underlying right of the paternal kin-group to the property owned by any of its members. We have seen that a man must obtain his brothers' or brothers' sons' consent before he can make over his property to a resident son-in-law (*maksu*), and that a childless widow cannot be designated as a man's heir at the expense of his close paternal kinsmen. Similarly, an emphasis on the latent joint-ownership of property by a father and his sons is expressed in the rule that a man setting up a new household with a second wife should retain no larger a share of his property than that received by any of his sons after an equal division of movable and immovable possessions between him and however many sons he may have.

The greater part of Sherpa property is passed on in the male line from father to son, elder to younger brother, or father's brother to nephew. But parallel to this inheritance of possessions in the male line runs a succession of property through women. A woman's valuable ornaments usually go to her daughters either as part of their dowries or gifts at other times, or after the mother's death. Similarly land, houses and cattle may be given to women as dowries, and in the next generation they may again form part of the property made over to a daughter on the occasion of her marriage. Whereas in Nepalese Hindu society a bride's dowry is merged with her husband's estate, Sherpas are very clear in the recognition of the principle that property can be held by both men and women and that it can be passed on either in the male or the female line.

4

Village Organization

A Sherpa village is a territorial as well as a political and ritual unit. Though the time when the majority of the villagers reside within the limits of the main settlement does not amount to even half of the year, it is nevertheless the only unit within which the integrating forces of Sherpa society can be observed in full play. Neither the clans extending throughout the whole of Sherpa land, nor groups of villages contained within a geographically determined region, such as Khumbu or Pharak, are structured in the sense that mutually dependent parts combine in an organized way for concerted action. The village, on the other hand, does not consist of a random accumulation of individuals and households but is a community of families, many of them interrelated by ties of kinship and affinity, which proves capable of acting in common for the preservation of natural resources, the maintenance of public peace and harmony, and for the performance of ritual activities essential to the material and spiritual well-being of the village as a whole.

Lying remote from the centres of state and district administration, and rarely visited by touring officials, Khumbu enjoys a measure of *de facto*, though not *de jure* autonomy, which has enabled the Sherpas to organize their tribal life with a minimum of outside interference. Delivery of the very modest land revenue through the villagers' own representatives, known as *pembu*, to the government treasury at Okhaldhunga, at least six days' journey from Khumbu, is their only positive obligation towards the State. Though there is a police outpost in Namche and cases of crime fall under the jurisdiction of the Magistrate's court at Okhaldhunga, a whole year may pass without any such cases being reported or any Khumbu Sherpa seeking the assistance of the legal machinery of the State.

Such disputes as arise between villagers or members of two villages are usually settled locally, and no outside authority intervenes in the internal affairs of any of the villages of Khumbu. The

Village Organization

control of these affairs lies in the hands of a number of village officials, elected by the villagers for terms of one year at a time, and a system by which authority and the burden of public office pass in turn from one householder to the other engenders a high sense of civic responsibility and a remarkable degree of discipline regarding matters affecting the common good. This civic sense is not confined to the Sherpa families settled in a village for generations, but has been imparted even to the more recent Khamba immigrants, who can gain social recognition only by gradually assuming their share in the discharge of public duties.

In the composition of their population the villages of Khumbu show considerable variations, but these variations do not influence the pattern of village government to any great extent. Before we can discuss this pattern, it will be useful, however, to describe in some detail the composition of *one* village, and to refer briefly to the deviations from this pattern in some of the other villages.

The village of Khumjung has a population consisting of a core of old Sherpa families associated with the village since time immemorial, a number of Sherpa families and individuals known to have moved to Khumjung from other villages of Khumbu and Solu, and of Khamba families immigrated from Tibet within the last few generations or even within the lifetime of their members. The number of households which represented these three categories in 1957 were 37, 9 and 45 respectively.

The Sherpa families of long local standing belong, with a single exception, to one of three intermarrying clans, namely Thaktu, Mende and Paldorje. Though tradition relates that Paldorje was the clan of the first settlers, the leadership of the village has for some generations passed to families of Thaktu and Mende clan. None of the three clans, moreover, constitutes an undivided group of kinsmen able to trace their descent from a common ancestry, but each is divided into a number of lineages (*kalak*). Just as a clan is not confined to a group of villages or single region, so a lineage may extend beyond the borders of one village and include families in the one or other neighbouring village. But its main strength is usually in one village, and in this sense Khumjung is the centre of several important lineages of Thaktu and Mende clan.

The importance of a lineage in village affairs depends not so much on its numerical strength as on the wealth and inherited social status of its members. Thus the most prominent Thaktu lineage, headed by Kushang, the owner of one of the two largest houses in Khumjung, in 1957, consisted of fifteen members. Ten of them were resident in Khumjung and one in Kunde, but only three of these were independent householders, the others being dependents or women married to men of other clans. The second prominent lineage of Thaktu clan consisted of twenty-eight members, many of them young children, and accounted for four of the householders of Khumjung and Kunde. There were five other lineages of Thaktu clan represented in the two villages, but two of them were without strong local associations, their presence in the area being of recent date.

The people of Mende clan were divided into four lineages, one of which was important owing to its wealth, and another owing to the number of householders among its members. Yet another was represented only by one family recently immigrated from Thamichok.

The members of Paldorje clan resident in Khumjung and Kunde were split up among no less than ten lineages. The largest of these consisted of twenty-five members, including women married to men of other clans; seven other lineages were represented by only a few individuals or even single households.

A Sherpa lineage, though of importance in the regulation of inheritance, is not a unit receiving recognition in the organization of a village. No right or office is vested in a lineage, and no public task allotted to it. Its members take their turn in duties and responsibilites in their capacity as householders, and not as representatives or nominees of their lineage. Theoretically there should be no difference in the government of a village consisting of two or three large lineages and a village where no two households belong to the same lineage.

The irrelevancy of clan- and lineage-membership to the individual householder's civic rights and duties is borne out by the position of immigrants from Tibet. These Khambas, who in 1957 accounted for 45 out of the 91 households of Khumjung, belong, of course, to none of the Sherpa clans and lineages. Many of them arrived in Khumbu much too recently for a growth of new lineages, and only in regard to Khambas settled in Khumjung for three and four generations can lineages be compared with the *kalak* of Sherpas.

Village Organization

When I inquired about Khamba *kalak* my Sherpa informants listed some 14 groups of Khamba families whom they considered as forming separate lineages, but I have never heard a Khamba referring to his or any other Khamba's *kalak*. The Khamba residents of a village though not the social equals of the old Sherpa families, play their part in the system of public responsibilities in proportion to their economic position and length of residence. In Khumjung, where most Khambas are fairly recent immigrants and only one Khamba family compares in wealth with the richer Sherpa families, this part is as yet a minor one in so far as offices involving authority are concerned. But public appointments involving duties and the obligation to incur expenditure for the common good go to Khambas no less than to Sherpas, according to a cycle of rotation based on the number of individual householders. The performance of these duties, and particularly the satisfactory discharge of the obligations involved, offer a Khamba the best opportunity of establishing himself as a normal member of a Sherpa village, and the Sherpas are sufficiently free of class prejudice and pollution fears to allow even Khambas of the semi-untouchable *khamendeu* class to take their turn in the discharge of civic responsibilities and to act even in the rôle of organizers of ritual performances.

The leadership of the old-established Sherpa families finds expression not so much in the formal aspects of the village organization, but in the greater weight of their voices in *ad hoc* discussions and, above all, in the economic control their greater wealth enables them to exert.

A situation similar to that of Khumjung prevails in Kunde. There the proportion of Sherpa and Khamba households is 33 to 11, and the control of affairs has remained firmly in Sherpa hands.

In Namche Bazar, on the other hand, a settlement founded by the grandfathers of the present generation, different conditions prevailed from the very beginning. For Khamba traders from Tibet were among the first men to build their houses on the new site, and Khambas have been prominent in the life of the village ever since. Being essentially a mercantile settlement Namche does not require of its inhabitants as high a degree of co-ordination of activities as villages dependent to a greater extent on agriculture and cattle-breeding, and the influence of elected village officials is thus over-shadowed by the economic power of the big traders, several of whom have establishments in the Tibetan town of Tingri as well as in Khumbu.

The situation in the villages of Phortse and Pangboche is different. In these settlements, lying off the main trade-route, agriculture and animal husbandry are the people's principal occupations, while trading is done only on a small scale to meet domestic needs; hence there is not the same scope for newly arrived Khambas as in such places as Namche or even Khumjung and Kunde. Yet, in both villages there is a large number of old-established Khamba families, immigrated four or even five generations ago, whose absorption within the Sherpa pattern of life is so far progressed that their stakes in the effective running of village affairs is as high as that of any Sherpa. Discrimination against Khambas in the allocation of public office has therefore practically disappeared, and the composition of these village communities is far more homogeneous than that of most other Khumbu settlements. The proportion of Sherpa and Khamba households is 40 to 15 in Phortse, and 44 to 17 in Pangboche. The distinction however has lost much of its significance in these two villages.

Whatever the composition of a village community, the guiding principle for its government everywhere is that authority is vested in the totality of its inhabitants. This authority is then delegated to officials elected for limited periods, and during the term of their office they may be guided by decisions on policy made by a public gathering but are not responsible to any superior body for the day to day administration of agreed rules. They have power to inflict fines and collect them as well as to grant exemption from general rules in cases of individual hardship. The village community as a whole cannot correct the actions of such an official, but can only express disapproval by withholding re-election or any future appointment.

The function of each village official, however, is strictly circumscribed, and large spheres of social life lie outside the jurisdiction of these officials. The settlement of disputes relating to these spheres is left to private mediation, and the inability—or unwillingness—of the village community as a whole to assume authority in dealing with such matters, is one of the peculiar features of Sherpa social organization.

Village Organization

THE *NAUA* OR VILLAGE GUARDIANS

In every Sherpa village of Khumbu there are two men known as *naua* appointed to control the use of the village land for purposes of agriculture and cattle-breeding. Their function is to hold a balance between the needs of these two branches of Sherpa economy, and prevent the carelessness or egotism of individuals damaging the interests of other members of the community.

The appointment of the *naua* coincides with the Osho, a rite aimed at surrounding the village with a magical boundary, and banning all evil spirits and malignant forces beyond this invisible fortification. The Osho takes place in the early part of May, when the period of germination and growth of cultivated plants begins. At this time the new *naua* arrange for the performance of the ritual and go in procession round the cultivated village land. It is owing to this association that they are described as *Osho naua* in order to distinguish them from the *shingo naua* or forest guards.

The method of the selection of *naua* is difficult to assess and even more difficult to describe on account of its casualness and the absence of any recognized customary procedure. There is no formal election by a gathering of villagers nor an appointment by any individual entitled to appoint village officials. The decision as to who should be the *naua* for the coming year is taken in informal consultations between three or four leading men of the village, and if their candidates are willing to serve, they take office without any possibility of rival candidates contesting their claims to the position of *naua*.

In Khumjung the selection of *naua* lay for many years in the hands of four or five men. These were the heads of the two richest houses, Kushang (Thaktu) and An Tandin (Mende), the *chorpen* Nima Teshi, the *chorumba*[1] Dorje Ngungdu and—until his death in 1955—Pemba Kitar of Thaktu clan. The latter's son, though no less rich than his greatly respected father, took no part in the appointment of *naua*, for he was a shy man and wealth alone does not carry influence in village affairs with it. The choice of these men was not put before the rest of the villagers even in casual consultation, and it is by no means clear from where they derived their mandate. But it seems that there was never any opposition to their decision,

---

[1] *Chorpen* and *chorumba* are officials of the village temple; their functions are described on pp. 113, 114.

even though the *naua* were chosen mainly from one section of the village community. The list of *naua* from 1952 till 1957 makes this clear:

1952 { Nima Teshi (Thaktu), *chorpen*.
       { Aila (Thaktu), son of Pemba Kitar.

1953 { Dorje Ngungdu (Thaktu), *chorumba*.
       { Phur Temba (Paldorje).

1954 { Jangbu (Thaktu), son of Kushang.
       { Sharap Lama (Khamba).

1955 { Pemba Kitar (Paldorje).
       { Ongcho Lama (Paldorje).

1956 { Lhakpa Choti (Thaktu).
       { Lhakpa Sonam (Khamba).

1957 { Ang Pemba (Paldorje), brother of Phur Temba, *naua* in 1953.
       { Ang Nurbu (Thaktu), brother of Dorje Ngungdu, *naua* in 1953.

We see from this list that of the twelve men who served as *naua* between 1952 and 1957, five were either members of the appointing group or linked to it by the closest of kinship ties, and that the two *naua* for 1957 were the brothers of the *naua* of 1953. Only two of the twelve *naua* were Khamba although the proportion of Sherpa and Khamba households in Khumjung was then 46 to 45.

Many of these men served within a comparatively short period also as forest guards (*shingo naua*), a fact which demonstrates that authority is by no means evenly spread over the 93 households of Khumjung. Most Sherpas explain the weak representation of Khambas among the village officials of the past six years by saying that—with a few exceptions—they lacked reliability and integrity. A correlation of the list of *naua* with a map of the village shows moreover that all those who served as *naua* had their houses in the older part of Khumjung, where houses and land are far more valuable than in the Khamba quarter built against the hill. This quarter has remained completely unrepresented, for even the two Khambas included in the list of *naua* live in the older part of the village; one of them has kinship ties with the head of the most important lineage of Thaktu clan, and the other is a lama and married to a woman of a respectable Sherpa family.

Village Organization

The duties of the *naua* are not very onerous, but their discharge calls for sound judgement as well as tact and firmness. Their main task is to co-ordinate the villagers' agricultural activities and to prevent any damage to the crops. Soon after their election they call all villagers to a meeting known as *yül-thim* ('village-law'). At this meeting it is decided how far cattle-owners have to remove their animals from the village land under cultivation, and fines for any breach of the relevant rules are laid down. For it is customary for the *naua* to banish all cattle from the village soon after the Dumje festival in early July, and the *yül-thim* serves to reach an agreed decision about the line beyond which the cattle has to be kept. This decision is laid down in a written document handed to the *naua*, whose duty it is to administer the rules as agreed to by this village assembly.

By a certain day after the Dumje, proclaimed by the two *naua* no yak, cow, sheep or goat may remain within the prohibited area and any one who by that time has not removed his cattle is liable to a fine. In cases of special hardship the *naua* may extend the time limit for a few days, and they can allow an animal with a broken leg to be kept in the village indefinitely. Pack-animals arriving from Tibet or from one of the high-altitude settlements may remain in the village for one night, but any one exceeding this time limit can by fined by the *naua*.

The detection of breaches of these rules is not entirely left to the *naua*, for other villagers may bring offences to the *naua*'s notice. Thus at the *yül-thim* in 1957 one of the *pembu* made great play with the fact that the year before he had been fined Rs.20 for keeping a milk-giving cow a few days longer in the village, even though the animal had done no damage whatsoever, and swore that in this year he would see that the *naua* applied the rules to others equally strictly.

While the ban on the keeping of cattle within the village land lasts from a few days after the Dumje until after the harvest, other restrictions to be enforced by the *naua* apply only for the period of the growth of the crops, i.e. from the end of the weeding in late July until the beginning of the potato harvest in early September. During this period of growth no one may enter a field, whether his own or that of another villager, no milk or curd should be brought near the fields, and even people who do the milking and churning should not come close to the fields. No green wood should be carried past the field and no green plants should be dried within the village boundary. Similarly the water mixed with dye for dyeing wool and cloth should not be thrown out in the village, and dyed materials must not be dried inside the village. No gun must be fired, because the smell of gunpowder would adversely affect the growth of the crops, and there should be no quarrel within the village.

Anyone who offends against these rules can be fined by the *naua*, and such a fine, whether paid in cash or in the form of beer is called *na-chang*.

The two *naua*, either on their own authority or in consultation with the leading men of the village, fix the day when the potato harvest may begin. Until then no one should enter a field even to pull out weeds, a task which precedes the digging-up of potatoes in order to prevent their seeds falling onto the field.

The final act of the *naua* is to permit the cattle back into the village after the harvest of both potatoes and buckwheat has been completed, and on the day of throwing open the village land they symbolically demolish a small wall which had been built across the main path which leads from the village to *gunsa* and *yersa* settlements.

The fines imposed by the *naua* during the cultivating season—and it is only during this season that they wield authority—are either paid in the form of beer, in which case they are consumed by the *naua*, or in all but trivial cases in the form of cash. Such cash fines are used for the upkeep of the village *gomba* or for other public works.

At the end of their term, a few days before the Osho, when their successors will be appointed, the *naua* go from house to house and collect as their fee about 2 lb. of maize or buckwheat and a small quantity of rice or other grain from each household. In the case of the twin villages of Khumjung and Kunde, these contributions are pooled between the four *naua*, and are partly used for beer to be drunk at the Osho, partly given to the officiating lama and partly divided among the four *naua*.

The material advantages a *naua* derives from his position are insignificant, but the office adds to a man's standing in the village. While there is no direct competition for the office, there are neither any signs that those selected have to be persuaded to accept the appointment. I have not heard of *naua* abusing their position by levying excessive fines from people against whom they had a

Participants in a meeting of the village-assembly

Members of the village-assembly of Khumjung

The abbess of Devuche and Ang Nima

Nima Teshi and his wife turning prayer-wheels

private grudge, nor do those fined express any personal resentment against the *naua* who had to impose the fine, though—as in the case of the Khumjung *pembu* already mentioned—they may consider a fine too severe.

Slackness or excessive leniency on the part of a *naua* may arouse popular indignation, and in Phortse dissatisfaction with the *naua*'s activities led, some fifteen years ago, to a change in the system of appointment. Until that time the *naua* of Phortse held office for more than one year, but one autumn several villagers brought a great many yak and cows into the village without waiting for the day appointed by the *naua* for the return of the cattle. The two *naua* ignored this flagrant breach of the rules and did not fine the offenders. At this the villagers got angry and went to Khumjung to seek the advice of one of their *pembu* and other influential men. In consultation with them they decided to appoint their *naua* only for a one year term. After their return to Phortse they made a list of villagers suitable for the office of *naua*, and the men on this list have since served as *naua* in strict rotation. At the same time it was decided that the fine for taking cattle into the village before the *naua* had granted permission to do so should be raised from Rs.10 to Rs.20.

In Namche Bazar three *naua* are appointed every year, but as the village has little cultivation and the number of people who keep cattle is comparatively small, their intervention is seldom required.

In the Thamichok area two *naua* are appointed for the villages of Thamu, Thami, Thamote, O-ang and Phurte, and two for the villages of Hilajung and Pare, which lie on the other bank of the Bhote Kosi. Their rôle is like that of the *naua* in Khumjung and Kunde, but I have no data on the families from which they are recruited. In 1953 the Thami *naua* fined six people for driving their cattle down from the higher settlements before the appointed day. The offenders had to provide beer and this was drunk at a gathering of some of the important villagers, to whom they apologized for their disregard of village rules.

If a *naua* dies during his term of office no new appointment is made, but a member of his household, preferably an adult son, or failing this even his widow, acts as *naua* for the rest of the year. Stress is laid on the fact that the substitute *naua* should be of the same house; a brother living in a separate house cannot automatically take over the function of *naua*.

SHINGO NAUA OR FOREST GUARDS

Besides the *naua* responsible for the control of the movement of cattle, and the co-ordination of the work on the fields, there are in every village officials in charge of the preservation of protected forests. These officials too are also known as *naua*, but as they deal with the husbanding of the community's wood and timber resources, they are referred to as *shingo naua*, *shing* being the Sherpa word for wood. Like the *Osho naua*, they ostensibly derive their mandate from an assembly of villagers, while their appointment is in reality the outcome of consultations within a comparatively small group of influential men.

The most important difference between the *Osho naua* and the *shingo naua* is the latter's longer term of office. Whereas no *Osho naua* ever serves for more than one year and there is no possibility of an early re-appointment, a *shingo naua* enjoying the villagers' confidence may hold the office as long as twelve years. This was the period Dorje Ngungdu served in this capacity in Khumjung, and he might have had an even longer term of office had he not resigned in 1957.

The following list of Khumjung's *shingo naua* during the years 1941 till 1957 shows the same tendency noticeable in the selection of *Osho naua*. The office is largely reserved for men of the old established Sherpa families, and the same men who served in the capacity of *shingo naua* may subsequently be appointed as *Osho naua* or vice versa:

1941–43
- Dong Nima (Mende)
- Da Tensing (Paldorje)
- Sange Lama (Chusherwa).

1944–46
- Kushang (Thaktu)
- Yülha Tarkia (Thaktu)
- Lhakpa Sona (Khamba)
- Ang Pemba (Thaktu).

1947–50
- Dorje Ngundu (Thaktu)
- Kitar (Paldorje), father of Phur Temba [cf. 1957]
- Kishung (Mende)
- Ngawang Tawa (Khamba).

1951–52
- Dorje Ngungdu (Thaktu)
- Aila (Thaktu)
- Tandin Sundokpa (Paldorje).

Village Organization

1953–56
- Dorje Ngungdu (Thaktu)
- Ang Nurbu (Thaktu), brother of Dorje Ngungdu
- Ongcho Lama (Paldorje)
- Kapa Kalden (Gurung); officiating Sharap Lama (Khamba).

1957–
- Lhakpa Choti (Thaktu)
- Phur Temba (Paldorje)
- Anulu (Thaktu)
- Pemba Nurbu (Khamba).

There is no objection to a man combining the offices of *Osho naua* and *shingo naua*. Thus Dorje Ngungdu held both offices in 1953, Aila in 1952 and Ongcho Lama in 1955.

The *shingo naua* are responsible for the protection of the reserved forest close to the village, and three to four men are appointed to serve simultaneously because continuous vigilance is needed to prevent wood-cutters from encroaching on the forest growth in the prohibited areas. It is within the *shingo naua*'s power to permit limited fellings in the protected forest for special purposes, such as house-building, and they do not interfere with the cutting of wood required for funeral pyres.

Their mandate is not confined to the punishment of offenders in the act of cutting wood in a reserved area or of carrying such wood to the village, but they may also inspect the stocks of wood in people's houses, and demand an explanation for any unusual quantity. The maximum fine for felling a tree in the protected forest (*keak-shing*) is Rs.15, but such fines are imposed only in extreme cases.

The fining of offenders takes place annually soon after the Osho rite when the *shingo naua* are re-appointed or new men take office. At that time the *shingo naua* responsible for the past year go round the village, collecting the fines imposed during their period of office and inspecting any suspicious stocks of wood. They then call the villagers to a meeting in the public assembly place, and anyone guilty of a forest offence has to bring a bottle of beer and confess his or her fault in public to the *naua*. If the offence is of a minor nature, such as the cutting of a few green branches in an area where only dead wood may be collected, the beer is accepted as an adequate fine, but cash fines are imposed for more serious breaches of the law.

The beer brought on this occasion is known as *shingi-na-chang* (wood fine). It is at once consumed by the assembled villagers, and under its mollifying influence the atmosphere at this *yül-thim* rapidly changes from that of a village court to the jollity of a minor festival.

The *yül-thim* usually lasts for two days, and those among the law-breakers who omitted to produce their *shingi-na-chang* on the first day have to bring twice the required quantity of beer, and apologize for the delay as well as for their offence. The excuses tendered on this occasion are often rather naive and often follow the pattern 'I saw others do it, and so did it too'. At the 1957 *yül-thim*, for instance, Atashi, a Khamba settled in Khumjung for the past eight years, brought forward the excuse that he had cut down only two trees, and they were just by the side of trees already cut down by other villagers. He said he used to go for wood beyond the Dudh Kosi (where wood-cutting is permitted) or to collect only dry wood, but when he saw others cutting green wood he succumbed to the temptation of saving time and labour and followed their example.

The *shingo naua* are entitled to use a small part of the cash fines which they collect for buying food and drink for a party at which they list the offenders and the amounts paid. The balance is either paid into the funds of the village *gomba* or employed in the furthering of public works, such as the reconstruction of a bridge.

The effective functioning of the *shingo naua* is of vital importance to the long-term well-being of a village community. In an area which lies close to the tree-line, and in a climate where wood is required not only for house-building and as fuel for cooking, but equally for heating, deforestation would be a danger to the very existence of many village communities. Only by protecting the forests situated close to the larger accumulations of population is it possible to prevent their destruction by youthful wood-cutters, too thoughtless and short-sighted to see the dangers that unrestricted fellings would involve for their own homes.

Compared with the forests of lower and climatically more favoured regions where peasants of Chetri, Brahman and Newar stock have in recent generations wrought enormous devastation, the forests of Khumbu are on the whole in good condition. This is mainly due to an efficient system of checks and controls developed

Village Organization

and administered by a society which combines strong civic sense with a system of investing individuals with authority without enabling them to tyrannize their fellow-villagers.

CHORUMBA AND CHORPEN: THE GUARDIANS OF THE VILLAGE TEMPLE

Though not every village possesses a *gomba* or temple of its own, every village participates on equal terms in the festivals celebrated in the *gomba* to which it is traditionally affiliated. Thus Khumjung and Kunde combine in the performance of the annual rites in the Khumjung *gomba*, and Pangboche and Phortse stand in a similar partnership of celebrating the annual festivals jointly in the *gomba* of Pangboche.

The officials in charge of these *gomba* are responsible not only for the religious performances, which will be discussed in another context, but also for the organization of village festivals and the administration of funds collected by the villagers and ear-marked for *gomba* purposes. In this sense, they are then village officials and their tasks include many secular activities. While the position of senior *gomba* priest or *umse* (cf. p. 146) is always held by a lama, the offices of *chorumba* and *chorpen* of village temples, though not of the *gomba* of monasteries, are invariably held by laymen.

Both *chorumba* and *chorpen* hold their position on behalf and with the consent of the village communities responsible for the upkeep of a *gomba*. The *chorumba* of the Khumjung *gomba*, Dorje Ngungdu, had in 1962 held the office for fifteen years, but his predecessor, Konje Chunbi, had served only for two years, and the *chorumba* before him only for one year. Yet, there is no limit to the number of years a *chorumba* may hold office, and the office of *chorpen* of the Khumjung *gomba* has for three generations been held by members of the family of the present *chorpen*, Nima Teshi. Though in this case the position is virtually hereditary, the villagers of Khumjung and Kunde would be within their rights to dismiss the *chorpen* and to appoint in his place a man of different clan and family.

Jointly *chorumba* and *chorpen* are responsible for the upkeep of the temple and the administration of temple funds. They arrange for repairs, and are entitled to use for such purposes the money collected as fines by the *shingo naua*. In Khumjung Dorje Ngungdu combined for many years the function of temple guardian and forest guard, but this overlapping of public offices was incidental, and as *chorumba* he remained entitled to the administration of fine-money even when he had resigned the office of *shingo naua*.

Apart from the responsibility for the temple finances, which he shares with the *chorpen*, the *chorumba* has also the difficult task of maintaining discipline during the Dumje festival. At that time he is not only empowered to fine people for creating disturbances, but he may also wield his long leather whip which he carries as symbol of his office. No one can complain of having been hit by the *chorumba* when he has to use force in restoring order, and this privileged position of the *chorumba* demonstrates the fact that Sherpa society will invest individuals with powers far greater than even the most influential man can attain without the authority of public office.

Another important function of the *chorumba* is the appointment of Dumje *lawa*, persons charged with the provision of food and drink at the time of the Dumje festival (cf. p. 185). Though the honourable and yet burdensome rôle of Dumje *lawa* falls in turn to every villager, fluctuations in the village population necessitate minor adjustments in the order of rotation, and the *chorumba*, who manipulates this order, has a task calling for considerable diplomacy.

The *chorpen's* function is in comparison far less exacting. He has to guard the *torma*, ritual objects and offerings set out in the *gomba* during the Dumje, and is hence expected to sleep there throughout the duration of the festival. He has also some minor ritual tasks, but bears no responsibility comparable with that of the *chorumba*.

The offices of *chorumba* and *chorpen* are mainly honorary, and their prestige is the incumbents' principal reward. On the occasion of festivals, such as the Dumje, the latter may receive some small dues out of the contributions of the *lawa* (cf. p. 186) but this is a very small recompense for the effort they expend for the common good.

CIVIC DUTIES BY ROTATION

The foremost principle underlying Sherpa village organization is the allocation of civic tasks by rotation. We have seen that in the village of Phortse the *Osho naua* take office according to a cycle of rotation laid down in writing. In Khumjung, on the other hand, the influx of large numbers of newcomers with different customs and standards has made it impossible to give all sections of the population an equal share in the government of the village. There the office of *naua* is held in turn by the members of families representing the old core of the village community as well as by those Khambas considered sufficiently assimilated to be entrusted with positions of authority. Tasks less vital to the well-being of the community, however, are allocated in rotation to all villagers irrespective of their social and economic status. Such tasks concern mainly the organization of festivals or religious performances, and the provision of food and drink for the participants. The most important of these is the organization of the Dumje festival, and the men chosen to undertake it are known as *lawa*. This term is used for anyone appointed to arrange for a public ceremony or even the annual reciting of holy scriptures at public expense. Besides the *lawa* in charge of the preparations for the Dumje, there are *lawa* concerned with the Yerchang, with the annual reading of the Kangyur, and the Tsirim rite, which serves to banish evil spirits from the village.

The number of *lawa* appointed for any such occasion depends on the magnitude of the task. The traditional number of *lawa* for the Dumje celebrated in the temples of Khumjung and Pangboche is eight, but there have been years when one *lawa* fell out, and others when nine were appointed to share in the task. The *lawa* are chosen from the two villages sharing one *gomba* in numbers approximately proportionate to the number of houses in the villages concerned. Thus there are usually five *lawa* from Khumjung and three from Kunde, whereas at the Pangboche Dumje four *lawa* from Pangboche and four from Phortse are in charge of the arrangements. In Khumjung and Kunde a man's turn to act as *lawa* comes about once in fourteen years, and the system of rotation operates in such a way that the household and not the individual is considered the unit. Thus the obligation to act as *lawa* may pass to a widow and a young son if it would have been the turn of the deceased head of the household. In a case of great poverty or illness a person may be excused from performing the duties of *lawa*, but such an exemption usually implies only a postponement of his turn for a number of years.

The duties of a Dumje *lawa* are by no means light. Apart from contributing to the materials required for the making of sacrificial cakes (*torma*) and the payment of lamas, a Dumje *lawa* has to entertain all the villagers with beer and liquor, and provide one meal to be served in the *gomba* to all those participating in the festival, i.e. to the entire population of the villages sharing a *gomba*.

The system of allotting the responsibility for the entire catering a village festival to one set of eight households after the other in rotation means in fact that for about thirteen years a Khumjung family can eat and drink their fill at the Dumje without considering the cost, but that in the fourteenth year they will have to bear the very considerable expense of providing food and drink for at least five hundred people. The quality of the food provided depends, of course, on a family's means, but the desire to gain prestige stimulates every *lawa* to exert himself to the utmost in collecting the materials for the great occasion when he is host to the entire community.

A result of this system of catering at festivals by turn is a spreading of resources throughout the community. Rich and poor alike partake during these days of the same meals provided by the eight *lawa*, and everyone has equal access to the large quantities of beer and liquor dispensed by the day's hosts.

At minor rites the *lawa* have not so much to provide food and drink at their own expense, but to give their labour in organizing the collection of public contributions and undertaking the preparation of food. Such an occasion is the annual reading of the 108 books of the Kangyur in the village *gomba*. As many as twelve lamas, most of whom are invited from neighbouring villages, are employed for this task, and they have to be fed during the days spent in reciting, as well as be provided with ample quantities of tea and beer. Thus the two *lawa* and some members of their families have to spend eight days or more in attending to the lamas, and though their expenditure on food and drink is reimbursed from public subscription, they still may have to forgo several days' earnings or work for their own benefit.

The idea behind all such arrangements is the same. A responsibility resting with the whole of the village community is passed on to a small number of individuals, who during the period of their appointment function as the representatives of the village. Rather than pay these representatives for their services, the Sherpas have evolved the system of rotation, which assures that irksome duties have to be discharged only for short periods and that every villager has sooner or later to take his turn in their performance. The system provides for efficiency as well as for social justice, for whoever acts as *lawa* is, so to say, a 'new broom', and the period of service is so

Village Organization

short that the eagerness to prove himself useful is not blunted by boredom or spoilt by impatience.

COLLECTORS OF LAND REVENUE: THE *PEMBU*

A Sherpa village with its *naua* to guard its fields and forests, its temple officials to arrange for worship and festivals, and the efficient system of public service by rotation would be virtually autonomous were it not that the State exercises the right to levy rent on the cultivated land. But unlike governments in other parts of the world, the Government of Nepal dispenses with a machinery of paid officials for the collection of this land revenue. It wisely relies on the Sherpas themselves to collect fixed amounts, and deliver the money once a year to the Treasury in Okhaldhunga. This system, admirably suited to the Sherpas' temperament, calls for men trusted by their fellow-tribesmen and government alike, and these men, who collect the revenue and pay the cash into the government's treasury are known as *pembu* or *misar*, the former term being Tibetan and the latter Nepali. But whereas in other hill regions of Nepal the revenue is usually collected by village headmen, known as *mukiya*, *taluqdar* or *misar*, the position in Khumbu is more complex, and the revenue is not collected on a village basis. There are at present seven *pembu* or *misar* for the whole of Khumbu, and each of these *pembu* collects the revenue from a number of clients (*misir*) scattered over several villages. Three of these *pembu* live in Namche, two in Khumjung, one in Kunde, and one, who until recently lived in Thamu, now lives in Solu, but continues to act as one of the Khumbu *pembu*. The villages of Phortse and Pangboche, and the whole of the Thamichok area, have today no resident *pembu*, and this uneven distribution of the *pembu* alone makes it clear that the *pembu's* rôle is not that of village headman. While in 1957 the number of *pembu* was seven, the traditional number of *pembu*-ships is eight, and the reduction in numbers is due to the recent combination of two *pembu*-ships in one person.

The origin of the institutions of *pembu* as well as the establishment of eight *pembu*-ships in Khumbu is obscure, but documents going back for more than a century, already refer to 'one *gembu* and eight *pembu*'. The position of *gembu* is today obsolete, but there remains the vivid memory of a time when a *gembu*, resident first in Thami and later in Namche Bazar, fulfilled the function of controlling the eight *pembu* and 'protecting the people against any oppressiveness on the part of the *pembu*'.

The oldest document I found, in the possession of one of the Khumjung *pembu*, was a government order dated 1885 Bikram era (A.D. 1828) addressed to the '*genbu* Pasang Tenu, *misar* Gordza, and the villagers of Khumbu'. Another document is dated the 6th Jestha 1894 Bikram era (A.D. 1836) and addressed to 'Ganba [*gembu*] Pasang Tendu and eight *misar*'. This document lists the amounts payable by the individual *misar* (*pembu*), but it is doubtful whether the names given are those of individuals or traditional titles attached to their respective *pembu*-ships. The number of houses under their control, and the amounts listed are as follows:

Nam Chunbi *misar*	—33 houses,	Rs.	212/4
Ildar *misar*	—23	,,	,,	158/–
Sumba *misar*	—18	,,	,,	132/–
Chitama *misar*	—14	,,	,,	102/–
Chumba *misar*	—21	,,	,,	156/25
Karta *misar*	—17	,,	,,	125/5
Gordza Sunamba *misar*				
	—23	,,	,,	170/75
Ngatashi *misar*	—20	,,	,,	142/50
	169 houses		Rs.1198/79

The document contains no reference to villages, but there is a tradition that four *pembu*, including the Karta and Gordza *misar* were associated with the Thamichok area and four with the rest of Khumbu. Though the titles of *pembu*-ships contained in this document are no longer in current usage, their link with certain posts is still remembered and the following list indicates the holders of their posts in 1957:

Nam Chimla	Shrita (Paldorje) of Namche
Ildar	Nima Dorje (Thaktu) of Thamu
Sumba	} Ang Chunbi (Paldorje) of Kunde
Chitama	
Chumba	Konje Chunbi (Thaktu) of Khumjung
Karta	Urkan (Khamba) of Namche
Gordza	Kazi (Gurung) of Namche
Ngatashi	Chopali (Gole) of Khumjung.

The Gordza *pembu*-ship passed only recently to a Namche man of Gurung descent. Until about 1950 it was held by Gordza Tarkia of Gardza clan of Thamote village, who when getting old gave the post voluntarily to Ngawang Cheten (Gurung) of Namche, on whose death it passed to his son Kazi.

The data contained in the documents stemming from the first half of the nineteenth century and the fragments of traditions remembered by the present *pembu*, enable us to reconstruct a sequence of events which, though partly hypothetical, explains the present situation to a considerable extent. The development seems to have been roughly as follows:

Ever since the government of the Gorkha kingdom established its right to the collection of revenue from the Khumbu area, it dealt with the Sherpas through a number of tribal leaders known as *gembu* and *pembu*. While the *gembu* acted as the representative of the whole of Khumbu, each of the *pembu* was responsible for the collection of a fixed amount of revenue from certain groups of households. It is probable that these groups were originally localized, and that each *pembu* collected the revenue of a specific area. The revenue was assessed partly in cash and partly in kind, and agents of government, known as *duari*, came once a year to Khumbu to receive the revenue from the eight *pembu*. At that time there was no survey of the cultivated land and the *pembu* were free to assess their clients according to their means and not in exact proportion to the area cultivated. As there was no rigid link between any particular land under cultivation and the payment of revenue a client could continue to pay the revenue to his traditional *pembu* even if he moved to another village. It seems that at this time the *pembu*-client relationship was more lasting and relevant than the association of a *pembu* with a specific area. The movements of families within Khumbu ultimately led to a situation when each *pembu* had clients in several villages, and the revenue of one village was collected by two, three or even four *pembu*, each levying the rent from his own traditional clients settled in the village.

From time to time the revenue payable by the people of Khumbu was raised in accordance with the change of monetary values, and the revenue for the whole region rose from Rs.750 in 1828, to Rs.1198 in 1836, and by gradual stages to Rs.4000 in 1939. A major change in the system of assessment, however, occurred only after 1941 when as a preliminary step towards a land survey, the government compiled lists of the cultivated areas under the control of the individual *pembu*. This procedure created a permanent link between a *pembu*-ship and certain specific pieces of land, and a man could no longer continue to pay his revenue to his traditional *pembu* wherever he cultivated, but the rent for every field had to be paid to the *pembu* who had collected the revenue of this particular area at the time of the preliminary survey.

A situation in which the clients and consequently the areas of land under a *pembu's* jurisdiction were dispersed over several villages was thereby perpetuated and deprived of all flexibility. When land subsequently changed hands, the purchaser had to pay the revenue to the *pembu* in charge of the land, and it thus came about that some people were no longer the clients of one particular *pembu*, but paid revenue to two or three *pembu*.

At the same time there was a change in the system of the remittance of revenue to the government. Instead of sending its agents (*duari*) to Khumbu, the government ordered the *pembu* to bring the collected revenue once a year to Okhaldunga, and pay it there into the district treasury.

Seen against this background of developments over the past 120 years, the present position of the *pembu* becomes understandable, and we are now able to explain the unusual dovetailing and overlapping of jurisdictions, which distinguishes the Sherpa *pembu* from the village headmen of such tribes as Tamangs, Rais, Limbus and Gurungs. The, as yet, unexplained eclipse of the position of *gembu* may have been partly due to a historic accident and partly to the increase of direct government control over the *pembu*.

The available documents indicate that even a century ago the *gembu* of Khumbu was the person to whom government orders were addressed. He stood above the eight *pembu* and some of his functions are still remembered. Thus it is believed that the *gembu* had authority to fine any *pembu* guilty of an irregularity, and that he had to be consulted and give his consent before a *pembu*-ship could be transferred from one person to the other. From time to time the *pembu* gathered in his house to discuss matters of public interest, and disputes between men of importance were settled by the *gembu*.

Pasang Tendu, the *gembu* mentioned in the documents of 1828 and 1836, was a man of Shangup clan, resident in Thami. His son, Kunga Hishi, and his grandson, Dorje, both held the office, but in 1895 Dorje was dismissed by a touring government official on the grounds of inefficiency and lack of co-operativeness. In his place Chopal of Gole clan, a Sherpa from Solu settled in Namche Bazar, was appointed *gembu*. In an attempt to curb the high-handedness of one of the *pembu*—Sun Tundu (Paldorje) of Phortse—and bring him to justice, he aroused the wrath of the latter's supporters, who in turn tried to murder Chopal. The plot was abortive but in the course of the resultant disturbances Dorje, the dismissed *gembu*, was wounded and two other people were killed.

Chopal, finding it unsafe to remain in Namche, went to Tibet and died in Lhasa. His son Pasang Gyalje succeeded him as *gembu* and at first he lived in his house in Namche but the opposition which had driven his father to Tibet continued to smoulder, and he ultimately moved to Gole, his family's ancestral village. From that moment he lost touch with Khumbu, and though nominally still *gembu*, could no longer exert any effective influence on local affairs. His son Lhakpa Gelbu retains only the title of *gembu* and is not recognized by the government, which now deals with the *pembu* without any intermediary. As an institution the office of *gembu* has ceased to be part of the Sherpa political system.

The control which the *gembu* exerted over the eight *pembu* is now replaced by closer supervision on the part of touring government officials, who are known to have investigated complaints and in recent years compelled one *pembu* to resign in favour of his son. The change-over, however, was largely nominal, and the father continued to act as *pembu* in all but name—a measure, incidentally, of the limitations of government control.

Succession to a *pembu*-ship has always been partly determined by the principle of heredity, and partly by considerations of personal ability. An analysis of the succession to the eight *pembu*-ships of Khumbu during the last three or four generations shows clearly that the office has seldom remained in one family for more than two generations. A *pembu's* sons or kinsmen who were not equal to the post, either refused to succeed or were soon replaced by men of greater drive and ability.

One of the *pembu*-ships, now held by Chopali (Gole) of Khumjung, changed hands nine times during the last eighty years, and two of the past holders were still alive in 1957. Most of the changes were due to resignations of men who found the work irksome, and prevailed upon one of their clients to take over the work for some years. This, however, was an exception, and the position of *pembu* is normally held for life.

There have been cases, however, of a *pembu* being displaced by one of his clients, who achieved this aim by instigating dissatisfaction among the other clients or by intriguing against the *pembu* with government officials.

Thus the Yülha Tarkia (Thaktu), the father of Konje Chunbi, one of the present *pembu*, obtained his *pembu*-ship by complaining to touring government officials about his *pembu*, Lhakia (Shangup) of Thami, and by bribing some of the latter's clients to support his complaint. Though Yülha Tarkia then lived in Namche and most of the *pembu's* clients were in Thami, he succeeded in his intrigue and was appointed in the place of Lhakia.

Similarly Gyalwa (Paldorje), the father of the present *pembu* Ang Chunbi, obtained his *pembu*-ship from Pem Putr (Mende), who was the adopted son of the *pembu* Munpuli (Thaktu). While Munpuli had been extremely rich and influential, Pem Putr was a spendthrift, and Gyalwa, who was one of his clients set out to arouse the other clients' dissatisfaction with the management of the *pembu*-ship. When he had thus prepared the ground for a change-over, he offered to work on Pem Putr's behalf, but later did not stick to the bargain and assumed the *pembu*-ship himself. His son Ang Chunbi not only inherited this *pembu*-ship, but acquired also another *pembu*-ship, previously held by Sange Lama, thus adding the latter's 105 clients to the 84 clients of his father's *pembu*-ship.

The attraction of the position of *pembu* is twofold. The clients of a *pembu* give him a certain amount of free labour, and he has the right to dispose of any land which has fallen vacant. The right to free labour cannot now be enforced, and rich and influential people may refuse to provide any free labour for their *pembu*, but the average client family provides annually one member to work on their *pembu's* fields for three days. Poor people who are anxious to gain the *pembu's* favour may do even more work on his fields, and the most frequent complaints against *pembu* is the exaction of excessive unpaid labour. The right to dispose of vacant land can also be manipulated to a *pembu's* advantage. When a man dies without heirs and kinsmen of the same *kalak*, his *pembu* is entitled to allocate the vacant house and land to anyone he chooses. The recipient usually pays a small fee to the *pembu*, but there are also many instances of *pembu* themselves taking possession of land which has fallen vacant. This procedure is in itself not illegal, but it can lead to the neglect of claims of distant kinsmen which under other circumstances might have been admitted as valid.

Both the possibility of increasing his holdings at little expense, and the authority of allotting vacant land to those he favours, can add greatly to a *pembu's* economic strength and influence. Thanks to this influence Ang Chunbi (Paldorje), for instance, had become the richest man of his village, though at the time when he left his father's house in Khumjung and settled in Kunde, he was well-off but by no means outstandingly rich. But his position enabled him to acquire land not only in Kunde, but also in Khumjung, Pangboche and Dingboche, and the services of his 189 clients made it possible to cultivate all this land without great expenditure on labour.

While in Khumjung the effective control over village affairs is shared by several wealthy men, who choose the *naua* and take the leading parts in the deliberations of a *yül-thim* meeting, in Kunde authority is concentrated in the hands of the *pembu*, Ang Chunbi. It is he who determines the selection of *naua*, but even though they are his nominees he often undermines their authority by disregarding their orders and thereby giving the villagers a bad example. In 1957, for instance, several Kunde people did not await the *naua*'s orders before beginning the potato harvest, and this was attributed to Ang Chunbi who was the first to begin with the work on his fields. It is obvious that any such offence against the *naua*'s orders weakens the whole system of controls, which is based on the voluntary delegations of authority to elected members of the community. The *naua*, who need not be men of great wealth and personal influence, are powerful only as long as the whole community supports their orders, and in the face of an overbearing *pembu* they are reduced to a more or less ceremonial rôle.

It is not unlikely that as long as there was an effective *gembu* too great an accumulation of power in the hands of a *pembu* was curbed. There is at least one case on record of the *gembu* apprehending an oppressive *pembu*, and handing him over to the government authorities. With the virtual abolishment of the *gembu*'s office there is no local check on the *pembu*, though major irregularities or widespread complaints by their clients may result in their dismissal.

Yet as a rule the *pembu* seem to enjoy their clients' confidence, and the fact that they are members of the village community and, for all social purposes, dependent on their co-villagers' good will, sets limits to any high-handedness. Compared with the rapacity of revenue collectors in many of the backward areas of India or in the Nepal Terai, the tendency of some *pembu* to further their own interests rather than those of their clients is not a very grave defect, and the institution as at present constituted does not give much scope for corruption.

A Sherpa *pembu*, moreover, is not just a collector of revenue, but his rôle vis-à-vis his clients is not unlike that of a senior kinsman. At the wedding of a man who has neither a father nor a father's brother he may act in the place of the father and may even bear some of the expenses. Similarly he should perform the funeral rites of a client who has no heirs or kinsmen of his own lineage (*kalak*).

A *pembu* represents, in certain respects, the community and its laws. Some fines for breaches of accepted customs are paid to the *pembu*, particularly in cases where there is no aggrieved party. Thus a man who marries his late wife's eldest sister must pay a nominal fine of one rupee to his *pembu*. The latter may also act as a trustee of compensation money. A man who wants to marry a girl betrothed by *dem-chang* to someone else, may deposit the customary compensation of Rs.105 with his *pembu* as proof that he is prepared and able to pay damages. Similarly a man whose father-in-law procrastinates over agreeing to the performance of the final wedding rite and is unwilling to accept a *rit* payment (cf. pp. 65–67), may pay Rs.6 to his *pembu* and take his betrothed by force to his house. All such payments to a *pembu* are resorted to in order to legalize a situation before agreement between the parties involved could be reached.

In disputes which defy the ordinary system of settling quarrels, the *pembu* of the parties involved sometimes try to mediate. They have no judicial powers, however, and cannot impose a settlement.

Another responsibility of the *pembu* is the control of the extension of cultivation, and of the establishment of new immigrants. Anyone who wants to cultivate a piece of waste land must consult his *pembu*, who may—but need not—increase his client's revenue. Newly arrived Khambas must obtain a *pembu*'s permission to trade or cultivate in Khumbu. For a payment of three to five rupees, known as *se-geup*, this permission is usually readily given. Some *pembu* even approach newly immigrated Khambas with a demand for this payment, and whichever *pembu* does this first gains the new settler as a client.

Monks and novices of Tengboche

Chörten and *gomba* at Tengboche

The houses of the monks surrounding the *gomba*

A function of the *pembu*, which is rarely exercised, is the purification of persons polluted by drinking from the cup of a *khamendeu* Khamba or by having had sexual intercourse with someone of *khamendeu* status. The procedure is simple. The *pembu* first drinks beer out of a cup, then lets the person to be purified drink out of it, and finally drinks again from the same cup, and passes it to other people present. The offender has to provide the beer and pay a fee of one rupee to the *pembu*. It is said that only those who unwittingly associated with a person of *khamendeu* status can be purified in this way, whereas those who have lived knowingly with a man or woman of *khamendeu* class become *khamendeu* themselves and can never regain *khadeu* status.

The whole idea of such a purification ceremony seems to be foreign to Sherpa concepts, however, and it seems that while everybody has heard about the possibility of being purified in this way very few people know of any concrete cases. No ceremony of this kind seems to have taken place in Khumjung and Kunde within human memory, and it is believed that in Namche Bazar, where one or two cases occurred some thirty years ago, the *pembu* concerned was not acting independently, but was assisted by a government agent. As such agents were often Chetris or other high caste Hindus, the whole idea of such a purification may be the influence of Hindu ideas of ritual purity and the need for its restoration after any polluting contact. Some Sherpas remember, for instance, that one generation ago a government official purified a Khamba, who was suspected of being *khamendeu* (though he posed as *khadeu*) and that by this act established him as *khadeu*.

In view of the manifold responsibilities of a *pembu*, it is remarkable that even in villages with resident *pembu* the actual leadership does not necessarily lie with them. Whereas Ang Chunbi (Paldorje), the *pembu* resident in Kunde, was in 1957 the undisputed leader of the village, the two *pembu* of Khumjung, Konje Chunbi (Thaktu) and Chopali (Gole), neither wielded great influence in village affairs nor ranked particularly high in the order of precedence followed on ceremonial occasions. Here the real authority lay with several men of wealth and long-established family prestige, who did not compete for public office but were, nevertheless, the ultimate power behind the village officers responsible for the day-to-day administration of village affairs.

5

Monastic Institutions and Priesthood

The village, with its inhabitants engrossed in the pursuit of husbandry and trade, represents only one side of Sherpa life. The other side is represented by monasteries and nunneries, by the lonely cave-dwellings of hermits and the small settlements of lamas within easy reach of the habitations of lay village-folk. Sherpa society embraces the laity as well as the many men and women who choose the religious life, and the one part is incomplete and incomprehensible without the other. Unlike the Brahman priest of Hindu society, whose place is invariably inside secular society, the Buddhist lama has the choice of either living in the midst of the laity, a villager among villagers, or of abandoning all secular ambitions and associations and devoting himself exclusively to spiritual pursuits. While personally withdrawing from lay society, he does not withdraw his services; indeed the monastery and its monks are forces of vital importance for Sherpa society and Sherpa culture.

There is no cleavage between the Buddhist doctrine practised in the monasteries and the religion of the ordinary villager. Both have their roots in Tibetan religious traditions, and the worship of local deities, foremost in the religious thought of the untutored layman, is not excluded from the ritual performances of the monasteries. The intellectual levels of the religious practices of monks and laymen are undoubtedly very different, but unlike in Tamang[1] society there is no trace of any conflict between village religion and the more sophisticated beliefs of learned lamas.

The historical development of Buddhism in Khumbu and Solu is a problem intimately linked with that of the age of Sherpa civilization in its present form. Strange as it may seem, none of the monastic institutions in Khumbu and Solu are older than a hundred years, and the two most prominent monasteries, Tengboche and Chiwong,

[1] Cf. C. von Fürer-Haimendorf, 'Ethnographic Notes on the Tamangs of Nepal', *Eastern Anthropologist*, Vol. 9, 1955/56, pp. 166–77.

were founded less than fifty years ago. That the last three generations have seen a most vigorous expansion of religious institutions cannot be doubted, and in Chapter I (pp. 10, 11) I have suggested that the great upsurge in religious activities had been made possible by favourable developments in the social and economic fields.

The Sherpas associate the oldest centres of Buddhist worship in Khumbu with the legendary figure of Lama Sanga Dorje, the sixth reincarnation of Changna Dorje (Vajra Pani), whose twelfth reincarnation is the present abbot of the Tibetan monastery of Rongphu. While all other reincarnations of Dorje Chang occurred in Tibet, local tradition has it that Lama Sanga Dorje was born in Mohang, a place on the path between Khumjung and Phortse, as the son of the great lama Bundachendzen. This lama, who is reputed to have been a Sherpa of Salaka clan, is himself the central figure of various legends. Thus it is said that the great country god Khumbu-yülha regularly visited Lama Bundachendzen in his *gomba* in Mohang, but that the latter's wife, made suspicious by her husband's long conversations with a mysterious visitor, once surprised the god, who departed in a flash of light and never again appeared at Mohang. There is also a story of a contest of magic between Lama Bundachendzen and another lama resident near Khumjung, and all these traditions point to the fact that Lama Sanga Dorje, although thought responsible for the foundation of the first village temple in Khumbu, is not considered the first great lama who lived in this region. While his father, Bundachendzen, was able to converse in person with the great country god Khumbu-yülha, Lama Sanga Dorje had the power to fly through the air and perform other magical feats.

There is a story according to which he and his two brothers were debating as to which of them was the more powerful lama. Lama Sanga Dorje won the resulting competition in magical feats by using a ray of sunlight entering a room through a crack in the wall as a line to hang up his cloak. His fame greatly exceeds that of his two brothers, though the latter are also believed responsible for the foundation of *gomba*, namely those of Kerok and Gomila.

Lama Sanga Dorje is reputed to have stayed for some time at the present site of Tengboche, where he built a small *gomba*. But once he slipped on a rock, which still bears the marks of his feet, and taking this as an inauspicious sign, he left Tengboche and moved to nearby Pangboche, in the valley of the Imja Khola. There he built a *gomba*, the first great temple in the whole of Khumbu. Soon he collected monks around him, and his teaching is believed to have laid the foundation for much of the Buddhist learning in Khumbu.

The people of Pangboche point to many landmarks as the products of Lama Sanga Dorje's miraculous feats. Thus they believe that the groves of old juniper trees to both sides of the *gomba* sprang from the hairs the saint cut from his head and scattered to the left and right of the site chosen for the temple. There is also a roof-like projection of rock, which he is believed to have pulled out of the mountainside to obtain shelter when he first arrived at Pangboche.

According to local tradition Lama Sanga Dorje's activities did not remain unopposed, and there is a story that a man of Jongdomba clan, alternatively believed to have been a *pembu* of Thamichok or a resident of Khumjung, sent out two men to murder the saint. But Lama Sanga Dorje, who at that time lived in a hermitage at Nagarjung above Dingboche, saw the two men approach and sent his two dogs, transformed into a tiger and a leopard, to kill the assassins.

Lama Sanga Dorje's death, like his life, was accompanied by miraculous events. He died not in Pangboche but at Tshou, a place close to Rongphu. His body was not cremated; it evaporated in the form of a rainbow, and only his eyes, tongue and heart remained. These were enshrined in a silver casket by the local Tibetans, but on hearing of the death of their saint, the Pangboche people devised a trick to acquire the precious relics (*kudung*) for their own *gomba*. Sixteen men went to the shrine where they were kept, and while eight of them made its guardians drunk with beer and liquor, eight others seized the casket with the relics and carried it across the Nangpa La. The Tibetans, when recovered from their intoxication, pursued the Sherpas, but were beaten back by a hail of stones from the latters' slings. The relics were installed in the Pangboche *gomba*, and a second attempt by Tibetans, aimed at recovering the saint's remains, was averted by negotiation. Ever since the silver casket with the relics has occupied the central place in the first-floor hall (*ser-song lha-khang*) of the Pangboche *gomba*, flanked by two caskets containing similar relics of two reincarnated Pangboche lamas, one of them the grandfather of Lama Ngawang Chotr, a man now in his early forties.

Monastic Institutions and Priesthood 129

Lama Sanga Dorje had gathered a group of monks, who were celibate like himself but, when after his death he was not reincarnated for three years, another lama, named Rigsing Totuk Wongbu, established himself at Pangboche. He was married and the monks, following his example, also took wives, so that since that time Pangboche is a *gomba* of married lamas.

Lama Sanga Dorje was reincarnated in Tibet, and the abbots of Rongphu monastery are considered the reincarnations of this saint, who—it must be remembered—was himself the sixth reincarnation of Dorje Chang. The present abbot of Rongphu is the twelfth reincarnation of Dorje Chang (and the sixth of Lama Sanga Dorje), and it is believed that there will be only two more reincarnations after which Lama Sanga Dorje will enter Devachen; i.e. the Western Paradise of Opame (Sanskrit: Amithaba), the Buddha of Boundless Light.

The inhabitants of Pangboche are not the only Sherpas to claim Lama Sanga Dorje as founder and patron of their religious institutions. The people of Thami, too, point to this great saint as the founder of their *gomba* and preceptor of the lama who became the ancestor of a long line of married head-lamas. The story goes that at the time when Lama Sanga Dorje was contemplating the foundations of Thami *gomba*, which originally stood on the site now occupied by the head lama's house, he saw one morning a rainbow leading from the summit of Khumbu-yülha to this place above Thami, and took it as an indication of where the *gomba* should be built. He then installed one of his disciples as the lama to be in charge of the new *gomba*, and the latter's descendants, who were not celibate monks but married lamas have held this office ever since. The head lama whom I met in 1957 had a record of fourteen generations of lamas of his own family, and he believed that the foundation of the *gomba* occurred some four hundred years ago. This estimate tallies roughly with the idea that since then Lama Sanga Dorje has been reincarnated six times.

Dr. David Snellgrove has suggested that Buddhism was introduced into Khumbu towards the end of the seventeenth century[1] and, if this proves correct, local ideas of the antiquity of the oldest *gomba* overestimate the time elapsed since its foundation by over one fourth, an error which may easily develop in a society with little sense of historic precision. In the context of our study the exact

[1] *Buddhist Himālaya*, Oxford, 1957, p. 213.

age of such *gomba* as those of Pangboche and Thami is of little relevance, but a phenomenon calling for an explanation is the proliferation of monastic institutions and the rapid increase in the numbers of celibate monks and nuns in the course of the past two or three generations.

Fifty years ago there existed in Khumbu no institution which might have been called a monastery or nunnery. There were the three ancient *gomba* of Pangboche, Thami and Kerok, and the more recently-founded *gomba* of Khumjung and Namche. Attached to each of these *gomba* were several lamas, and in the case of the Thami and Kerok *gomba* one particular family of lamas had been in charge of the *gomba* for several generations. All the lamas were married men, and there were, as it seems, no monks (*thawa*) who had taken vows of permanent celibacy. Besides these married lamas there were hermits, who for a number of years occupied a cave-dwelling or solitary hut high above the inhabited valleys, but none of them seem to have attempted to turn their personal retreat into a settlement where others might join them in their life of meditation.

It was only in 1923 that Lama Gulu, the member of a prominent family of Khumjung and, as it seems a powerful personality, inspired the people of Khumjung to support him in the foundation of a *gomba* on the model of Tibetan monasteries. Lama Gulu did not embrace a religious career early in life. He married and had six children, five of whom died in childhood. It was only when he also lost his wife that he devoted himself more and more to the active practice of religion. He went to study in Tibet, and subsequently retired to Chamgaon, a small settlement on the slopes of Khumbuyülha, some 800 feet above Khumjung, where convenient rock shelters easily convertible into cave-dwellings had sometimes served hermits and religious-minded women as a temporary retreat from village life. It was there that he secluded himself for the traditional period of three years, three months and three days, and his example gradually led other men and women, to seek peace and spiritual advancement in the vicinity of so inspired a teacher. More and more people settled at Chamgaon, until it became a regular settlement of twelve to thirteen houses where people of Khumjung devoted themselves to religious practices.

Yet, these men and women who lived there without formal organization and discipline, did not form a regular monastic com-

Monastic Institutions and Priesthood 131

munity. Only in his old age did Lama Gulu begin to contemplate the foundation of a proper monastery with an organized and disciplined religious life.

It was in connection with the founding of Tengboche that the abbot of Rongphu recognized Lama Gulu as a reincarnation of Lama Bundachendzen. The fact that his nature as a reincarnate lama was not discovered in childhood was explained by reference to an accident he had suffered in infancy. Old people remembered that as a small child Lama Gulu had fallen into a latrine, and this unfortunate defilement by human excrement was believed to have veiled his character as Lama Bundachendzen's reincarnation. When the two men met the abbot of Rongphu is said to have asked Lama Gulu not to salute him with the usual obeisance due to a reincarnate lama, for as Lama Gulu was a reincarnation of Lama Bundachendzen (the father of Lama Sanga Dorje), he stood to the abbot of Rongphu, the reincarnation of Lama Sanga Dorje, in the relationship of father. As Lama Bundachendzen is far less famous than Lama Sanga Dorje and Lama Gulu's nature as his first reincarnation for several hundred years is not widely known, the reincarnate abbot of Rongphu is nevertheless regarded with greater reverence than Lama Gulu's reincarnation, the present abbot of Tengboche. For Rongphu is the mother-institution, to which the young monks of Tengboche used to go for study and inspiration, and the charter of Tengboche, containing an account of the foundation and an enumeration of the rules governing its monastic life, bears the seal of the abbot of Rongphu.

The costs of constructing the newly founded *gomba* of Tengboche were borne mainly by four men: Kushang (Thaktu) of Khumjung, Lama Karmamundu (Lama) of Junbesi, Chepal (Gole), the *gembu* of Khumbu, who lived in Namche, and a kinsman of his, Sun Chopal of Gole. To pay for the wall-paintings and other items of interior decoration as well as for the images Lama Gulu collected subscriptions in all the villages of Khumbu. So great is the Sherpas' generosity for religious purposes that an impressive three-storeyed building with a large paved courtyard surrounded by galleries arose within two months on a site several hours' walk from any permanent village. For all the villagers of Khumjung, Kunde, Phortse, Pangboche and Namche came to help with the work, giving their labour free of charge.

As soon as the *gomba* was completed, Lama Gulu built a house for himself and other men, attracted by the prospects of an organized religious life, built small houses around the main temple. These houses were and still are individually owned, and may be sold by one monk to another. It is only in the event of a monk breaking his vows of celibacy and leaving the monastery that his immovable property within the *gomba* precincts falls to the monastery, from which it may be purchased by other monks.

The first members of the new monastic community of Tengboche were Lama Gulu's brother's son and three other men of Khumjung, one man of Kunde, one man of Pangboche, one man of Namche, and one lama of Junbesi. Several of these men had taken monastic vows in Rongphu monastery, and were living in Dzamda, a small settlement situated on a high and lonely site north of Thami, of a character similar to that of Chamgaon. While in Dzamda there was no *gomba*, Tengboche offered the chance of leading a full monastic life under the guidance of a lama renowned for his learning and saintliness throughout Khumbu.

Within the first decade the number of monks in Tengboche had increased to twenty-five, and the monastery rapidly became the focal point of religious activities within a wide area. But ten years after its foundation a catastrophe occurred which might well have daunted the spirits of a people less resilient and devout than the Sherpas of Khumbu. In the great earthquake of 1933 the main temple collapsed and Lama Gulu, then eighty-five years old, died shortly afterwards of shock. He was cremated in the ruins of the monastery, on the very site where the great hall (*duang*) of the *gomba* had stood.

The villagers of Khumbu again came to the help of the young monastery and, giving money and free labour, they rebuilt the *gomba*, making it even bigger than it had been before the earthquake. And only three years passed before it was found that Lama Gulu was reincarnated in the son of a Khamba couple of Namche. The child's utterances about his former home in Tengboche had aroused first the parents' and then other people's attention, and when the monks of Tengboche placed some of Lama Gulu's clothes and other personal possessions, mixed up with similar articles of different origin before the child suspected to be a reincarnation of their late abbot, the little boy, then four years old, picked out all the genuine articles, saying that they belonged to him.

Monastic Institutions and Priesthood

Satisfied with this proof the monks brought the child to Tengboche, and one of the higher monastery officials, the *umse* Gyaljen, who was Lama Gulu's brother's son, took the boy into his own house and devoted himself to his education. As the first reincarnate (*tulku*) lama of Tengboche, the Khamba boy was regarded with veneration from the very beginning. At the age of sixteen he was taken to Rongphu for further studies and when in 1956 he returned to Tengboche he was ready to assume—or in the Sherpas' view to reassume —his place as the head of the monastery.

In 1957 Tengboche had not only a young man as its head lama, but the average age of the monks was not more than thirty. Since its foundation thirty-four years previously many boys and young men of the villages of Khumbu, and particularly of Khumjung, Kunde and Namche, had come to the monastery to learn and to become initiated into a religious life. Not all were temperamentally suited to the contemplative existence of a monk. Some left the monastery to return to secular occupations, some married and settled down as village lamas, but others remained true to their monastic vows, content to make Tengboche their permanent home.

Even those monks who have no intention of returning to a secular life do not permanently live in an ivory tower. Many are the occasions when they are called to the one or other village, to recite from sacred scriptures for the benefit of a sick person, to participate in funeral ceremonies and memorial services, to conduct a rite in a village temple, and to help with the annual reading of the Kangyur. On all these occasions they are in close contact with the lay villagers, and they freely visit their families and kinsmen, staying for some days in their houses and advising them on practical as well as religious problems.

Similarly lay folk from all villages of Khumbu as well as many parts of Pharak and Solu occasionally visit the *gomba*, anxious to obtain the reincarnate lama's blessing or intent on commissioning the performance of a sacred rite, be it to gain merit (*sönam*) or to honour the memory of a deceased kinsman, and smooth his path in the world beyond.

In this manner there is a continuous two way traffic between the monastery and the lay world, and the learning of the monks is a source of inspiration to the village lamas as well as to the more educated among the laymen. The great monastery festival, known as

Mani-rimdu, places even before the most simple of villagers some basic notions of Buddhist doctrine in the form of dramatic and most impressive representations.

The monk community of Tengboche might have grown to even greater size had it not been for the presence of a settlement of nuns, known as Devuche, less than half an hour's walk north-east of the monastery. Four years before his death Lama Gulu agreed to the foundation of a nunnery in a pleasant valley a few hundred feet below the ridge of Tengboche, and there some of the wealthy families of Khumjung, Kunde and Namche built small houses for daughters or sisters attracted by the prospect of a religious life close to the revered abbot of Tengboche. But the proximity of young monks and young nuns had consequences perhaps not foreseen by Lama Gulu, and the high rate of marriages between Tengboche monks and Devuche nuns formed a serious brake to the growth of the new community of monks.

But before we deal in detail with the social composition of these two religious settlements we must briefly consider contemporary developments in the western part of Khumbu. At Thami, the largest village in the valley of the Bhote Kosi, a family of married or *gyupi* lamas had for many generations—fourteen generations according to their own estimate—been in charge of a *gomba* tracing its origin to Lama Sanga Dorje. This *gomba* was a small building, and the only lamas living in the neighbouring houses were members of the present head lama's lineage. Even when Lama Tundu, the latter's father succeeded to the position of abbot there were no celibate monks at Thami, and several lay families dwelt in the settlement clustering round the small *gomba*. But in the year 1920 Lama Tundu decided to shift the *gomba* to a place where a bigger structure could be erected, and the reincarnate abbot of Rongphu, the same man who had chosen the site for Tengboche, encouraged him in this undertaking. The completion of the three-storeyed building in its present shape prepared the way for the development of the Thami *gomba* from a family institution to a monastic establishment catering for a wider circle of students and lamas.

Young men desirous of becoming monks soon collected. Most of them came from the villages of Thamichok, and small houses, built into the rocks of the steep mountain slope, began to spring up round the new *gomba*. Among the first novices were several sisters' sons of

Monastic Institutions and Priesthood

Lama Tundu, but others had no ties of kinship to the lama's family, but gathered there on account of Lama Tundu's reputation and the facilities for a communal religious life provided in the newly built *gomba*. By 1957 Thami *gomba*, the official name of which is Gon-de Dziri-chu-ko, had grown into a monastery comprising married lamas as well as celibate monks, or *thawa*, with a full complement of monastery officials, and the facilities for staging performances of the great Mani-rimdu dance festival.

The inspiration for this development—like the inspiration for the foundation of Tengboche—clearly came from Rongphu, the famous monastery of the Nyingmapa sect on the Tibetan side of the Mount Everest group, and no year passed without some of the Thami monks going for several weeks, or even months, to Rongphu for study and religious practices. It was in Rongphu that these *thawa* first took their vows and later received instruction in the ritual dances of the Mani-rimdu. The first performance of this festival at Thami monastery took place in 1942, but for several years it was confined to the *gomba* services and the blessing of the crowd by the abbot. Only from 1950 onwards were the monks able to stage also the elaborate dramatic dances, which give the Mani-rimdu the character of a colourful folk festival.

The first half of the twentieth century saw the emergence of monastic institutions not only in Khumbu, but also in various parts of Solu. Monasteries and nunneries have sprung up at Chiwang, Trakshindo, Tolaka, Gole and most recently Todhung. Their foundation within the past fifty years tends to show that the establishment of monasteries at Tengboche and Thami at about the same time cannot be due to purely local cause

THE COMPOSITION OF MONASTIC COMMUNITIES

Before we enter upon a discussion of the organization of a monastery such as Tengboche, it is appropriate to analyse the composition of such a small and closely-knit community of men and boys, who have renounced secular life in familiar surroundings in order to devote themselves to the practice of religion. Does such a community constitute a random aggregation of individuals united solely by the common desire for spiritual advancement, or are some of the *thawa* linked by ties of kinship, and do family connections play a part in setting young boys on the path to a monastic career? An analysis of the community of *thawa* in Tengboche provides the answer to some of these questions.

In 1957 there were, apart from the reincarnate abbot, thirty-two monks in Tengboche. Eight of these came from Namche, two of them being step-brothers while one was the father's brother's grandson of Kushang (Thaktu), who had provided part of the funds for the construction of the monastery. Only three of the monks resident in 1957 came from Khumjung, but judging from the large number of ex-*thawa* born in Khumjung and living in various villages, Khumjung provided in earlier years a much larger percentage of the Tengboche monks. Kunde was the home-village of seven *thawa*, two of these stood in the relation of uncle and brother's son, two were brothers, and with one of these monks lived his widowed father, a lama who in his youth had also been a monk in Tengboche. Pangboche, a village with a high percentage of lamas, was represented only by three monks, and Phortse, though at no great distance from Tengboche, surprisingly only by one *thawa*. It is understandable, on the other hand, that only one of the monks came from Thami, a village with its own flourishing *gomba*. Finally there were two young step-brothers of the reincarnate abbot among the student monks. They were the sons of his father and a Tibetan mother, and had grown up in Tibet, where their father had settled after separating from the *tulku* lama's mother. The latter lived with her son in Tengboche, an exception from the ban on women being made in the case of a reincarnate lama's mother, and with her was her twelve-year-old son from a second husband. This step-brother of the abbot also received training in Tengboche and in August 1957 he went to Rongphu to take monastic vows. It thus seems that a reincarnate lama has the tendency to attract members of his family to the monastery in which he resides.

This analysis of the community of Tengboche monks in 1957 shows the close link between a monastery and the villages in the vicinity. With the exception of the abbot's Tibetan step-brothers not one of the monks hailed from any village outside Khumbu, and the vast majority came from the three villages of Namche, Khumjung and Kunde. It shows moreover that many monks have kinship ties to at least one other member of the community, and this tendency becomes even clearer when we include in our consideration those monks who either died or left the monastery. For we then see

Monastic Institutions and Priesthood 137

that among those *thawa* who in 1957 had no close kinsmen in the monastery, some came to Tengboche at a time when they could share the house of a close relative.

The picture of the composition of the monk community gains greatly in depth if we extend our analysis over the thirty-three years between the foundation of the monastery and 1957. In that period 91 *thawa* were admitted to the *gomba*; 8 died there, one founded a monastery of his own at Trakshindo, and 44 *thawa* either voluntarily left Tengboche to return to secular life and marry, or were compelled to leave on account of clandestine associations with women brought to the *gomba* officials' notice. The large number of *thawa*, who left the monastery for the one or other reason, leads us to the conclusion that the state of monk is not considered as a man's final choice, but that in many cases it is but a phase in a career, comparable almost to some years spent in an institution of higher education.

If we add all the figures of *thawa* who had passed through Tengboche to those resident in 1957, we find that altogether 17 came from Namche, 18 from Khumjung, 13 from Kunde, 9 from Pangboche, 2 from Phortse, one from Thami, 4 from Solu and Pharak, and 2 from Tibet.

Many are the families of Namche, Khumjung and Kunde which furnished more than one *thawa*. Thus we find among the past and present *thawa* three brothers of Chusherwa clan of Kunde, four members of one Thaktu family of Khumjung, a man of another Thaktu lineage of Khumjung, as well as four cases of father and son. Kinship connections with one of the senior *thawa* greatly facilitates a boy's entrance into the monastery and reduces the financial burden to his parents. For in such a case a boy will usually stay with his relative for several years and may ultimately even inherit his house. Considering that the majority of the *thawa* of Tengboche come from the wealthier and more prominent families of the three villages Namche, Khumjung and Kunde, it is obvious that the web of consanguineous and affinal kinship ties connecting most of these families extends also to the monk community of Tengboche. It is noteworthy, however, that the reincarnation of Tengboche's founder Lama Gulu, who had belonged to one of the leading Khumjung families, occurred not within the same circle, but in a family of Khambas recently immigrated from Tibet.

The same social stratum from which most of the monks in Tengboche were recruited, also provided the majority of the nuns (*ani*) of Devuche. In 1957 there were twenty nuns resident, but only nine of these had the qualifications to take an active part in the services in their *gomba*. The others were either devout women without sufficient learning, who had not taken any vows, or nuns disqualified by a breach of their vow of celibacy. Fourteen of the nuns had never been married—though two of these had had *themba* children—and six had been married but came to Devuche after their husband's death or the break-up of their marriage. Nine of the nuns came from Khumjung, seven from Namche, three from Kunde and one from Phortse. Neither Pangboche nor the Thamichok area was represented in the small community. Among the twenty nuns there were four pairs of sisters, and one mother and her daughter. The percentage of nuns who had remained for the whole of their lives in Devuche was no greater than that of monks who had resisted the temptations of a secular life. Since the foundation of Devuche in 1930 fourteen nuns had left the nunnery and got married, and in ten of these cases they had married ex-*thawa* of Tengboche. But the number of nuns in Devuche remained fairly stable, for there was a hard core of those unlikely to find husbands even if they were thus inclined, and novices took the place and acquired the houses of those who left the nunnery.

One of the principal factors determining the composition of a community of monks as well as that of a nunnery, is the general rule that monks and nuns must provide for their own maintenance and their own lodgings. Unlike the members of religious institutions in some other societies, the monks in a Sherpa monastery, though provided with tea during the daily services, have each their own household maintained by two or three *thawa* living in one house. The parents of a novice either buy or build him a house, or arrange for him to live with an older kinsman or friend. They provide the young *thawa* with food and other necessities, and when it seems probable that he will persist in a monastic career they give him a share in their property similar to that given to an elder son at the time of his marriage and separation from the parental household. Whatever immovable property a monk receives as his share he usually sells, investing the money in such a way as to give him a steady income of agricultural produce. The high rates of interest paid by Sherpas—25 per cent being the usual rate—enable a single man to live on the income from even a modest capital and, as there is always a demand for cash loans, no monk or nun has difficulty in finding borrowers who will promise annual deliveries of provisions as a form of interest payment.

This system allows only the sons of fairly wealthy people to enter a monastery as a *thawa*, and the same applies to the nuns wishing to settle at Devuche. A poor man can maintain himself in a monastery only if he finds work as the servant of a more affluent *thawa*, but such opportunities are limited. Few monks are rich enough to maintain such a servant; there are usually younger kinsmen only too willing to serve a father's or mother's brother in return for instruction and their keep. Among the monks resident in 1957 there was none who had to maintain himself by serving the other monks, but a Tibetan *thawa* without any income of his own, had lived in Tengboche for many years supporting himself by carrying water and doing other menial jobs for his fellow monks. He had nevertheless the same status as other monks and remained in Tengboche until his death.

What are the motives which determine a young Sherpa to enter a monastery? In trying to answer this question we must distinguish between boys of perhaps not more than twelve or thirteen sent to a monastery by their parents and usually left in charge of an older kinsman, and young men who become *thawa* on their own initiative. In the former case parents of some means may wish their sons to receive a sound education, leaving them the option of staying in the monastery and in due course taking religious vows, or of returning to their home and employing their learning perhaps in a career of village lama. The presence among the monks of a senior kinsman facilitates a boy's maintenance at a monastery, and such family connections obviously play a rôle in deciding parents to detail one son to a career of religious studies. The prestige value of learning and religious knowledge is certainly not without influence in such a decision, but an equally strong motive is the genuine conviction that a life spent in the service of religion and devoted to the accumulation of merit predestines a person for a desirable fate in future lives.

Family circumstances are, of course, also taken into consideration. A rich man with much property to pass on to his children is not likely to encourage an only son to become a *thawa*, but if there are several sons the departure of one leaves no gap and may even ease arrangements for the management of the paternal property. If we consider the boys and young men of Khumjung and Kunde who, in 1957, had either already become *thawa* or intended to take up a monastic career in Tengboche we find that out of twelve only one was the sole son of his parents. But in this case there was the strong motivation that the boy's father's brother had acted, during the reincarnate lama's minority, as head of the monastery and wanted his nephew to live with him. Two of the prospective *thawa* were second sons out of three sons; one the third son among seven; three the second sons out of two; and one the fourth and last son. In one case both the eldest and the second sons of a rich man had become *thawa*, but there were three younger brothers to remain with the parents.

The way in which an elder kinsman can attract a boy to a monastic life is exemplified by the case of the eldest son of Phur Temba (Paldorje), a moderately prosperous man of Khumjung. This boy was being taught how to read and write by his maternal uncle Jangbu, who was a monk in Tengboche. It was understood that if the boy proved intelligent and Jangbu liked him he would leave him all his property, which included a house in Tengboche and sufficient investments to support him. His sister's son, if willing to take monastic vows, would thus have a home and adequate means to lead a life free of worldly cares.

Where the decision to enter a monastery is taken by a young man himself, a predilection for intellectual pursuits is probably one of the most frequent motives. A young Sherpa of more than average intelligence, whose interests lie in the literary sphere rather than in trade, finds in a monastery more scope for his special talent than in any other environment. Whether he has a bent for a contemplative life, enjoys the study of scriptures, proves skilful in the organization of ritual performances or has a talent for the running of monastery affairs, as a *thawa* he can follow his interests and finds ample opportunity for the development of his intellectual gifts. The attraction of a materially rather comfortable life is not likely to rank high among the incentives, for young men wealthy enough to be able to maintain themselves at a monastery, would not suffer any hardships even if they remained in their parental houses. Far more important is, no doubt, the prospect of attaining to positions of dignity and influence, for the social status of a lama reputed for his learning is high. Sherpas will vie with each other in inviting such a person for

The reincarnate abbot of Tengboche

Altar with sacrificial dough and butter figures

Chapel in the temple of Tengboche monastery

the performance of rites and will consider it an honour to offer him hospitality and generous gifts.

Yet we would misinterpret Sherpa mentality, if we assumed that expectations of worldly success and recognition were the main motives that led young men to choose a career as monks and lamas. There is no doubt a deeply religious strain in Sherpa society, and the conviction that the acquisition of merit assures future bliss no less than present peace of mind and joyousness, is not confined to a few hermits and reincarnate lamas. One has only to spend a few days in a Sherpa monastery to realize that the expectation of a happy and contented life is no illusion. The monks one meets there, old as well as young, seem so cheerful and full of zest that one can hardly doubt their satisfaction with the mode of life they have chosen. Though the direction of their endeavours may be 'other-worldly' they enjoy to the full the permitted pleasures their monastic life has to offer, and the artistic merits of their immediate environment are proof of a highly developed and basically life-affirming sense of aesthetic appreciation.

There is, moreover, the important fact that the youthful enthusiasm of those attracted by a life of study and religious practices has not to contend with the scepticism of a more worldly minded majority, for although only a few Sherpas are prepared to follow Buddhist doctrine in all its implications, no one doubts its validity and the superiority of a life of renunciation and 'other-worldliness' to the secular life of the ordinary villager.

Neither are the two types of life mutually exclusive and choices once made irrevocable. The example of the founder of Tengboche shows that even those who for many years were householders and family men, can embrace a religious life and attain to such high spiritual perfection that they take re-birth as reincarnate lamas. Conversely there are many monks who after some years in a monastery return to secular life, but continue to study and practise their knowledge of ritual performances, and even strive for the gain of new merit by periods of fasting and long isolation.

The composition of a monastic community is therefore never static. As some members quit the monastery to seek satisfaction of natural desires permissible only in the outside world, without however abandoning faith in religious practices, others join the monastery either in early youth or in middle age after having tasted of secular life and finding it wanting in emotional or intellectual satisfaction. There is even provision for those too old to join the monastery as *thawa* and take the regular vows. Mature men can join the monk community as *korba* or lay members, and in this capacity they can lead a life of study and religious practices without sharing in all the privileges and responsibilities of regular monks. It is not unusual for widowed village-lamas to enter a monastery in this capacity. Even lamas, who in their youth had been *thawa*, but left the monastery in order to marry, may be allowed to rejoin the monks' community in the capacity of *korba*. In order to do that they must either be widowed or must have formally separated from their wives. As *korba* they may not participate in *gomba* services and consequently receive none of the tea and food served to the *thawa* at the expense of the monastery. Neither do they receive any share of the donations given to the monks. They are free, however, to act as lamas and participate in rites and ceremonies performed outside the monastery.

In Tengboche there were in 1957 two *korba*, Ngawang Chundu and Ngawang Yönden. The former was one of the seven original *thawa*, who had to leave the monastery on account of an association with a woman of Pangboche. When she deserted him, he sought and obtained permission to live in Tengboche as *korba*. The other was Ngawang Yönden, who had also been a *thawa*. After leaving the monastery and marrying twice, he returned to Tengboche and shared the house of his son, who was a regular monk. When re-entering a monastery as *korba* such a lama must once more take a vow, but whereas a middle-aged man who had never been a *thawa* can be accepted as a proper monk, no one who has once broken his vow of celibacy can be accepted in any other capacity than as *korba*.

In distinction to the *korba*, the fully privileged monks are described as *tshowa*, which means literally 'those who partake of *tsho* (offerings)'.

MONASTIC VOWS AND MONASTERY ORGANIZATION

While young boys may be sent to a monastery for the purpose of study without committing them to a clerical career, no one can be a full member of a monastic community without having taken vows of celibacy and abstention from certain worldly occupations. The superior vows can be administered only by reincarnate abbots or other lamas of high spiritual achievements, but a preliminary vow, which a prospective monk has to take when entering a monastery, can be given into the hands of any senior lama. Few formalities are connected with its administration. No questions are put to the candidate, and his future preceptor simply says: 'From now on you will have a new name and be called so-and-so; you must now promise not to engage in tilling the soil and not to marry.' The candidate promises to observe these rules, and is henceforth known as *gyengi* ('living upon virtue') and is entitled to participate in *gomba* services.

Not all monks pass through the stage of *gyengi*. Some young men who have studied privately, while living in their parental homes until the age of eighteen or twenty, may omit taking the vow of *gyengi*, and begin their monastic career by at once taking the next higher vow, known as *rabdzung*. The only qualification for admittance to this vow is the ability to read Tibetan, and once a young man has taken this vow he is considered a *thawa* or monk, even if his learning is still very rudimentary.

The vow of *rabdzung* must be administered by a 'great' lama over thirty years of age, assisted by four other lamas all of whom have themselves taken the next higher vow (*gelung*). As in 1957 the reincarnate abbot of Tengboche was in his early twenties, and there was no other lama of adequate status and age in Khumbu, candidates for the administration of the vow of *rabdzung* had to go to Rongphu or await the visit of a Tibetan lama of high status. Such a visit occurred some years ago, when the abbot of a Sakyapa monastery visited Tengboche, and conducted the initiation of several *thawa*. It was more usual, however, for candidates to make the journey to Rongphu. In August 1957 twelve young boys and one girl from Khumbu went to Rongphu and there took the vow of *rabdzung*, which the reincarnate abbot of that monastery administered during the same ceremony to about sixty prospective monks and nuns. It is obvious that during a mass initiation of this kind, the questions put to the candidates are asked for the sake of formality rather than to elicit information about the young men's and women's qualifications for a religious life. But the traditional procedure is observed and the abbot's first assistant begins the male candidate's interrogation with the following question:

'Have you ever committed any crime? Have you killed one of your parents or a lama?' Such a murder is an absolute bar to the administration of the *rabdzung* vow, while other types of murder and manslaughter can be expiated.

If the answer is satisfactory, the second monk asks:

'Have you any grey hair on your head?' (A candidate with grey hair cannot be admitted to this vow, as men and women past middle age are not to be ordained. It must be remembered, however, that most Sherpas retain black hair until well over the age of fifty.)

The third monk then asks:

'Are you free of any marital tie? Have your parents permitted you to become a monk?'

If the candidates can give positive answers to both these questions, they are asked by the fourth monk:

'Are you free of debts? Are you under no obligation towards any government authority? Has no court of law pronounced any order against you?'

When these questions have also been satisfactorily answered the senior lama conducting the ceremony asks:

'Are you prepared to shave your head and to have a new name?'

The candidates affirm their willingness. The lama then confers upon each his *thawa* name, and invests him with a monk's habit, which the candidate or his parents have handed to the lama before the beginning of the ceremony. The lama also burns a piece of paper, on which is written the candidate's previous name. If the candidate had previously been made a *gyengi*, he may be given the same or a new name. The lama finally admonishes the candidates not to commit any sins, to remain celibate and to abstain from trading and the cultivation of the land.

Each candidate solemnly promises to observe all these rules, and by taking the *rabdzung* vow he becomes a proper *thawa*. There is no definite age a candidate must have reached before taking this vow, but before he can proceed to the next vow, known as *gelung*, he must at least be twenty years old. In practice, however, most *thawa* are of mature age before taking this vow. It is only a confirmation of the previous vow, and the questions asked by the 'great' lama and his four assistants are virtually the same. But those who have taken the *gelung* vow, and are therefore sometimes referred to as *gelung*, can themselves act as a 'great' lama's assistant in administering the vow provided they are not less than thirty years old.

In September 1957 there were in Tengboche monastery five monks who had taken the *gelung* vow, and nineteen who had taken the vow of *rabdzung*. At that time there were no boys, who had taken the initial vow of *gyengi* only, for even *thawa* of fourteen and fifteen years of age had already had the opportunity of going to Rongphu and taking the *rabdzung* vow.

In the small monastery of Trakshindo, founded in 1946 by a monk of Tengboche, there were in 1957 thirteen *thawa* who had taken the *rabdzung* vow and two—exclusive of the founder, Lama Chuldim—who had taken the vow of *gelung*. These two, as well as six of the former, had made the journey to the Tibetan monastery of Rongphu for the purpose of taking their vows, whereas seven had their *rabdzung* vows administered by the abbot of a Sakyapa monastery on the occasion of his visit to Tengboche. Apart from these fifteen *thawa* there were three who had taken only *gyengi* vows administered by Lama Chuldim.

Just as the ritual performances in the monasteries of Tengboche and Thami are replicas of the corresponding performances in Tibetan monasteries of the Nyingmapa sect, and the monks study and recite from books identical to those used in such places as Rongphu, so the organization of these institutions has been modelled according to the Tibetan monastic pattern. But whereas in the large monasteries in Tibet there were hundreds and even thousands of monks and students, the numbers of *thawa* in Sherpa monasteries are small, with the result that in order to fill all or most of the traditional offices as many as 25 or 30 per cent of the monks must serve as monastery officials.

The abbot of a monastery is either a reincarnate lama, known as *tulku* lama and never referred to by his name, or a head lama (*lama che*) such as the hereditary lama of the Thami *gomba*. An abbot usually does not concern himself with the day-to-day administration of monastery affairs, but spends his time in studying religious scriptures, teaching some of the monks, receiving pilgrims and visitors and presiding at major rites and festivals.

It is obvious, however, that the founder of a monastery, such as Lama Gulu, must take a more active part in shaping the new community of monks than an abbot who succeeds to the headship of an established monastery. Yet, even such an abbot impresses his personality on the monks under his authority and the fortunes of a monastery depend to no small degree on the leadership of its abbot.

Next in rank to the abbot is an official known as *loben*. He has no definite function, but advises other monks in matters of ritual, and sits at ceremonies above the other *thawa*, without being directly in charge of the proceedings. Whenever the abbot is absent and during the years of a reincarnate lama's minority, the *loben* officiates as the head of the monastery.

The official immediately below the *loben* is the *umse*, who conducts all the services in the *gomba*, leads the recitation and is generally in charge of the ritual. While the *loben* is usually one of the most senior monks, and may hold the office for many years, the *umse* can be a comparatively young man knowledgeable in scriptures and historical matters, and his appointment is usually for three years.

The monastery official next in rank to the *umse* is known as *gerku*. He is responsible for the maintenance of discipline, has the right to punish offenders against monastery rules, settles disputes arising between *thawa*, and keeps the accounts of monastery funds. He is usually elected for one year only, but may be re-elected if the abbot and the other monks are satisfied with his conduct of affairs.

Responsible to the *gerku* are one or more officials known as *nierwa*. They are in charge of the trading and other economic affairs of the monastery, and may be described as managers or stewards. The *nierwa* hold the cash, but have to show accounts to the *gerku*. They are elected for one year, and can normally not be re-elected. If there is a profit from the trading deals they have conducted it goes to the monastery, but if they have incurred a loss through their own fault they may be asked to make it up out of their personal property. In small monasteries there may be only one *nierwa*, but in monasteries which have landed property and cattle and engage in trade, the number of monks dealing with business matters must be at least two, one in charge of the internal management, and one free to go on trading journeys which may extend over several weeks at a time.

In Tengboche, which compared with Tibetan monasteries is by no means big, there were in 1957 no less than seven monks with the title of *nierwa*. One was in charge of the kitchen and the regular *gomba* services; one was specifically responsible for the making of the tea, which plays so great a rôle in sustaining the *thawa* during the long ritual performances; one was in charge of the money offered by benefactors for *mang-se*, i.e. the supply of tea to the monks, and having invested such contributions had to collect the interest; two *nierwa* were responsible for the maintenance and repair of the buildings and one of them collected for this purpose contributions within Khumbu and Solu, whereas the other travelled to Tibet and Kalimpong to raise funds for the monastery. Finally there were two *nierwa* in charge of the cattle and the land owned by Tengboche.

The need for men specifically responsible for the management of a monastery's economic assets becomes obvious if we consider that some gifts of wealthy men are neither in cash nor in goods suitable for direct consumption. Some twenty years ago, for instance, a rich trader of Namche donated to Tengboche a herd of one hundred yak, and to care for such a herd requires considerable organization.

A monk may gradually pass through all the ranks of monastery officials, and finally be senior even to the *loben* without holding any specific office. Thus in 1957 the second son of the abbot of Thami *gomba* ranked above all the *thawa* and was the chosen successor of his father, while his youngest brother held the post of *loben* and his eldest brother's son acted as *gerku*. In Tengboche where, unlike in Thami, there are no married lamas and the succession is by reincarnation instead of by lineal succession, elderly monks who have passed through all the higher posts, but made room for younger men, have no clearly defined status, and are usually referred to by the title of the last senior post they held.

Apart from the higher ranks connected with administrative responsibilities there are ranks of lower order, through which the younger *thawa* have to pass before they become eligible for one of the responsible posts. These ranks are named after the part played by the various *thawa* at *gomba* services. For the first three years after his admission a boy works as *cha-de* or server of tea, and it is usually only after one or two years that he advances to *majen* or cook. When he has done his apprenticeship in these menial capacities, he is promoted to *nga-wa* or drummer, and from now on he sits in the *gomba* in the line of monks reciting and playing instruments. He remains *nga-wa* for one or two years, and then rises to the rank and function of *sang-dung-ba* or blower of long, telescopic horns. This rank he will normally hold for two or three years, until he gains promotion to *geling-ba* or flageolet player, a rank he may hold for about three years.

The lower ranks are attained in accordance with the knowledge of books a monk has mastered and with the acquisition of such skills as the making of ritual requisites. Any monk who has reached a certain stage in his studies may present himself before the abbot, *loben* and *umse* and give proof that he has attained proficiency in his subjects. If he passes this test, he becomes eligible for promotion. There are no public examinations, as those held in the great Tibetan monasteries, and in a small community like that of Tengboche the senior officials are undoubtedly well aware of the progress and qualifications of the individual junior monks, and it seems that at times they even dispense with the formal test to be held before the abbot. By the time a monk has attained the rank of flageolet player (*gelingba*), he is eligible for election as *nierwa* or even *gerku*.

The age at which a monk may attain one of the higher posts depends on the size and composition of the individual monastic community. In the recently founded monastery of Trakshindo, for instance, there were in 1957 not sufficient even middle-aged monks to fill the majority of senior posts. It was a community of young men; the *loben* was forty-two years old, the *umse* thirty-one, the *gerku* twenty-eight, and the only *nierwa* twenty-three.

In small monasteries where officials and junior *thawa* are daily in close contact, and many of the inmates, recruited from a few nearby villages, are linked by ties of kinship or traditional friendship, there is not the same need for the enforcement of strict and impersonal discipline as in the giant monasteries of Tibet. Yet, there exists nevertheless provision for the punishment of those who offend against the monastery discipline or disregard the orders of the officials. In the case of an offence having been committed, the *gerku*, who is responsible for discipline, investigates the case, and then consults with the *umse* regarding an appropriate punishment. To expiate a minor fault the offender is usually ordered to provide tea for all the monks, and this punishment is known as *mang-se*. Money fines are imposed for major offences, and if someone is very obstinate and does not submit to their punishment, the *gerku* may even order him to be flogged. This, however, is a most exceptional occurrence, and I have not heard of any concrete case where corporal punishment was inflicted. Monks are not supposed to smoke at all, and they may not drink liquor or beer within the monastery precincts. Breaches of these rules are subject to fines, but if it becomes known that a monk has relations with a woman he is expelled from the monastery. Anyone who has proof of such a violation of a monk's vow of chastity may remove from the *gomba* the offender's personal cushion on which he used to sit during services and which is symbolic of a man's status of *thawa*. The case is then reported to the *gerku*, who will compel the offender to confess his sin to the abbot, and ask for his discharge from the monastery. For in such cases there is no alternative to expulsion.

In the event of a *gerku* being found guilty of a breach of monastery rules, all the *thawa* must sit in judgement on him, and the punishment to which he is liable is twice that to which an ordinary *thawa* would be subjected had he committed the same offence.

Expulsion of a *thawa* on account of relations with women involves confiscation of any immovable property the offender may possess within the monastery precincts. If he owned a house, this falls to the monastery and the expelled owner has no right to sell it.

If, on the other hand, a monk wants to leave his monastery in order to join another institution, he may get leave to do so and sell his house provided he pays a fee of Rs.40. To the monastery which he wants to enter he has also to pay a fee of at least Rs.40, and he must, moreover, offer scarves to the *loben, umse* and *gerku*.

A change-over from one monastery to the other is not a frequent practice, but it occurs occasionally when a monk has quarrelled with his abbot or when he is attracted by a new foundation close to his home village. Thus the present *loben* of Trakshindo monastery was for ten years a monk in Rongphu, but as a native of Ringmo, a village close to Trakshindo, he returned to Solu to participate in the development of a new monastery in his home district.

Visits to other monasteries, on the other hand, are a regular feature in the lives of many monks. Until the time when the Chinese communists destroyed monastic life in Tibet, it was usual for the *thawa* of Thami to go to Rongphu for further study, and during their stay there they had to hire a house and provided their own food. But they could take part in the services, and Tibetan lamas coming to Thami were granted the same privilege. Periods of foreign travel and study were sometimes very prolonged. Of the eighteen *thawa* of Trakshindo, two spent six years in monasteries of the Tibetan province of Kham, and seven received some training in Tengboche. Many of the Sherpa lamas are widely travelled, and the universality of Tibetan Buddhism enables them to feel at home wherever its doctrine is practised and the same scriptures form the basis of monastery ritual.

The organization of nunneries is modelled on that of monasteries, but communal activities and services are fewer, and the discipline is, on the whole, less strict. There is no figure corresponding to a reincarnate lama or permanent abbot, but the head nun, known as *loben*, is elected from time to time. There are also nuns holding the posts of *umse* and *gerku*, but—at least in the small nunneries of Khumbu—none in the lower ranks corresponding to *cha-de* or *nga-wa*.

Before a girl can be admitted to a nunnery as a proper nun (*ani*), she must take the same *rabdzung* vow as that taken by monks. In August 1957, for instance, when twelve young men went to Rongphu to take this vow, one girl of Kunde, sister of a rich man, attended the same initiation ceremony, and took the *rabdzung* vow which enabled her to enter the nunnery of Devuche.

Nuns guilty of a breach of their vow of chastity are excluded from the *gomba* services, but they sometimes stay on in their houses, and —when they leave the nunnery—have the right to sell these to other nuns. Although occasionally a 'great' lama may perform a rite of 'Life-Consecration' (*Tshe-wong*) in the *gomba* of a nunnery, the nuns are capable of conducting all the normal services including such rites as the Niungne, and on these occasions they play the same instruments as those used by lamas. Like monks the nuns of Devuche are sometimes invited to perform a mourning or memorial rite in one of the villages of Khumbu, and in such a case they proceed in a body to the house where their services are required, and perform the ritual in much the same way as lamas.

MONASTIC ROUTINE IN TENGBOCHE

The charter of the Tengboche monastery, a document bearing the seal of Lama Tenzing Nurbu of Rongphu, the fifth reincarnation of Lama Sanga Dorje, lays down the rules according to which the life of the community should be organized. The formulation and arrangement of these rules appear somewhat haphazard, and it is obvious that they do not by any means represent a complete code of behaviour to be observed by the monks. But as a reflection of what the reincarnate lama of Rongphu and the founder of the monastery must have considered important points, they are worth quoting. In the original document the rules are not numbered, but in summarizing the points it will be convenient to arrange them under the following numbers:

1. The *thawa* must be punctual in attending the *gomba* services, and assemble as soon as the gong is sounded. Any *thawa* who is late must prostrate himself 100 times.
2. No woman may live within the precincts of the *gomba*, and no *thawa* may anywhere share a house with a nun.
3. When a *thawa* is alone he should meditate on his own chosen divinity.
4. Every *thawa* should observe a fast on the fifteenth and thirtieth day of each month.
5. Every *thawa* must learn by heart the three books Deshags-Kundü[1], Ngundru-ral-tso and Cho-tse.
6. Every *thawa* should study the books Konchok-chündi,[2] Rena, Thukdub, Drowa-Kündröl,[3] Rigsin, Zangthal, Gyaldzen-lak-len, a book of instructions and Gurutangmar, a book of texts for ceremonies.
7. Every *thawa* must learn to make *torma*, play cymbals, drums, trumpets and flageolets.
8. Every *thawa*, after learning all these skills must show before the abbot, *loben* and *umse*, that he has mastered them, and if he passes the test he shall be promoted.
9. Every *thawa* must learn to recite the book Dombsun-seta. (*domba*—vow, instruction for monks).
10. During *gomba* services the *thawa* must wear sleeveless gowns. It is desirable that *thawa* should wear sleeveless gowns even outside the monastery.
11. At the first blowing of the conch shell all *thawa* must file into the *gomba* hall, and start reciting without talking to each other.

From these rules it appears that attendance of the *gomba* service, normally held in the morning, is on ordinary days the only compulsory corporate activity of the members of a monastery. For the

[1] 'Unity of All the Blessed', (Tib. *bDe-gshegs kun-'dus*).
[2] 'Union of the Precious Ones', (Tib. *dKon-mchog-spyi-'dus*).
[3] 'Universal Saviour', (Tib. *'Gro-ba-Kun-sgrol*).

rest of the day the monks go about their individual business, reading books, studying with their preceptor or teaching pupils, meditating, engaging in one of the religious crafts, such as painting, or dealing with more practical tasks of monastery management, catering, accounts or trade. As each monk has his own household, there is, except at the *gomba* services, no occasion for common meals, and gatherings of monks for purposes other than formal worship are confined to casual visits of individual monks to each other's houses.

At the time of planting or harvest the younger monks work in groups on the monastery's fields, and at that time they mess together in the houses belonging to the *gomba* in such places as Dingboche. But the duration of such activities is short, and during other times of the year co-operation in practical matters is limited to such incidental tasks as the building of a bridge across the Dudh Kosi or the repair of the monastery buildings.

Regular co-operation of all the monks is compulsory, however, in the various rites and ceremonies traditionally held at fixed times of the year. An abstract of the calendar of rites and festivals will give an idea of the manner and frequency of such co-operation:

Dawa Tangbu (corresponding approximately to March)
- (a) *Losar* celebrations on the 1st to 3rd day of the month.
    - 1st day: a service is held, *torma* are made, and the abbot entertains all the monks to a meal.
    - 2nd day: the monks are entertained from *gomba* funds.
    - 3rd day: the monks hold a common meal to which all have subscribed.
- (b) *Tsedub duwa*, a prayer service performed for the benefit of the country, the king and all the people, lasting for ten days.
- (c) *Tsho*, a memorial rite for the late abbot of Rongphu, lasting from the 17th to the 19th day.

Dawa Niwa (April)
No special rites.

Dawa Sumba (May)
No special rites.

Dawa Shiwa (June)
No special rites.

Dawa Ngawa (July)
The abbot and many monks go to Namche Bazar and celebrate the Dumje festival for five days.

Monastic Institutions and Priesthood

Dawa Tukpa (August)
   Niungne rite lasting for three days.
Dawa Dümba (September)
   Dorsung-duwa, a *tsedub* rite lasting for ten days.
Dawa Gyepa (October)
   No special rites.
Dawa Guwa (November)

From the 15th *Dawa Ngawa* to the 15th *Dawa Dümba* the monks observe *yerne dembu* (summer retreat).

The last day of this month is the first day of the *Mani-rimdu* festival.

Dawa Chuwa (December)
  (a) *Mani-rimdu* rites and dance festival from the 1st—15th day:
     1st—5th day: *torma* making and recitations
     6th—11th day: recitations
     12th—13th day: dancing
     14th day: *Jinsak* (fire-sacrifice)
     15th day: *Tshe-wong* (rite of 'Life-Consecration')
  (b) 29th day: Recitation of *Kangso* throughout the night; this is a rite of propitiation of local gods.

Dawa Chuchikpa (January)
  (a) 29th day: *Sherab ninpo*, a *kurim* rite.
  (b) Last day of the month: first day of the *Tsho*, memorial rite, for the late abbot, Lama Gulu.

Dawa Chuniwa (February)
  (a) 1st—3rd day: *Tsho* (=*gong-dzok*, memory of death)
  (b) 25th—29th day: *Lokpar*, a rite identical with the Dumje festival performed in village temples in Dawa Ngawa.
  (c) 30th day: *Delakunjung lhapsang*, a *kurim* rite.

Apart from the above seasonal feasts and rites there are ceremonies held throughout the year on specific days of the month. Thus on the eighth day of every month a *lhapsang* known as *Gyenga-lhapsang* is performed, and on the twenty-fifth day, a *tsho* rite held. In the days of the late Lama Gulu there was also a *tsho* rite on the tenth day of every month, but this practice was abandoned as a measure of economy. I was told, however, that the present abbot was anxious to resume the celebration of this monthly rite.

The summer retreat (*yerne dembu*), which lasts from the 15th of Dawa Ngawa to the 15th of Dawa Dümba, is a period of intensified religious concentration. During these two months no woman may enter the monastery precincts except with special permission of the abbot, and the monks may not leave Tengboche unless there is an emergency. But even in this case, they should be back before nightfall. The prohibition of killing any living being extends during this time even to plants. The monks may not remove weeds from their gardens and should not even pass urine on the grass lest they harm it. There are two daily services in the *gomba* during this time, and the monks are served at monastery expense twice a day with tea and once with gruel (*koli*). At the end of this period, i.e. on the 15th of Dawa Dümba, there is general feasting, playing and dancing, and this day of rejoicing when everyone may do what he likes is called *gyakye tongup*.

As long as the members of a monastic community have to provide for their own maintenance, they must inevitably be allowed a great deal of liberty in the way they spend their time outside the regular *gomba* services. Though this system of individual independence has its positive features, it undoubtedly militates against the planning of scholarly and religious activities under a central authority. The young reincarnate abbot of Tengboche seems to have realized this weakness of the accepted system, and he has recently made an attempt to counteract it by an innovation designed to give him more direct control over a nucleus of monks selected for their intellectual abilities. His aim is to provide from a special fund for the maintenance of a small élite group, throughout the year, and to exercise over their studies and other activities of this group a much closer control than over those of other monks.

Such monks entirely maintained from monastery funds and known as *seta to-up* were a feature of many Tibetan monasteries, and add, as it seems, greatly to the prestige of an institution. When I last visited Tengboche in October 1957, the *seta to-up* group consisted of nine young monks and had been in existence for only two months. The fund to maintain them, which was separate from the general monastery funds, was not yet large enough to provide these monks with their entire board, but the reincarnate abbot was hopeful of collecting sufficient contributions ultimately to maintain fifteen *thawa* in this way.

The members of the *seta to-up* group were to spend most of their time in studying, and were to be given leave only twice a year, during the months of Dawa Shiwa (June) and Dawa Gyepa (October). At these times of the year they were to be allowed fifteen days' leave, to collect money and provisions, either from their parents' house, or by going round the villages and collecting the interest of their investments or even charitable contributions.

Though fed by the monastery, even such *seta to-up* have to provide their own clothes, and to buy or build their own houses. They must therefore have some private means, and the system of *seta to-up* is certainly not designed to open the monastery to the sons of very poor families, but to give the abbot a more direct control over a group of monks freed from the petty cares of their supplies of food.

REINCARNATE LAMAS AND LAYMEN

In Tibet the principle of reincarnation seems to have determined the succession to high ecclesiastic office for at least half a millenium. The earliest authentically documented case is that of the first Grand Lama of the Gelugpa Church, Geden-dub, who died in A.D. 1475. According to contemporary belief he was reborn in a child identified by oracular signs, and this boy was duly installed as the second Grand Lama. The heads of the Gelugpa Church, who since 1640 were also the temporal rulers of Tibet, have ever since been chosen on the basis of the belief that the deceased priest-king is reborn in an infant recognizable by his ability to identify objects associated with his previous life. This manner of establishing an uncontested succession to major ecclesiastical posts soon spread throughout Tibet, and countless reincarnate lamas functioned as the heads of monastic institutions. They were known as *tulku*.

The Sherpas too believe in the principle of reincarnation. They have long been used to revere the abbot of Rongphu monastery as the reincarnation of their patron saint Lama Sanga Dorje, but it would seem that the appearance of reincarnate lamas in Khumbu and Solu is a comparatively recent phenomenon. Until the foundation of monastic institutions during the first half of the twentieth century, there were indeed no ecclesiastic personalities of sufficient eminence to make their rebirth in a child a matter of public concern, nor would a reincarnate lama have found the proper setting for his activities.

All this changed, however, with the foundation of monastic institutions not only in Khumbu, which is only a few days' walk from

Rongphu, the seat of a famous succession of reincarnate lamas, but even in Solu, the southernmost projection of the Buddhist sphere. In 1957 there were within these regions four publicly recognized reincarnate lamas, and the monastery of Chiwong had only recently lost its reincarnate lama to the larger and more important Tibetan monastery of Tathyo.

To understand the principle of succession to office by reincarnation we must briefly anticipate the discussion of eschatological concepts (cf. p. 246). According to the ideas current among Buddhists of the Nyingmapa sect, a man's personality (*sem*)[1] after death takes one of six paths leading to the six spheres of the world beyond. On the fork of three paths Urken Rimpoche awaits the departed and sends everyone according to his merit along one of the seven paths. But when a great lama, whose merit would entitle him to go to Devachen the 'Abode of Gods', arrives at the fork, Urken Rimpoche leads him only a short way along the white path to heaven. He then arrests his progress and tells him: 'Your time to go to Devachen has not yet come. You must take rebirth again and return to your task on earth. In future times you may go to Devachen.'

Such a lama, though fully entitled to heavenly rewards for past merit, is then reincarnated for the benefit of humanity, but unlike other beings in a new birth, he retains his knowledge of past experiences. His wisdom is hence superior to that of any lama relying on the learning of a single life.

An example of the competition between monasteries for the presence of a reincarnate lama (*tulku*) is the career of Karma Ongel (Salaka), a young Sherpa held to be a reincarnation of Lama Tensing Nurbu, an abbot of Rongphu, who was himself a reincarnation of Lama Sanga Dorje, or—as some believe—even of the famous translator Vairocana. He was born in 1938 in Changmitang near Tengboche as the *themba* son of an ex-nun of Devuche. His mother Ani Lhamai was of Lama clan and came from the Solu village of Thalsa. Her paternal father was Phinzo Lama, who—as we shall see presently—was also reincarnated. Lama Tensing Nurbu, though abbot of a Tibetan monastery, was himself from Solu, and stood to Ani Lhamai in the classifactory relationship of father's brother. Karma Ongel's father was a Salaka man from

[1] *Sem*, written in Tibetan *sems*, is the equivalent of the Sanskrit *chit*, and means literally 'mind'.

Novices in Tengboche monastery

Frescoes in a private chapel

Frescoes in the temple of Pangboche

Solu, who at first paid little attention to his *themba* son, and did nothing to support the mother. After she had to leave Devuche, she lived in a minute house in Changmitang, and added to her small income by working for other people.

The story goes that when the boy was about three years old, he began to say that Changmitang was not his home, that he was a Rongphu lama, and wanted to go to Rongphu. Often he cried, because his mother would not take him to Rongphu, and at first she used to scold and even beat him, when he pestered her in this way. But ultimately she told other people about the boy's odd behaviour and they advised her to take the child to Rongphu. When they arrived in Rongphu, the child said at once: 'This is my *gomba*, these are my books', and seemed to recognize many things in the monastery. The monks in Rongphu, who no doubt were looking out for a reincarnation of their late abbot, listened sympathetically to the mother's account, and agreed to go with her and the child to Khumbu, and to arrange there for the usual test. Taking the beads and some of their late abbot's other belongings with them they went to Khumbu, and there confronted the child with a collection of articles containing among many of similar type also those of the Rongphu lama. The child chose without hesitation the genuine articles, and thus proved himself as a reincarnation of the late abbot.

Under normal circumstances the boy and his mother would have been invited to take residence in Rongphu, but in this case the matter was complicated by another claimant, born in Tibet, who at about the same time had successfully passed a similar test. Double, and even triple reincarnations are by themselves not unknown for every personality is made up of *ku* (body), *sung* (voice) and *tü* (heart), and the theory is that these components can be reincarnated separately. Many of the Rongphu monks favoured the Khumbu-born *tulku*, but the problem had to be referred to Lhasa, and it is said that the father of the other claimant was a man of some influence, and hence brought about a decision in favour of his son, who was duly installed as abbot designate of Rongphu.

Ani Lhamai, in the meanwhile, took her son to Solu and lived with relatives near the monastery of Chiwong. There is a story, according to which the boy, who continued to demand to be taken to Rongphu, once, when about ten years old, accompanied some Sherpa monks to Tibet, and at a place called Singi-tak near Shigatse met some of the nuns of Rongphu. Seeing him, the nuns began to cry, protesting that they knew him to be the true incarnation of the heart (*tü*) of Lama Tensing Nurbu, but that now an inferior reincarnation had taken his place in Rongphu. But the young lama said: 'Do not cry, I will still remain with you, and I shall build a *gomba* in this very place.' At this, all those present marvelled, for at Singi-tak there was neither water nor suitable building material. But the boy thrust his stick into the ground and said: 'Dig here and you will find stones for building a *gomba*.' And when the people dug, they found stones excellent for house building. But they pointed out that there was no water, and again the reincarnate lama pointed to a place on the ground and, when the people removed a little soil, they found an ample current of water. Then a small *gomba* was built there, and the young *tulku* lama stayed there for some time, attended by the nuns and supplied by the local population.

But finally the monks of Chiwong offered him the abbotship of their monastery, and it was there that he received his formal education. When I met him in Chiwong in 1953 he seemed a cheerful, though slightly self-conscious boy, not very different from other student monks of his age. But two years later he went for further studies to Tibet, and the abbot of the monastery of Thatyo, a monastery one day's journey from Rongphu, was so impressed by his personality that he offered him the succession to the abbotship of Tathyo. Being over eighty years old, the abbot soon withdrew from active affairs, and in 1957 the young reincarnate lama was de facto abbot of Thatyo. As Thatyo was a monastery with over eighty monks, while in 1957 there were only fifteen resident monks in Chiwong, this position was of far greater importance than the one which the reincarnate lama had held in Solu. It is said, moreover, that he was also offered the position of abbot of the Naphta monastery in Tibet. Regrettably he succumbed to an illness in 1958, but on his death-bed he foretold an early reincarnation.

There is some indication that reincarnations may, so to speak, run in a family for Phinzo Lama, the grandfather of Ani Lhamai, the young *tulku* lama's mother, was himself reincarnated in Ngawang Yönde Nurbu, the younger brother of Lama Tundu, the late abbot of Thami *gomba*. Ngawang Yönde Nurbu went to live in Chiwong, but when he began an association with a nun related to the family of Sange Lama of Phaphlu, the patron of Chiwong, he came into conflict with this powerful personality, and left Chiwong for the newly-founded monastery of Toloka. He married the nun, whose name was Giami, and lived in Toloka until his death some fourteen years ago. Giami then married Randul Lama (Gole), a disciple of her late husband, and a son she bore to him was found to be a reincarnation of Ngawang Yönde Nurbu. The boy, who in 1957 was twenty-one years old, is generally recognized as a *tulku* lama and after studying for three years in Tibet, he lived at Toloka in the monastery known as Tar-ling. This monastery seems to be modelled on the pattern of Thami *gomba* rather than on that of Chiwong or Tengboche. Among the inmates there are married lamas as well as *thawa*, and I was told that even the reincarnate lama might marry, but that if he did so he could not ordain *thawa* such as the reincarnate abbot of Tengboche would soon be able to do.

The even more recently founded monks' community of Thodung *gomba*, built by Lama Dawa Kipa of Lama clan in 1948, prides itself also on having a reincarnate lama, a small Sherpa boy born to the west of Solu, but recognized as the reincarnation of a Drugpa lama.

Reincarnations are not confined to the abbots of monasteries. Even lamas and nuns of less exalted status may be reborn in children, who recall some experiences of their past life. Thus Lama Kiri (Sherwa) of Khumjung, a lama of learning and repute, but without monastic affiliations, was reborn in the son of Lama Lhakpa of the Kerok *gomba*. The child's mother was from Khumjung, and distantly related by marriage to Lama Kiri. When she brought her son to Khumjung, he pointed out the house in which Lama Kiri had lived, and insisted that it had belonged to him. He remembered also certain incidents of Lama Kiri's life, but as no question of succession is involved in such cases, there are no tests like those required to establish the claim of a reincarnate abbot.

In Rongphu there was, in the last generation, a case of reincarnation which supports the Sherpa idea that a monk's marriage and return to secular life, if permitted by his preceptor, does not necessarily involve a very serious loss of merit. The *loben* of Rongphu, who was obviously one of the most senior and highly respected monks, asked permission to marry a nun with whom he had fallen in love. Leave was granted and the couple got married. Both died after a few years of married life, and both were reincarnated at about the same time. Their reincarnations are now again a monk and a nun, and it would be of interest to know whether any bond of sympathy reflects their love in a previous existence.

Even laymen without special claims to sanctity are sometimes reincarnated in children conscious of their previous life. Such reincarnations, however, are of little practical importance. While a reincarnate abbot takes over the personal property as well as the official position of his predecessor, the reincarnation of a layman has no claim to the property owned in his previous life. Yet, there is some indication that such a claim would not be considered entirely fantastic, for the heirs, who inherited the property, usually give to the new incarnation of their late father or kinsman a set of new clothes in recognition of his right to a share in the property.

In the village of Khumjung there were in 1957 two generally known reincarnations of this type, as well as two children considered as reincarnations only by a small circle of relatives. The best known case was that of Lama Karma (Thaktu), a young man about thirty years old. The story goes that a nun in Devuche, who had a *themba* son who died before she entered the nunnery once asked the abbot of Rongphu in what shape her child might have been reincarnated. The reply was that in one of the highest houses of Khumjung there lived a lama, and that in his son—the present Lama Karma—her child was reincarnated. This indication was corroborated by the small boy himself, who several times spoke of his mother who was a nun and lived in Devuche. The nun was delighted to know of her child's rebirth and presented the boy with clothes and other gifts. But with this ended the acknowledgement of their connection in the child's previous life, and there are no signs of any lasting relationship of intimacy and mutual affection between the nun and Lama Karma.

The other lay-reincarnation in Khumjung, is Phu Dorje, the son of a Khamba couple of rather humble status. When the boy was four years old he said that he had been the father of the then very important and influential *pembu* Yülha Tarkia (Thaktu). When he saw the *pembu* riding past his parents' house, he shouted from the window: 'This is my son, and this is the horse I used to ride.' The parents, fearing the *pembu*'s anger, tried to prevent the child from making such remarks. But the boy was not to be restrained, and went on to describe the property and the house he had owned in his previous life. The child's strange remarks came to the *pembu*'s ears, and he fetched the boy to his house and gave him a present of

Monastic Institutions and Priesthood

clothes. The *pembu*'s son, who told me the story, said that the boy claimed to be a reincarnation of his grandfather, expressed no wish to remain in the house he had owned in his previous life, but that in Tibet such a reincarnation of a layman may be accepted as a member of the reincarnated person's family and brought up in his former home.

Less well known than these two cases is the alleged reincarnation of a lama and a nun of Phortse in the two small daughters of Ngawang Tundu (Mende), an ex-monk of Tengboche, married to an ex-nun of Devuche. The fact that a man should be reincarnated in a girl-child is not considered an entirely improbable event, for reincarnations are known to have occurred in children of the opposite sex. I do not know, however, what would happen if the abbot of a monastery was found to be reincarnated in a girl-child.

Whereas the reincarnations of laymen are unusual and unforeseen events, the kinsmen of a lama of learning and a reputation for holiness sometimes expect him to be reborn and wait for the appropriate signs. Thus it was told of Lama Ngawang Chotr of Pangboche that he expected his father, who had died two years previously, to be reincarnated before long. His father was a highly respected lama, and the son of a reincarnated lama, whose heart, eyes and tongue were enshrined in a silver casket in the Pangboche *gomba* by the side of the similar relics of Lama Sanga Dorje. Ngawang Chotr had kept the heart of his father, no doubt with a view to placing it in the *gomba* as soon as there were sure signs of his reincarnation.

THE VILLAGE CLERGY

While the monasteries are today the main focal points of Sherpa religious life, the performance of seasonal and domestic ritual is mainly the responsibility of the lamas resident in the villages. The position of such a village lama must not be confused with that of a priest who is the hereditary or appointed representative of the community in the religious sphere. There is in a Sherpa village no position comparable either to that of a parson or priest appointed by a superior religious authority, or to that of a priest with hereditary ties to locality gods such as found in many Indian tribal societies. A village lama is simply a person who has received religious instruction enabling him to perform certain rites and is resident in the village as a householder. He may have been taught by another village lama or he may have spent some years as a novice or a *thawa* in a monastery before returning to secular life. A village lama need not have taken any vows nor does he require to be elected or appointed like one of the secular village dignitaries. The fact that he is available in the village and capable of ministering at such seasonal rites as Osho, Dumje or Yer-chang, as well as at the usual domestic rites assures him employment whenever there is need for the services of lamas.

At the beginning of his career a village lama will act as assistant at rites conducted by a senior and more experienced lama. But as his knowledge and his skill in the reciting of liturgical books increases, he will gradually assume rôles of greater responsibility, and may even be asked to perform minor rites independently. If there are several experienced lamas in a village, such a chance may nos come early, but where there is a shortage of lamas, even a young and not very learned lama may have to minister on many occasions.

Virtually all village lamas are married and in many cases it is the desire to legalize an irregular union which induces a monk to give up his monastic career and settle down as a married householder. Some such ex-monks are today highly respected village lamas, whose services are much in demand even outside their own village community.

But marriage and his position as householder and owner of land and cattle do not prevent a village lama from striving after further spiritual perfection, and the honour and prestige which goes along with virtue and wisdom. The recognized manner of acquiring further knowledge and spiritual power is the practice of *tsam*, which involves isolation in a hermitage or, more rarely, seclusion in one's own house. The duration of a *tsam* may be of any length, but the most effective is an isolation for three years, three months and three days, referred to as *losum, dasum, sheaksum*. During such a period of isolation a lama may be visited only by a disciple, servant or kinsman, who brings him supplies of food and ritual accessories, and by superior monks or lamas, who can guide him in his spiritual exercises. Part of the practice of *tsam* are times of fasting when the hermit takes no other nourishment than three times a day a small quantity of milk mixed with water and certain herbs. While in isolation a lama spends his days in the study and recitation of sacred scriptures, and in meditation.

Monastic Institutions and Priesthood

In 1957 there was no lama in Khumbu engaged in a long period of *tsam*, but in a cave above the village of Jorsale (Sherpa: Thumbu), a few hours walk south of Namche Bazar, there was the hermitage of Lama Nurbu of Salaka clan, who was engaged in a *tsam* of three years, three months and three days. He had built himself a fairly substantial hermitage, which stood in the mouth of a large cave, and in his house ten minutes' walk below lived his wife and children. His youngest son, a boy of eighteen, looked after the lama's bodily needs, brought him food cooked in his house or cooked for him in the hermitage. This period of *tsam* was intended as a temporary exercise and the lama's wife told me that after its completion her husband would rejoin his family and the company of people.

A different type of *tsam* was being practised by an ex-monk of Tengboche, who lived as her seventh husband with Ngawang Samden, in a small, but comfortable house above Pangboche. For one whole year he did not leave this house and its small garden, but he had the company of his wife and received visitors. Ngawang Samden told me that at the end of her husband's *tsam*, she would observe the same voluntary seclusion and her husband would maintain the connection with the outside world and bring up supplies.

There are many married lamas who have never undergone the rigorous discipline of a prolonged *tsam*, but such lamas are considered incapable of conducting independently rites for which great spiritual powers are required, such as the rite of 'Life-Consecration' known as *Tshe-wong*. Hence there is not only a spiritual but also a social incentive to embark on the arduous enterprise of nearly total isolation from the world of laymen. The lama who has successfully completed his seclusion of three years, three months and three days, can be sure of the increased respect of his co-villagers and his fame is likely to spread throughout Khumbu and Pharak. His services will be more in demand and more generously rewarded than those of village lamas of lesser reputation, and material rewards will thus follow upon the spiritual progress resulting from the practice of *tsam*.

Yet even village lamas of lesser achievements in the sphere of learning and meditation have often a very full programme of ritual duties. The extent and nature of such duties as well as their material rewards can best be demonstrated by a specific example. During my stay at Khumjung in 1957 Sharap Lama, a popular and well situated, but only moderately learned lama of Khamba origin had from the end of April until early October the following engagements:

28 April	Co-operation in the performance of the *tsirim* rite, aimed at the expulsion of evil spirits, in the *gomba* of Khumjung.
1–2 May	Co-operation in the recitation of *Totup* on the occasion of the death of Ang Tenzing.
3 May	As above and co-operation in the funeral of Ang Tenzing.
4–7 May	Co-operation in the performance of *napur* for Ang Tenzing.
10 May	Co-operation in a rite connected with the death of Ang Teshi (Thaktu) in Kunde village.
11–13 May	Co-operation in the performance of *shetu* rite for Pasang Putr in Namche Bazar.
14–19 May	Co-operation in the *napur* rite for Ang Teshi (Thaktu) in Kunde.
23 May	Co-operation in a *tsho* rite commissioned by the widow of a Khumjung man for her late husband's benefit, and performed in the Khumjung *gomba*.
25 May	Co-operation in a similar *tsho* rite performed in a private house of Khumjung.
26–27 May	Co-operation in recitation of *do-dzunga* in the house of the late Ang Tenzing's son.
28 May–1 June	Co-operation in *napur* rite for Mingma (Paldorje), who had died on an expedition.
2–5 June	Co-operation in *shetu* rite for Ang Teshi (Thaktu) in Kunde.
6 June	Completion of *shetu* and *gyewa* for Ang Teshi in Kunde.
7 June (morning)	Recitation of *kurim* in the house of Lama Kiu who was seriously ill.
7–9 June	Co-operation in *shetu* rite for Ang Tenzing.
10 June	Completion of *shetu* and *gyewa* for Ang Tenzing.
11–15 June	Co-operation in a *shetu* rite commissioned by a man of Namche Bazar in the name of his wife and father.

Monastic Institutions and Priesthood 165

15 June	Completion of *shetu* rite in Namche Bazar and *gyewa*.
16–17 June	Co-operation in recitation of *Dordzi chopa* for Chortin, recently drowned.
20 June	Co-operation in funeral rites of Lama Kiu.
21–23 June	Recitation of *niti* in his own house on the occasion of his eldest daughter's 25th birthday.
27 June–1 July	Co-operation in *shetu* rite for Chortin.
4–10 July	Co-operation in the rites and ceremonies of the Dumje village festival.
12 July	Co-operation in *lhapsang* rite performed by the abbot of Tengboche in order to purify the house of Dawa Tenzing, whose son Mingma and wife Chortin had died in accidents.
14 July	Co-operation in *Tshe-Wong* rite performed in the Khumjung *gomba* by the abbot of Tengboche.
16–19 July	Co-operation in *shetu* rite for Lama Kiu.
20 July	Completion of *shetu* and *gyewa* for Lama Kiu.
21 July	Recitation of a *kurim* in the house of Urken (Khamba) for the welfare of his household.
24 July	Recitation of a *kurim* in the house of a sick man.
25 July	Recitation of a *kurim* for the benefit of a woman entering her 49th year.
31 July	Journey to Machherma.
1–6 August	Performance of *Yer-chang* rite at Machherma.
7 August	Journey from Machherma to Khumjung.
10–11 August	Recitation of *doma* in his own house for the benefit of a sick man.
15–19 August	Some hours of each day spent in the recitation of *doma* for the general welfare of his own family. (This was done because there was no other work).
22–24 September	Recited with seven other lamas the 16 volumes of *Bum* in a private house of Namche Bazar; this was done as *kurim* rite for the benefit of the son of the house, who was ill.
1–3 October	Recited with eight other lamas the 16 volumes of *Bum* in a house of Namche Bazar, whose

	owner commissions every year such a recitation for the general welfare of his family.
4–6 October	As above in the house of another man of Namche Bazar.

From the above list it appears that Sharap Lama was engaged in ritual tasks on 26 days in May, 25 days in June, and 18 days in July. During these months there occurred the deaths of several well-to-do persons, and the subsequent funerary rites account for the greater part of Sharap Lama's and other lamas' activities. These months can therefore hardly be taken as normal, but neither do the three days spent in September in reciting sacred scriptures in the house of a wealthy merchant of Namche Bazar represent the normal ritual activities of a lama during a full month. The average lies in between these extremes, and we can assume that most village lamas will spend between one half and one third of their time on purely ritual tasks, whereas for the rest of the time they are free to devote themselves to agriculture or trade.

A lama's income from participation in the performance of rites is modest. When reciting *shetu* in the house of a rich man, Sharap Lama received about Rs.1½ in cash per day, which is only 50 per cent more than the wage of a farm labourer, but part of the reward consists in the lavish food and drink with which the lamas are entertained throughout a performance. Yet, on the whole it appears that village lamas no less than monks are modest in their demands on the laity, and that they will readily participate in the performance of rites in private houses whenever called upon, and accept whatever fee the host or organizer of the rite is prepared to pay them. They do not, moreover, expect cash payments when performing any of the village rites, but usually receive a share of the grain or other food offered at the time. Often an individual will give a lama a quantity of beer with the request to recite a *kurim* in furtherance of any specific prospect. Thus an oldish rich man of Khumjung who set out on a journey across the Nangpa La at the time of the monsoon presented Lama Lakba of Kerok *gomba* with beer made with about 10 lb. of maize and asked him to recite the book of *Dorje kotop ngabum* to obtain good weather for the two days of the journey across the pass. The lama accepted the commission and the weather duly improved.

Monastic Institutions and Priesthood

Similar requests to village lamas are by no means infrequent, for in Sherpa belief there are few activities which cannot benefit from the recitation of the one or other *kurim*, and it is in illness, misfortune and many a risky activity that a Sherpa turns to lamas for help. In the choice of those whom he invites to his house or commissions to recite a specific text in their own home, he is not bound by any hereditary ties or village custom. He can turn to one of the lamas of his own village, or approach a lama of a neighbouring village or the abbot of a monastery. There is no institution comparable with the tie between a Hindu and his family priest (*purohit*) nor does residence in a village give a lama any specific right to employment by the people of the locality.

A lama does not by virtue of his religious knowledge and skill hold any position of authority in the village in which he resides, and even the *gomba* dignitaries, such as *umse*, *chorumba* and *chorpen* may be laymen. Thus in Khumjung all three of these offices were filled by laymen, and the village lamas, though called upon to act at ceremonies and rites held in the *gomba*, had no status in its administration. In his capacity as a householder any village lama may, however, be elected to one of the village offices, and lamas may thus function as *Osho naua, shingo naua* or *pembu*. But their function in such a position is quite separate from their priestly tasks.

Village lamas, in other words, are not village dignitaries, but act as private practitioners providing their priestly services wherever they are required. They do not hold any recognized or traditionally defined position within the village community, and owe any influence they may possess solely to their personality or reputation of knowledge and saintliness. Though a village without some resident lamas must inevitably experience many difficulties, there is no organized effort on the part of the village community as a whole to attract lamas or get some of its own members instructed in Buddhist scriptures and ritual. This is left to the initiative of individuals and hence more or less to chance.

There may be times when a village community comprises several eminent lamas, and others when that same village depends for all more important rites on the ministration of lamas from neighbouring villages. The position in Khumjung has recently undergone such a change.

In 1953 there were in Khumjung the following lamas: Kusho

Kapkye, a Khamba, who immigrated from Tibet some thirty years previously, and had the reputation of considerable learning, Lama Kiu of Gardze clan, then eighty years old, Sharap Lama, a Khamba, who had immigrated from Tibet some twenty-five years previously, Lama Karma of Thaktu clan, who was the son of a lama of Kunde, and Ongchu Lama, a man of Solu, and son-in-law of Sange Lama, who was one of the Khumjung *pembu* but had retired to Tengboche. Kusho Kapkye ranked as the senior lama, and presided at major rites. When he died in 1955, this rôle fell to Lama Kiu, who despite his great age and frailty presided at *gomba* rites and funeral services as late as May 1957. When he died in June of that year, there was no lama of sufficient status to conduct the service at his funeral, and an old lama from Phortse had to be called. In November 1957 Sharap Lama died suddenly, thus leaving the village with only Lama Karma and Ongchu Lama, both of whom were rather worldly personalities and lacking the spiritual status which qualify a lama for the independent performance of major rites. In the neighbouring village of Kunde, which shares with Khumjung one *gomba* and co-operates in the performance of all village rites, there was only one lama, Lama Jangbu, a widower with grown-up children, whose reputation for learning was also not very high. Yet, he was senior to the two lamas of Khumjung, and in the absence of lamas of higher status it fell to him to preside at ceremonies in the *gomba*.

Yet, even at the celebration of the Dumje festival, which occurred shortly after the death of Lama Kiu, and at a time when Sharap Lama was alive and in excellent health, the organizers of the festival felt that the help of a more experienced lama was required, and they prevailed upon Gelung Ngawang, a former *loben* and acting head lama of Tengboche, who then lived in a hermitage above Dingboche, to undertake the journey to Khumjung and preside at the Dumje rites. Similar arrangements will presumably have to be made until Khumjung has once more a resident lama of learning and high spiritual status.

Not every man qualified by education and experience actually practises as a lama. In Khumjung, for instance, there was Ngawang Tundu, who for many years had been a monk at Tengboche but who returned to secular life on account of his marriage to an ex-nun of Devuche. Though he had the full religious training of a monk and like many other ex-monks of Tengboche, could have set up as a respected village lama, he devoted himself entirely to the care of his large herd of yak and the cultivation of his land, and never even joined the lamas of the village in their recitations at village rites.

Unlike the clergy of an organized church or the monks of a Buddhist monastery, the village lamas are not subject to any ecclesiastic authority. Yet, co-operation at all ritual occasions appears to function smoothly, and there seem to be no quarrels over the question of precedence. Greater knowledge of texts and ritual practices is readily recognized and this, together with the reputation and spiritual status gained by the practice of *tsam*, determines a lama's place among other village lamas co-operating in the same ritual. The most senior lama, who formally conducts the rite, always sits nearest to the altar, and the others take their places in order of seniority.

The use of the title Lama for the ordinary village priest is somewhat inconsistent with the monastic practice of reserving this title, which corresponds to the Sansksrit *guru* or master, to the abbot of a monastery, who is usually referred to as *lamache* or 'great lama'.[1] The ordinary monks are not described as lamas, and if someone speaks, for instance, of the 'Tengboche lama' he means inevitably the abbot. All those clerics resident in villages who engage regularly in the performance of religious rites, on the other hand, are freely accorded the title lama, even though some of them may be much less learned than the average monk. The qualifications which entitle a religious practitioner to the courtesy title of Lama are not clearly defined, and at the early stages of a village lama's career there will be some villagers who refer to him already by this title while others continue to call him by his ordinary name. But as he establishes himself as an experienced performer of rites and ceremonies, he will gradually become known as Lama 'so-and-so', or the title Lama will be affixed to his name. In Khumjung there were in 1957 several men with some knowledge of sacred books and ritual practices who were never referred to as lamas, though on the occasion of funerals or certain other services they might sit in a line with the lamas and join in the recitation of liturgical texts. Most prominent among them was the painter Kapa Kalden, who though a man of learning no less than of artistic gifts, never aspired to the title of lama, and never undertook independently any ritual task. Some of

[1] Cf. also L. A. Waddell, *The Buddhism of Tibet*, p. 173, London, 1895.

the others, however, occasionally accepted the commission of reciting a text for a private purpose, and they were also employed at the annual public recitation of the Kangyur at village expense. It is not unlikely that the one or other of these young men will continue his studies and ultimately qualify for the tasks of a regular village lama.

While the nuns of such nunneries as Devuche correspond to the monks of the monasteries, there are no female counterparts to the village lamas. Among the inhabitants of most villages there are no doubt one or two religiously-minded women described as nuns (*ani*), who shave their hair and dress like the nuns of a nunnery, but they do not play any active rôle in ritual performances and are often virtually illiterate. Unable to join a nunnery on account of poverty, or unacceptable to a nunnery because of their lack of learning, they lead within the village a devout and celibate life, and usually help in the houses and in the fields of kinsmen who provide for their bodily needs. Even if learned in the sacred scriptures such an *ani* resident in a village can never attain to a position comparable to that of a village lama, and the only commission she might occasionally be entrusted with is the recitation of a *kurim* for the purpose of warding off illness or any specific danger. The nuns of an established nunnery are occasionally invited to perform one of the mortuary rites, but Sherpa religion provides no scope for ministrations of individual women following a religious calling.

VILLAGE TEMPLES

In every main village there is either a temple (*gomba*) or at least a building which contains a giant, brightly painted prayer-wheel. Such religious buildings are invariably painted a dull pink, and their roof is surmounted by a gilded spire. While the structures housing prayer-wheels only serve the private devotions of those squatting before the wheel and turning it to the accompaniment of their prayers, the village temple is the centre of many celebrations which have their secular as well as religious aspects.

Most temples consist of a courtyard surrounded by galleries the main hall containing the altar and library of sacred books, and one or two minor buildings in which the kitchen and storerooms are accommodated. The position of these main features depends on the character of the site, but a description of the temple in Khumjung will give a general idea of a Sherpa *gomba*.

Monastic Institutions and Priesthood

This temple stands in a small grove of juniper trees at the foot of the hill slopes rising on the northern side of the village. Five stone steps lead to a double-leaved wooden door set into the stone wall of the courtyard, and through this door one enters the covered gallery surrounding an open courtyard 35 feet square. The gallery covered by an inward sloping roof of wooden planks is about 5 feet wide and raised 2 feet above the level of the courtyard. In its centre stands a flagpole.

On the right side of the courtyard, and accessible only through it, stands a double-storeyed house for the sacristan (*konier*). Its two ground-floor rooms are used as kitchen and store whenever rites performed in the temple necessitate the preparation of food.

Three steps lead from the courtyard to the single entrance door of the main hall (*duang*) of the temple, which is approximately 40 feet square. Passing through this door one faces the main altar. At a right angle to this stand two long benches, on which at rituals lamas and prominent villagers sit facing each other. The roof of the *duang* rests on four stout wooden pillars, on each of which hangs a painted banner (*thanka*), the gift of a villager long dead.

The large central figure on the altar represents the 'Lotus-Born' Buddha Padmasambhava, a historical figure connected with the establishment of Buddhism in Tibet, who is known to the Sherpas as Guru Rimpoche ('Precious Master') and regarded as a manifestation of Pawa Cheresi. Other statues of divinities arranged on an altar-table running along the entire back wall of the main hall are those of the Great Saviour Pawa Cheresi (Sanskrit: Avalokiteśvara), of the Saviouress Drolma (Sanskrit: Tara); of Mandārāva and the 'Goddess Ocean of Wisdom' Kando-ye-shes-chogyel, the two wives of Guru Rimpoche, and of an unnamed reincarnate nun. On a separate altar in the right hand corner stands a large statue of Jambhala (Nor-lha) the god of wealth.

These statues, which are made of plaster and painted in gold and various colours, are not of high artistic merit, and compare unfavourably with the many exquisite frescoes in Tibetan style, painted by Sherpa painters, which adorn the temples and private chapels of Khumbu.

The entire side wall to the left of the entrance is lined with wooden shelves in the shape of pigeon holes, each of which contains a volume of the temple library. The latter consists of Tibetan block prints of the 108 volumes of the Kangyur, the Buddhist canon, of part of the Tengyur, the commentaries, and several other sacred works. Most of the books, as well as several of the statues, are gifts of individual villagers. To donate ritual objects or works of religious art to a temple is a usual way of acquiring merit, and even the restoration of temples or individual statues is often paid for by pious persons anxious to add to their store of merit or to express their gratitude for rescue from danger. Thus in 1957 a young Sherpa, who had survived a serious illness contracted on a mountaineering expedition, paid for the regilding of the faces of some of the statues in the *gomba*.

Among the ritual objects deposited in the temple are the carved, wooden masks worn by dancers representing divinities and demons at the time of the Dumje festival. Some of these are hung up on pillars while others lie on a special shelf.

Built on to the main hall of the *gomba*, but not accessible either from this hall or even the temple courtyard, is a structure 27 feet long and 12 feet wide, which houses a prayer-wheel 8 feet high and 6 feet in diameter. While the frescoes in the hall of the *gomba* are not remarkable, and indeed of much poorer quality than many frescoes in private chapels, the walls of the interior of the prayer-wheel house bear frescoes of much better style. Among these are panels featuring the Great Saviour 'Glancing Eye' Pawa Cheresi (Avalokiteśvara), the 'Precious Master' Guru Rimpoche (Padmasambhava), the 'Lord of Death' Shinje-chogyal (Yamaraj); Tungsha Tonba, the five celestial Buddhas; Guru Trakpo, the fierce aspect of Guru Rimpoche, and the Supreme Buddha 'All Good' Kuntubzang-po (Samanthabhadra).

Whereas the *gomba* itself is shared by the people of the two villages of Khumjung and Kunde, the latter village has a prayer-wheel house of its own, which stands in a central place and is the only purely religious building of that village.

A century ago there were in Khumbu only two temples, namely the one at Pangboche, believed to have been founded by Lama Sanga Dorje, and a small temple at Thami. Only in those two villages was the Dumje festival celebrated, and the people of Khumjung, for instance, went for the celebration of the Dumje to Thami. Not until the end of the nineteenth century—no exact dates are available—was a village temple built in Khumjung, and the one in

Procession during the Osho rite

Sprinkling libations during the Osho rite

Penitents circumambulate a *mani*-wall and *chörten*

Participants in the Niungne rite of Khumjung

Namche Bazar is of an even more recent date. Khumbu was then without any monastic establishment, and it was only in the first half of the twentieth century, that the great and elaborately decorated *gomba* of Thami and Tengboche were built.

Roughly at the same time which saw the construction of these new temples, many wealthy men of Khumbu built houses with elaborately furnished and painted private chapels, and all along the paths sprung up religious structures, such as *chörten*, *mani*-walls, rock engravings, and houses containing water-driven prayer-wheels. *Chörten* are stupa-like monuments consisting usually of a square base built of stone, a semi-spherical stone structure enclosing printed scriptures and sometimes some relics of a great lama, and rising above this a short spire, sometimes carrying a crescent moon. In most main villages there are one or two such *chörten*, usually standing close to a principal path leading into the village, but *chörten* are also found near subsidiary settlements and even on paths far from human habitation. The same applies to the *mani*-walls so characteristic of all the Buddhist regions of Nepal. They consist of an understructure of rough stone supporting innumerable upright stone slabs. The inscriptions on these slabs, carved in relief, include the sacred formula *om mani padme hum* and other prayers, and their erection provides merit for the person who bears the cost of the construction and of the work of carving the tablets.

The economic effort required for the construction of all these religious buildings and structures within a comparatively short span, must be rated all the higher as the population of Khumbu, numbering 2,205 in 1957, was even one generation ago undoubtedly still considerably smaller. For quite apart from any natural growth the population increased rapidly owing to the immigration of numerous Khamba families which settled in Khumbu only within the last thirty or forty years.

Out of the surplus of income over domestic expenditure the farmers and traders of Khumbu not only paid for the construction of temples, monasteries and religious monuments, but they also maintained a growing number of monks and nuns, who did not directly contribute to production. In 1957 the number of monks and lamas in Tengboche and Thami *gomba* was sixty, and that of nuns in Devuche and Thami *gomba* twenty-five. Apart from these there were in all the villages of Khumbu lamas who, though householders and landowners, devoted only part of their time to the farming of their land, and spent days and often weeks in ritual activities, for which they received payment by the laymen of the community.

Thus the economic efforts of some 500 lay-households provide sufficient food and other necessities to support entirely some eighty-five monks and nuns, and contribute to the maintenance of several village lamas, much of whose income is derived from the fees paid by other householders for ritual services.

Although Buddhism has been well established in Khumbu for at least 300 years, the foundation of monasteries and nunneries as well as the construction of new village temples and many religious monuments have taken place within the last fifty to eighty years. This points to economic events which favoured a sudden spurt of non-productive activities, and in my opinion there can be little doubt that these events were brought about by the introduction of the potato and the resulting increase in agricultural production. Obviously the sudden development of a surplus in food supplies must be regarded as permissive and not as causative of the flowering of the religious life. It would seem that among the Sherpas, as among Tibetan Buddhists, the religious impulse is so strong that any margin of resources left after essential needs have been met is largely devoted to religious purposes. This seems to have happened not only in Khumbu, but also in Solu where no less than five monastic establishments—Chiwong, Trakshindo, Gole, Tolaka and Thodung—have sprung up during the past forty years when the development of potato cultivation did not only improve the local food supplies but provided a commodity for a profitable export trade to India.

6

The Practice of Religion

The religious beliefs of the Sherpas are basically those of Tibetan Buddhism and Sherpa lamas use for the performance of private as well as public rites the liturgical texts current among members of the Nyingmapa or 'Old Sect'. A general discussion of either the doctrine or the ritual practices of Mahayana Buddhism lies outside the scope of this book, but reference may be made to David Snellgrove's *Buddhist Himālaya*[1] which contains a detailed analysis of certain ritual performances in the Sherpa monastery of Chiwong (or Jiwong) in Solu. In this chapter I shall confine myself mainly to a description of ritual practices which apart from expressing religious beliefs exemplify the co-operation of the members of a village community, or of persons drawn from several village communities, in organized religious and ritual activities.

Organized and more or less spectacular ritual performances are only one side of Sherpa religion. The other consists of private prayer and meditation, the turning of prayer-wheels and circumambulation of *gomba* and *chŏrten*, and the many other acts individually performed for the purpose of obtaining merit (*sönam*). No lamas are required to assist in the daily ritual of those whose houses contain private chapels (*lhang*),[2] but members of the family light incense or butter lamps there, and every morning change the water in the brass bowls arranged on the altar.

Whenever a domestic or public rite of greater importance is to be performed, there is a need for ritual experts to prepare the altar and appropriate accessories, and to conduct the invocation of the deities to whom the worship is directed. An indispensable part of all such ritual performances are the *torma*, figures made of dough and butter, shaped to symbolize deities and spirits as well as offerings to be presented to the deities invoked. The ability to mould such

---

[1] Oxford, 1957.
[2] A contraction of *lha-khang* ('god's house').

torma is one of the skills every lama has to acquire, and many laymen are also capable of making the simpler *torma*.

The *torma* which occupy the centre of the altar at such major rites as the Dumje festival or the *shetu* mortuary rite are elaborate structures, built up of several layers of dough or boiled rice compressed to a solid, sticky mass, and surmounted by flat wooden boards, which have been decorated with patterns of butter dyed in different colours. The exact shape of such a *torma* depends on the liturgical text to be recited at the rite. The central *torma*, which in any set of *torma* is described as *kingur* or *paldor*, for instance, may symbolize Guru Rimpoche or Lama Rigsin (Milaräpa).

Each rite has its appropriate set of *torma*, and there are handwritten and painted pattern books which show the exact shape of every *torma*. When a ceremony has been completed the *torma* are broken up and distributed. The parts made of dough and boiled rice are then eaten, but the butter mixed with dyes is no longer fit to be consumed and is used for anointing the hair or for softening leather.

An altar prepared for the performance of a major rite must bear not only the appropriate *torma*, but also a number of prescribed offerings and ritual objects. Most prominent and also decorated with coloured butter are three cups made of human skulls which contain the so-called *mera* offerings of beer and blood, the latter being usually represented by tea. There are, moreover, the *chin-tse*, the 'essential' offerings, which consist of drinking-water (*chö-ön*), water for washing feet (*zab-sel*), flowers (*me-tok*), incense (*dupó*), a lamp (*mar-me*), perfumed water (*ti-chab*), food in the form of a *torma* (*shal-se*), and cymbals (*rol-mo*). The last of these may be omitted and the texts, therefore, speak of the seven essential offerings. Apart from these there are five objects known collectively as *nang-che*, which stand as offerings for the five senses, namely a mirror for the sight, an instrument producing sound for the hearing, incense for the smell, food for the taste, and a cloth for the touch. In addition to these prescribed offerings, there are shallow brass cups, usually numbering five or seven, some of which contain rice or maize, while others are filled with water.

The lamas preparing such an altar normally place on it also a *dorje*, representing a thunderbolt, a bell, a miniature *chörten*, a sacred book, a jug for holy water, a sacred wand dressed up with silk streamers in five colours (*dādar*), a metal mirror, a small and a large pair of cymbals, a conch shell trumpet and sometimes also a thighbone trumpet. All these ritual implements are used during the act of worship, and their number is not strictly prescribed. Lamps filled with butter, or failing this with oil, are used in most performances and at major rites up to a hundred such lamps consisting of small brass bowls may be burning at one time.

Common to all acts of worship are certain set features. First the deities are summoned to the feast and this invocation is accompanied by loud music and the clash of cymbals aimed at attracting their attention. Each deity is then invited to be seated, and thereupon follows the presentation of offerings. Recitations in praise of the deity occupy much of the time, and these alternate with the repetition of the appropriate *mantra* (magical spells). Moreover there are prayers of different kinds, and many rites close with a benediction, when the participants bow before the senior lama, who touches their heads with his hand or his *dādar*.

Invariably there are numerous pauses in the proceedings, and during these the lamas are served tea, beer and food, and there is usually a great deal of chatting. The most solemn performance may thus be interspersed with light-hearted conversation and even the most ribald jokes. During the funeral service for Ang Tenzing of Khumjung, the over eighty-year-old Lama Kiu entertained in the intervals of chanting the assembled lamas with stories of the adventures of his youth. No one thought it odd or shocking when he related the most intimate details of a love affair with the mother of another lama who was participating in the service, nor was the latter in the least put out by these stories about his mother's amorous experiences. Such mundane talk in the intervals of a serious ritual is considered neither irreverent nor in bad taste, and any suggestion that it might affect the efficacy of the rite would be met with astonishment.

SEASONAL RITES

Besides the rites which may be performed at any time of the year when the propitiation of supernatural powers seems indicated, there are several ceremonies the celebration of which recur regularly and are the responsibility of the entire village community or of groups of families residing at the time in one of the subsidiary settlements.

The Banishment of Evil Spirits

Twice a year, once in April, soon after the beginning of the agricultural year, and again in October, when the harvest has been brought in and the herds and herdsmen have returned from the high pastures, a rite known as Tsirim is performed in the village *gomba*. The purpose of this rite is to drive off all evil spirits which may threaten the community. The organization of the rite lies with two *lawa* or organizers, who are appointed from among all householders in rotation. Those to serve in April are selected in the previous October, and at the April performance new *lawa* are appointed for the rite in October. It is the duty of the *lawa* to collect contributions of grain from all villagers, and to arrange for tea and food for the lamas ministering at the rite. The grain contributed is partly consumed at a feast prepared in the temple, and partly it is used to meet the expenditure on tea, beer, butter and other materials for the entertainment of the lamas, and the preparation of *torma* and offerings. Sometimes the *lawa* may be out of pocket, for the contributions are voluntary and no specific quantity of grain to be given is stipulated, but more often some grain remains and this is equally distributed among the lamas, who are not paid any fee in cash.

In the temple kitchen the *lawa* and their helpers prepare fried bread, potatoes, beer and tea, which are consumed by the lamas, and those who helped to prepare the feast. Other villagers who attend the rite are offered beer, but no food.

The Tsirim rite, which does not require the ministration of a lama of great spiritual power, is usually performed by the lamas resident in the village, and there is normally no provision for inviting lamas from outside. But at least two lamas *must* officiate, and when I attended the Tsirim in Khumjung three lamas were engaged in the ritual (cf. p. 252).

With the public Tsirim performed twice a year the village community as a whole wages a preventive war against evil spirits, while it is left to individuals to commission private rites of exorcism (cf. p. 254) designed to beat off the spirits' attacks on the health and welfare of specific families. Public and private performances follow basically the same pattern, but while the former are always held in a *gomba* the private rites take place in individual houses. Often after nightfall one can see small processions of torches emerge from such houses and hear shouts of 'ho-ho-ho' intended to chase away malignant spirits and ghosts.

The Rite of Protecting the Village Land

A village rite which follows the beginning of the agricultural season and aims at providing supernatural protection to the newly sown crops is known as Osho, a term the derivation of which I was unable to discover. It is performed in late April or early May, but no definite date is prescribed, and the year I was in Khumjung the celebration already arranged for May 2 was postponed for five days on account of the death of one of the villagers. The performance of the Osho is the last public act of the *naua* or village guardians, and on the evening of the day of the rite the new *naua* for the subsequent year are selected. These *naua* are consequently referred to as *Osho naua*, in order to distinguish them from the *shingo naua* or forest guards, and the Osho thus marks the beginning of the period of office of new village officials.

On the morning of the day appointed for the Osho, a rite of worship is held in the house of one of the *naua*, and in the twin villages of Khumjung and Kunde this performance takes place alternately in the one and the other village. In 1957 it was Kunde's turn, and the four *naua* assembled in the house of one of them for the performance of this rite and the preparations for the subsequent procession. In one of the windows a small altar with two tiers of *torma* had been prepared, and a lama of Kunde recited from a book, his chanting being punctuated by the clashing of cymbals and the sound of a drum. Apart from this lama, the four *naua* and the family of the host, few people were present, and the villagers obviously contented themselves with the knowledge that their chosen representatives were performing the rite on behalf of the whole community.

While the lama recited prayers inside the house, the owner and some helpers erected a tall pole with a new prayer flag, and three other flags, usually kept in the village temple, were temporarily tied to the same pole. Those who had helped with these preparations were then entertained to a meal in the *naua*'s house, and when this had been eaten, a procession formed which was to encircle the cultivated land of the twin villages. It was headed by some young boys carrying the three square temple flags, and behind them followed two girls in bright, festive clothes. Next came two lamas, playing cymbals, one old man carrying a brass plate with four *torma* representing the *gyal-dzen-deshi* or guardians of the four quarters, and three men—one of them a *naua* and another a *naua*'s son—carrying books tied up in coloured cloth. Three of the four *naua* actually went with this procession, and one was represented by his brother, who—sharing his house and being married to the same wife—counted for social and ritual purposes as the substitute of his brother.

Apart from these men only very young boys and a few children of both sexes joined the procession. It first went to a rock outside Kunde, on which one of the *torma* was deposited to the beating of drums and cymbals. One of the Kunde *naua* had provided some beer, and this was offered to the *gyal-dzen-deshi* and then drunk by the adult men present. The procession then left Kunde and went towards Khumjung, halting now and then to give the lamas time to recite a blessing for the benefit of the newly planted crops. This blessing of fields and crops is considered the principal purpose of the procession, which encircled the whole village land including the terraced fields carved into the hill-slopes above the houses. The people of Khumjung took comparatively little notice of the procession. True, some had lit fires of juniper branches to provide clouds of incense, but no one joined in the circumambulation. At the two corners of the village land, where *torma* were to be deposited, women awaited the lamas with flasks of beer, and there was one more halt when near the southern entrance of Khumjung more beer was offered to the participants in the procession.

The last of the *torma* for the guardians of the four quarters was set up on Kunde land, and the procession then returned to the house of the *naua*, from which it had set out. By this circumambulation the entire village land had been surrounded with an invisible wall against evil forces and magical dangers.

Niungne—The Rite to obtain Forgiveness of Sins

At the end of May or early in June all those villages which have a temple of their own arrange for the performance of a rite believed to benefit not so much the village community as a whole but the individual participants. The specific purpose of this rite, which is known as Niungne, is to cleanse the worshippers of sin and add to their store of merit (*sönam*). The origin of the rite is ascribed to the action of a famous lama, who tamed some man-eating ogres and taught them how to expiate their guilt. The story of his feat is briefly as follows:

Once upon a time there were seven *dü* (demons) who killed many men. One of these was Adakpalum, and she had five hundred children. They were all *dü* like their mother and every day they killed and ate 500 men and women. Then Lama Dzi-chen Rimpoche caught and hid one of Adakpalum's sons. In her search for her son the mother also approached Dzi-chen Rimpoche and implored him to help her find her lost son. The lama said: 'You and your children have been killing 500 men and women a day, and now you have lost one of your sons you are so distressed. If you promise not to kill any more people, I shall help you to find your son.'

Adakpalum promised to desist from devouring human beings, and the lama restored to her the lost son. Having experienced the grief and sorrow of losing one son, Adakpalum realized how much suffering she and her *dü* companions must have caused to the parents and brothers of their victims, and persuaded the other six *dü* also to desist henceforth from man-eating.

Lama Dzi-chen Rimpoche then advised them to perform for three years the Niungne rite in order to cleanse themselves of their sins, promising that if they did so, they would be able to enter Devachen, the Paradise of 'Boundless Light'. They followed his advice and instruction and finally reached Devachen. As the Niungne rite proved effective in removing so great a sin, the tradition of its regular performance was established, and men too can now be cleansed of all sins and gain a great deal of merit.

Though the Niungne benefits individuals rather than the whole village community, the arrangements for its performance are nevertheless a village responsibility, and the village officials appoint annually three *lawa* to organize the rite. Their task is to provide the required ritual accessories, such as butter lamps, to invite and reward those lamas who came from outside the village to minister at the rite,[1] and to prepare food and drink to be served in the temple. The expenditure incurred by the three *lawa* who acted in Khumjung in 1957 was Rs.50 each. They had all volunteered for their rôle,

---

[1] The lamas resident in the village receive no cash payment, but Gelung Ngawang received in 1957 between Rs.2½ and Rs.7 from each of the three *lawa*.

though one of them, a widow, was by no means well off. The number of villagers actively participating in the rite of expiation is not necessarily large and many attend the rite only once in several years. It is usually only elderly and particularly pious persons who participate regularly in the Niungne rites. In 1957 sixty-two men and women, drawn from Khumjung and Kunde, took part in the entire procedure of fasting and worship, which extended over three days and ended with a ceremony attended by many more of the villagers.

On the morning of the first day the participants assembled in the temple, and the lamas and more important men occupied the two rows of seats which stand at right angles to the altar. All the women and the less prominent men sat on the floor of the central aisle and in the space behind the two rows of benches. Gelung Ngawang, a former monk of Tengboche, who then lived as a hermit above Dingboche, had been invited to preside over the proceedings, and led by this greatly revered personality, the five lamas then resident in Khumjung and Kunde recited in the course of the celebration the books *Gelung-maha-palmo-yi-luk* and *Tsho-tuk-dze-chen-tshom-po-yi-niungne*. There was no playing of instruments on that day, and the lamas did not indulge in the usual loud and heavily accented recitations. There was a low hum of prayers, and lamas as well as laymen appeared solemn and completely serious. There was certainly none of the bandying of jokes lamas are prone to, even in the performance of funerary rites.

The first day of the Niungne is not a day of fasting and the participants ate a substantial meal of wheat flour dumplings served with *ghi* and sugar, boiled rice, potato curry and tea. This meal, prepared by the *lawa* and their wives and paid for from public funds, was served in the temple, and constituted the last solid meal the worshippers would eat on that day and the next. Early in the afternoon the participants went in procession to the great *chörten* and *mani*-wall at the south side of Khumjung and twice circumambulated the long wall. A few women wanted to gain special merit by doing a third circumambulation, whereas some very old and frail people did not join in the procession and circumambulated the temple only. All participants were barefoot throughout the performance of the Niungne, and this underlined the procession's character as an act of penance.

Before re-entering the temple the participants sat down in the open space outside the temple walls and the *pembu* of Kunde and one of the lamas read out a story from what appeared to be a recently written manuscript. The story related to the origin of the Niungne, but the atmosphere at this reading was relaxed and cheerful, and it was clear that it did not form part of the liturgical proceedings.

Afterwards all returned to the temple and took up their seats. Three times on that day, and three times on the following day, the participants had to recite a long prayer for the forgiveness of sins, and while doing this they had to prostrate themselves repeatedly, touching the floor with their foreheads. This is known as *chak-cho-lu*, and when I counted the number of prostrations during one recitation I found that most of the worshippers prostrated themselves 90 times. This however, is not a prescribed figure, and some of the older participants and even the leading lama prostrated themselves only at greater intervals, altogether perhaps 25 times. Each of the three times the *chak-cho-lu* is performed, the appropriate prayer is recited 21 times, i.e. 63 times a day. The prayer begins with an invocation of various gods and saints. The worshippers describe themselves as sinners and pray to be freed of all sufferings. They offer their lands and their wealth, their images and shrines to the gods, they invoke Ngawa Taiye Urkien (an aspect of Padmasambhava), they invoke the serpent deities (*lu*) of the four quarters and pay respect to the fierce, man-eating spirits (*dü*). They revere Pawa Cheresi (Avalokiteśvara) and pray that their bodies and minds may become one with Pawa Cheresi. To him they offer everything visible and audible and beg that in the future their minds may become like those of gods.

Not all of the worshippers know this whole prayer by heart, and those who do not repeat a few phrases with the same intention. But the more educated of my lay informants emphasized the urge to identify themselves with Pawa Cheresi and thereby to obtain release from the effects of all sins. I do not know of any single other rite regularly performed by laymen in which there is so strong a stress on the expiation of sins, although obviously every merit-producing act serves to balance to a greater or lesser extent the ill-effects of sinful acts.

Throughout the second day of the Niungne the lamas and lay participants remained in the temple, except for a circumambulation of the great *mani*-wall. Though they recited and chanted, they were not supposed to speak to each other or any one else. They observed a strict fast, and did not even drink water. Some of the worshippers took the ban on swallowing anything so literally that they even spat out accumulated saliva rather than swallow it.

The three appointed *lawa* saw to it that there were always sufficient butter lamps burning, and they and their wives also busied themselves with preparations for the next day's *tsho*, which involved the offering of great quantities of food. Numerous *tsho-torma* already stood on the altar and more and more food offerings were placed in front of it. There was great activity in the temple kitchen, and now and then groups of women brought gifts of food for the *tsho* and deposited them inside the temple wall.

The celebration of the Niungne incidentally coincided with the last two days of the annual recitation of the Kangyur, and the lamas engaged on this task had to be moved to the covered gallery surrounding the temple courtyard. Their payment and ceremonial send-off with many cups of *yangdzi* beer had to take place in the temple kitchen because the main hall was occupied by the Niungne worshippers. The latter spent the whole night in the temple, sleeping, as well as they could, under blankets or in mountaineering sleeping-bags. Before going to sleep and again early in the morning, they did the prostrations connected with the *chak-cho-lu*, but there was no service during the night.

Next morning the worshippers went to their houses, broke their fast, put on shoes and, in some cases, hats, and later in the morning returned to the temple. With them came many of the villagers, who had not taken part in the Niungne, and the temple was soon filled. Great quantities of potatoes, buckwheat cakes, puffed maize and *tsho-torma* made of boiled rice had been placed as offerings before the altar, and this *tsho* food was now distributed to all comers.

This was followed by a brief service with recitations and the playing of instruments, and the Niungne *lawa* then offered *yangdzi* beer to the two most senior lamas. Next the lama who had acted as *chorpen* of the Niungne rite began the preparation for the *Tshewong*, the rite of 'Life-Consecration',[1] to be conducted by Gelung Ngawang, the senior lama. The first to receive the blessing and the 'communion' were the *lawa* and their wives, and then followed all

[1] This rite is described in greater detail on pp. 214–16.

others present. There was a good deal of good-tempered pushing, as everybody pressed forward, but something like a queue finally formed, and every one passed the lamas, to be touched in blessing by Gelung Ngawang with a ritual wand (*dādar*) and receive holy water, life-pellets (*tshe-ril*) and consecrated beer from the other lamas. This concluded the celebration and the crowd dispersed.

Dumje—The Great Festival of the Village Temple

Whereas Osho is a rite performed for the benefit of the village community, but conducted by only a few *ex officio* participants, and the Niungne is a purely religious rite, benefiting those who join in the prayers and fasting but of little concern to the majority of the community, the Dumje, usually held within a month after the Niungne and never much later than the first part of July, is the one festival which involves nearly every member of the village community and serves as an annual expression of the unity of all those who share one temple. For six days the Dumje celebrations absorb the entire energy of the villagers and all other work rests. Only a very few men and boys, indispensable for looking after the yak herds, remain at that time at the high *yersa* settlements, but by taking turns in helping each other, even those herdsmen manage frequently to join in the Dumje celebrations for at least one or two days. It is during the Dumje that the villagers are united the last time for many weeks to come. Immediately afterwards begins the general exodus to the summer settlements in the regions high above the tree-line.

The Dumje is a true village festival in the sense that the preparation of food and drink for its celebration is not left to individual initiative, but is a responsibility of the village community as a whole, discharged through a number of appointed representatives, known as Dumje *lawa*. Although *lawa* are appointed also to arrange for the Niungne and various minor rites, the tasks of the Dumje *lawa* are incomparably more onerous and important, for to them falls the provision of food and ample drink for the entire community throughout the duration of the festival.

The significance of the Dumje is far from clear. The Sherpas themselves take it to be the celebration of the anniversary of the death of their patron saint Lama Sanga Dorje, comparable perhaps with the Tsho ceremonies held annually in honour of the founder and late abbot of Tengboche monastery. This, however, does not tally with the fact that in Tengboche a rite similar to the Dumje (but there referred to as Lokpar) is performed in the month of Chuniwa, which is approximately February, without any reference being made to Lama Sanga Dorje. A few weeks earlier an annual memorial rite is performed for Lama Gulu, and any similar observance in honour of Lama Sanga Dorje would certainly be described specifically as such. In view of its central position in the social life of a village, it might be interpreted as a Buddhist adaptation of an older seasonal festival, preceding the annual dispersal of the village community over the high pastures. Against such an interpretation stands the evidence of the essential link between the Dumje rite and the village temple. While the Osho, a seasonal rite connected with the welfare of the crops, as well as the *lhachetu* after the return of the herds in the autumn, are performed in all villages and do not include any temple ritual, the Dumje can only be performed in a public temple. The earliest Dumje celebrations in Khumbu were held in Pangboche and in Thami, and just as the people of Phortse, who have no village temple of their own, still attend the Dumje at Pangboche, so the people of Khumjung and Kunde used to go to Thami. Once there was a quarrel over the celebrations, and the people of Khumjung and Kunde decided to build their own temple and celebrate the Dumje independently. Namche Bazar took the same course, and today the Dumje is celebrated in Pangboche, Thami, Kerok, Khumjung and Namche Bazar.

For the celebration of the Dumje Khumjung and Kunde act as a single unit and the *lawa* are chosen from a combined list of the householders of both villages which is kept by the *chorumba* of the temple. Service as *lawa* goes strictly by rotation and every year eight *lawa* have to be chosen, and sometimes a ninth is elected to allow for emergencies. A householder's turn to act as *lawa* comes approximately once in fourteen years and the task is allotted to a household rather than to its individual head. If the selected *lawa* dies between appointment and the Dumje his task has to be taken over by the widow or any son who had been living in the father's household. People know when their turn is likely to come and many men have to save for a long time to be able to meet the expenditure incurred in acting as *lawa*. The lavishness of the entertainment of the villagers varies, of course, with the economic resources of the individual *lawa*, but an expenditure of about Rs.500 on rice, beer, feeding and payment of lamas and provision of the raw materials for *torma* is normal for a householder of average means. There have been cases of Khamba immigrants who left the village rather than face the obligations of a *lawa*, but when it is the turn of a really poor man to act as *lawa* the leading men of the village may change the order of rotation so as to give him some respite. Permanent exemption from the duties of *lawa*, however, is irreconcilable with full membership of the village community, and it is a matter of pride even for poor men to discharge their obligations of *lawa*, and to repay thereby the free food and drink provided in past years by other villagers acting as *lawa*.

For all those not acting as *lawa* the Dumje is a carefree occasion, and one when rich and poor join in the celebrations on equal terms. The Dumje is also a time of gaiety and merry-making, and the young people, never very restrained in joking and flirtations, enjoy a special licence for horseplay and amorous adventures.

The Dumje lasts for eight days, the first two of which are taken up with preparations that concern only the *lawa* and the lamas engaged in the ritual performances. In view of the importance ascribed by the Sherpas to the Dumje celebrations which are a highlight of the year and in a sense comparable to Christmas in Western countries, a descriptive outline of the procedure as I observed it in Khumjung in July 1957 will not be out of place.

The customary number of *lawa* is eight, but as in 1956 one *lawa*, a Khamba immigrant, had evaded his duty, the leading men of the village decided to appoint for 1957 altogether nine *lawa*. Three of these were men of Kunde, and the rest were Khumjung people. Among these were two widows who had to act as *lawa* because it would have been their husbands' turn had they lived, and the widows represented their respective households. One of the selected *lawa*, the old Lama Kiu, had died some weeks before the Dumje, but the duty of acting as *lawa* passed automatically to his heirs living in his house and was discharged by his *maksu* son-in-law. The three *lawa* of Kunde moved for the duration of the festival to the houses of kinsmen or friends in Khumjung. This is a general practice and no Kunde *lawa* ever entertains in his own village, though it is only about ten minutes' walk from Khumjung to Kunde, but moves with his entire family and large quantities of provisions and drink to a borrowed house in Khumjung.

The first day of the Dumje is known as *Koma-bang-up*,[1] and in the morning of this day the village lamas practised the recitation of the liturgy. The death of Lama Kiu, the most senior lama of the twin settlements, had left a gap in the ritual life of Khumjung and Kunde, and the other lamas, missing his guidance, took advantage of the presence of an experienced lama of Phortse to rehearse the recitations. They sometimes interrupted the chanting to discuss doubtful points, and marked their books in pencil. Among them were two men well in their fifties and the care with which they prepared for the ceremonies was proof of a sense of responsibility, in sharp contrast to the attitude of Nepalese village Brahmans, most of whom will recite Sanskrit texts without worrying about the exact meaning of individual passages. The Sherpas, on the other hand, do not, on the whole, chant automatically, but are anxious to understand the text they are reciting.

After the Kunde *lawa* had moved to Khumjung in procession, all the nine *lawa* assembled in the house of the *chorpen* of the temple. Each *lawa* had brought a bottle of beer, and one was provided by the *chorpen*. A little beer from each of these bottles was mixed together in a flask and sprinkled to the accompaniment of a blessing. After much of the beer had been consumed, the *lawa* proceeded to fix the sequence in which they would entertain the villagers. The *chorpen* produced nine small stones, different in shape and colour. Every *lawa* selected one of these stones, which were then placed into a flat dish. A young man, both of whose parents were alive, then held the dish above his head and drew out one stone after the other, and produced it before the *lawa*. The sequence in which the stones had been drawn indicated the sequence in which the *lawa* were to discharge their responsibility of acting as host to the village.

Subsequently the selection of *lawa* for the various tasks connected with the driving out of evil spirits and the disposal of the Lokpar *torma* (cf. p. 201) on the seventh day took place in a similar fashion, though at this time pieces of wool were used instead of stones.

The *chorpen* should have provided the butter required for the decoration of the *torma*, but as he had failed in this duty, three of the *lawa* brought the required amount as a personal contribution. This butter was finally mixed with red dye and kept ready for use in the fashioning of *torma* on the following day.

[1] *Koma* is a red dye used in the preparation of *torma*.

Burning the Lok-par *torma* at the Dumje rite

A festive crowd in Khumjung

Weighing butter for the Yer-chang offerings

Dorje Ngungdu re-dedicating a yak at the Yer-chang rite

At this first meeting of the nine *lawa* there prevailed an air of friendliness and complete informality. One of the chosen *lawa*, a Khamba of *khamendeu* class, was clearly socially inferior to the other office-bearer, but no outsider seeing him joke and laugh with the *chorpen* and the other office-bearers would have thought that he was not their social equal.

The second day, known as *Gentako-up*, was devoted mainly to the decoration of the wooden boards used in the construction of *torma*. The three lamas of Khumjung, and Kapa Kalden, the well-known painter, gathered in the house of Dorje Ngungdu, who not only acted as *lawa* but also held the more permanent office of temple *chorumba*. Each of the *lawa* then brought about 2 lb. of butter, which was weighed and then passed on to the lamas making the decorations for the *torma*. The butter was mixed with various dyes, and each lama placed lumps of coloured butter on a brass plate. They thus proceeded to cover flat wooden boards, to be used in the construction of the main *torma*, with layers of butter in different colours. This is a task requiring both skill and aesthetic sense. Butter is not a particularly easy medium for the modelling of intricate patterns, and every lama had a brass bowl filled with cold water, and into this he dipped lumps of butter before giving them any particular shape. One of the lamas arranged cones of coloured butter on a tablet, like colours on a palette, and then moulded flower petals and leaves of butter in various pastel colours and arranged them in a floral design on one set of boards. Kapa Kalden, the painter, on the other hand, painted scrolls of black ink on to a pattern of tile-like butter-pats.

Throughout these activities, which lasted for most of the day, there was an atmosphere of conviviality and quiet gaiety. Beer and tea were served, and everybody drank a good deal, but no one got drunk. There was conversation, and now and then some laughter, but no one was distracted from the work in hand. In the course of the proceedings Gelung Ngawang arrived after a two days' journey from his hermitage above Dingboche. He was exhausted after the long climb from the Dudh Kosi to Khumjung, but said that it would have been a 'sin' to burden a pony with his heavy weight—if he had done so, he might have to carry the pony himself in his next life, when the rôles might be reversed.

When the work on the butter decoration was over, guests were entertained with food and drink, provided by all the nine *lawa*.

Theoretically all inhabitants of the village could have come and joined in the meal, and had they availed themselves of this right, the food prepared would have been inadequate. In practice only a few close friends and neighbours of Dorje Ngundu came in and partook of the food.

At dusk groups of young boys and girls gathered in open spaces, and amused themselves with the rough horse-play and wrestling beloved by the young of both sexes in Khumbu. There were shrieks of laughter as boys and girls tumbled over each other in struggling heaps, and older people watched the play with tolerant smiles. An elderly woman explained to me that at the time of Dumje anyone may join in such horse-play and even middle-aged matrons would not resent being pulled about by drunken men.

The third day of the Dumje, known as *Drup-shak*, was devoted mainly to the making of the *torma* and the setting up of the altar in the village temple. The wooden boards, completely covered with patterns and mouldings in vivid colours, which had been prepared the previous day, had been deposited there already the evening before, and so cool is the climate of Khumbu, that even at the height of the summer the delicate butter mouldings had remained fresh and firm. Now the lamas began the construction of the dough figures to which these boards were to be attached. For this task they were joined by several helpers and the great hall of the temple of Khumjung was soon transformed into a workshop where huge quantities of parched barley-flour were mixed with water and butter, and then kneaded into a stiff dough of a brown colour. This and rice, cooked so long until it formed a solid, sticky mass, were the raw materials from which the great *torma* for the centre of the altar as well as a multitude of minor figures were to be moulded.

Each major *torma* has to have a form prescribed by tradition in every detail of design and symbol, and even experienced lamas work with the help of coloured hand-painted pattern books.

They first build up the main structure of such a *torma* by moulding barley dough or boiled rice into flat blocks and cubes, and placing these one on top of the other. A wooden stick on which each layer is impaled serves as a support for the whole structure, and the basic shape of most figures thus formed is a kind of stepped pyramid. But the spire-like upper part moulded around the upright stick has a more elaborate form depending on the divinity with which the *torma* is to be associated. The various layers may alternatively be parched barley-flour and rice, but when the figure is completed neither the brown nor the white material remains visible. For as soon as the dough figure is complete it is partly covered with a thin layer of coloured butter and partly painted red. Then the curved, wooden boards decorated with butter design are attached to the figure and frame it like a halo. An important feature of the decoration is very thin circular and moon-shaped discs of uncoloured butter; these are attached not only to the principal, elaborately constructed *torma* but even to the smaller ones representing minor divinities and sacrificial offerings. For the Dumje four great *torma* are constructed, known as Rena, Rigsin, Thukdubans and Drowa-Kundröl. The first two symbolize the saints Rinsing Rena Lingpa, a disciple of Guru Rimpoche, and Lama Rigsin (Vidyādhara, 'Knowledge Holder'), whereas the latter two are associated with two books of the same name. It is a general practice to make for every rite the *torma* appropriate to the books to be recited.

On the occasion of the Khumjung Dumje rite each of the senior lamas undertook the task of constructing one of these *torma*, but another lama specially skilled in the modelling of butter designs helped with the final decoration in one or two cases. The painter Kapa Kalden, in the meanwhile, was busy constructing the Lokpar *torma*, which symbolizes the demon whose ritual destruction forms the climax of the Dumje rites. This figure was quite different from other *torma* and made not of rice and *tsampa* dough, but of the darker buckwheat dough. It was painted black and red, with scrolls representing hellish flames, and miniature models of human skulls were hoisted above it on thin poles.

While the lamas shaped the principal *torma*, other helpers busied themselves making small dough models of various sacrificial animals and innumerable conical *torma* to be used as offerings. Throughout the day the lamas and their helpers were served beer, tea and food, provided by the *lawa* of the day. As there was an uneven number of *lawa*, only one had been appointed for this day, when the ceremonies are not yet in full swing, whereas two *lawa* were in charge of the arrangements for each of the subsequent four days of the festival.

The day was well advanced when all the *torma* were at last completed and the altar could be set up. The colourful principal *torma*, now resplendent with their decorations of butter-covered wing-like boards, were placed on the highest tier. Below them were representations of minor deities and still lower were set out the offerings for the deities to be invoked in the ritual: those appealing to the seven senses of benevolent calm deities, and those more horrific demanded by bloodthirsty fierce divinities. While the texts of the liturgy prescribe offerings of blood and human flesh, the gentle and sophisticated Sherpas, as indeed is nowadays the practice also throughout Tibet, substitute for these such inoffensive substances as tea and barley dough, modelling from the latter realistic representations of human limbs. Three cups made of genuine human skulls must always be present, and they are made more gruesome by the addition of teeth and soft parts modelled in butter of various colours.

The brass lamps filled with butter were now lit, and their flickering light played on the *torma* and newly gilded faces of the temple statues throughout the ceremonies. Whenever a set of these lamps had burnt out others were filled and lit, and the number of those burning was increased during the actual services.

A *mandala* painted on a cloth was firmly suspended above the altar like a canopy, and half an hour later the first rites of the Dumje began. The lamas, the nine *lawa* and a small crowd of villagers formed a procession, and walked round the *gomba* clockwise, the lamas offering a libation (*sirkim*) and playing instruments. Four *torma*, representing the guardians of the four quarters (*gyal-dzen-deshi*), were set up on stones at the four corners of the *gomba*, and in this way the temple was made safe from supernatural dangers.

The procession then entered the courtyard, which was now crowded with people. Two lamas blew the long, telescopic horns (*sange*), and the other lamas played cymbals, a large drum and a thigh-bone flute. Then followed the stabbing and burial of a figure made of *tsampa* dough which represents the evil spirit, whose destruction is thought of as one of the main purposes of the Dumje ritual. The disposal of the *tsampa* doll did not take long, however. Gelung Ngawang, the senior lama standing in the temple courtyard just outside the door leading into the main halls of the *gomba*, was given the dough figure, and pierced it with his ritual dagger. He then threw it into a small pit excavated in front of the steps, and the other lamas placed earth and water on it, and then covered the pit with three flat stones, one on top of the other. All lamas then stood round the pit, reciting and playing instruments, and finally placed their feet on the cover-stone.

The *tsampa* doll buried in the temple courtyard is the first of three such figures to be destroyed in the course of the Dumje. They are all representations of the fiend referred to in a book recited several times in the course of the rites.

The full title of this text is *Tamdzen-dzi-kangso chen-mo go-det re-kong-tin-le khi puti rana ling-pi yar-tam zukso*. The following summary of the contents is not based on a literal translation, but represents the meaning ascribed to the text by the Sherpa lamas of Khumjung.

Like other liturgical books this text begins with instructions to the performers. It begins with the promise that anyone afflicted by enemies and evil spirits will attain protection if this text is recited. Then follow some *mantra* in Sanskrit the exact meaning of which is not known to the Sherpa lamas. Next the text instructs the lamas to burn the fat from the heart of a goat—an instruction which is not carried out in Khumbu—and to wave pieces of red cloth while reciting.

The next pages contain invocations of gods which according to the book's instructions should be impersonated by lama dancers wearing masks. In Khumjung such masks are worn only on the day of Jinsak (cf. p. 200) but the liturgy seems to allow for their wider use. Several pages are then devoted to detailed descriptions of the gods, and my informants thought that these were recited in order to prove to the deities, believed to suspect their worshippers of being ignorant of their true nature, that the lamas are well aware of their appearance and character.

Then comes the phrase: 'This service of blessing is meant not only for you' (i.e. Tamdzen, the god invoked by name), 'but also for other gods—you distribute our tribute among yourselves. I am offering you the things which you eat, now you must do whatever I demand. This is not *my* order, but you have promised to work for me in the beginning of time. If there is a war, lead the forces for me; if there is trade, do the trade for me. Give me whatever I need. I shall remember you, if you do all this for me.'

The text then instructs the lamas to blow conch shells, beat drums and cymbals.

Thereupon follows a recitation in which the offerings are described: 'I am offering you a *torma* as it was in the age of Bhagwan; I am offering you *amrit* (represented by liquor and beer) as it was in the age of Bhagwan; I am offering you the fat of a goat's heart, and the hides of leopards and tigers to please your eyes. Since the age of Bhagwan your residence has been in Tibet.' The seat of the god is then described in detail.

The next sentences are devoted to the praise of the deity: 'I am not the only one who worships you, but all gods, *lu* (serpent-spirits), *shrindi* (evil ghosts) worship you.'

The lama is then instructed to beat his drum from the reverse side, like a spirit-caller (*lhawa*).

Up to this part of the text, the invocations were directed to the god Tamdzen, but the following pages contain similar invocations of other gods. They are begged to help in the fight against the fiend in such phrases as: 'You who are riding on a lion, confound the enemy who is troubling me; collect all the warriors from this land, kill the enemy, and destroy his wife, children and fields.'

Next the reasons for the fight against the enemy are given: 'Because he hinders the recitations of great incarnate lamas, and troubles the ordinary people, he must be overcome. I shall give you all the weapons you need in this fight: spears, swords, guns, medicines to make people lose their reason, ropes to tie the vanquished. Bring him in fetters before me.'

The next section of the book assumes that the demonic enemy has been vanquished by the gods and brought before the lamas in fetters. The enemy has now to be tried and sentenced, and all the great gods are called to witness the trial. 'Before all these witnesses I declare that I was engaged in religious work for the benefit of the people, but this enemy interfered with my devotions.'

The enemy is tried and the unanimous verdict is that he is a criminal and shall be killed and buried in a pit. The next passage is directly addressed to the vanquished fiend: 'You had a bad dream today, because you are to be buried. As you are a criminal there is no one to help you. You are completely ruined.'

Thereupon follows a Sanskrit *mantra* which the lama is to recite holding a dagger in his hand. During this recitation a triangular pit is to be dug.

The following passages are again addressed to the vanquished fiend: 'You are not the only being to be buried here; all other evil beings are buried with you; all those who gave trouble to great lamas and to the common people.' The text then explains that the fiend used to appear in many shapes, sometimes in human and sometimes in animal shape. He did much harm to traders and damaged household property, and he misled many lamas, making them believe that they stood on level ground, when they were on precipices, and thus caused their death. He killed old people before their time, and turned the dead into *shrindi* and *norpa* (two types of evil ghosts). 'But now you will not be able to do further mischief, because you are fettered and you are going to be buried in a triangular pit. You are now tied up in a black cloth, tied with threads of five colours and sealed five times.'

All lamas should then grasp some weapons. The following sentences again taunt the fiend: 'You have dreamt to dwell in a house built of conch shells, but this is not a house of conch shells, but it is the skull of a dog into which you have been put.' (In practice the *tsampa* doll representing the fiend is usually not buried in the skull of a dog or any other animal.) 'In your dreams you have seen rafters, but these are now the seals with which we have enclosed you. You dreamt of wearing many ornaments, but these are the five coloured threads with which you are tied. You dreamt that you slept in a pleasant cave, but this is a triangular pit.'

The text here contains an apparent diversion, which begins with a description of the god Jambal Nagpu. This god is believed to have given instructions regarding the occasion when the text is to be recited and the rite of burying the demonic fiend performed. This section contains instructions not connected with the Dumje, such as the advice to perform the rite in times of epidemic or in the event of a series of amorous intrigues between monks and nuns, such as may be caused at the instigation of the enemy.

The final words to the enemy run approximately as follows: 'On account of your misdeeds you are going down to hell, and Shinjechogyal (Yama Raj, the Lord of the Dead) will remind you of your crimes.'

Then follows an invocation of all the deities present. They are not specifically addressed by name, but are requested to keep watch over the pit. 'Guard over this enemy until the crows grow white feathers, the dogs grow horns, and sun and moon fall from the sky. Only if the enemy abandons thoughts of evil deeds and becomes a devotee of Chum-dende (Bhagwan) may he emerge from the pit in the shape of the syllable HUM.'

With these words ends the part of the text which relates directly to the burial of the *tsampa* doll in the temple courtyard. The rest of the book describes in much the same vein the destruction of the fiend by burning, and this part is appropriate to the disposal of the Lokpar *torma*.

At the Dumje celebrations in Khumjung the rite of burying the representation of the demon was followed by the return of lamas, *lawa* and other villagers to the hall of the temple. The lamas installed themselves on seats placed parallel with the altar, and the prominent men of Khumjung occupied the two benches standing at right angles to the altar. Kunde was represented by one lama and the three Kunde *lawa*, but otherwise none of the more prominent men of Kunde attended this part of the celebrations.

A short recitation by the lamas opened the proceedings. It appeared that they were not very familiar with the text, for now and then they had to search for the appropriate pages. Then followed the distribution of food and drink by the *lawa* of the day, a widow of moderate means who could not afford to serve rice but had prepared large quantities of flat cakes made of buckwheat and potatoes as well as some maize beer. Her relatives and friends handed out the food to the men and women seated in the temple hall, and ladled out the beer into the drinking cups, which people bring along with them on all such occasions. This distribution did not take long, and as soon as it was completed, the *chorumba* and the *chorpen* got up from their seats, and Dorje Ngungdu, as the *chorumba*, unrolled a long scroll of Nepalese paper, which contained the rules governing the celebration of the Dumje. Two men with lamps lit up the document, and Dorje and a few others then read out its contents.

This document, known as *cha-yik*, is very old and believed to stem from the days of Lama Sanga Dorje. It is always in the safe-keeping of whoever holds the office of *chorumba*, and is read out publicly on the occasion of the Dumje. Its contents can be summarized as follows:

1. It is forbidden: to quarrel in the *gomba*,
    to take weapons to the *gomba*,
    to wear the pigtail wound round the head during *gomba* services,
    to take empty cradles into the *gomba*,
    to spin thread in the *gomba*.

2. The *chorumba* is entitled to punish offenders against these rules with up to 100 strokes of his whip (which he wields at festivals as a sign of his office).
3. No one may complain about the punishments meted out by the *chorumba*. If anyone resists his authority, all the villagers shall combine and bring him before the authorities of the state.
4. May whoever obeys these rules receive wealth as ample as the flow of a river in the month of Dawa Tukpa (i.e. during the rainy season).
   May the wealth of those who offend against these rules be like a water-course running into sand.
5. If someone disobeys the rules seriously and opposes the *chorumba*, he shall be whipped; if he commits a minor offence he shall be fined according to the *chorumba*'s discretion and shall prostrate himself one hundred times in the *gomba*.

After the reading of these rules, beer from two vessels standing in front of the altar—one provided by the *chorpen* and one by the *lawa* of the day—was served to selected men who, standing in the aisle between the two benches, faced the altar and sang a solemn chant of the type sung also at the Niungne.

Soon afterwards most of the congregation dispersed. Only the lamas and *chorpen* and *chorumba* stayed on for the performance of a *tsho*, a sacrificial rite, which lasted until midnight.

On the fourth day of the Dumje, known as *Thē*, two *lawa*, Dorje Ngungdu, who was also the *chorumba*, and Urken, a Khamba of *khamendeu* status, acted as *lawa*. The rice they had provided was cooked in the courtyard of the temple, and when cooled made into balls similar to those distributed at memorial feasts. In the morning, there were some minor recitations inside the temple, but public ceremonies started only in the early afternoon, when an altar-table was set up in the courtyard in preparation for the performance of a *lhapsang* rite. Low tables and seats for the lamas were then arranged in such a way that the lamas, turning their backs to the *gomba*, faced the altar and the great prayer flag raised in the centre of the courtyard. While they recited a *sirkim* and then a *lhapsang* text, the villagers arrived singly and in groups, each carrying a flag, known as *lungtar tarshing*, consisting of a thin bamboo pole with squares of white and coloured cloth attached to it. These they tied to the main flag-pole, threw some offerings of rice over the altar and bowed to the senior lama. A few old men of prominent status were invited to sit down next to the lamas, but all others joined the rapidly growing circle of spectators.

The lamas' recitation had gone on for some time when there was suddenly a rush of young boys for the *tarshing* tied to the prayer flag. Each took two or three and carried them out of the temple courtyard. About half were put up on a shrine immediately in front of the temple, and with the other half the boys climbed the hill-slope above the village, as far as a big rock, on which there were still the tattered remains of the flags put up the previous year. None of the lamas had left the temple courtyard, but the *chorpen*, and a young man carrying a bottle of beer and some incense, had followed the boys. They all climbed the rock, burnt incense and sprinkled beer, and then put up the new flags in the name of Khumbu-yülha, the mountain god worshipped as the local protector of Khumbu.

While the *tarshing* were erected on the rock sacred to Khumbu-yülha the lamas continued the recitation of the text of the *lhapsang*. At one juncture, a dispute arose about a technical point in the procedure. Two of the lamas maintained that a *lhang-ma* offering should be thrown to the evil spirits (*shrindi*), whereas two others maintained that this was not required by the liturgy. Gelung Ngawang, the hermit and revered ex-monk of Tengboche, though senior to all and nominally presiding over the rites, did not express an opinion in order to avoid offending either side. Sharap Lama, who had drunk an enormous amount of beer, got exceedingly angry, and folding up his book, was about to rush away in a huff. Several bystanders tried to placate him and would not let him get up. The other lamas started intoning their chant, and Sharap Lama, gradually calming down, re-opened his book and soon joined in the recitation.

During the afternoon most of the villagers visited the houses of the two *lawa*. There they were entertained with liquor and beer. The serving of the drink was done in a very formal way. Each seated guest was handed a filled cup, and the men serving, usually two or three, then stood in front of him, holding a flask, and sang a short chant, at the end of which the guest had to empty the cup, which was at once refilled. Though guests are not expected to stay too long, but to make room for other villagers, there was heavy drinking in both the houses of *lawa*, as well as at many private parties.

Most of the villagers were therefore in a gay mood when before sunset they streamed back towards the temple. Old and young were dressed in their best, and a holiday spirit animated the crowd despite the intermittent rain usual at that time of the year. The main hall of the temple was soon packed with the prominent men sitting in the two central benches, and all the rest of the crowd on the floor. While the lamas resumed their recitation the crowd awaited the distribution of the rice prepared by the two *lawa*. The prominent men sitting behind low tables were served their share on brass plates, these plates being handed through the crowd with shouts of their owners' names. Most other people were given rice-balls, intended to be taken home, the crush in the temple virtually excluding the possibility of eating a meal then and there.

While this distribution, by itself a rather noisy affair, was in progress, there were suddenly angry shouts from the part of the hall where the Kunde men were sitting. Several of them stood up, and shouted abuse at some of the men of Khumjung. The *chorpen* and *chorumba* tried to quieten the men, but failed at first to make much impact. The noise grew rapidly as more and more men took sides, and suddenly there was a scuffle at the back of the temple hall. Calls to order were of no avail, until Dorje Ngungdu suddenly jumped up, seized his *chorumba* whip, conveniently hanging on the post next to his seat—and with astonishing speed and energy belaboured the unruly elements. As the leather thongs of the whip cracked through the air, it seemed for a moment as if there would be a free fight, and anxious women quickly sheltered near their husbands.

A few well-aimed strokes of the *chorumba*'s leather whip brought the crowd to their senses, and the tussle between those at the back of the hall came to a stop. Shouting continued, but those itching for a fight were held back by wives and friends, and the distribution of rice was resumed. The lamas too, who had been helpless spectators of the brawl, resumed their interrupted recitations.

The incident, which had released a feeling of antagonism between the men of Kunde and Khumjung, seems to have been trivial. It sprang from a chance remark made in jest by the *chorumba*'s brother, a somewhat eccentric bachelor, which was taken seriously by some Kunde men. Peace-makers were soon busy reconciling the opponents, and particularly one of the *pembu* excelled in these efforts. The man, who had shouted most abusively at the *chorumba*'s brother, was finally persuaded to come forward and bow before him in a gesture of reconciliation.

Though my informants tended to belittle the incident by explaining that the trouble-makers had been drinking too much, the outburst seemed symptomatic of a rivalry between the two villages which is normally not apparent.

On the fifth day of Dumje, which is also known as *Thē*, there was a somewhat similar commotion, but this time the Kunde men seemed to have a genuine grievance. They demanded that only lamas and those who contributed to temple funds, either by gifts of butter or otherwise, should be allowed to sit in seats of honour, whereas the *gomba* officials, all of whom were Khumjung men, allowed certain of their co-villagers to continue in the use of the benches, even though they no longer helped in meeting temple expenditure. This time the Kunde party was led by the powerful *pembu*, Ang Chumbi, and another rich man. Harmony was restored with difficulty, and there remained for a while a feeling of bitterness about the quarrel. Otherwise the procedure of the fifth day of Dumje was similar to that of the previous day. The two *lawa* responsible for the day's arrangements entertained the villagers in their houses and distributed food in the temple.

In the late evening, however, there was the performance of the Jinsak rite which symbolized the destruction of the fiend described in the book. In the temple courtyard, close to the steps leading into the *gomba*, a raised triangular platform of earth was moulded, and one of the lamas drew on this, within a few minutes, a rough design of white flour.[1] Above this triangle a tripod bearing a frying-pan was set up, and the pan filled with butter.

In the covered gallery along the front of the *gomba* a seat for the lamas was then prepared. They emerged from the temple hall dressed in rich Chinese silk robes. All reading the same book, the lamas began to recite, but at one point interrupted the recitation unable to decide about a passage in the text. Finally one of the lamas brought another copy of the same book, and with the help of this the problem was solved and the reciting continued.

A fire was lit on the triangular 'altar' and various substances

[1] In Namche Bazar where the reincarnate abbot and the monks of Tengboche perform the Dumje celebration, this altar for the burnt offerings is covered with an elaborate sand painting in several colours.

such as grain, butter, honey and grass were burnt in it as offerings.¹ A human figure moulded in *tsampa* dough was then placed before the lamas, and they were handed, one after the other, miniature weapons which form part of the Dumje requisites. Gelung Ngawang as the senior lama hit and pierced with each weapon the *tsampa* representation of the demonic fiend; the mangled parts of the figure were finally thrown into the fire.

The lamas then rose and stood in their shiny silken gowns close to the glow of the fire. Gelung Ngawang then threw a measure of the strongest liquor into the frying-pan and, as the alcohol caught fire, an enormous sheet of flame shot up. This was repeated three times, and as the flames lit up the courtyard there were loud shouts of joy over the burning of the fiend. Finally the lama wearing a blue mask danced for a few moments, and then ran into the temple accompanied by shouts and cheering. By that time it was long past midnight and the villagers slowly dispersed to their houses.

The sixth day of the Dumje, like the fourth and fifth, is called *Thē*. *Pung-chang* was served in the houses of the two *lawa* of the day, one of them being a house lent for the purpose by a resident of Khumjung. Both *lawa* provided only cakes made of buckwheat and potato for distribution in the temple, and there was no repetition of the two previous days' quarrel. The seats for the prominent men were carefully kept unoccupied until after the Kunde men's arrival, and as Ang Chumbi, the *pembu* of Kunde, did not attend, his small son, aged some eight or nine years, sat in one of the seats of honour close to the altar.

The distribution of the cakes was followed by the preparation for the disposal of the Lokpar *torma*, which represents the universal enemy. The *torma* was carried from the temple hall into the courtyard, and the lamas installed themselves with their books in a row of seats facing the *torma*. They recited from the book *Tamdzen-dzi-kangso* the passages relating to the burning of the demonic fiend. In this numerous gods are begged to be present and asked to help in the fight against the enemy. When they have been summoned, various tasks are allotted to the gods, and clapping their hands the lamas say: 'May illnesses and epidemics go to the enemy, may skin-disease and the twenty-five diseases which produce madness go to the

---

¹ These were the same as those burnt at a funeral on the pyre, except that seven instead of five pieces were burnt of every item. Cf. p. 233.

enemy, may all *sem* (spirits of dead men) and all *lu* (serpent-spirits) attack the enemy, may you (i.e. the invited deities) curse the enemy and smite him with arrows and swords.'

The same book describes in detail the procedure to be followed in the final disposal of the Lokpar *torma*, and lays down that a human figure moulded of dough should be placed near the *torma* and ultimately destroyed.

This phase of the ritual requires the presence of a man dressed in a sheepskin coat, worn with the fur outside, and a conical cap made ostensibly from the skin of a *yeti*. This person, known as *gemaka*, is armed with bow and arrow, and carries a round shield. The rôle of *gemaka* is not popular, and in Khumjung a poor Khamba was hired to play it for a wage of Rs.$4\frac{1}{2}$. He stood throughout the ceremony at the entrance door to the temple courtyard, and later accompanied the procession to the village boundary where the Lokpar *torma* was burnt. The function of the *gemaka* is obscure, and the Sherpas know only that his presence at this rite is prescribed by custom.[1]

As soon as the *gemaka* had taken his stand at the gate, two boys dressed in white and representing *rurang* or skeletons came out of the temple and danced about in the courtyard crowded with spectators. They were soon joined by other dancers wearing demon masks. Their dancing was the untutored jumping about of amateurs, in no way comparable to the skilful and disciplined dancing of the lamas of monasteries. Though built into a ritual context, and no doubt inspired by the dances which the Khumjung people see in the monasteries of Tengboche and Thami, those dances at the Dumje were clearly intended to amuse the spectators, and there was a good deal of horse-play incompatible with the character of a ritual dance. As at the Mani-rimdu at Thami, there also appeared a dancer, wearing the mask of a very old man, and supporting himself on a stick. This figure, representing extreme old age, was greeted with a burst of laughter. Even small boys took part in the fun, donning masks much too large for their size, and hopping about in the temple courtyard.

The dancing lasted only about twenty minutes, and when it had come to an end the lamas had completed their recitation, a pro-

---

[1] There is possibly a connection between the *gemaka* and two men in similar attire who act as 'scape-goats of the *glud*' gong ceremony during the New Year celebrations in Lhasa. Cf. R. de Nebesky-Wojkowitz, *Oracles and Demons of Tibet*, s'-Gravenhage, 1956, p. 508.

cession formed very similar to that concluding the Tsirim rite (p. 254). A Khamba, paid a fee of half a rupee for the task, lifted the Lokpar *torma*, and carried it out of the courtyard. He had a scarf bound in front of his mouth, in order to minimize contamination by the representation of evil. Followed by the *gemaka*, the lamas and a small crowd of men and boys, he carried the *torma* to a place outside the village close to the path to Namche Bazar, where a deep pit had already been dug.

Here the Lokpar *torma* was put down, and at some distance from it the *tsampa* figure of the evil spirit. Lamas and boys then threw stones at the figure, symbolically killing the fiend. The lamas recited from a book and, as it was raining heavily, two men sheltered it with a small tarpaulin. The lamas' chant was a renewed invocation of the gods, whose help was required to conquer the universal enemy. It concluded with the words, 'You gods in heaven, you serpent-spirits (*lu*), I do not coerce you. If you wish to help me, do so, if you do not want to help me, remain quiet. If the enemy is already present, I shall throw the *torma* on him, if he is not here, then bring him here, while I throw the *torma*.'

Uttering threatening shouts, lamas and *gemaka* brandished weapons, and the senior lama shot an arrow from an ancient bow in the direction of the shattered *tsampa* figure. Finally a fire was lit in the pit, and as the flames were shooting up, the senior lama threw the Lokpar *torma* into the blaze.

With shouts of victory, the procession left the flames to consume the Lokpar *torma* and returned to the temple. There the lamas resumed their usual seats, and continued their recitations accompanied by the playing of bells, cymbals and drum. Simultaneously the men began to sing dance-songs, and formed a line of dancers in the space between the benches and the door. The wife of a wealthy man, who was not one of the *lawa*, served beer, and one of the lamas handed round a plate of food left from the offerings.

By 11 p.m. the dancing was in full swing, and the lamas had completed their recitation. A line of about forty male dancers was joined by a smaller line of women dancers, who danced with their backs to the book-shelves containing the volumes of the Kangyur, the Buddhist canon. Men and women sang at first alternately, but later their songs mingled, though the lead in the singing continued to alternate between men and women.

Half-grown boys and girls, who did not dance, teased, pinched and pulled each other around, and some young nuns were not immune from these rather crude advances of the boys. Nearly all the butter lamps had burnt down, but the dancing and the amorous play of the very young continued in semi-darkness until late into the night.

Normally there is dancing also out of doors, but during the Dumje, which I attended, it unluckily rained every night, and this hampered the extension of singing and merry-making to the open spaces, where people dance in fine weather.

The seventh and last day of the Dumje is called *Ong-shop*, and on this day a rite of blessing, presided over by the senior lama, crowns the ritual side of the festival. The morning was spent in visits to the two remaining *lawa*, and in the afternoon followed the distribution of food in the temple.

Before the rite of 'Life-Consecration' (*Tshe-wong*) many of the villagers brought plates of maize and buckwheat as gifts for the lamas. This rite was conducted by Gelung Ngawang, and after the usual incantations and offerings, all the villagers filed past him to have their heads touched with his ritual wand (*dādar*).

The *Tshe-wong* was followed by the appointment of the *lawa* for the next year. They had already been chosen by *chorpen* and *chorumba* in accordance with the system of rotation, and they now stood in front of the main altar, each carrying a brass tray containing a white scarf. These scarves were then thrown up to the statue of Guru Rimpoche in such a way that they hung over his arms or shoulders. The new *lawa* were then each given one of the smaller *torma*, and these they took to their houses.

As the altar was being cleared, the three skull-cups were taken off their stands, and old and new *lawa* drank the contents of these gruesome vessels. Finally the large *torma* were lifted down from the altar. Two of them were at once dismantled, and the rice and *tsampa* parts cut up and distributed among the villagers present.

The *torma* Drowa-Kündröl and Thukdub, however, were left intact and given respectively to the verger (*konier*) of the temple, and to the *chorumba* in his capacity of the *lawa* in whose house the decoration of the *torma* had taken place on the first day of the festival. As he carried the *torma* through the temple and the courtyard, worshippers touched its base with their heads in greeting, and this suggests

Dance of the heralds during the Mani-rimdu at Thami

Monks playing flageolets

Monks blowing conch-shells

that as long as the *torma* retains its shape it also retains some measure of sanctity, and that this is dispelled only in the moment of its break-up. Though by that time temple officials, lamas and *lawa* were all extremely tired, small drinking parties were held in various houses, and the *chorumba* himself sang and played on a guitar-like instrument, while his daughter and her friends danced until late at night.

The ritual procedure of the Dumje had come to an end, and the following day most of the villagers returned to their ordinary activities. But the *lawa* gathered on the evening of that day once more in the house of one of their number, and entertained the lamas and some friends at a party where rice and beer were served.

How heavy then is the burden which falls on each *lawa* during the tenure of his office? The expenditure the *lawa* have to meet cannot be easily calculated in money. Men who have ample supplies of potatoes and buckwheat grown on their own fields, or stores of home-made butter, need not purchase any of these commodities, while just the poorer *lawa* have to buy for cash whatever they contribute. Conversely the less affluent *lawa* feed the villagers with the comparatively cheap buckwheat and potato-cakes, whereas richer people take pride in providing large quantities of rice.

There are certain items of expenditure which are met jointly by all the Dumje *lawa*, and rich and poor contribute to these alike. The table on p. 206 shows the joint expenditure of the *lawa*, one ninth of which was borne by each *lawa*, as well as the contributions made individually.

Thus each *lawa* had to spend at least Rs.$31\frac{3}{4}$ before he even started to pay for the food and drink which he had to dispense in entertaining his co-villagers on the day when this task falls to him. Here the expenditure varies according to a *lawa*'s means.

Dorje Ngungdu spent about Rs.400 alone on some 470 lb. of rice, whereas those *lawa* who distributed buckwheat bread spent only some Rs.120 on buckwheat. Dorje Ngungdu spent moreover some Rs.10 on the food and drink for the lamas during the half-day when it was his turn to act as host, and Rs.6 worth of butter for lamps lit on the day. He also spent some Rs.10 on feeding his helpers. The beer dispensed at his house was worth about Rs.30, and whenever people gathered in the house to discuss the preparation for the Dumje they were offered potatoes, which came from his own store.

Adding up these items Dorje Ngungdu's expenditure must have

been close to Rs.500, while the poorer among the *lawa*, who economized by distributing buckwheat bread instead of rice, may have managed within Rs.220. Even that is a large sum for a poor farmer, but the expenditure has to be borne only once in perhaps fifteen years, and whoever has served as Dumje *lawa* knows that for many years to come he and his family will enjoy the year's most important festival without any anxiety about the provision of food and drink.

A. *Joint expenditure in cash:*

Fees to lamas and temple officials	Rs.18
Extra fee to Gelung Ngawang, the senior lama	,, 3
Fee to four lamas and three laymen for decorating *torma*	,, 7
Fee to Khamba acting as *gemaka*	,, 7½
Fee to carrier of Lokpar *torma*	,, ½
	Rs.36

B. *Individual contributions of each* lawa *in kind:*

Butter worth	Rs.6
Rice ,,	,, 6
Tsampa ,,	,, ¾
Beer for second day worth	,, 3
Cash to purchase rice and *tsampa* for the construction of *torma*	,, 6
Wheat flour and eggs to feed the lamas	,, 6
	Rs.27¾

The Dumje, more than any other festival, strengthens the ties between those with a common stake in a *gomba*. Such a community, comparable to a parish, may consist of a single village, such as Namche Bazar, of two twin villages, such as Khumjung and Kunde, or even two villages situated at a considerable distance, such as Pangboche and Phortse. In all these cases the responsibility for holding the Dumje is distributed equally among all the parishioners. The lamas conducting the rites do this not in the capacity of principal organizers, but on behalf, and one may almost say, in the employ of the parishioners. For the senior lama need not even be resident in the parish but may be invited to come from outside and preside over the rites.

The Practice of Religion

Neither the *pembu* nor such secular village officials as the *naua* have any function in the preparation or conduct of the Dumje rite, though as residents they naturally take part in the proceedings and, when their turn comes, act like anyone else as *lawa*.

The religious function of the Dumje as seen by the Sherpas is the control and destruction of those evil forces which threaten the bodily and spiritual well-being of the community. It differs from that of the Niungne in so far as the individual worshipper is not expected to make any personal effort for closer union with the divine powers. Their worship is largely left to the lamas who strive to enrol the gods in the struggle against the universal enemy.

A social function of the Dumje which has gained increasing importance with the settlement of numerous Khamba among the Sherpas of Khumbu, is the integration of new residents within the fabric of a parish. Once an immigrant has served as Dumje *lawa* he is truly a full member of the community, and a conscientious discharge of his responsibility as *lawa* raises his standing among the other villagers, who, however rich and important, have on one occasion enjoyed his hospitality. Failure to take on this responsibility, on the other hand, makes a man unfit to remain in the parish, and this was shown by the example of the Khamba who left Khumjung, where he had been resident for years, in order to escape from his obligation (cf. p. 33).

The Dumje is thus one of the principal focal points of the spirit of corporateness which pervades a Sherpa parish, and its timing is particularly appropriate to emphasize and enliven this spirit before the Sherpas' annual dispersal to their high pastures. At the same time it seems to have sometimes a cathartic effect in bringing into the open hidden tensions among the members of the parish. In the crowded gatherings in the temple, when everyone has had a great deal of drink, inhibitions fall away, and emotions of rivalry or frustration may be given expression. But outbursts, such as those I watched in the Khumjung temple, occur under conditions when the control and eventual reconciliation of antagonists can be comparatively easily affected. The *chorumba* with his whip symbolizes the restraining forces of society, and the authority vested in him for the duration of the festival guarantees that he will be able to maintain order. People may thus give vent to their feelings without risking any serious conflagration, and the spirit of general good fellowship pervading the Dumje celebrations facilitates the task of peacemakers never absent from a Sherpa community.

Yer-chang: The Rite of Summer

After the Dumje all cattle-owners leave the village, and move with their herds to the one or other of the high-altitude settlements. It is there, among the pastures and glacial moraines, that the Sherpas celebrate the rite known as Yer-chang, which means literally 'summer-beer'. This rite aims mainly at securing the welfare of the herds, and those families that own no cattle and remain throughout the summer in the village content themselves with a pale imitation of the festivities devoid of their ritual core.

Most yak-owners own houses and land in more than one summer settlement (*yersa*), but though their movements from one to the other do not necessarily conform to a fixed routine, it is usual for a family to celebrate the Yer-chang year after year in the same locality and in co-operation with the same neighbours.

The Yer-chang celebration which I attended in 1957 was held in Machherma, a settlement well above the 15,000-feet line, high above the right bank of the Dudh Kosi. Six yak-owners of Khumjung are in the habit of performing the Yer-chang in this place, and as there is no lama among them, they invited Lama Sharap to minister at the rites. One among the six householders functions as *lawa* of the rite, and as such he is responsible for the payment of the lama and for providing certain ritual accessories. On this occasion the function of *lawa* is not onerous, for all the householders make equal contributions in the shape of raw materials for *torma* and offerings.

The main rite was held on August 1, the sixth day after new moon, but this date is not prescribed and people in some other settlements had performed the Yer-chang two days earlier. On the first day an altar was set up in the open at the foot of a square stone structure surmounted by *tarshing* flying small prayer flags. While the lama prepared for the making of *torma*, each of the six householders brought his contribution of butter, *tsampa* and unrefined sugar. As he arrived at the altar, the butter was weighed and the *tsampa* measured so as to assure that everyone contributed exactly the same quantity. All the six men then set about mixing the ingredients and producing a stiff dough known as *phema*.

The lama then made a *Lhapsang Kingur torma* as well as *torma*

The Practice of Religion

representing Guru Trakpo and Sengdroma, whereas the laymen fashioned six big *torma* symbolizing Khumbu-yülha, Longyok, Pari, Lapchi, Dzamdrak and a *lu*. Moreover they modelled yak, sheep and goats, but significantly neither oxen nor horses. All these *torma* were set out in the altar and the lama tied yellow and blue primulas to his wand.

The lama then began the recitation of a *lhapsang* text, and the other men occasionally joined in the chanting, one of them beating a large drum. Later the six householders, each carrying a brass plate containing rice-grains and some red and white ribbons, stood in a line close to the altar. One of them, who for the occasion had donned a yellow silk robe and a flat yellow Chinese hat, produced a small book, with the title *Lachopi rimba*, and recited from this the appropriate *lhachetu* invocations. These consist of long enumerations of the names of gods, lamas and saints, the recitation of each section being followed by the phrase 'to you all I offer these grains' and the scattering of rice-grains. First the Buddhas Cheku Ngawang Taye (Sakya Muni), Lungu-tudze-chembu (Avalokiteśvara mahakaruna) and Tulungu Pemadzun (Urken Rimpoche, i.e. Padmasambhava) are invoked. Then follow groups of names of saints of Tibet, of India, and of China, names of defender deities (*srungma*) and of *kangdo*, of the mothers of *srungma*, and of such locality gods as Khumbu-yülha, and then the names of deities worshipped by specific Sherpa clans. Finally there is an invocation of the unspecified deities of mountains, trees, water, cliffs, summer settlements and winter settlements.

The recitation of this text is always done by a layman, whereas a lama is required to perform the *lhapsang* rite at the altar.

At the end of the ritual all the yak belonging to the six householders celebrating the Yer-chang were driven past the altar, and then into their owner's enclosures. For now followed the re-dedication of such yak as had once been dedicated to Khumbu-yülha or any other mountain deity. In Machherma there were three such animals, and for each a private rite was performed by the owner. Dorje Ngungdu, who owned a white female yak once dedicated to Khumbu-yülha, approached the animal first with smouldering incense, then tied red ribbons to the yak's ears, shoulder hair and tail, put dots of butter on its head, back, sides and feet, and finally poured milk on its back. While doing this he recited prayers, and his wife held the burning incense. At the end the yak was released and the whole herd driven out of the enclosure.

Later in the day all the members of the six families assembled once more at the altar, and every man, woman and child received a large ball made of the *phema* mixture. Curd, contributed by all householders, was now ladled out into cups and bowls which people had brought with them. Everyone sat down to drink the curd and eat part of his share of *phema*. Finally the altar was dismantled, and the *torma* was distributed among those present. Each householder received one of the six big *torma* and a random number of smaller ones.

This day and the following five days the six families entertained each other in turn. Large quantities of beer had been made or brought up from Khumjung, and each party started with a ceremonial offering of beer to one guest after the other. As a guest takes the filled drinking bowl, which contains about a pint, in both hands, the hostess and all the men present intone a chant containing a reference to Guru Rimpoche. The guest is expected to drink first part of the bowl's contents, and when it has been refilled by the hostess, empty it in one draught. For women a somewhat smaller bowl may be used, and very young boys and girls are not compelled to empty a bowl completely. A lavish meal of rice and stew follows the ceremonial serving of drinks, but more beer is available after the meal, and every party ends with singing, even though in the small houses of a *yersa* settlement there is not sufficient room for dancing.

While the ritual is confirmed to the first day, the feasting continues for as many days as there are families celebrating the Yerchang together. At this time the herds do not require a great deal of care, and the grass-cutting and hay-making has not yet begun. The herdsmen and their families can therefore indulge in a short spell of feasting and drinking, but the supplies of beer and grain brought from their villages are soon exhausted, and for the remainder of their stay in the high summer settlements they lead a very frugal life.

Mani-rimdu—A Monastery Feast of Ritual Dances

Apart from the rites performed in the village temples and attended by the normal congregation of such *gomba*, there is one ritual per-

The Practice of Religion

formance which attracts men and women from all the villages of Khumbu. This rite, known as Mani-rimdu, is held annually at the Thami monastery in the month of May, and at Tengboche in November. The liturgical basis is similar to that of the Dumje, but whereas the Dumje can be performed by a small number of lamas supported by the lay-members of a village community, the celebration of the Mani-rimdu requires the setting and the resources of a monastery. The complete enactment of the rite includes ritual dances performed by monks who dress up in elaborate costumes and wear masks representing deities and spirits.

Until the establishment of monastic communities in the first half of the twentieth century, the Mani-rimdu had never been celebrated in Khumbu, but many if the inhabitants had seen performances in the Tibetan monastery of Rongphu, and it was there that the monks of Khumbu learnt the ritual dances. In the lifetime of Gulu Lama, the founder of Tengboche, the celebration of the Mani-rimdu in that monastery was on a very grand scale, but in Thami *gomba* this rite was first performed in 1940, and the enactment of the appropriate dances was begun only in 1950, some seven years before the performance I watched in May 1957.

The performance was on a much more modest scale than the Mani-rimdu celebrations in Rongphu and other Tibetan monasteries which had served as prototypes, but one could nevertheless clearly discern that this rite was basically of the same nature as the Tibetan mystery play described by L. A. Waddell.[1] According to Waddell the play was known to unsophisticated Tibetans as 'Dance of the Red Tiger Devil' (s'Tag-dmar-ch'am), a deity of the pre-Buddhist Bön religion of Tibet, and it is indeed probable that elements of very ancient Tibetan ritual survive as features of this rite. The Sherpas of Khumbu know it only under the name of Mani-rimdu, and consider it unquestioningly an integral part of Buddhist religious life.[2] They explain that the performances aim at increasing the general welfare of the people, and do not serve any such specific purpose as, for instance, the celebration of the Niungne. For laymen

---
[1] *The Buddhism of Tibet*, pp. 516–39, London, 1895.
[2] For descriptions of comparable performances in Tibet and Ladakh see also J. Bacot, *Representations Théatrales dans les Monastères du Tibet*. (*Les Classiques de l'Orient*, Tome III), Paris, 1921, and H. H. Godwin-Austen, 'Description of a Mystic Play as performed in Ladekh Zasker', *Journal of the Asiatic Society of Bengal*, pp. 71–9, Vol. 34, Part I, 1865.

to be in attendance at the Mani-rimdu is considered meritorious, and many of those present at the rites try to gain further merit by offering gifts of money to the presiding lama or the community of monks, and by distributing food among the pilgrims.

A detailed description of the proceedings during the four days of the Mani-rimdu celebrations would fill an entire chapter, and here only an outline of the ritual performances can be given.

The first day, which in 1957 fell on May 8th, was devoted mainly to a final rehearsal of the ritual dances. Only a few visitors and pilgrims had arrived, and the courtyard of the monastery was empty of spectators. It consists of a roughly square terrace, partly cut out of the steep hillside and partly built up of stone-work. On the hillside it is bounded by the *gomba*, and on two other sides by low galleries with flat roofs. On the fourth side there is a precipice and looking down over the wooden railing one sees several hundred feet below the houses and fields of Thami sprawling along a glacial stream. Towering above the valley there are the snow-capped mountains flanking the Teshi Lapcha—a high pass leading to the Rolwaling area—and this background of dazzling snow heightened the impressiveness of the ritual performances enacted on so magnificent a stage.

Early in the morning the younger monks busied themselves with carrying benches, chairs and low tables from the interior of the temple into the courtyard. They arranged them so as to provide elevated seats on the *gomba* side of the courtyard. During the following three days these seats remained the same, but in the centre of the courtyard tables for offerings and other ritual arrangements were set up and changed again according to the rites to be performed.

Although the first day's performance was in the nature of a rehearsal, and the dancers wore neither masks nor costumes, it was nevertheless done with all solemnity, and the incantations were obviously intended as true prayers. It began with a fanfare of trumpets and the entrance of the head lama, a stout man in his seventies who wore a yellow jacket, red robe and white scarf draped over one shoulder, and a peaked cap of dull red. The latter, however, was later replaced by a black-fringed eye-shade. Behind the head lama walked several other lamas and monks, including two of his sons.[1]

---

[1] For the personnel of the Thami monastery see pp. 134, 135.

The head lama was installed in the central seat of a row of benches put up along the *gomba* wall, and the other lamas arranged themselves on both sides of him. Before them stood low tables, and that in front of the head lama was covered with a Chinese carpet in blue and yellow; on this was now placed a lacquer tray bearing hand-bell, *dorje* and a small drum. A large *torma* draped in a white scarf, a plate with rice-grains, prayer-books and several pairs of large cymbals were distributed over the other tables.

The lamas who were to provide the musical accompaniment for the recitations and dances were seated in two groups: one on benches placed at right angles to the 'high table' of the head lama, and one in a gallery on the side of the courtyard facing the first group. The former included two players of enormous telescopic horns, and the other the players of large double-membrane drums, which were suspended from the roof of the gallery. Most of these musicians had books in front of them, and in the intervals of playing their instruments they joined in the recitations.

The proceedings were introduced by prayers led by the head lama and the lamas sitting beside him. Whenever there was a pause, young monks served tea to all the seated lamas, and as the morning wore on individual villagers approached the head lama with offerings of chillies, beer and coins. All these were put to one side, but afterwards the chillies were distributed among all the lamas.

After a brief interval the sound of a thigh-bone trumpet, blown on the top storey of the temple, announced that the dancers were ready, and this signal was answered by a blast on a similar instrument played by one of the lamas in the gallery of the courtyard. Heralded by a slow rhythm played on the telescopic horns, cymbals and hand-drums six lamas emerged one by one from the temple door, and came down the steps with slow deliberate movements. At each step they turned towards the head lama, and by bowing 'asked his permission to dance'.

They wore their usual purple sleeveless cassocks and heavy felt boots, but though they were not professional dancers they executed the ensuing dance with surprising assurance and nimbleness. This and the other dances will be described as they were executed in full costume on the third day of the Mani-rimdu. A comparison between the two performances showed that the rehearsal, known as *tsam-ki-bulu* ('dance of showing'), was an exact replica of the full ritual, complete with ritual accessories, incantations and music, but without masks, costumes and an audience. It lasted until the late afternoon, and though by the end one or two of the monastery dignitaries were slightly the worse for having drunk too much of the beer provided by the faithful, the solemnity of the proceedings remained undiminished up to the end when, accompanied by lamas blowing trumpets, the head lama returned to the temple.

The second day began with the usual morning service in the *gomba*. Immediately after its close the head lama, proceeded by two trumpeters and lamas carrying plates with chillies, and followed by two boys carrying offerings of maize, came out of the temple and walked to his own house built on a ledge above the temple.

Later in the morning crowds of villagers from Thami and visitors from as far as Namche Bazar came up the steep, winding path to the monastery. They were dressed in their best clothes, and among them were old grey-haired people as well as a great many children. On arrival they first circled the *gomba*, and some of the older people, turning silver prayer-wheels as they walked, repeated this circumambulation several times before they settled down in the courtyard. Outside the gate several women had taken their stand with large barrels of maize beer, and every newcomer was pressed to refresh himself with a free drink. By this and similar dispensations of drink and food lay people acquire merit as well as prestige and popularity.

In the meantime lamas arranged seats and tables for the performance of a rite known as *Tshe-wong* ('Life-Consecration'), which is preceded by the presentation of offerings to the head lama by the laity and consists of a general blessing and distribution of sacred food to all those present.

By the time the head lama and his suite were to take their seats at the 'high table', the courtyard was crowded with pilgrims, some squatting and some standing. His entry was heralded by trumpeters wearing orange caps crested with high yellow tufts, and as the old man took his seat the other lamas filed into a lower row of seats facing the 'high table'. There was a blast of trumpets and a clash of cymbals, and clouds of incense from burning juniper branches floated through the air.

After a sequence of incantations accompanied by the full orchestra of instruments, the presentation of gifts by laymen began. Each

The Practice of Religion

donor had to push his way through the densely packed crowd squatting in the courtyard, and then stood in front of the head lama's throne with his back to the line of lamas on the lower seats. He presented a white scarf to the head lama, and was then made to hold up one by one a three-tiered structure of silver inlaid with turquoise and covered with rice, known as the 'magic offering of the universe' or rice-*mandala*, a brass figure of a Buddha (*ku*), a small book (*sung*) and a brass *chörten*. After holding up all these objects he placed his gift, which consisted of either cash or grain, on the table before the head lama. But this elaborate form of presentation was used only in the case of prominent donors most of whom gave substantial cash gifts. Ordinary people handed small bags of grain to two laymen of Thami who, acting as unofficial helpers, conveyed these gifts in a continuous stream to the head lama.

Apart from the donors of cash or grain, there were men and women who brought flasks of beer and kept filling the cups of lamas. Indeed refreshments were continuously served, and the lamas' tea-cups were never allowed to remain empty for long.

It was late in the afternoon and dusk was falling when the presentation of gifts and the recitation of prayers ended. The moment for the rite of 'Life Consecration' had now come, and in preparation of this final rite several lamas went through the crowd with brass jugs containing holy water (*tu*) mixed with red powder. This liquid they poured into the cupped hands or the drinking cups of the assembled people, who sipped from it and put the rest on their heads.

The *Tshe-wong* rite of 'Life-Consecration', described by L. A. Waddell[1] as the 'Eucharist of Lamaism', is intended to bestow on the recipients the blessing of long life, and this is symbolized by the distribution of life-giving liquids and pills. In a recent detailed description of this rite as observed in the Dolpo region of Western Nepal, David Snellgrove[2] points out that the intention of this 'Life-Consecration' is the nourishing of the 'supernatural' life (*bla-tshe*) distinct from the normal life force. The invocation forming part of the ritual which he quotes makes it clear that the *bla-tshe* to be strengthened is indeed, as suggested also by Nebesky-Wojkowitz,[3] comparable with the detachable 'life' or 'soul-force' which plays

---
[1] Op. cit., p. 444–8.
[2] *Himalayan Pilgrimage*, Oxford, 1961, p. 143.
[3] *Oracles and Demons of Tibet*, s'-Gravenhage, 1956, pp. 481, 482.

so great a rôle in Indian tribal folklore and the straying of which does not involve immediate physical death.

The liturgical text[1] used at this rite contains invocations of Padmasambhava ('Lotus-Born') and the divinities of the lotus-family with which he is identified, but both these invocations and the consecration of the life-giving substances were lost on the majority of the crowd, which eagerly awaited the distribution of these substances at the hands of the lama sitting on both sides of the abbot.

When finally the rite had reached this stage, the crowd surged towards the head lama's table, and several lamas tried to control it with the help of a wooden bar held in such a manner that only a few people at a time could file past the line of lamas seated behind the high table. As each person passed the lamas he received from the first a drop of holy water (*tu*), from the second a life-pellet made of flour and spice (*tshe-ril*), from the next a spoonful of beer mixed with sugar (*tswe-chang*), from the head lama a blessing conveyed by the touch of a sacred wand (*dādar*), and from the last lama a small red pellet made of rice-flour (*mani-rhil-bu*). Some lifted up children or supported old persons, and the master of ceremonies (*chortimba*), who wielded a stick with a white scarf attached to it, supported by the younger lamas was hard put to it to maintain an orderly progress past the 'high table'. A few young men, who had imbibed more than their fair share of beer, used the surge towards the head lama to whip up an atmosphere of excitement. Finally, however, all those present had received the blessing believed to ensure long life, and the lamas could retire to the *gomba*.

The third day of the festival was devoted entirely to the performance of the ritual dances rehearsed on the first day. Festive crowds, even more numerous than the day before, filled every corner of the courtyard, and the flat roofs of the two galleries were packed with spectators. Two *chortimba* wielding long leather whips cleared the centre of the courtyard and saw to it that the crowds did not encroach on the space required for the dancers.

Even before the dance ritual started there was a bustle of men and women serving beer. Generous donors had placed a whole battery of large wooden barrels in a corner of the courtyard, and from these the thick brew was ladled into flasks and jugs, which in turn were carried to fill bowls and drinking cups. This activity

---

[1] Tib.: *dkon-mchog-spyi-'dus ts'e-dbang mts'ams-sbyor.*

continued throughout the day, and the donors of drink and all sorts of dry food, determined that their gifts should reach the spectators, seemed to mind little whether the distribution disturbed the atmophere of the sacred dances.

The entrance of the first six dancers was nevertheless impressive. They were dressed in orange and yellow silk jackets worn over their wide purple robes, had high, crested yellow hats and accompanied their measured movements with the clash of big brass cymbals. These dancers are known as *sua-sol-ten* ('heralds') and their dance, which does not form part of the traditional sequence of dramatic dances and lasts only a few minutes, is considered a merely ornamental introduction and known as *rul-tsam*.

The sound of a thigh-bone trumpet from the inside of the *gomba* subsequently announced the first of the dances of the traditional sequence. The six lamas performing this dance are known as *surzi-ngawa* ('dancers of the four directions'). They solemnly came down the steps of the temple to dance the *sirkim* or 'libation dance'. They wore wide-brimmed black hats (*shenok*) made of a kind of lacquered papier mâché by the Khumjung painter Kapa Kalden, each topped by a three-pronged structure bearing the painted design of a human skull. Criss-cross patterns of green bands covered the top of the wide brims, the other side of which was painted red. The wide flowing robes of the six dancers were in Chinese style and consisted of silks in various bright colours, orange, green and magenta in two of the robes, yellow, blue and red in two others, and black, red, green and blue in the remaining two. One by one the dancers circled the courtyard first with slow movements and then with faster turns, till all six dancers were arranged round the centre pole, next to which stood a table with offerings and *torma*. Tied to the centre post was the dried leg of a sheep, and as animal sacrifices have no place in Buddhist ritual, this ritual use of the limb of an animal may be an element belonging to the supposed Bön background of the ritual. In the shamanistic ritual of Tibetan oraclepriests animal sacrifices and the ritual use of the animal's severed leg are used even today.[1]

The *chorpen* then distributed to the dancers small brass cups containing flour-balls and filled them with beer. Holding these cups

[1] Cf. R. de Nebesky-Wojkowitz, *Oracles and Demons of Tibet*, 's-Gravenhage, 1956, p. 551.

the dancers executed several turns, and then flung flour-balls and beer into the air as an offering to the spirits. This they repeated twice and in between they performed a number of dance movements including a rapid whirl reminiscent of a pirouette.

The identity of the figures represented by these dancers is by no means clear. The Sherpas consider the *surzi-ngawa* as divine beings, somehow associated with the four quarters, but not identical with the four *gyal-dzen-deshi*. Elsewhere similarly attired dancers, however, have been described as 'black-hat magicians' or Bön-priests, and Waddell speaks of them as 'the pre-Lamaist black-mitred priests, clad in rich robes of China silk and brocade'.[1]

After a dance lasting nearly twenty minutes, the six dancers returned two by two into the *gomba*. There was a short interval used for the distribution of refreshments, and then four dancers wearing masks and known as *king-dzi* came running out of the *gomba*. The *king-dzi* represent jesters in the paradise of Sundokpari, but have also associations with the four directions. The one wearing a white mask comes from the east, the bearer of the green mask from the south, that of the red mask from the west, and that of the yellow mask from the north. Two of them accompanied their dance with the playing of cymbals and two beat hand-drums. This dance was fast and full of movement, thus contrasting sharply with the dignified and restrained dance of the black-hatted priests.

The number of *king-dzi* is not prescribed; while in Thami and Tengboche only four appear at the Mani-rimdu, there were eight in Rongphu, and according to the texts there should ideally be one thousand, a figure which can hardly ever have been reached even in the biggest Tibetan monasteries.

Next a dancer wearing the mask of Raja Dorje Tolo was heralded by a fanfare of trumpets played by lamas wearing high yellow hats. Raja Dorje Tolo is described as an aspect of Guru Rimpoche, but the huge mask the dancer wore seemed more appropriate to a dangerous demon than to the revered Buddhist saint. The basic colour of the terrifying face was a dark brown with the features outlined in yellow; on the forehead there were representations of three skulls, and above the mask there was a shock of brown hair

---

[1] Waddell, op. cit., p. 522. R. de Nebesky-Wojkowitz also mentions a dance of black-hat magicians (*zhva-nag*) as part of a feast serving the propitiation of the protective deities. Cf. *Oracles and Demons of Tibet*, p. 422.

tied up in a top-knot. In his right hand the dancer carried ribbon streamers in green and yellow, and in his left hand a large dagger. He wore a blue gauze skirt bordered in gold, and as an apron a *thanka* painted on cloth. His large shawl was yellow, red and green. The movements of this dancer, hampered by his huge mask and clothes, were slow and this was in keeping with the royal status of Raja Dorje Tolo. After some time he was shown to a seat, and a lama presented him with a *torma* as an offering.

After the appearance of Raja Dorje Tolo there was an interval, when most people had something to eat. Men and women with baskets containing various types of fried bread and sweets went through the crowd and freely distributed these eatables, without discriminating in any way between the various spectators. Beer also continued to flow freely, and the gain of merit was the ostensible reward for those dispensing such lavish hospitality.

This lunch break was also the time for one of the humorous interludes which now and then enlivened the proceedings. A man dressed in a blue robe and wearing an enormous white mask with a benign smile appeared on the temple steps, but seemed too weak and tottery to come down into the courtyard. Two lamas went to his aid and tried to keep him from falling. This figure is called *Hyabo-mi-tsering*, and represents extreme old age. The idea is that a very great age will be reached by those who do good works, but whatever the figure was to symbolize, the part of *mi-tsering* had turned into that of a jester, whose antics were intended to make the audience laugh.

When the musicians resumed their playing it was to accompany the dance of two lamas representing skeletons (*rurang*). They wore cream-coloured masks with red, eyeless sockets, gaping mouths and nostrils, and fan-like ears. Their dress consisted of white cotton trousers and tunics, and there had been some attempt to paint the bones and ribs in red on to the costume. The whole attire failed to make a terrifying impression, and the crowd considered the dance of the *rurang* more with amusement than with awe, even when the two skeletons produced a small doll representing a naked human body, and flayed and tormented it while dragging it around the courtyard. The scene symbolized the torments which humans may suffer at the hands of evil spirits unless they are aided by the powers of Buddhist saints and divinities.

After this four dancers known as *gon-dzen*, wearing masks and robes of dark blue with long pointed sleeves, took the stage. The monks were vague about the meaning of their dance but one of my informants explained that the *gon-dzen* represent the legendary Lama Lhalung-paldik-dorje, who hid a bow and arrow in his sleeve and killed Du-lang-tarma, who had been reincarnated as an evil spirit and had inflicted much suffering on the people of Tibet. This legendary figure may be represented by any number of dancers, but there is no attempt at any dramatic representation of the incident which established the lama's fame.

A dancer wearing a red mask with three eyes and a skull above the forehead then entered in the company of two attendants wearing pinkish masks with cat-like features. The main figure, who went through movements similar to those of Raja Dorje Tolo, represented Shelunga, a local god worshipped near Rongphu. As the Thami lamas learnt the Mani-rimdu dances at the Rongphu monastery, they also adopted this sequence, although Shelunga plays no rôle in the cult of Khumbu.

The next dance, known as Tidzam, brought four deities armed with swords on to the scene. Their masks, two blue and two brown, were similar to those of the *gon-dzen*, and at the end of the dance a small human figure made of dough was produced in a triangular box, and cut into pieces by the dancers' swords. This action is reminiscent of the destruction of the dough figure at the Dumje rite (p. 201), and the figure, known as *linga*, represents a hostile spirit.[1]

During another long interval in the ritual performance a jester, known as Tong-den and acted by the *gerku* of the monastery, made his appearance in the courtyard. This figure wore a mask and clothes suggestive of an Indian sadhu or fakir. His untidy copper-coloured, curled hair was tied up in a top-knot, and he carried a rattle-drum and a stick. His buffoonery included imitations of the serious performances of the day, such as a parody of a libation and food-offering.

---

[1] Cf. R. de Nebesky-Wojkowitz, *Oracles and Demons of Tibet*, p. 360.—Waddell (p. 527) mentions that in the course of the Tibetan mystery play such a dough figure is stabbed by four 'cemetery-ghouls', and it seems that at the Mani-rimdu as performed in Thami this symbolical destruction of the enemy of Buddhism is enacted twice in a slightly different form; once in the dance of the *rurang*, who torment a doll made of fabric, and once in the Tidzam dance, when the effigy to be destroyed is made of dough.

The abbot and senior monks of Thami

Dance of the skeletons at the Mani-rimdu

Dancer representing Raja Dorje Tolo

Dorje Ngundu reciting at the Yer-chang rite

The Practice of Religion

By the time the music and dances restarted it was getting dark. After a dance of two pairs of masked figures known as Hlang-ma and Sur-dzem, and dressed in ceremonial robes of Chinese pattern, there was finally a dance called *tsam-na* ('all dance together') or *lok-tsam* ('go out dance'). For this final dance all the available costumes, masks and dancers were gathered, and nine lamas, wearing the costumes of *gon-dzen*, Tidzam and other benevolent beings (but not the two divinities Raja Dorje Tolo and Shelunga) appeared in the courtyard, and danced a round dance expressing the people's joy over their liberation from the forces of evil.

During the last two dances one of the two *chortimba* showed signs of possession by a god. This layman, who had doubtless drunk a great deal of beer, suddenly began to tremble and utter strange sounds. Several men tried to restrain him, but he shook them off, rushed to join the dance with untutored but vigorous movements, flinging his arms about and several times coming into the way of the masked dancers. Though everyone agreed that a god had come upon him, the crowd seemed more amused than awed. The possession left him as soon as the music stopped and no further notice was taken of his experience.

The day ended with general shouts of *lha-rgyal-lol!*, a cry of victory, and as the lamas went back into the temple and the crowd thinned, the young men among the visitors started a round dance of their own, and continued dancing and singing in the way usual at social occasions until late into the night.

The day after the ritual dances is traditionally devoted to a ceremony known as Shiwi Jinsak, which is the Buddhist version of the Hindu Hom offering. The preparations for this rite begin with the construction of an altar in the monastery courtyard on which the offerings are to be burnt. This altar (*tapkun*) consists of a raised square shaped out of mud, which is enclosed within wooden boards until it has hardened and a sand painting has been drawn on its surface.

The *chorpen* of the temple, helped by another lama, was in charge of this task. Using a long metal funnel, from which if gently knocked a tiny trickle of coloured sand issues, he drew five concentric circles, three red alternating with two white ones. In the centre he drew four figures known as 'flower-petals', and in each of the four corners of the altar he drew on a blue background a yellow moon and standing in its curve a *dorje* or *vajra*. Before anyone, except a few children, had admired this sand painting, known as *pema-dama-shi*, it was covered with cakes of dried cow dung, and thus remained invisible until the flames of the burnt offerings had destroyed it.

The *chorpen* also brought two *torma*, one representing a serpent-spirit (*lu*), which was later to be thrown into a stream, and one known as *chotr*, adorned with representations of flower petals. The latter was to be burnt on the altar.

Benches and tables were arranged to form a square enclosing the altar. On a table to the right of the head lama's seat, offerings, *torma* and ritual objects were set out, and all these preparations extended over most of the afternoon. The sun was sinking when the head lama took his seat and the other lamas settled down on the benches, bringing with them books and the usual instruments for the accompaniment of recitations.

Within the square there were also a few seats for laymen, and a prominent villager of Thami and his wife brought a large container filled with loaves made of *tsampa*, and proceeded to serve them to the lamas and the children who were the sole spectators of the rite.

Prayers and chanting went on for a long time. When the full moon lit up the open courtyard, the head lama and one of the oldest monks donned Chinese silk robes and head-dresses known as *ringa*. These consist of five painted leaves showing the figures of the five Dhyani Buddhas known to the Sherpas as the *Gyelwa-ringa*.

Finally the *chorpen* lit the butter lamps inside the pile of dung cakes on the altar, and soon the whole structure stood in flames, fanned by a strong wind and now and then fed with small wooden sticks. Using a spoon with a specially long ladle the head lama first poured molten butter into the fire, and then a number of articles known as the 'essential seven offerings' were dropped on to the altar and consumed by the flames. One of these was a *torma* which took a long time to burn and necessitated the addition of more sticks of wood.

In between the burning of the offerings there were recitations and music, and as it was now too dark to read from the texts, the lamas chanted from memory.

When all the offerings were completed, the fire was allowed to die down, and the lamas returned to the temple and their houses. The ritual surrounding the Mani-rimdu celebrations had come to an end.

The sacred texts recited at the Mani-rimdu are largely the same as those forming the liturgical background of the Dumje (cf. p. 193), and several features such as the symbolic destruction of the effigy of an evil spirit and the offering of burnt sacrifices on a temporary altar form part of both these rites.

The rôles of the two ceremonies in present-day Sherpa society, however, are basically different. The Dumje is an occasion for giving ritual expression to the unity and interdependence of all the members of the congregation of a village *gomba*, a community which may comprise the inhabitants of either a single village or of two closely linked villages. The Mani-rimdu, on the other hand, is not focused on any individual village community. Whatever the purpose of the original Tibetan mystery plays may have been, the Sherpas think of this monastery festival as a rite performed for the general well-being of the people. They ascribe its initial celebration to Pawa Cheresi (Avalokiteśvara), known also as Kurwan-tu-che-shang-bu (Tib. *Thugs-rje chen-po* 'of Great Compassion'), to whom my informants referred to as 'the god of the Mani-rimdu'.

Though neither lamas nor laymen were able to give a consistent interpretation of the individual dances and masked figures, they unanimously described the whole performance as a dramatic enactment of the victory of the divine and human protagonists of Buddhist doctrine over the forces of evil. As such the dances serve as visual reassurance of Sherpa ideology, and to those who from childhood onwards have frequently watched the Mani-rimdu either at Thami or Tengboche, the figures representing Buddhist saints and divinities become familiar and as much invested with reality as biblical personalities to the spectators of mediaeval Christian mystery plays. The message they convey is unconnected, however, with day-to-day morality, for though they affirm the existence of positive as well as negative spiritual forces they do not elaborate the theme of virtue and sin which link men with the one or the other of the hostile camps.

As one of the principal social events of Khumbu the Mani-rimdu, drawing together large crowds from several villages, offers to the wealthy ample opportunity of attaining religious merit and at the same time social prestige by offering gifts to lamas and the monastery, and by dispensing food and drink to all comers. Thus wealth is displayed conspicuously to the benefit of the many poor who eat and drink to their hearts' desire at the expense of wealthier fellow pilgrims.

Participation in the sacred mystery depicted in the dances is superficial on the part of the laity. None of the awe and religious fervour noticeable among the worshippers at a rite such as the Niungne is noticeable among those who watch the Mani-rimdu. The performance of the dancers, all of whom are known to be lamas, is viewed as a spectacle rather than as a ritual act, but the way in which the members of the crowd will chat and enjoy the distributed eatables while the personifications of deities and spirits move about the stage, implies neither disrespect nor disbelief in the supernatural beings represented by the masked dancers. The laymen take the view that the propitiation and worship of the deities are safe in the hands of the lamas conducting the rite and reciting from their sacred texts the prayers and incantations appropriate to every phase of the ritual. Pilgrims and spectators have hence no other function than to attend the performance and contribute by their gifts to the material basis for celebration. To them the Mani-rimdu is a festival rather than a ritual occasion, and they are satisfied with their gain of merit by the mere fact of their attendance without feeling an urge to participate more actively in the lamas' activities directed to the worship of specific gods. Religious fervour manifests itself only when on the day of the 'Life Consecration' the crowd presses forward to receive from the hands of the lamas the sacred liquids and substances, and benefits from the sanctifying touch of the head lama's wand.

Individuals, moreover, may be moved to states of religious ecstasy at the time of the ritual dances, and the possession of laymen by one of the divinities invoked during the rite is an occurrence which causes little surprise and is thought of as in keeping with the nature of the Mani-rimdu.

RITES OF DEATH

Among the *rites de passage* there is but one which requires the ministrations of lamas and has all the characteristics of a truly religious rite. While in the celebrations associated with birth, betrothal and marriage religious elements are little more than secondary aspects of basically social functions, death brings man face to face with those figures and forms of existence to which all religious

The Practice of Religion

practice and thinking is directed. It is when death strikes a family that the surviving members set into motion a series of rites and ceremonies which, though embedded in a framework of social obligations and customs, are of an essentially religious nature. These rites are performed according to certain sacred Tibetan texts, some of which are available in English translations. In so far as their original content is concerned, I can do no more than to refer the reader to the texts and the commentaries provided by the translators and editors.[1]

My main concern in this context, however, is to describe, and as far as possible, analyse, the Sherpas' reactions and attitudes to the rites of death. The popular beliefs regarding their efficacy are in certain respects clearly different from the ideas contained in the texts recited by the ministering lamas. Scholars familiar with these texts may keep in mind, therefore, that the account here given does not represent an interpretation of the funeral rites as it emerges from a study of the texts, but a picture as it presents itself to the Sherpa layman and to the comparatively naïve village lama, who recites the texts without any critical thought as to their ultimate implications.

As soon as a sick person is considered to be dangerously ill, Sherpas shun no expense in seeking the help of spirit-callers (*lhawa*) to discover the cause of the affliction. If the suggested remedies prove fruitless, they may commission lamas and monks to recite various *kurim* (Tib. *sku-rim*) for the patient's benefit, and the sums distributed on such occasions among senior lamas and monasteries may run to several hundred rupees. Lamas may also be called to the house to drive away malignant spirits, and to recite such books as Gyaldö, Gyapshi or Dzendö for the benefit of the patient. There is, in such matters, close co-operation between spirit-callers and lamas, and the books to be recited as a *kurim* are often indicated by the spirit-caller.

A rich man may call as many as thirty lamas to his house, and when in 1953 the wife of the *pembu* Ang Chumbi of Kunde lay dying, the entire main room of his house was occupied by some twenty-five lamas, who were reading aloud from the 108 volumes of the Kangyur in an attempt to avert the woman's death.

[1] The book most relevant to this section is W. Y. Evans-Wentz's *The Tibetan Book of the Dead*, London 1957. Also important is the section on 'Guiding the Consciousness after Death' in David Snellgrove's *Buddhist Himālaya*, London, 1957, pp. 262–74.

If all such intercessions are fruitless and the patient dies, the corpse is covered with a white cloth, and must not be touched until a lama has been consulted. The bereaved family then calls a lama and one man to prepare the corpse. No member of the household should undertake this task, and there are in every village several men experienced in handling corpses. They are not professionals and anyone, irrespective of clan- or kinship-ties, may prepare the dead body, provided he does not belong to the household of the deceased and is not of lower social status, i.e. of *khamendeu* class, if the deceased was *khadeu*.

As soon as the lama arrives, and before the corpse has been touched by anyone, he recites a prayer known as *pho-giaū*, which is contained in the book Sal-deū. A great lama called in on such an occasion, may pull out a few hairs from the dead person's head, in order to produce an opening through which his spirit (*sem*) may leave the head. While doing this, the lama pronounces a spell aimed at sending the *sem* straight to Devachen, the heaven of 'Boundless Light' (Opame) and the *pho-giaū* prayer has ostensibly the same purpose. But the Sherpas themselves seem very doubtful about the efficaciousness of this procedure, for all the subsequent mortuary rites are based on the assumption that for forty-nine days after death the *sem* lingers in an intermediate state in which he can profit from the advice and the prayers of the living.

After reciting five times the *pho-giaū* prayer the lama consults an astrological manual, known as *tsi-pi*, as well as a calendar (*dadu*), with a view to discovering where and in which manner the corpse should be disposed of. In his calculations the following factors are taken into consideration:

1. The age of the departed.
2. The year of the *tolo*-cycle (of twelve years) in which he was born.
3. The year of the *kam*-cycle (of eight years) in which he was born.
4. The day of month and week and the time of death.
5. The constellation of stars at the time of death.
6. The position of Pum-dung, a bird-like creature with a human body, who often changes its location. Its position at any time of the year is given in the printed *dadu*.

As a result of his calculations, the lama indicates by whom the body may be touched, which direction is open for its disposal and whether it should be cremated, buried or thrown into a river. As cremation is the only respectable way of disposing of the corpse of an adult, the relatives responsible for the mortuary rights usually insist on cremation, even if the lama advised another type of disposal. Those who have been born in the same *tolo*-year as the departed may not touch the corpse, and those born in the same *kam*-year are usually also excluded.

Astrological calculations sometimes narrow down the number of those who can handle the corpse without danger to such an extent that serious difficulties may arise, particularly if death occurred in a remote *yersa* settlement. In such a case a device known as *thap kiru* is employed in order to enable persons who should not touch the corpse nevertheless to assist in the funeral without danger to themselves. They must disguise themselves by painting one cheek white and one black, by putting on their clothes inside out, by wearing one boot only, and behaving in every possible way in a manner opposite to usual practice. If a body has to be cremated in a place lying in a direction excluded by the astrological calculations the same device of *thap kiru* is used by the mourners.

As soon as the lama has made his pronouncement, the man called in to prepare the corpse ties it up in a sitting position with the help of a rope, and places it in front of a temporary altar erected by the side wall of the main room opposite the entrance. Wrapped up in white cloth, the corpse is encased in a square structure, on top of which is laid a painting or a print known as *sipa kholu*. This contains a combination of calendrical and other auspicious symbols, and is believed to protect the corpse against *dü*, *shrindi* and other evil spirits, who flee at the sight of these magical signs.

The lama meanwhile make the *torma* appropriate to the book of Drowa-Kündröl ('Ritual of the Compassionate Saviour of All Beings') or—if the mourners want to shorten the proceedings—those appropriate to a book the full title of which is 'Showing the Spheres of Existence for the Benefit of the Departed and in Reliance on the Great Compassionate One.'

The altar erected behind the corpse consists of at least two tiers. On the higher tier are arranged the *torma*, usually six in number, representing the deities appropriate to the service recited, as well as a mirror and a whisk for sprinkling holy water. On the lower shelf there are brass cups, some filled with water and others with maize, a *torma* to be eaten by the people of the house and another known as *gyak*, which together with odd bits of food is to be thrown out as an offering for the evil spirits. In front of the corpse, no part of which is visible, there is a small table bearing butter lamps and a number of food and drink offerings. Two baskets, one containing fried bread and the other puffed maize to be distributed among the mourners at the funeral, are placed on the floor close to this table.

For the service which begins as soon as the *torma* and the arrangement of the altar has been completed, only one lama is strictly necessary, and this lama in charge of the service recites morning and evening Drowa-Kündröl, and during the day Bardo Thödol, a book known to the Sherpas as *Totul*.[1] The whole service is hence referred to as *Totul shetu*. All those who can afford the expense employ several additional lamas and these recite simultaneously *Dorje-diksha*, which consists of the five volumes of *Dorje chepa* and the ten volumes of *Diksha-serki-puti*. While their incantations are addressed to various gods, with the aim of relieving the departed from the burden of sin, the text recited by the senior lama is addressed direct to the *sem* of the dead person.

In the Bardo Thödol the departed is told about the regions of the nether world through which he will have to pass. There he would meet many *srungma* deities of frightening appearance; he should not be afraid, but bow to them with folded hands, and remember that these deities are his protectors. He is told too how to find the path to Shinje-chogyal and how to recognize this deity who sends the dead to one of the six spheres of the wheel of life or directs them on the path to Devachen. Shinje-chogyal, the King of the Dead, corresponds to Yama Raja, the lord of the underworld in Hindu mythology.

The period between death and the cremation of the corpse should be at least three days and three nights. This period is sometimes shortened to two for reasons of convenience, though such a procedure is contrary to the instructions of the scriptures. There is no

[1] Bardo Thödol (Tib. *bardo t'os-grol*). Cf. W. Y. Evans-Wentz, *The Tibetan Book of the Dead or The After-Death Experiences on the Bardo Plane*, London, 1957.

The Practice of Religion 229

harm, on the other hand, in delaying the cremation for up to six days, if no auspicious day can be found earlier. I have even heard the view expressed that it would be preferable to keep the corpse seven or eleven days in the house; and that as this could not be done without the corpse decomposing an effigy (*ten*) is made for the post-cremation rites as the next best alternative.

During the recitation of Drowa-Kündröl the senior lama must not drink beer or liquor, nor eat meat or animal fat, but should be served with milk, curd and vegetarian food instead. This restriction, however, does not apply to the rest of the day, but only to the intervals in the recitation of the Drowa-Kündröl.

While the corpse remains in the house, and the lamas are engaged in their solemn recitations, suitably accompanied by the clash of cymbals, the beating of drums and the blowing of a thigh-bone trumpet, relations and friends of the departed visit the house to express their sympathy to the mourners and give some offerings to the deceased. The most usual gift on this occasion is beer or liquor, and this is known as *kem-chang*. The visitor entering the house with his flask of beer or liquor first pours a little into the cup of the senior lama, then fills a small brass cup to be offered to the deceased, and thirdly serves a drink to the chief mourner. The libation for the deceased remains only for a few minutes on the table in front of the corpse, and is then either given to the senior lama or poured into another vessel. The visitor and all those gathered there then drink of his gift which is usually consumed on the spot. The gift of *kem-chang* need not necessarily be beer or liquor, but some people present the mourners with other presents, such as grain or even pieces of cloth. Until the day of the funeral the lamas remain in the house of mourning, and are supplied with food and large quantities of tea and beer throughout the time of their stay.

The most usual form of the disposal of the dead is cremation. Only children are buried, and the bodies of exceedingly poor people, or of those who leave neither property nor any kinsmen responsible for their mortuary rites, are thrown into a river. Unless the lama consulting the *tsi-pi* finds strong counter indications and the mourners do not overrule their advice, it is normal therefore to have a corpse cremated as soon as an auspicious day for the funeral can be found.

Unlike the funerals of many other peoples, the cremation of a

Sherpa is not a performance to be attended by large numbers of mourners. The proceedings are entirely in the hands of the lamas, and all that is required are a few helpers who will prepare the pyre, carry supplies to the cremation ground and provide for the lamas' bodily needs by making tea and serving food. These helpers need not be the next of kin, and are often young men, standing to the deceased in the relationship of grandsons, or brothers' sons. Women never attend a cremation.

At the funeral of Ang Tenzing (Paldorje) of Khumjung, for instance, none of his four sons were present, though three of them were at the time in Khumjung and its vicinity. Even Anulu, his youngest son, in whose house he had lived and who, as chief mourner, was responsible for the entire expenditure, did not attend the cremation, though a few hours afterwards he took part in a *demchang* celebration. Such absence of the nearest of kin is not a sign of indifference, but by making the material arrangements for the performance and employing lamas to conduct it, they have done all that custom requires.

A funeral procession usually leaves the house of mourning at sunrise, and proceeds to one of the cremation places indicated by the lama consulted about the manner of the funeral. The sound of a thigh-bone trumpet heralds the emergence of the mourners from the house of the dead person. In front walks a junior lama carrying a prayer flag; he is followed by the other lamas, and then comes a man, who may or may not be a lama, carrying on his back the corpse, still wrapped in white cloths and tied up for the journey. His payment for this service is called *robla* (*ro* = corpse) and usually includes the clothes in which the corpse was dressed.

On the way to the cremation ground, which usually lies high above the village, the lamas recite parts of the book *Lam-chu* ('path showing'), and this recitation, accompanied by the playing of rattle-drums, is intended to show the deceased the 'path' to Devachen, the 'heaven' of Sherpa belief. It is believed that this recitation serves also to purify the corpse which by this time may have begun to smell.

As soon as the procession has reached the place of cremation, which may be high above the village at a distance of as much as half an hour's walk, the corpse is put down close to the pyre. This has usually been prepared, but on occasion more branches are gathered while the lamas prepare their temporary altar. Most people are burnt on the one or other of the ordinary cremation grounds, of which there are several near every village, but for the cremation of a senior lama, a more solitary place which had never, or at least not recently, been used, may be chosen. This was done for the cremation of Lama Kiu of Khumjung. The site was on a sloping spur, close to a waterfall, and there was so little level ground that pyre, altar and cooking place were at different levels, thus necessitating continuous climbing up and down of the men engaged in the conduct of the rites.

The altar is made of stones arranged in two tiers and covered with a yak-hair blanket. On the upper tier are placed the same *torma* which stood on the altar inside the house, some butter lamps, a cup filled with liquor, and whisks for sprinkling holy water. The lower tier is for the ritual paraphernalia required during the recitations: books, a hand-bell, conch-shells, plates with rice-grain, loose maize for offerings, and cups for beer.

A few feet from this altar are set out a number of rough *tshotorma*, moulded out of boiled rice. They are later partly thrown on the pyre as offerings to the deceased, and partly consumed by the lamas and mourners.

As soon as the altar has been completed, the lamas begin with the recitation of the Drowa-Kündröl. The senior lama wields bell and *dorje* (thunderbolt), another lama plays cymbals, two lamas play flageolets (*gelung*), and one lama beats the big drum. There may be also two long trumpets (*sang-dung*), but these are not obligatory, and are played only at the funerals of very rich people who employ more than the usual number of four or five lamas.

While the lamas begin their recitation, other helpers carry the corpse to the pyre and undress it. The senior lama then sprinkles some water on it and recites a short text known as *Tosul*, while the corpse-bearers pour more water over the corpse. Seven square pieces of paper bearing block prints of certain prayers are then attached to the head, throat, chest, navel, knees and feet of the dead body. A larger piece of paper (*sakhil*), bearing the imprint of a simplified wheel of life with the syllables *o, ma, ne, pe, me, hun*, in its six compartments and the syllable *shri* in its centre is placed below the pyre. Above the head of the corpse is placed another print, known as *namkhil*, which represents a wheel of life surrounded by flames. The corpse is then built into the pyre in a sitting position, and a cross-frame of split logs constructed around it. The pyre is finally covered with juniper branches. At this stage one of the lamas throws away a small *torma* of rice-flour, known as *gyalse*, as an offering to the Lords of the Soil (*zidag*).

At the cremation of important persons poles with prayer flags of white, red and blue cloth are erected at some distance from the pyre. The number of these flags is not prescribed and the only time I observed this practice—at the funeral of Lama Kiu—they formed a triangle enclosing the pyre.

The lama acting as *chorpen* of the service then throws part of one of the *tsho-torma* on the pyre as an offering to the deceased. Brass dishes containing pieces of *tsho-torma* and other food are served to the lamas, and then begins the distribution of pieces of *torma*, boiled potatoes, buckwheat bread and puffed maize to all those present. It is not unusual for a number of small boys, not connected with the deceased, to attend a cremation mainly for the sake of this *tsho* food.

At this stage the lamas interrupt the service at the altar, and go close to the pyre, and standing there chant a special part of a book entitled *Nelung*. Another small *torma*, known as *gyak*, is thrown away as an offering to the evil spirits, and one of the lamas, who is not necessarily the one conducting the service, produces a pack of *tsagli*, small pictures approximately the size of playing cards, which represent the following deities and symbols:

1. Pawa Cheresi (Avalokiteśvara).
2. The *mantra* of Pawa Cheresi known as Paw Sung.
3. Lhayi-thuba, god of Lha-yül, the sphere of gods.
4. Lhamayin-thuba god of Lhama-yül, the sphere of titans.
5. Mi-thuba, god of Mi-yül, the sphere of men.
6. Chosung-thuba, god of Tundu-yül, the sphere of animals.
7. Yidak-tuba, god of Yidak-yül, the sphere of suffering spirits.
8. Nyeli-thuba, god of Nyela, the sphere of hell.
9–12. Gomadzi, the gods of the four quarters. (These may be on separate cards, or combined in one painting.)
13. Thang-lha, the god of the plains.
14. Man-dün, seven protective female spirits.
15. Tashi-takye, symbols of the seven perceptions.

16. Dzuki lhamu, six symbols including a wheel and three precious gems.
17. Guru Asara, provider of long life and disciple of Guru Rimpoche.

The senior lama displays one of these cards after the other, and while doing so, chants the appropriate text from the book *Nelung*, which instructs the departed about the phenomena he will encounter in the world beyond.

This chant also advises the *sem* of the deceased not to hanker after the possessions he had in this life, and to detach himself from thoughts of his house and family. He should go happily to the world beyond, and not trouble the living as a restless spirit. The text is, of course, not as simple as that, but the lay-folk believe that the words chanted in a solemn and soothing tune, very different from the usual invocations of deities, have roughly this meaning.

For the phase which then follows a book called *Nang-che-nima* is recited by the lamas. The use of this book was introduced only some forty years ago, by a lama who brought a copy from Lhasa. It replaced a simpler service, and is now generally used throughout Khumbu.

When the lamas return to the altar, and there resume their chanted recitations, the funeral pyre is set alight. This must not be done by a son, brother or husband of the deceased, but a son-in-law may light the pyre. More usually, however, this task is left to the corpse-carrier. Though some three hours may have passed between the beginning of the service on the cremation ground and the lighting of the pyre, this is by no means the final phase of the ritual, for now begins the elaborate presentation of a large variety of offerings (*zedza*) to Mela, the god of fire. While the pyre burns, the lama acting as *chorpen*, throws into the flames offerings of many kinds, comprising several types of grain, two kinds of grass, butter, honey, sesam, betel-nuts and the red paste used in preparing *pan*[1] as well as small sticks. He carries each item on a long iron ladle from the altar to the pyre, and another lama loudly counts out five portions of each item to be put on the ladle. There is no definite limit to the number of these offerings, for until the flames have consumed the body, more and more offerings are thrown into the fire, even if the sequence of sacrificial items has to be repeated several times.

[1] These offerings are made though Sherpas do not chew betel and *pan*.

While the pyre burns one of the lamas performs the *lhangma* rite, the fourth stage in every sacrificial performance; he takes a small dish containing the tip of a *tsho-torma*, as well as potatoes and rice, holds it up in a position of presentation, and then throws the contents away. The same process is repeated with the two *torma* known as *chindö* and *tema*, which are thrown away 'as an offering to all gods'.

As the flames slowly consume the body, a process which may take over two hours, and is hastened by the addition of new fuel to the pyre, the onlookers watch to see whether any charred pieces of bones become visible. One of these is picked out with the help of a stick, to be ground into powder and mixed with clay and water, and made into a *tsawar* figure (cf. pp. 236, 237).

The lamas end their worship by the act of *tashi*, the throwing of rice as an offering to all the gods invoked. The *torma* remaining on the altar are then cut up and distributed to the mourners, who may eat them at once or take them home. As a last offering the *chorpen* then sprinkles some milk into the pyre.

While the pyre burns down the lamas pack up their ritual objects, and the whole company moves away from the cremation ground. They return to the house of mourning where all those who attended the cremation, including small boys, are given a small gift (*geza*), which may be money, salt, chillies or any other available commodity. The lamas who officiated also get this gift in addition to the payment for their co-operation in the whole mortuary ritual, a payment called *bulup* for senior lamas and *te-rup* for junior lamas.

After their return from the cremation ground the lamas recite a book called *Tonak*, which is a kind of *kurim*, read for the benefit of the living members of the family.

All those who can afford to employ the lamas for a further period, commission them to perform a rite known as *napur*. This rite may be held either immediately after the funeral, if this has been held on the 3rd day after the death occurred, or on either the 7th or on the 11th day. Only rich people choose the 11th day, because in the intervening time the lamas continue to recite the Bardo Thödol and have to be fed and paid.

The book used for the *napur* rite is the *Nelung*, part of which has already been recited at the cremation. Before the *napur* can be performed some of the deceased's clothes and jewels are draped over a stool or rough framework in such a way that they can be taken for

The Practice of Religion

a figure to represent the dead person. This figure is known as *ten*, and its preparation is referred to as *ten-zu*. During the performance the lamas offer some of the food and drink with which they have been served to this figure, in the same way in which food and drink was offered to the corpse during the *Totul shetu*, the recitation of Bardo Thödol. In addition to the effigy a 'name-card' (*changpar*) is prepared, which consists of a piece of paper with the imprint of a prayer and a human figure, on which there is left space for the deceased's name. This is attached to a small stick, like a miniature flag, and this stick is erected in a vessel filled with grain, which is placed close to the *ten* figure representing the departed.

The lama conducting the service then begins the recitation of the *Nelung*, and calls upon the departed to present himself on the name-card and remain there until he directs him where to go. Next the lama addresses himself to the serpent-spirit (*lu*) of the locality, asking it to release the departed if he has fallen into its power, and to take instead a *torma*, which is a much more valuable offering. He then threatens to cut the *lu* into a hundred pieces, if it refuses to set the departed free.

Next he proceeds to assure the departed that he would cleanse him from all sins he had committed in this life, and free him from all worldly obligations.

The lama then produces six painted cards, each representing one sphere of the wheel of life. These he places in a row, between two lines of six *torma*. The vessel with the name-card is then first placed close to the card representing Nyela, and the tortures of this hell are described. One of the *torma* to the left is then thrown away as an offering to the *lu*, and one *torma* to the right taken up by the lama as an offering to the gods.

The departed is then released from rebirth in Nyela; the card representing Nyela is taken up, and the name-card is moved to the card representing Yidak-yül, the sphere of unhappy spirits. There the same procedure is repeated, and one more *torma* from each row is removed. In like manner the name-card is moved from one sphere to the other until at last it reaches the card representing Lha-yül, the sphere of gods. Since suffering extends even to this sphere, the lama frees the departed from rebirth in Lha-yül too, and the last card is taken up and the last *torma* are offered.

The lama then admonished the departed to be attentive when he shows him Pawa Cheresi, as big and as white as the snow-mountains. He should pray to him with folded hands, and if he does so he will receive whatever he desires. Next the lama shows him the gods of the four directions, who will act as his protectors. He assures the deceased that he himself is great and powerful like Pawa Cheresi, and that he can guide him to good places. If the departed does not follow his advice, he will suffer much.

The lama then blesses the *ten* figure, in the same way as living persons are blessed at a *Tshe-wong* rite, and offers it food. 'There is so much food here,' he says, 'that you cannot eat it all, the more you eat of it, the more it increases.'

The ritual now draws to its close, and the lama despatches the departed to Devachen, 'as fast as an arrow flies from a bow-string'. The final admonitions urge him to go to the west where the Buddha Sange Ngawang Tai Sakya Muni is dwelling. To his right he will see Pawa Cheresi (Avalokiteśvara) and to his left Tudze-chenbu (Avalokiteśvara mahākāruna). All these are benevolent divinities who will nourish and help the deceased.

'Your body has been burnt,' he is finally told, 'and only your mind (*sem*) is here. You are now like the letter A, and my (i.e. the lama's) *sem* is like HUM.[1] A and HUM are now mingled. With an arrow's speed now go to the place where I am sending you—*phoi, phoi, phoi!* There is nothing left here—your *sem* has gone too. Do not be afraid. I shall burn this piece of paper like a feather, of which no ash remains.'

Remaining in his seat, the senior lama now takes the name-card in one hand, dips a thin piece of wood in melted butter, lights it and with this flame burns the name-card. He then says: 'Your *sem*, which is like A, has now been taken up by the gods.'

From the moment of the burning of the name-card, the name of the departed should no longer be mentioned, and most people are indeed extremely reluctant to pronounce the name of any dead person.

The ashes of the name-card are gathered and mixed with a little *tsampa* and water, to be later mixed with the powdered bones of the deceased and some clay. The mixture is then pressed into a wooden mould and allowed to harden. The resultant figure, known as *tsa-*

---

[1] HUM is a mystical syllable which occurs in many magical spells and is untranslatable.

Lamas at a cremation rite in Khumjung

Lamas reciting the prayers for the departed

The distribution of money at a memorial rite

Guests at a memorial rite in Kunde

war, may have the shape of a seated Pawa Cheresi or simply of a *chörten*. It is deposited either in some isolated spot, where an overhanging rock protects it from rain, or is placed in a *gomba* or the building containing the prayer-wheel.

The popular view of the purpose of the *napur* is that it helps the departed to gain freedom from rebirth in any of the sections of the wheel of life, and to find his way to Devachen, the heaven presided over by Opame (Amithaba). Sherpas are well aware that only very few persons of exceptional merit reach this highest aim, but they think that even if the *napur* rite does not have this most desirable effect, it will nevertheless serve to improve the fate of the departed in the worlds beyond. Wealthy people commission *napur* rites to be held in various monasteries, and such rites are performed in addition to the *napur* which takes place in the house of mourning. On the day of this *napur* kinsmen and friends of the family are invited to a meal, and there is a rule that no part of the food served should be taken outside the house.

Irrespective of the date of the *napur*, a ceremony known as Dedzongu is performed on the 8th day after death, and this ceremony serves to rid the house of the evil spirits (*shrindi*), who may have caused the death. This rite is not strictly part of the mortuary rites, and it is very frequently performed in order to drive out spirits suspected of bringing disease and other misfortune. It is basically similar to the Lokpar rite held on the 7th day of the Dumje.

We have so far dealt with the funerary rites which follow a normal death. In cases of accident, when a person's body could not be discovered, there can, of course, be no cremation, and certain minor adjustments in the timing of the other rites may be required. By chance I had an opportunity to observe the procedure in two such cases, for during my stay in Khumjung a young man was killed by an avalanche while serving as porter on a mountaineering expedition, and a few weeks later his mother slipped on an emergency bridge across the Dudh Kosi and was drowned. In neither case was the body recovered, and hence there could be no funeral in the usual sense.

The proceedings began with the visits of friends and relatives to the house of mourning with gifts of beer and liquor. Such gifts are known as *semsun* and, unlike the *kem-chang* gifts offered if a corpse is in the house, these *semsun* gifts have no ritual significance, but are intended merely as an expression of sympathy. Their presentation is accompanied by words of comfort. The mourners are begged not to grieve too much, and they are reminded that all men must die some day. They are then encouraged to drink of the beer or liquor and thus soothe their sorrow.

As soon as lamas have been called together to perform the mortuary service, a *ten* figure is prepared, and from that moment on gifts of *kem-chang* can be brought in the usual way, part of the beer or liquor being offered to the *sem* of the deceased.

The lamas begin the ceremonies by reciting the book Dorje diksha, but not Bardo Thödol,[1] and this leads up to a performance of the *napur* rite. There is no difference between these proceedings and those that follow a normal funeral, for the departed is in both cases represented by the *ten* figure, and his name-card (*changpar*) is burnt in like manner.

For the young Sherpa killed in a mountaineering accident his mother commissioned additional *napur* rites to be performed in the three *gomba* of Tengboche, Thami and Kerok, but when she shortly died herself, the only *napur* held was that performed in her house.

With the completion of the *napur*, the lamas in charge of the funeral rites leave the house of mourning, and there is usually a pause in the sequence of ritual performances. But all except the very poor prepare during this pause for another set of ceremonies, which must be completed within forty-nine days, the period during which the spirit of the deceased is believed to be in a transitional state and capable of profiting from the prayers and offerings provided by the members of his family.

It is therefore during these forty-nine days that the final rites for the deceased's benefit are performed. These fall into two parts: the *shetu*, a solemn rite of worship accompanied by the repeated recitation of a short text, and the *gyewa*, the distribution of food and/or money in the name of the departed.

The essence of the *shetu* is the recitation of a text from the book known as Konchok-chindü (Union of the Precious Ones),[2] part of which must be recited at least a thousand times. The daily procedure

---

[1] In Solu it is customary to recite Bardo Thödol also on such occasions.
[2] Tib.: *dkon-mchog-spyi-'dus*. The full title of this book is *The Liturgy of the Union of The Precious Ones and Their means of expression in The Tranquil and Fierce Divinities*.

The Practice of Religion

is to recite the first part of the book (*majok*) only once in the morning, to recite the part known as *shetu gyewa*, morning, midday and evening, and to recite a short part known as *shetu dua* as often as possible and usually about twenty-five times during the day. Interspersed between the recitations of this section are short texts known as *sheawa*. To recite *shetu dua* and one such *sheawa* text takes about fifteen minutes, and by employing ten lamas for simultaneous recitation, the number of times the text has to be recited is divided by ten, and if twenty lamas can be gathered the time required is again halved. Wealthy people commission two or three thousand recitations of the *shetu dua*, and the whole performance may take five to six days.

Before they begin their recitations the lamas make a set of *torma* much more elaborate than those made for *Totul shetu* and *napur*. Together with the offerings and ritual objects these *torma* occupy six tiers of an altar put up on the far side wall of the main room. Even in houses containing a private chapel (*lhang*), the *shetu* is always held in this room which alone can accommodate all the lamas as well as the mourners and their friends and kinsmen. On the highest tier there are three great *torma*, representing Guru Rimpoche (in the centre), his fierce aspect Guru Trakpo (to the left), and his female manifestation Sengdroma, the lion-headed Dakini (to the right). Flanking these on each side are two minor *torma*, and separating the three central *torma* are cups containing offerings of beer and tea, the latter representing blood.

The tier below this contains thirteen *torma*, most of them representing *srungma* deities. A step further down is a row of butter lamps and symbols of the six perceptions, namely a book, a piece of cloth, some food, a conch shell, a pair of small cymbals and a mirror. Below this is a tier bearing a *torma* known as Wongbumedok (or Ongbu gonga), which stands for eyes, ears, tongue, heart and nose, and consist of more or less realistic representations of these organs to be offered to the fierce divinities. On the same tier there are incense, scented herbs, cymbals and two lamps. In front of this there are three cups made of human skulls, and given a more gruesome appearance by the addition of rows of teeth and other anatomical detail made skilfully out of butter dyed in different colours. Two of these skull-cups contain beer and one tea, which represents blood. On the same level there are numerous *torma*, known as *gaktor*, which serve as a kind of tally for the number of times the *shetu* text has been recited.

On the floor, below this altar, are baskets with offerings of grain and other food, and vessels of beer. In wealthy houses numerous lighted lamps stand on the altar, and as the butter burns out in a lamp, a new one is filled and lit to take its place.

From the hearth to the altar the whole room is given up to the lamas who sit in rows behind low tables bearing books, instruments and cups, kept always full of tea by the women of the house. At a *shetu* I attended at Kunde, held in the house of Dhanami (Thaktu) for the benefit of his father, there were thirty-four persons reciting, and these were seated in four rows: one on the window-bench, one against the back wall, and two facing each other across low tables along the centre of the house. There were all the lamas of Kunde and Khumjung, nine monks of Tengboche, seven lamas of Pangboche, five of Phortse, and one lama of Milingbo. In addition to professional lamas five men with the learning, but not the status, of lamas had also been invited, and their recitations counted on this occasion as equal to that of the lamas.

The *shetu dua* text was to be recited three thousand times, and as each lama's recitation counts separately, and more than thirty men were reciting simultaneously, less than one hundred recitations of the text were required. As each day's performance included about twenty-five repetitions of the *shetu dua*, four days were sufficient to complete the stipulated number of recitations.

The number of individual recitations (*dzar*) is counted by a tally which works in the following manner.

Every time the *shetu dua* has been recited, the *chorpen*, who on that occasion must be a lama, moulds a *torma* from a heap of cooked rice, cuts off the top and offers it to Guru Rimpoche represented by the central *torma*, known as *kingur*, and then puts the pieces aside. If there are ten lamas the text should have been recited for a thousand times as soon as the hundredth *torma* has been made in this way, but to allow for a margin of error—in case a lama fell asleep or otherwise missed a few recitations—the recitations are continued until the tally amounts to 108 *torma*.

Every time the *chorpen* offers a *torma*, he also pours a libation of beer into a small pot. This is later on emptied into a bigger vessel, and the beer is finally fed to the lamas. In addition the *chorpen* puts a handful of maize or rice on the *mendal*, the three-tiered silver object used for the 'magic offering of the universe',[1] and lights one lamp.

Thereafter the *chorpen* recites one of the *sheawa* texts, and while he does this—and the other lamas pause in their recitations—the members of the household prostrate themselves three times before the altar.

As soon as this act of worship is completed, the lamas resume the recitation of *shetu dua*, at the end of which the procedure just described is repeated in exactly the same form.

The lamas engaged in the performance of a *shetu* have to be provided with food and drink, and this constitutes a major item in the expenditure connected with the mortuary rites. A day's menu will give some idea of the rather lavish entertainment expected by lamas on such an occasion:

At dawn: Tea and *tsampa*.
Later and throughout the day: Beer and tea.
- 9 a.m.: *Getuk*, a Tibetan dish consisting of noodles of wheat flour, meat and greens.
- 12 a.m.: Boiled rice with some meat or vegetable stew, followed by beer.
- 3 p.m.: *Rildoksen*, i.e. mashed potatoes mixed with buckwheat flour.
- 8 p.m.: Stew of potatoes, meat and vegetables.

The provision of such a diet for up to thirty lamas during several days requires a considerable effort even for a wealthy household, and usually it is found necessary to construct a temporary cook-shed outside the house, and to call in kinswomen and friends to help in the preparation of the food.

The greatest expenditure of wealth, however, is connected not with the performance of the *shetu* rites, but with the final funeral feast known as *gyewa*. This too has to be held within the forty-nine days following death, and the Sherpas believe that the departed benefits directly from the wealth distributed in his or her name on the occasion of the *gyewa*. Usually the *gyewa* is held immediately after the conclusion of the *shetu* recitations, but there are cases when the *gyewa* takes place during a pause in the performance of the *shetu*.

[1] For a description and illustration of this ritual object, the rice-*mandala*, see L. A. Waddell, op. cit., pp. 296, 398.

The *gyewa* is basically not a religious rite, but a dispensation of charity to villagers and people from neighbouring villages. No personal invitations are issued, for the theory is that anyone attending the feast must receive a share of whatever is available for distribution. In fact, however, rich people preparing a *gyewa* let it be known that people from neighbouring villages are expected to come to the feast, while those of moderate means cater only for the inhabitants of their own village. The commodities customarily distributed at a *gyewa* are balls of cooked rice, clarified butter, salt and cash in coins or, of late, even in currency notes. While very rich men may provide all of these commodities as well as cash for distribution, less affluent men may have to be content with distributing only salt or rice.

A *gyewa* held on June 6, 1957, in Kunde village in honour of Ang Teshi of Thaktu clan can be taken as typical of the more lavish performances. The deceased's younger son Dhanami, who had lived in his father's house and acted as the donor of the feast, was himself fairly wealthy and moreover he spent on the funerary rites a recent gift which his father had received from his eldest son who was established as a trader in Lhasa.

The preparations for the *gyewa* began at about 10 a.m. At that time the *shetu* recitations were still continuing in the house of mourning, but in front of the public building containing the great prayer-wheel enormous cooking-pots had been installed on improvised hearths, and members of Dhanami's family helped by friends and kinsmen were busy with boiling large quantities of rice. The boiled rice was heaped on mats and several young people moulded it into large balls. These had to be of equal weight, and as one ball was finished it was weighed against another on a pair of simple scales. The rice-balls were then placed into carrying baskets and stored in the porch of the prayer-wheel building. At about midday two large cauldrons were placed over slow fires, and members of Dhanami's family emptied large tins of clarified butter into these cauldrons.

In the house of mourning kinsmen and close friends were entertained with liquor and a dish of stew and noodles which the visitors ate with chopsticks. Those accepting this hospitality placed a few coins on the table where the host was sitting, and such immediate payment for hospitality is considered courteous and in no way detrimental to the host's prestige.

Some of the donor's helpers then prepared for the seating of the crowds expected to come for the distribution of rice. On the large open space in front of the prayer-wheel building they drew long lines of powdered reddish earth, and as the *gyewa* guests began to arrive, they were asked to sit along the lines, but before the guests were directed to the space marked out for the people of their village, they were offered a drink of beer ladled out from large vessels kept at the approaches to the site of the *gyewa*. Among the guests were people from Namche Bazar, Phortse and Pangboche as well as from nearby Khumjung and, of course, from Kunde itself. They grouped themselves according to villages, and whereas the people of Khumjung and Kunde had turned out almost completely, it seemed that from Namche Bazar mainly the poorer people had come.

At about 4 p.m. the chanting and playing of instruments in the house of mourning stopped, and the lamas came to the open place, where by that time the guests were seated in orderly rows. Two lamas placed long, telescopic horns in position and others brought their flageolets. A tremendous blast from both types of instruments announced the beginning of the *gyewa*, and late-comers from Kunde and Khumjung hurried to sit down beside their co-villagers. All the lamas were then installed on blankets and low tables were brought and placed in front of them.

When this was done, the general distribution of gifts could begin. With baskets and cauldrons heaped with rice-balls the host's helpers walked through the rows of seated guests, and handed to each one of the large balls of cooked rice, while others carried cooking vessels filled with heated, liquid butter, which they ladled into vessels and tins brought by the guests. Each guest received nearly half a pint of this precious liquid.

Last came the distribution of money, and this was done by Dhanami, the donor of the *gyewa* himself. Accompanied by a lama of Khumjung, who carried a plate with rupee notes covered with a white cloth, he passed through the rows of guests, distributing one rupee notes from large bundles. The idea was to give to each person one *mohar*, i.e. the standard coin worth half a rupee, but as it had been impossible to obtain so many *mohar* coins Dhanami used the expedient of giving a one rupee note for two persons, and as more than one member from every family had come, this procedure did not cause any difficulties. Adults and babies in arms received the same amount, and altogether 580 rupee notes were distributed to 1,160 recipients constituting just over half of the total population of Khumbu.

When the distribution was over the guests got up, and without looking back streamed away in the direction of the villages. While otherwise the offering and the receiving of hospitality is accompanied by endless courtesies, the distribution and acceptance of the shares handed out at a *gyewa* takes place entirely mechanically and unaccompanied by any expression of appreciation or gratitude. By accepting whatever is offered the guests are believed to benefit the departed, and it would be discourteous not to attend a *gyewa* held by the heirs of a deceased co-villager.

Apart from the Rs.580 Dhanami distributed in cash, he spent at least Rs.1,500 on the provision of rice, clarified butter and beer. As not quite enough rice had been boiled, the lamas, who were to stay on in any case, and a number of late-comers who came for their share after the distribution was over, received the equivalent of the rice-balls in uncooked rice.

An expenditure of over two thousand rupees on a *gyewa* is not unusual, and within a month of the *gyewa* held by Dhanami of Kunde, Dawa Tenzing, a wealthy expedition *sirdar* of Khumjung, distributed at a *gyewa* held in memory of his late wife Chortin Rs.750 in cash, rice-balls at a cost of nearly Rs.600 and salt worth Rs.700. In addition to this expenditure he spent approximately Rs.550 on the payment and entertainment of the lamas employed for the performance of the *shetu* rite.

After the distribution of the gifts at the *gyewa*, yet another rite has to be performed in the house of mourning. This is known as *kongdzok*, and after its completion all the *torma* are broken up. Finally one of the lamas recites a prayer known as *mani kulup*, and kinsmen and villagers join in this service, either reciting the same text as the lama or, if incapable of doing so, repeating only the words Om mani padme hum.

Though not every *gyewa* needs to be performed on as lavish a scale as the *gyewa* in honour of Ang Teshi of Kunde, even the distribution of a single commodity is beyond the means of poor families. The very poor may have to omit any comparable performance, but those capable of affording the expenditure of brewing a quantity of beer, will carry a whole barrel to a path outside the village. There they offer a drink of *chang* to every passer by until the barrel is empty, and this modest dispensation of charity is known as *kor-chang*. The element common to *gyewa* and *kor-chang* is the undiscriminating distribution of food or drink. To invite a specific number of kinsmen or friends to a meal would count as ordinary hospitality and would lack the meritorious character of the dispensation of charity to all comers, be they the crowds attending *gyewa* or the incidental passers by on a public path.

Whether a *gyewa* or a *kor-chang* was held, on the fiftieth day after the cremation the piece of bone recovered from the ashes of the fire is pounded to powder and mixed with clay. The resulting mixture is then moulded into a small model of a *chorten* or other sacred symbol, and deposited in a *gomba*, prayer-wheel house or minor sacred structure, and this rite is known as *tsawar gyaup*.

As the last action in the long sequence of mortuary rites, the chief mourner approaches the senior lama who conducted the *shetu* with a present of one measure of rice, one rupee coin and one *mohar* coin, and informs him of the amount he had spent on the funerary rites and could do no more. In popular Sherpa belief the lama is supposed to convey this message to the departed. This final act is known as *ngo-shop* and concludes all that for the time being a mourner can do for his deceased parent, brother, wife or child.

The elaborate and costly rites which precede, accompany and follow the funeral of a Sherpa are clear evidence of a vivid belief in the dependence of those recently deceased on the ministrations of the living. Popular belief conforms with the doctrines expressed in such Tibetan books as the Bardo Thödol, commonly known as the 'Tibetan Book of the Dead',[1] and it appears that there is very little, if any, distinction between Sherpa and Tibetan eschatological ideas.

The same incongruities which have struck L. A. Waddell[2] occur also in the rites of the Sherpas, for the attempt to send the *sem* or spirit of the deceased straight to Devachen, the paradise of Opame (Amithaba), which a lama undertakes immediately after death, is obviously inconsistent with the belief in the intermediate state of forty-nine days between death and the deceased's entry into his or her next existence. But the Sherpas are not concerned about such

---

[1] For a translation and commentaries see W. Y. Evans-Wentz, *The Tibetan Book of the Dead*, 3rd edition, London, 1957.
[2] Op. cit., p. 492.

inconsistencies, and follow the principle that in a situation of uncertainty, provision must be made for all eventualities.

There is, above all, the general conviction that the departed, faced by unfamiliar surroundings and unknown dangers, is in need of the advice and support the lamas conducting the mortuary rites are capable of giving him. The ideas about the transitional state of forty-nine days, however, are vague, and to some extent conflicting. Some of my informants expressed the view that during this period the *sem* of the deceased was lingering on this earth, and this would be consistent with the practice of offering to the deceased both food and drink all through the rites performed in the house of mourning previous to the funeral as well as serving similar offerings to the *ten* figure during the *napur* rite after the cremation.

Yet, Sherpas believe at the same time that the departed is wandering through the regions of the nether world, and I was told explicitly that the recitation of the *shetu* helped the *sem* a great deal. For on the way to Shinje-chogyal, the King of the Dead, the *sem* might fall into the clutches of some malevolent spirit, and the purpose of the *shetu* was to counteract such a misfortune and to set the *sem* free.[1] Once the *sem* of the deceased has reached Shinje-chogyal, and has been sent to be reborn in one of the six spheres, the *shetu* cannot benefit him any more.

In all my conversations about the rites of death and the fate of the departed, I had the impression that lamas and educated laymen alike thought of the King of the Dead and other figures met by the *sem* as real beings, irrespective of the passage in the *Sidpa Bardo*, one of the texts recited in the course of the funeral rites, which denies their reality in that sense, and contains the following advice to the departed: 'The Lords of Death are their own hallucinations ... Apart from one's own hallucinations, in reality there are no such things existing outside oneself as Lord of Death, or god, or demon, or the Bull-headed Spirit of Death. Act so as to recognize this.'[2]

I do not know how Sherpa lamas interpret that particular passage, but I have no doubt that most, if not all of them, think of deities, demons and spirits as possessed of independent reality. Specifically Shinje-chogyal, the Lord of the Dead, is imagined as a figure of

---

[1] *Shetu* or *shetul* is said to be derived from the word *tul* 'to free, to liberate'.
[2] Translation by Lāma Kazi Dawa-Samdup in W. Y. Evans-Wentz, *The Tibetan Book of the Dead*, London, 1957, pp. 166, 167.

importance and power, and the ritual of the *napur* is specifically designed to exempt the deceased from rebirth in any of the six spheres to which this judge of the dead might send him, and thus to enable the deceased to enter Devachen. Automatic success of this rite would seem to conflict with the belief in the inexorable effect of a person's *karma* on his next existence, and would even frustrate the function of Shinje-chogyal as an impartial judge, who sends everyone to the sphere appropriate to his deeds in his life on this earth.

I discussed these inconsistencies with lamas as well as laymen, and most of them were of the opinion that the performance of rites and the charity dispensed by the surviving kinsmen could help the departed during his wanderings in the nether world, but that his final fate depended on his own merit or demerit. It was the purity of the heart of the departed, and not the expenditure of wealth by the survivors which would secure entry into Devachen or to Lha-yül, the desirable sphere of the gods. While some laymen are inclined to put excessive faith in the effectiveness of costly mortuary rites, the more learned lamas have no illusions about the power of their own ministrations. Ngawang Chotr of Pangboche, for instance, a lama well known for his learning, told me explicitly that *napur*, *shetu* and *gyewa* were useful only to those who had acquired merit (*sönam*) in their earthly life, while those whose records showed little merit but many sins would not profit at all from any such performance.

It is nevertheless the duty of a person's heir or spouse to afford the departed on its way through the nether world as much ritual support as possible. The surviving kinsmen are not in a position to know whether the departed would be able to profit from their exertions, but have to proceed on the assumption that there was scope for assistance through ritual performances and the dispensation of charity.

Among clerics without the control of a central authority deciding questions of doctrine it would be surprising to find no inconsistencies in beliefs as well as practice, and inconsistencies do exist in the lamas' ideas of man's fate after death. In contrast to the purist view that the balance of merit and sin alone determines a person's fate after death is, for instance, the belief that the recitation of the *kansu*[1] of the god Shingdzong-seang-dong was once effective in freeing a person already in hell (*nyela*) and sending him to Devachen,

---
[1] A text recited during *shetu*.

and it is in memory of this event that the *kansu* appropriate to this god was incorporated in the *shetu* recitations. This idea is not peculiar to the Sherpas, but corresponds to the Tibetan belief according to which those suffering the torments of hell can be released by the performance of certain elaborate rites, a belief stemming, as it seems, from the *Avalambana sutra*.[1]

The necessity to complete the funerary rites within forty-nine days after death arises from the belief that only during this period, when the departed is in a transitional state previous to a further incarnation or entry into Devachen, the ministrations of the living can reach and benefit those who have died. This belief, held by lamas and laymen alike, is not easily compatible with the custom of marking the anniversary of a person's death with a sacrificial rite, known simply as *tsho*, which is thought to benefit the person in whose memory it is performed.

Unlike *napur*, *shetu* and *gyewa*, the performance of a *tsho* rite in honour of a deceased parent or spouse is not considered obligatory even for those of ample means. But it counts as an act of piety and affection, and gives prestige to the donor as well as comfort to the departed. The only *tsho* I had the opportunity to observe was one commissioned by Puruwa Diki, a Khamba widow, whose husband had died in an accident about a year previously. This husband was of *khamendeu* status, and by marrying him Puruwa Diki had herself sunk to the level of *khamendeu*. She was a woman of very modest means, but had collected about Rs.400 to pay for the *tsho* rite in memory of her deceased husband. In her case there was no question of aiming at the gain of social prestige, but affection and a sense of duty towards her deeply mourned husband were the only motives for incurring the expense of the rite. It was held in the *gomba* and food and drink were provided on a fairly lavish scale. It is possible to perform a *tsho* in one's own house, and in that case only the officiating lamas and those specifically invited have to be fed, but Puruwa Diki wanted to do more and held the *tsho* in the village temple.

The ritual followed the usual pattern of Buddhist worship, which comprises the invocation of the deities concerned, the presentation

---

[1] This *sutra* tells how on the advice of the Buddha his disciple Māndgalyāyāna rescued his mother from the purgatory of the *preta*. Cf. L. A. Waddell, op. cit., pp. 98, 99, 493.

of offerings, hymns in praise of the deities, prayers for special benefits and finally a benediction.[1]

Few villagers were present during the performance of the ritual, but someone from every house came to receive his share of the cooked food, and it is believed that by eating of this *tsho* food one can benefit the person in whose memory the rite was performed. As the villagers came at their convenience the serving of drink and food continued until late in the evening, and next morning Puruwa Diki was still engaged in pouring out drinks and serving food. Among the last guests was one of the richest and most prominent men of the village, and the fact that Puruwa Diki and her husband were of *khamendeu* status and of very little consequence in Khumjung society did not deter him from eating a large meal.

According to popular belief a *tsho* is an offering to divinities and demons for the benefit of the departed, in whose honour it is held. As a person's next existence must long have been decided by the time a *tsho* is performed to mark the anniversary of his death, there can be no question of averting an unhappy rebirth but I have heard it said that by the performance of *tsho* the kinsmen of a deceased can shorten the period of his suffering in the sphere of unhappy spirits (*yidak-yül*) or in hell (*nyela*). The purpose of a *tsho* becomes more obscure, however, when its performance is in memory and honour of a lama whose reincarnation in human form has already been recognized. Thus the monks of Tengboche celebrate every year a *tsho* for Lama Gulu, the founder of their monastery, although Lama Gulu is reincarnated in their present abbot and lives in their midst. In that case one can hardly think of the rite as benefiting the person in whose memory it is performed, and it must be considered a memorial rite in the narrower sense, namely as a rite honouring the memory of the founder of the monastery in his incarnation as Lama Gulu. *Tsho* rites of this type seem to be regularly performed in most monasteries, and I was told that in Rongphu, too, every year a great *tsho* was held in honour of the past reincarnate abbot.

Among lay-folk, on the other hand, *tsho* rites in memory of deceased spouses or relatives are rare, and the *tsho* which Puruwa Diki commissioned in memory of her late husband was the only *tsho* performed that year in the village temple of Khumjung. Unlike Hindus

[1] Cf. Waddell, op. cit., p. 430.

the Buddhist Sherpas normally do not engage in any ritual comparable to the *sraddha* which could be described as ancestor worship. Great as the expenditure on *napur*, *shetu* and *gyewa* may be, in most cases these rites and perhaps a *tsho* at the first anniversary conclude the ritual preoccupation with the deceased, unless—as we shall see below (p. 265)—the unhappy spirit of a kinsman who failed to find rest in a new birth, visits his heirs or relatives and has to be pacified.

7

The Control of Invisible Forces

As Mahayana Buddhists the Sherpas of Khumbu believe in the great divinities, Buddhas and Bodhisattvas of the lamaistic pantheon, and the scriptures on which this belief is based are those used by all members of the Nyingmapa sect throughout Tibet and the adjoining regions. The attitude of the Sherpa towards the divinities whose pictorial representations cover in colourful profusion the walls of temples and private chapels is one of deep reverence and humility, but on the whole he does not think of these great figures of the transcendental world as likely to influence events affecting individual men and women as long as they live on this earth.

In his striving for spiritual perfection and the merit which will assure him a desirable rebirth and advance him on the path to Devachen, the realm of ultimate bliss, the Sherpa relies on the benevolent aid of the great Buddhist divinities Opame (Amitābha, 'Boundless Light'), Pawa Cheresi (Avalokiteśvara, 'Glancing Eye') and their human form the 'Precious Master' Guru Rimpoche (Padmasambhava, 'Lotus-Born') as well as on the host of protector deities (*srungma*). But when his material interests or his and his family's health are threatened he neither expects direct assistance on their part, nor does he reckon with the possibility that the wrath of any of these exalted figures may have caused his misfortune. He will think it very likely, however, that he or any other member of his household may have offended one of the minor earth-bound deities or spirits, and he will make every effort to discover in what manner such beings can be appeased or exorcized. According to Sherpa belief there are several categories of invisible beings, whose attention can be dangerous to man, but who can be controlled and rendered innocuous by those who know the appropriate means.

Most persistent in their attacks on men and women are the malignant spirits known as *shrindi*. Their number is legion, and people have always to be on guard to ward off their attacks, and drive out those whose evil influence has been identified. It is an eternal battle in which man can never comfortably relax, but in which he relies on the efficacy of well-established ritual, and the aid of two kinds of experts, the lamas and the spirit-media. Sherpas distinguish between *shrindi* who have never been human, and those *shrindi* or *norpa* who were men guilty of great sins and became malignant spirits instead of being reborn in one of the hells. As *shrindi* they are excluded from future rebirths, and one of the lamas of Khumjung ventured the explanation that by becoming *shrindi* they had sunk so low that they had forgone all chances of new incarnations. It is not clear, however, why some sinners should be born in one of the hells and there face a limited period of suffering while others become *shrindi* to roam the earth eternally, ever anxious to inflict harm on the living.

RITES OF EXORCISM

The rites to control the *shrindi* can be divided into public rites performed in the village temple in order to protect the entire community from the attacks of evil spirits, and private rites held in the house of individuals at a time of illness or in order to fortify the house against further misfortune, after a death or accident had already occurred.

In Khumjung a public rite of exorcism known as *tsirim* is held twice a year; once at the end of April and once in October. Its purpose is to rid the village of evil spirits (*shrindi*) and every year two officials (*lawa*) are appointed to organize the performance of the *tsirim* and to provide food and drink for the lamas. They collect contributions of grain from the villagers and this is used partly to pay the fees of the lamas, and partly to compensate the *lawa* for the expenditure of butter, tea and other provisions.

The *tsirim* is held in the village *gomba* and at least two lamas are required for its performance. In Khumjung three lamas resident in the village shared in the work of the preparations and in the subsequent rites, but if no local lama with sufficient knowledge is available outsiders may be brought in.

The preparations of *torma* and offerings took the three lamas several hours. The three main *torma* on the highest tier of the altar represented Guru Rimpoche, his fierce aspect Guru Trakpo and Sengdroma, the lion-faced goddess always associated with Guru Rimpoche and Guru Trakpo as *kañdo* or female counterpart. On the middle tier were *torma* representing Gombu Maning, Zida, Tema, Za, Thamchen, Chēndo and Ham-trhāng. Apart from this set of *torma* arranged on the altar, a special *torma* known as Lokpar and representing the *shrindi* to be expelled from the village was set up in a large iron dish standing on an iron tripod. This dish was filled with earth and in its centre was erected a three-headed figure moulded of dough and painted black; the three heads were those of a pig, an ox and a tiger. A fence of wooden spikes coloured red surrounded this figure, and inside this fence several multi-coloured thread crosses and three paper flags with red designs were stuck into the earth. This Lokpar *torma* symbolizes the *shrindi*, and the rite is intended to induce them to take their seat in it.[1]

The recitation from parts of the Konchok-Chündi ('Ritual of the Union of the Precious Ones') and the offering of the usual gifts of food to gods and spirits followed the same pattern as in such rites as the Dumje, but while the chanting of the lamas was of all due solemnity, the atmosphere was totally informal, relaxed and even gay. The lamas and other participants were confident that their incantations and spells would force the *shrindi* into the Lokpar *torma*, and there was no feeling that it might be dangerous to handle this receptacle of malignant forces. One can hardly imagine mediaeval Christian priests proceeding to the casting out of devils in so amiable and unruffled a frame of mind, but though those Buddhist priests and laymen certainly believed in the presence of evil spirits as firmly as any friar may have believed in the presence of devils, their usual gentle, cheerful and courteous manners were evident even in their dealings with *shrindi*.

The climax of the lengthy rite was reached when the senior lama called upon all the *shrindi* to enter the Lokpar *torma*, and on the floor of the temple another lama made a pattern of flour, and from this design a path of flour leading out of the temple into the open. Several young boys, carrying *kukri* and swords, then posted themselves before the Lokpar and three times rushed shouting along the

[1] This *torma* described by the Sherpas as Lokpar *torma* is obviously identical with the *Nag-po-mgo-gsum* image described in detail by Nebesky-Wojkowitz, in *Oracles and Demons of Tibet*, pp. 514, 515. I doubt, however, whether the Sherpa lamas are conscious of the symbolism according to which each feature of the three-headed image is intended to counteract specific evil forces. They rather see in it a general representation of the spirits inimical to man, and they destroy it to effect the downfall of the spirits.

flour path to the temple door. This was repeated several times, until the senior *lawa* lifted the Lokpar figure and carried it outside the temple precincts. Lamas and laymen followed him shouting and brandishing swords. The procession went as far as the southern end of the village, and there close to a *mani*-wall the Lokpar *torma* was put down, and two small boys were told to strike at it with their weapons. This completed the driving out of the *shrindi*, and every one returned contentedly to the *gomba* where the edible *torma* were distributed among the participants of this rite of exorcism.

Though no one doubts the efficacy of this public *tsirim* rite, it is yet accepted that *shrindi* are numerous and persistent, and anyone falling victim to an illness or other misfortune is easily inclined to attribute his affliction to the dreaded attention of a *shrindi*. By consulting a spirit-medium or a soothsayer[1] such suspicion can be confirmed, and the accepted way of diverting the evil influence of a *shrindi* is the performance of a private *tsirim* rite in the house of the affected family. Such a rite follows basically the same pattern as the public *tsirim* rites held in the village *gomba*, and the co-operation of at least one lama is essential. *Torma*, thread-crosses and other ritual objects are arranged on an altar, and there is invariably a Lokpar *torma* which eventually is carried out of the house and deposited outside the village.

While I lived in Khumjung, on many an evening I heard the drumming and shouting that accompanies the driving out of *shrindi*, and later in the night I would often see a procession of torches emerging from a house and moving towards the village border.

Particularly if there has been a misfortune in a house, such as the death of a child, it is considered advisable to rid the house of such evil influences as might have brought about the disaster, and to hold a *tsirim* rite in order to prevent future attacks by malignant *shrindi*.

SPIRIT-MEDIA AND SOOTHSAYERS

In his struggle with the evil spirits endangering human welfare the Sherpa relies in the last resort on the powers and techniques of lamas. But before the invisible enemies can be brought to battle they have to be identified and understood, and in this task Sherpas are helped by experts different from lamas and monks. These experts are the spirit-media or oracle-priests (*lhawa*, Tib. *lhapa*), and the soothsayers

[1] Cf. p. 262.

(*mindung*). Both *lhawa* and *mindung* are capable of seeing spirits, but only the former do so in a state of trance, during which spirits and gods take possession of the medium's body and speak through his mouth.

Compared with the number of lamas the number of spirit-media is small. They do not occupy a prominent place in Sherpa society by virtue of their special abilities, for unlike lamas, whose power is due to learning and spiritual achievements, the spirit-media are only the channels through which the spirits and deities manifest themselves to men. While anyone can be trained as a lama, only people of special psychic gifts can develop the skill of a *lhawa*, and turn their close relations with the spirit world to the advantage of their fellow men. Often a *lhawa* is virtually chosen by supernatural visitations and pressed into the rôle of medium irrespective of his own inclinations. However, the gifts of a medium may also be inherited, and there are families several members of which have acted as *lhawa*. Thus Pasang, a *lhawa* living in Jharo above Namche Bazar, had learnt the skill of establishing contact with spirits from his father's brother, who in turn had been the son of a famous medium of Thamo.

A-Tutu, a *lhawa* of Khamba origin settled in Khumjung, had had no direct contact with kinsmen proficient in spirit-mediumship. True, his mother's father had also been a *lhawa*, but A-Tutu had never seen him, and there were no other *lhawa* in the family. In 1957 A-Tutu was thirty years old, and told me that he had been a *lhawa* for about twelve years. As a youth he used to have confused visions which he could not interpret. They came upon him without warning, and made him feel ill and distraught. When he was walking through the hills, he would suddenly see no more mountains but be surrounded by level and nondescript country, or he might be in a house and see himself abruptly faced by crowds, but without being able to distinguish any details.

These visions distressed him so much that finally he approached the reincarnate abbot of Rongphu with the request to cure him of his affliction. The *tulku* lama examined A-Tutu and asked him to describe his visions. He then made him concentrate on a mirror, and asked him to describe what he saw in it. The lama then explained to A-Tutu that the confused cloud-like images he saw were gods and spirits, and suddenly the images became clear and A-Tutu saw the shapes of gods. The abbot also told A-Tutu that the visions he was having were caused by the influence of a certain god, whom he named. He moreover taught A-Tutu to distinguish the various elements of his visions, and how to work as a *lhawa*. All this instruction was completed in a single day, and no other lamas or monks took part in it; 'for only reincarnate lamas can see what is in men's minds'.

From that time onwards A-Tutu no longer suffered from involuntary trance-experiences, and began to practise as a *lhawa*. He fell into a trance only when he called his own familiar god. When he looked into the mirror used at all seances he could see his god, and the picture became gradually bigger and bigger and the room and the people therein smaller and smaller, till finally he saw his god as big as a great mountain. Then he could see other deities and spirits. The gods and serpent-divinities (*lu*) he saw in his bigger mirror, and the evil spirits (*shrindi*) and witches (*pem*) in a smaller mirror. The spirits (*shrindi*) of dead persons looked as these persons had looked when they were alive, and the *pem* had the appearance of the witches from whom they emanated. Gods and spirits spoke through his mouth, and whatever pronouncements he might make were derived directly from them, and were not his own conclusions. Though in his trance he might see distant places, he did not concern himself greatly with such visions but relied on what the gods and spirits might tell him.

Unlike the shamans of other Himalayan tribes[1] *lhawa* do not travel to the world of the spirits, but induce the spirits and gods to come to them and to speak through their mouths. They are able to discover which evil spirits may have caused an illness or other misfortune, and to indicate the manner in which they may be expelled or propitiated.

Lhawa have different ways of bringing about the state of trance in which gods and spirits take possession of them, but drumming plays an important rôle in inducing disassociation and a metal mirror is the main requisite used in focusing their visionary power. Almost invariably *lhawa* also don a head-gear (*ringa*) consisting of five leaf-like papier mâché tablets bearing paintings of the five Buddhas of Meditations, known as the *ligelwa-ringa* (Dhyani Buddhas). Attached to the band on which these tablets are strung are usually

[1] Cf. my 'The After-Life in Indian Tribal Belief', *Journal of the Royal Anthropological Institute*, Vol. 83, 1953, pp. 42-4.

The Control of Invisible Forces 257

also several bundles of feathers or ribbons. *Lhawa* are otherwise not dependent on any specific implements or ritual objects, but when preparing for a seance they usually erect an improvised altar with such offerings as bowls of water and rice-grains not unlike the altars put up for the worship of local divinities.

The procedure at a *lhawa*'s seance runs along certain traditional lines, but no two performances are exactly alike and each *lhawa* has his specific peculiarities. One of the seances I attended was held when my cook, Sonam, was ill through gorging himself with very high dried mutton and was obviously suffering from food poisoning. The Khamba *lhawa* A-Tutu was called in, but before he came Dorje Ngungdu applied some ritual first aid by burning, on a small stone slab, incense and a few woollen threads from the cloak of a great lama and waving the slab with smouldering wool round the patient's head, calling upon evil spirits (*shrindi*) and witches (*pem*) to depart. He then took the slab out of the house, placed some butter on the smouldering embers, surrounded the slab with other food offerings, and chased away the spirits with vehement spells, throwing dust and dirty leaves after them, and finally bolted the door.

When A-Tutu arrived he at once occupied himself with the prostrate Sonam. He had not brought any of his paraphernalia and first called for a rosary. This was fetched from a neighbouring house, and the *lhawa* then let the beads pass through his hands, and finally pronounced that a *shrindi* had attacked Sonam. This *shrindi* or *norpa* was the ghost of Lakba Gelbu, the late owner of the house in which we were living. Lakba Gelbu had been killed by an avalanche some twelve years previously and it was common knowledge that he had turned into a malignant ghost. The fact that Sonam was shivering and felt cold to the touch was connected with Lakba Gelbu's death in the snow.

When I asked A-Tutu to discover a way of propitiating the *shrindi*, who was causing Sonam's illness, he sent for the requisites used in every seance. They were brought in a basket and from this A-Tutu took two large brass cups and seven small zinc cups, a large and a small brass mirror, and the crown-like head-dress (*ringa*). He then asked for two small tables and improvised a stepped altar using one of my table-cloths as a covering. Next he asked for a lamp, filled it with butter and placed it on the altar in the middle of the seven zinc cups. One of these was filled with beer, one with milk and the remaining five were filled with rice; rice-grains were also put on a plate together with two strips of white cloth and two strips of red cloth. A-Tutu then put butter marks on the two metal mirrors and placed them on the altar.

When the altar had been prepared a large double-membrane drum was fetched from the *gomba* and erected next to the altar. Juniper twigs and pieces of smouldering wood were placed on a shovel and put next to the *lhawa*'s seat.

The scene was now set and the seance could begin. Standing upright in front of the improvised altar and holding the large mirror and a white cloth, A-Tutu began to chant in a low voice. He repeated this holding the smaller brass mirror, and then put the two mirrors into the two brass bowls filled with rice. Holding the plate with rice he then sprinkled rice-grains over the altar calling at the same time on various divinities and inviting them to come.

A-Tutu then sat down facing a low table, which had been placed at right angles to the altar. In this position he continued to chant and now and then scatter rice-grains. Soon he began to tremble, breathe heavily and to utter occasional grunts. Trembling, he took the head-dress and put it shakily on his head. He then grasped a bundle of ribbons and holding it in his left hand, hid his face in the ribbons, while with his right hand he beat out a rhythm on the drum. His knees trembled all the time as he sat cross-legged and his head swayed from one side to the other. A thin singing sound turning now and then into a high falsetto alternated with hissing and noisy blowing through the nose. Gradually his face, which had borne a tortured expression, assumed a peaceful and happy look.

Dorje Ngungdu, who sat facing the *lhawa*, tied a white ribbon to the other ribbons of the *ringa* head-dress, and put some rice-grains into A-Tutu's hand. The *shrindi* was now believed to be visible in the mirror, and three women present at the seance saluted the *shrindi* with folded hands, prostrating themselves before it.

I was then asked to provide a small silver coin, and this was placed on the altar as an offering to the *shrindi* who was requested to enter the *lhawa*'s body.

A-Tutu then violently shook his head until the head-dress slipped down. This was necessary, for the head-dress belonged to his tutelary god, and it had to be removed before the way was clear for the *shrindi*. The drumming then stopped, and the *lhawa* fell backwards, as if doubled up with pain, and threw himself about. He shivered violently and seemed to suffer the same pain as Sonam. Eventually he raised his arms, and as he opened his mouth, he breathed heavily like someone under an almost intolerable strain. At last he began to speak.

Dorje Ngungdu and the women present asked questions, and the *lhawa* replied haltingly between sighs and whistles. The ghost of Lakba Gelbu now spoke through A-Tutu's mouth, and he began by blaming Sonam for having come to live in the house which belonged to him. He then asked for a specific carpet, which had belonged to him, and this was found in the store-room and placed before the *lhawa*. All the time shivering and trembling A-Tutu then rubbed his thighs and back. The *shrindi* then called for beer, and this was poured into a cup, and the *lhawa* drank of it. But the *shrindi* did not relish the beer, saying that it was bad, and called for *rakshi*, i.e. distilled spirit. This seemed to satisfy him.

The ghost of Lakba Gelbu, always speaking through the mouth of A-Tutu, then said that by midday he would have carried Sonam away, but because of the offerings given by Dorje Ngungdu early in the morning, he now relented and would spare Sonam's life.

Further questions put in a calm and matter of fact tone by Dorje Ngungdu and the three women elicited long and rapidly spoken replies by Lakba Gelbu's ghosts. He pointed out that he had not been an ordinary person, but the son of a *pembu*, a rich and important man. He wanted only the best of food as offerings and would accept them only at the hands of Dorje Ngungdu himself, and not at the hands of Khambas whom he disliked. He complained that for days beer and strong liquor had been drunk in his house, but that no one had given him any offerings. He also expressed anger about the behaviour of his widow and his son, who had left and allowed the house to remain empty—a circumstance which incidentally had enabled me to hire it for the period of my stay in Khumjung.

Suddenly A-Tutu fell backwards, then raised his arms and with a quick movement indicated that the *shrindi* of Lakba Gelbu had departed. This, however, did not mean that the seance had come to an end.

The *lhawa* resumed the beating of the drum and began to chant in a different way. Gradually his expression changed, and he whistled and chanted with protruding lips, his face assuming a savage mien: a *dü*, a female demon, had possessed him. This possession did not last long, and soon gave way to possession by a *lu*, a serpent spirit. Soon the *lu* too was gone, and two different *dü* possessed A-Tutu in quick succession.

Next the *lhawa* was possessed by a monkey; he climbed one of the wooden shelves and made the movements of a monkey plucking fruit. Hardly had the monkey left him, and he had resumed his seat, when he was possessed by a bull, walked on all fours, pawed the floor and drank water in animal fashion from a bowl.

After these exhibitions A-Tutu was possessed in turn by Cho-sum, a god of Pangboche, by Kim-dang-kalar-karbu, a god from Tibet, who was A-Tutu's own tutelary deity, and by Deling-kandzi, a goddess of Darjeeling, who always appears at the end of a seance. While these divinities were present, the three women asked them questions not connected with Sonam's illness, and received out of A-Tutu's mouth reassuring news about their absent husbands, welfare.

One and a half hours after the beginning of the performance A-Tutu suddenly came out of his trance, and without much ado packed up his ritual objects, and the rice which was his perquisite. He also was paid four rupees, and kept the half rupee coin offered to one of the gods.

Then several branches of juniper were brought into the house, and Dorje Ngungdu prepared the feast for the ghost of Lakba Gelbu. The dead man's own carpet was put on the place where he used to it, and a meal consisting of stewed meat and rice, a cup of tea, as cup of beer and a small cup of liquor was set out on the low table. Dorje Ngungdu and A-Tutu then stood before the table and offered, one after the other, the food and drink to the *shrindi*. After having been formally presented each offering was thrown out of the window. Finally A-Tutu took the juniper twigs off the table, and waved them over the patient, who seemed calmed and comforted by the performance.

Both Dorje Ngungdu and A-Tutu then left the house carrying with them smouldering incense, and some minor offerings for the spirits and deities that had spoken through A-Tutu's mouth. The latter pretended to remember nothing of what he had done or said during his trance, and it is generally accepted that a *lhawa* acts simply as the mouthpiece of the gods and spirits coming upon him, and that afterwards he has no knowledge of the pronouncements which he had made while in a state of possession. In this state a *lhawa*'s voice usually undergoes a change, and he speaks or chants in a thin falsetto voice which sounds as if it were produced under a great strain.

The diagnosis of a *lhawa* is sought in most illnesses and other misfortunes, and there is no conflict between this approach to invisible powers and the approach made with the help of lamas. *Lhawa* often advise their clients to commission the recitation of sacred texts by lamas as one of the means of averting the wrath of an offended spirit or deity, and similarly lamas may suggest the consultation of a *lhawa*, if an illness does not show signs of improving as a result of the recitation of the appropriate scriptures. A *lhawa* may even point out what particular text should be read as a *kurim*, or he may discover the presence of an evil spirit and indicate that it can be expelled only by a Do-zongu rite performed by a powerful lama.

Lhawa never administer medicines, while some great lamas both manufacture and administer medicines of various sorts. Conversely no lama may ever act as a spirit-medium. The two vocations are exclusive, although they do not stand in a relationship of rivalry.

The importance of the spirit-media for the beliefs and world view of the Sherpa lies in the fact that deities and spirits manifest themselves in their seances and assume the reality of beings comprehensible through the senses. While in the rites conducted by lamas the presence of the divinities invoked is generally assumed, the presence of the deities, demons and spirits that possess a *lhawa* are directly experienced, and their utterances heard from the lips of the medium. No Sherpa doubts their reality nor the relevance of their pronouncements for the solution of personal problems.

A *lhawa* may also assist in crystallizing a latent and unexpressed public sentiment; thus he may confirm suspicions of the presence of a witch among the members of a village community. A witch (*pem*), though still alive, may speak through the mouth of a medium or of the *lhawa*, who, while in a state of trance, may see the face of a witch and recognize her. He may then identify the witch and indicate the means of warding off her attacks, but although the persons present at the seance may hear this and pass their knowledge on to others, care will be taken not to let the witch know that her nature has been recognized. Hence the *lhawa*'s discovery will not result in any public condemnation or prosecution of the witch, but individuals will be careful not to expose themselves to her harmful attention.

While *lhawa* can see in their trance all the inferior earth-bound gods and spirits, they cannot see the great divinities of Devachen (Tib.: *nub-p'yogs-bde-ba-can*), the western paradise of Opame. It is only great lamas and particularly reincarnate lamas who have gained so much merit that they can see the gods of Devachen. The *lhawa* are always involved in the affairs of the six spheres of the wheel of rebirth, and Sherpas therefore consider it unlikely that a *lhawa* can gain entry to the heaven of Opame. Perhaps it is the involvement with evil spirits and inferior, earthbound gods inseparably linked with the work of a *lhawa* which accounts for the fact that the vocations of lama and spirit-medium are considered incompatible.

In many respects similar to the rôle of the spirit-medium is that of the soothsayer (*mindung*) who has the power of clairvoyance without the need for a state of trance and possession by supernatural beings. The process of soothsaying is known as *tabyo*, and the art of the *mindung* may be practised by laymen and women as well as by lamas. Some *mindung* require no properties, while others use beads or a combination of lamp, mirror and rice-grains. A *mindung* in Khumjung used to put rice-grains into the hand of the client who had come for consultation, then took them back and threw them against a mirror. In this mirror he would then see whatever he had been asked to discover. Another *mindung* told me that when he was called to a patient he usually saw in front or behind the sick person the shape of the spirit or witch who had caused the affliction. Sometimes he would see this even in front of the messenger calling him to the sickbed. If he did not have such a vision spontaneously he used beads in order to discover whether a *lu*, *dü* or *shrindi* had attacked the patient. People consult *mindung* not only in the event of illness, but also in order to know whether a trading transaction will be profitable, or where a lost object can be found. The advice given by soothsayers is not very different from that offered by spirit-media; *mindung* may tell that a *norpa*, *shrindi* or *lu* has to be propitiated and what type of offerings would be acceptable.

Some great lamas, too, have the gift of clairvoyance and this is called *sundak-sho*. They never use properties but simply close their eyes and meditate for some time before giving their answer. They sometimes combine this process with astrological devices, ask for the client's day and year of birth, and then consult a book. A lama known for his gift of clairvoyance is consulted about the suitability of house sites, the choice of marriage-partners, the prospects of trade-deals as well as about the care of sickness. For such consultations people pay, according to their means, fees ranging from Rs.2 to Rs.5, and there are lamas who derive an appreciable income from such consultations. The art of *sundak-sho* cannot be learnt, but lamas of great spiritual power acquire it spontaneously.

WITCHES (*PEM*)

The practitioners who aid the Sherpa in his struggle with invisible malignant forces often come up against the baneful influence of witches and there is the widespread belief that much illness and other misfortune is caused by their activities. A witch is known as a *pem* or *sondim*, and normally it is only women who develop the power and urge to harm others through the invisible influence of their mind (*sem*) while they are still alive. Some of my informants were of the opinion that very rarely even a man may develop such malignant powers, but I have never heard of a concrete case.

No woman is ever born as a *pem*, but she may turn into a witch through envy, jealousy and evil thoughts and deeds. The *sem* of such a woman can act independently of her body, and is believed not to be fully under the control of her consciousness. Thus it is thought that the *sem* of a witch may visit other places and attack people, not only when she is asleep, but even while she is awake and at work. While the woman developing such powers is aware of her nature as a *pem*, she is believed not to be conscious and in control of all the doings of her *sem*. Thus the condition of a witch may be regarded as an affliction comparable to the evil eye rather than as a wilful manipulation of malignant forces. Yet, no good-natured woman kindly disposed towards her fellow-villagers is in danger of turning into a *pem*. This process is always set in motion by a wilful malicious act or persistent evil thoughts. Of one well-known witch of Khumjung it was said, for instance, that she became a *pem* when she poisoned some of her relations, and even her nearest kinsmen were so afraid of her that they did not dare accept food in her house.

The end of this particular *pem* occurred at the time of my stay under dramatic circumstances. First her son was killed by an avalanche while on a mountaineering expedition, and a few weeks later the woman herself slipped on a bridge across a swollen stream and was drowned in full view of her companions. Her body disappeared in the turbulent waters of the Dudh Kosi, and though later it was seen wedged between two rocks no attempts were made to recover it, for the lamas consulting their astrological manual had found out that it would have been extremely unlucky for anyone to touch the body.[1]

A *pem* wandering about and attacking people is sometimes accompanied by the *lu* of her house, and some witches send ahead their *sapta*, a dangerous type of earth-spirit, in the same way 'as kings send their soldiers ahead of them'. The evil influence of a witch can make itself felt at a great distance, and there are many stories of Sherpas who offended a woman having power of a *pem* while on a journey far beyond Khumjung and suffered her revenge long after returning home. If a spirit-medium identifies such a *pem*, she is placated with offerings, and these may be given near the afflicted person's home, however far away the witch may live. Similarly a *pem* dwelling in the vicinity is propitiated with offerings in the same way as the spirit of a deceased person, and no approach is made to the woman who has been recognized as a witch.

The Sherpas' attitude to *pem* is very different from the treatment witches receive among many Indian populations. Neither is a witch accused to her face of her doings on the evidence of spirit-media or seers, nor will any attempt be made to expel a woman identified as *pem* from the village where she resides. This may partly be due to the belief that an embittered witch could do more harm from a distance than she is likely to do when left unmolested, and partly to the belief that a woman may turn into a *pem* without her own volition. Consideration for the feelings of the other members of her family may also play a rôle in determining a community's attitude. In the case of the witch who died by drowning during my stay in Khumjung respect for her husband, who was a successful and well known *sirdar* of many mountaineering expeditions, had certainly played a part in muffling any public expression of condemnation of her activities. On the other hand, it was said, that her son had left

[1] Cf. p. 226.

the village and accepted employment in India largely because he was conscious of her reputation and felt awkward living in Khumjung.

MALIGNANT GHOSTS (*NORPA*)

Whereas some afflictions and individual misfortunes are attributed to the attacks of witches, a much larger part of human suffering is thought to be caused by the malignant ghosts of certain dead men. These ghosts are known as *norpa*, though in casual speech they are frequently referred to by the more general term *shrindi*. In contradistinction to a *pem*, who is the perverted *sem* of a living woman, a *norpa* comes into being if the *sem* of a dead man or woman is not reborn in any of the six worlds but wanders about on this earth without finding rest. Such a fate may be the result of evil deeds or thoughts in the person's last life, or it may be brought about by the manner of death. People who died in accidents are liable to become *norpa*, but if they had not been guilty of particularly evil conduct they may after a time cease being *norpa* and achieve rebirth in another sphere. The surviving kinsmen of such a person can aid him to escape from the existence of *norpa* by commissioning lamas to recite prayers for his benefit. The young son of the witch mentioned above, for instance, was believed to have become a *norpa* on being killed by an avalanche, and when he spoke through the mouth of a spirit-medium, he asked for warming food and drink because he was suffering from the effect of the snow and ice under which his body was buried. He also blamed his parents for having urged him on to engage in the dangerous occupation of high-altitude porter, and this pronouncement made through a *lhawa* corresponded to the general view in Khumjung that the young man's ambitious and greedy mother had forced him to take up expedition work against his own inclinations. The *norpa* thus said what was commonly believed to be the sentiment of the deceased, and in this case it was also thought that the *sem* turned *norpa* might sooner or later be released from this condition and attain another rebirth.

Generally a *norpa* does not move about alone but is accompanied by a *gyap-tak*, who may be a demon (*dü*), serpent-spirit (*lu*) or a locality spirit of malignant inclination. In the case of a person killed in an accident the locality spirit of the place of death is likely to assume the rôle of *gyap-tak*, and when a *norpa* is propitiated with offerings separate gifts are usually also offered to the accompanying *gyap-tak*.

The mortuary rites, and particularly the recitation of the *Nelung* text, aim at preventing the *sem* of the deceased from turning into a *norpa*. But these attempts are sometimes of no avail, and the probing of spirit-media may reveal that even a person highly respected in his last life suffered the fate of becoming a malignant, earth-bound ghost. Thus I found in 1957 that Kushyo Kapkye, whom four years previously I had come to know as the senior lama of Khumjung, was believed to have turned into a *norpa* and had appeared as such to more than one *lhawa*. This situation seemed all the more ironic as I remembered well a conversation in which the old lama had explained to me most earnestly that the performance of mortuary rites and memorial feasts could not benefit a dead man unless he had had a pure heart; the final determinant of a man's fate after death were not offerings and recitations but purity of heart.

SERPENT OR WATER-SPIRITS (*LU*)

To an order of normally invisible beings entirely different from that of *pem* and *norpa* belong the serpent or water-spirits known as *lu* (Tib. *klu*). But in their effect on men these *lu*, which correspond in some respects to the Indian *naga*, and are referred to as *naga* by Sherpas speaking in Nepali,[1] share some of the characteristics of *pem* and *norpa*, and the techniques employed to ward off the attacks of witches and ghosts are used also to diagnose and neutralize the unwanted attentions of an offended *lu*.

According to the Tibetan iconographic tradition followed by Sherpa painters, *lu* are depicted as men or women with a snake's tail in the place of legs, and there is the general belief that *lu* are closely associated with water. Yet, in Sherpa ritual practice, *lu* are treated as house-spirits rather than as water-spirits, and every family should normally have a house-*lu* and offer it regular worship.

A *lu* is potentially of benevolent disposition, but if neglected or offended can turn malicious and dangerous. The Sherpas visualize the changes in a *lu*'s temper as a change of colour; a *lu* can be

[1] R. de Nebesky-Wojkowitz is probably correct in suggesting that the Tibetan *klu* were originally water-spirits who have been identified with the *nāga* of India, and that consequently many a well-known *nāga* or *nāgi* is today included in their numbers. Cf. *Oracles and Demons of Tibet*, 's-Gravenhage, 1956, p. 290.

black, piebald or white; a black *lu* is malevolent, a piebald *lu* indifferent, and a white *lu* benevolent. There are male as well as female *lu*, but only the latter are dangerous to humans. The Sherpas believe that many *lu* migrate to Tibet during the summer and rainy season and return to Khumbu for the winter. This explains why in places such as Namche Bazar there is less water in the summer, although it rains then, than during the winter months. Individual *lu* have different names, and two prominent male *lu*, Gaphu and Zogphu, are described as *lu-gyelbu*, i.e. kings of the *lu*. Another important *lu* is Ham-thrang, the *lu* of a place where Guru Rimpoche (Padmasambhava) hid a sacred text, instructing the local *lu* to guard the book with the promise that the *lu* would be worshipped in return for this service.

There is a general belief that *lu* have a greater affinity to women than to men, and it is indeed the women who worship their house-*lu* most regularly. In view of the attachment of the house-*lu* to the women of the family special precautions are taken to prevent such a *lu* from following a bride when she goes to her husband's house. Before a newly married bride leaves her parental house the shrine of the family *lu* is covered with a cloth, and young girls and children sing and dance round the *lu* shrine in order to detract the *lu*'s attention from the bridal procession.

A man who sells his house and moves to another house or locality, however, will open his *lu* shrine, take the *lu* pot contained in it with him and enclose it in a new shrine built near his new home. A *lu* pot contains various substances symbolizing the eyes, hands, heart, liver, kidneys, lungs and intestines of the *lu*, as well as grains of maize, wheat, barley and rice, and pieces of gold, silver and beads. There is the belief that if a *lu* shrine is well maintained the *lu* appears as a young woman, whereas the *lu* of a neglected shrine appears to spirit-media and seers as an old, shrivelled woman. Such a *lu* can be rejuvenated by proper care of the shrine, just as the regular propitiation of a *lu* can bring about a change in colour.

A married son who separates from his parental household and moves to another house will not attempt to take the house-*lu* with him, but will consult a *lhawa* in order to discover where an unattached and unclaimed *lu* can be found. It is not absolutely necessary to build a shrine for a *lu*. Dorje Ngungdu, for instance, had been living in his house for many years without having built a shrine.

With the help of a *lhawa* he had found a *lu* and was worshipping it under a tree. He said that in order to install this *lu* in a shrine he would require an earthen pot from Tibet, for he was not sure whether a *lu* would take residence in a pot made in Nepal.

The Sherpas think of *lu* as real house-spirits who live in close proximity to the human inmates of the houses. Through the mouths of spirit-media the *lu* can make their wishes known and complain of actions which cause them discomfort. During a seance which I watched in Khumjung in 1953 the *lu* of the house, who had possessed the medium, blamed the members of the family for throwing their boots on the floor and thereby hitting its body. This complaint was launched in a most dramatic form; the *lhawa* possessed by the *lu* wept and whimpered on account of the pain inflicted on the *lu* by the throwing about of boots which had hurt it and polluted its home. The inmates of the house eventually satisfied the *lu* by removing the boots from the corner on the ground floor into which they used to throw them, and by placing an offering of butter into the fire of their hearth. The patient, a young girl for whose sake the seance was being held, prayed to the *lu*, asking for forgiveness of deeds which she had committed not on purpose, but out of ignorance, and concluded with the words: 'Please do not kill me, but let me live'. This final rather pathetic plea seemed to be somewhat inconsistent with the general belief that *lu* may cause swellings of the limbs, pain in the head or stomach, inflammation of the eyes and similar ailments, but neither a fatal disease nor a fatal accident.

Although an offended *lu* can become dangerous, the association with one of these water-spirits seems nevertheless advantageous, for otherwise a Sherpa would hardly go to the trouble of inducing his house-*lu* to move with him to a new house site or of finding an unattached *lu* who can be installed in a new shrine. If properly worshipped and kept in a good temper *lu* can be valuable allies in the fight with ghosts and evil spirits, and I have heard a *lu* who spoke through a *lhawa*'s mouth offering to drive away a troublesome *norpa* in return for worship and offerings. A favourably inclined *lu* also helps with the growth of crops and benefits the welfare of the cattle.

A popular prayer to the *lu* runs as follows: 'May all black *lu* become piebald, may all the piebald *lu* become white, may the white *lu* increase in kindness and benevolence.'

The water-spirits known to all Tibetan speaking people as *lu* (*klu*) are usually classified as a distinct category of *dregs-pa* or protective deities, but among the Sherpas, as also among other Bhotia populations, they have assumed the character of spirits very closely associated with individual families and houses. This association invests them with an importance in the esteem of the average Sherpa far surpassing that of most other classes of gods, and the maintenance of friendly relations with its house-*lu* is a vital concern of every family.

CONCLUSIONS

Though *shrindi* (spirits), *norpa* (ghosts) and *lu* do not represent the only categories of potentially malevolent invisible beings known to the Sherpa, they are those most frequently impinging on human affairs and consequently a target of the defensive efforts of lamas and spirit-media. To enumerate the many other ferocious and dangerous divinities and demons, the belief in whom the Sherpas share with all members of the Nyingmapa sect, would largely mean a duplication of the studies of such Tibetologists as David Snellgrove[1] and R. de Nebesky-Wojkowitz,[2] without materially adding to an understanding of the world-view of the average Sherpa. Lamas as well as laymen are conscious of the existence of a great number of demons as well as of the fierce aspects of the great divinities commonly represented on the walls of temples and frescoes, and some of the minor demons sometimes take possession of spirit-media and speak through their mouths. The most dangerous of these are the *dü*, equated with the *rakshasa* and *rakshasi* of Indian mythology, and we have seen that a man-eating *dü*, tamed by Lama Dzi-chen Rimpoche, is traditionally associated with the institution of the Niungne rite. Another category of malevolent deities are the *sapta* (Tib. *sa-bdag*), earth-spirits whom the Sherpas regard as somewhat similar to the *lu* but more dangerous in disposition. This is clearly a popular simplification, and Nebesky-Wojkowitz has shown that above the *sa-bdag* listed in the Tibetan astrological compendium *Vaidūrya dkar po* can be divided into a number of distinct categories.[3]

---

[1] Cf. *Buddhist Himālaya*, Oxford, 1957, and *Himālayan Pilgrimage*, Oxford, 1961.
[2] Cf. *Oracles and Demons of Tibet*, 's-Gravenhage, 1956.
[3] Op. cit., pp. 291-8.

Like all Mahayana Buddhists the Sherpas are confident that the forces of evil, in whatever form they may be manifested, can be brought under control by the exertion of spiritual powers. Just as the 'Precious Master' (Guru Rimpoche) tamed the indigenous deities of Tibet and forced them to accept the rôle of protector deities (*srungma*) so lamas of highest spiritual standing have the power to ward off the attacks of demons and evil spirits. Every sacrificial rite performed in the temples and private houses of Khumbu serves in part towards the propitiation or control of invisible beings potentially dangerous to man. The ultimate triumph of the true doctrine, as ceremoniously symbolized by such ritual performances as the Mani-rimdu, is never in doubt but in the Sherpa's daily life the services of humble village priests and spirit-media are frequently needed to ward off the threats of such minor enemies as a disgruntled ghost or offended serpent-spirit. Once diagnosed the evil influence of such a creature can be bought off even by laymen tendering the appropriate offerings, and only if a spirit proves refractory may a lama of high spiritual power have to be called in to perform a rite of exorcism.

8

Values and Moral Concepts

The Sherpa's world-view is a complex combination of a naïve belief in countless personal beings inhabiting this earth and the five other spheres of the Buddhist universe with the highly sophisticated conviction that man's ultimate fate is determined not by his relations with these personal beings but by his attitude to certain impersonal principles to which both men and gods are subject. The former aspect of the Sherpa's view of nature is not fundamentally different from that of many more primitive tribal populations of Nepal. The mountains, valleys and rivers of his environment, in many parts so forbidding and empty of human inhabitants, are enlivened with a throng of hill-deities, earth-spirits, water-spirits and other spirits partly hostile and partly friendly to man. Their cult and periodic propitiation has been referred to in the previous chapters, where we have seen that the Sherpa is conscious of the beneficial as well as the harmful influence these invisible beings can exert on his bodily and material welfare.

His fate in the life to come, however, is not dependent on the attitude or grace of any divine or demonic powers, but solely on the balance of merit and guilt which he accumulated in the course of his life on this earth. It is his moral conduct which ultimately determines his next reincarnation or—in the rare cases of great saints—his entry into Devachen, the Paradise of Opame (Amitābha, 'Boundless Light'), while his skilful manipulation of the gods and spirits assures his prosperity and worldly success. Expressed in this way, the distinction between secular and spiritual aims is perhaps too clear cut, and does not adequately take into account those acts of worship directed to such divinities as Pawa Cheresi (Avalokiteśvara) which aim specifically at the elimination of sins and the acquisition of religious merit. Rites such as the Niungne (cf. p. 180), though relating to personal beings, are certainly not thought of as furthering worldly purposes, but as increasing the religious merit of the participants.

MERIT AND SIN

The examination of the idea of 'merit' (*sönam*)[1] is the obvious point of departure for an analysis of Sherpa morality. Sherpas believe that every act of virtue (*gewa*) adds to an individual's store of *sönam*, whereas every morally negative action or 'sin' (*digba*) decreases this store. Addition and subtraction of *sönam* are thought of in more or less mechanical terms. Throughout a man's or woman's life, good and bad deeds make their marks on the person's record sheet, and this process is imagined as the action of two anthropomorphic beings, believed to be born with every individual and sitting invisibly on his right and left shoulder. The former, known as *lhen-cig-kye-wai-lha*, is the person's good genius who marks every deed of virtue with a white mark, while the latter, known as *lhen-cig-kye-wai-dre*, is his evil genius, who strives to lead a man along a downward path and marks every sin with a black sign.

At a man's death the account is made and the balance of white or black marks determines his fate in the next world. It is therefore everybody's endeavour to accumulate as much *sönam* as possible, and to avoid actions likely to diminish the stored-up merit. Moral prescriptions may thus be seen as a guide to the acquisition of *sönam*, and the acts they enjoin are teleological in character. Yet unlike the object of socially approved conduct in the ideologies of many less sophisticated tribal societies, the desired end-state of Sherpa ideology is not this-worldly but clearly transcendental. There is no promise of well-being and prosperity in this life as the result of *sönam*-gaining actions, but the promise of bliss or release in the world beyond.

Closely linked with the idea of rewards and retributions in the world beyond is the concept of reincarnation. This concept, basic to much of Hindu religious thought, is not peculiar to the Sherpas or even to Tibetans in general but, unlike Hindus, the Buddhist Sherpas and Tibetans give social recognition to the belief in the reincarnation of individual persons and reincarnate lamas play a vital rôle in the religious system. Persons who have gained so much *sönam* that they would be entitled to the final release, or in Sherpa words to the entry into Devachen (Tib. *nub-p'yogs-bde-ba-can*, 'Paradise of the West'), a kind of super-paradise beyond the world

[1] The term *sönam* is used by lamas and others familiar with Tibetan texts; the equivalent in colloquial Sherpa is *pei*.

Values and Moral Concepts

of the six spheres, may return as reincarnate lamas to the position they held in their former life and, as they are supposed to retain all the knowledge gained in previous lives, they are attributed with a degree of sanctity far exceeding that of even the most devout person in his first life.

Morally positive acts, which add to a person's *sönam*, include conduct ranging from the building of religious monuments to small acts of kindness to animals. Unlike monotheistic religions, such as Christianity, the Sherpas' ideology does not provide a motive for moral acts comparable with such ideas as the 'love of God' or 'obedience to the commands of God'. Though the one supreme motive for leading a good life is in Sherpa eyes the wish to acquire *sönam*, this motive is not directly linked with a belief in a personal deity to whom man is responsible for his behaviour. Similarly 'sin' is not seen as an act which offends any particular deity, but as an offence against a moral order existing independently of any of the gods whom the Sherpas worship.

The nature of behaviour believed to produce *sönam* can be understood, however, from a list of acts described as meritorious by my Sherpa informants. Sherpas are usually not very systematic in enumerating such acts, but here I have grouped them into three main categories: religious and ritual acts, acts in relation to persons, and acts in relation to animals.

All prayer and the recitation of sacred scriptures fall into the first category. It is meritorious to read and recite any of the sacred books, as well as to pay others to recite them. Thus the 108 volumes of the Kangyur, kept in a village temple, are annually recited by lamas paid from a fund which the villagers raise by public subscription. All those subscribing derive merit from this reading of the scriptures, and there are many occasions when individuals or groups may commission recitations of that type. Different from the mere reciting of scriptures, is the performance of rites which, in addition to the recitation of the appropriate liturgical texts, involve the presentation of food offerings and butter lamps, and the playing of musical instruments. Thus an individual may employ lamas to perform a *songu-tongu* which resembles, in outward form and the shape of the appropriate *torma*, the *shetu* rite (cf. p. 238), though this rite is not for the benefit of deceased kinsmen, but in order to obtain merit for the person commissioning the performance. Similarly a *tsho* rite may be performed for the same purpose, and such a rite is held either on the 15th, 25th or 30th day of the month. These are auspicious days when sins should be avoided and meritorious acts are particularly efficacious.

Minor religious practices productive of *sönam* are the burning of lamps and incense either in a *gomba* or a private chapel (*lhang*), the offering of water on one's house-altar, as well as the turning of prayer-wheels and the circumambulation of religious monuments.

The construction of *mani*-walls and *chörten*, even more than their circumambulation, is a source of great merit for those commissioning the work. The Sherpa country is full of *mani*-walls, bearing stone tablets with engravings of the sacred formula *om mani padme hum*, and of rock inscriptions containing this and other sacred formulae. The *sönam* produced by their construction or carving goes to the person who paid for the work, and not to the workmen or the artisan. Monks will sometimes carve rock inscriptions on speculation, and then 'sell' them to whoever wishes to acquire the *sönam* created by the carving. Similarly the building of bridges and rest-houses, benefiting countless travellers, is considered meritorious work of high order. In 1957 Gelung Ngawang, an old lama of high reputation, who had left Tengboche monastery and lived in a hermitage high above Dingboche, was collecting funds for the construction of rest-houses along the route across the Nangpa La, and it was common knowledge that he did this work in order to atone for his liaison with a nun, on whose account he had departed from Tengboche, the monastery whose acting head he had been throughout the infancy of the reincarnate abbot.

The construction of bridges and rest-houses, meritorious because of their benefit to the whole community, leads to the category of merit-producing acts which relate to interpersonal relations. All kinds of charity produce *sönam*. Gifts to lamas, whether they are in need of them or not, as well as alms to the poor result in the gain of *sönam* by the giver. It is particularly meritorious to feed those lacking food, and to clothe those inadequately clad. On the occasion of religious festivals wealthy people distribute food and drink in the expectation of gaining *sönam*.

It is considered meritorious to act as peace-maker. Many quarrels are settled by persons without official status, who far from deriving

Values and Moral Concepts

any profit from their activities in the interest of social harmony, incur considerable expense in providing the drink necessary to bring the parties together. What they gain is *sönam* and social approval. It is significant that Sherpas admire a skilful mediator and man of peace more than a 'strong' man. Their ideal is not the heroic personality, but the wise, restrained and mild man.

This emphasis on the virtue of mildness is particularly apparent in the Sherpas' attitude to animals. Acts of kindness to animals are a source of *sönam*, and I was told specifically that a person about to hit a dog or a cat, which has stolen meat or butter, may pause and let the animal get away with its ill-gotten gains for the sake of acquiring *sönam*.

These examples of *sönam*-producing actions reflect the type of conduct considered ideal for laymen. The members of monastic communities have additional means of acquiring *sönam*, not the least important of which is the voluntary renunciation of sex and family life.

The injunctions of a moral code are usually matched by corresponding interdictions, and one might well assume that the actions regarded by the Sherpas as 'sin' can also be divided into three major categories. It seems, however, that at least in the consciousness of the majority of Sherpas—and I have no material on the attitude of the more sophisticated and learned clerics—there is no concept of a 'sin' outside the sphere of personal relations and the relations of man to other animate beings. In other words, the wide range of religious and ritual acts producing *sönam* is not matched by sins relating to purely religious and ritual realities and not involving other human beings. The Sherpa layman is not conscious of the possibility of committing a 'sin' by offending any of the numerous divinities he worships and it would seem that even a neglect of their cult is interpreted as forgoing an opportunity of acquiring *sönam* rather than as a breach of the moral code. In the case of monks and nuns the position is different in so far as a violation of their vows of chastity is clearly described as sin. For them sexual congress is sinful, quite irrespective of the status of the other partner, and their action is not judged according to the rules regulating conduct between persons. The monk who consorts with an unmarried woman sins only because he breaks his vows of celibacy, and his partner sins because she causes him to sin. Were he not bound by his vow, sexual relations between the two persons concerned would be considered morally neutral.

The problem arises therefore whether the behaviour of the unchaste monk is wrong, simply because it violates an undertaking freely contracted, or whether it is sin because it offends any higher power. The question posed in this form can probably not be answered because Sherpas view morality not in relation to any personal legislator and upholder of a moral code, but against the background of an impersonal moral order. And according to this order the breach of a vow is 'sin', irrespective of whether any harm is done to another person.

Most of the actions considered 'sins', however, concern the relations between individuals and result, in particular, from any infringement of the rights or dignity of another person. The way in which Sherpas view such infringements is demonstrated by the following list of sins enumerated spontaneously by one of my lay informants:

1. All quarrelling is sin.
2. To steal is sin.
3. To cheat in trade is sin.
4. To talk ill of someone behind his back is sin, particularly if what one tells about him is not true.
5. To kill any living creature is sin. If someone kills a cat he commits so great a sin that he cannot make up for it even by burning as many butter lamps as the cat had hairs on its body. To kill yak and sheep is sin, even for the butchers, but not for those who buy the meat.
6. To have sexual relations with another person's spouse is sin.
7. To have sexual relations with a nun is sin, because the man involved contributes to the sin committed by the nun.
8. To threaten children or make them cry is sin, whatever the reason.
9. To marry a girl who is unwilling is sin both for the husband and for her parents, who arranged for the marriage.
10. To hit any animal is sin.
11. To fell trees is sin, though on occasion it is inevitable; even to pluck flowers is sin, and it is sinful to set fire to the forest.
12. For a monk it is a sin to drink too much and get intoxicated.

13. To cause a spirit long associated with a locality to be driven out is sin for the person who commissions the exorcizing, but not for the lamas who execute it.

This list, though by no means systematic, is illuminating in so far as it reflects the ideas which arise in a Sherpa's mind when he thinks about sin. A more complete list, compiled from the statements of all my informants, would cover several pages, but without substantially adding to our understanding of what Sherpas consider wrong and morally reprehensible. A characteristic feature of Sherpa morality is the idea that certain types of sin cannot be avoided, but that those who commit such sins make up for the loss of *sönam* by undertaking meritorious works. Thus yak-breeders have to castrate their yak-bulls, though it is sinful to inflict pain on animals, and it is necessary to fell trees even though plant life cannot be destroyed without incurring sin. The Sherpa overcomes this discrepancy between the desirable and the possible by comforting himself with the idea that good works can outweigh such minor sins. Perhaps it is this emphasis on the balance of merit remaining after all evil actions have set off by good works which takes the sting out of the distaste of such avoidable sins as adultery. For if all sins can be outweighed by good actions and a layman cannot lead the normal life of a farmer without committing a certain number of sins, there is no overwhelming incentive to avoid some of the more pleasurable sins. For these too will simply be added to the sum of sins which can be cancelled out by a somewhat larger sum of good works. The idea of this perpetual adding and subtracting from a balance of *sönam* is totally different from the dramatic contrast between the states of grace and mortal sin of Christian theology. Though Sherpas are often conscious of having committed sins and will engage in such ritual practices as the Niungne in order to cancel them out, I do not think that any Sherpa ever experiences a 'state of sin' in a sense comparable to the Christian concept of a loss of grace. Just as the belief in an unending chain of existences deprives the individual's fate after this life of the quality of finality, so the idea of a somewhat mechanical balancing of merit and demerit results in a view of sins as entries on the debit side of a ledger rather than as dramatic outrages against an accepted moral order.

There are many actions, moreover, which although socially

undesirable, do not fall within the category of sin. Moral and social evaluations do not by any means coincide. Thus it is sin to have sexual relations with a nun, but for the man concerned this offence has no adverse social consequences. On the other hand, it is *not* sin for an unmarried man to sleep with an unmarried girl of inferior, i.e. *khamendeu*, status, but persistence in the relationship deprives a man of his own superior status, and he sinks to that of the girl concerned. While it is sin to marry an unwilling girl, and even graver sin to impose sexual relations on her, no adverse social consequences result from such an arranged marriage, except of course the likelihood of its early break-up.

The consideration shown for a girl's wishes reflects the exceptionally high regard for the dignity and independence of the individual personality. Any action encroaching forcibly on this independence of another person is considered sin. Respect for the independence of the individual is expressed also in the attitude to those known to have committed sins. Their actions are held to be their own affair, and no public notice is taken of what is recognized as a violation of the moral code. In the village of Khumjung there were an ex-monk and an ex-nun who had left Tengboche and Devuche and lived as man and wife, farming the land the ex-monk had inherited from his father. Though my informants were unanimous in describing the violation of their vows of celibacy as sinful, they said that this was a matter of no concern to the villagers. The offending couple might suffer in the next world, but there was no reason why the neighbours should object. Indeed there were no signs of any cold-shouldering of the couple by other members of the village community, and when I asked whether they would be asked to weddings, my informants vigorously discounted any likelihood of discrimination, insisting that it would be uncharitable and wrong to hurt their feelings.

This attitude brings out the difference between 'sins', which result in a diminishment of the offender's store of *sönam* and may expose him to retribution in the next world, and civic offences, which may not reduce a person's *sönam*, but affect the interests of the community and are therefore punished by the elected village officials. Such morally neutral but socially reprehensible acts are violations of the rules regulating the use of grazing grounds or of publicly owned forest reserves. The Sherpas' attitude in these matters is perhaps comparable with a European's view of parking offences or the evasion of customs duty, which only those with the most tender conscience will regard as sins.

The whole sphere of sexual behaviour, which among all the Hindu communities of Nepal is rigidly controlled by numerous interdictions, is according to Sherpa ideology only partly subject to ethical ordinances. Basic to the Sherpas' attitude to sex is the view that sexual relations between those bound neither by marriage ties nor monastic vows are morally neutral. Sexual intercourse of such persons is neither considered 'sin' nor is it socially disapproved of. Even a girl already formally betrothed may sleep with unmarried men other than her fiancé, and such behaviour arouses no unfavourable comment. The pregnancy of an unmarried woman may be an economic embarrassment, but does not subject her to either social or supernatural sanctions.

Neither a sense of 'sin' nor a sense of 'shame' attaches to premarital sexual relations, and even extra-marital relations do not provoke severe condemnation on the part of society. No doubt adultery is considered 'sin', but it is a sin far less serious than say the killing of a cat, and its detection does not expose those concerned to strong social disapproval. Even the deceived spouse can be placated by a small payment or perhaps only the presentation of a bottle of beer or liquor offered together with the offender's apology.

There is no feeling that adultery offends any supernatural being or exposes the perpetrators, or even the whole community, to any specific danger. The idea widespread among Indian populations that certain breaches of the moral code draw disaster upon the heads of the offenders as well as the community to which they belong finds no echo among the Sherpas.

In sharp contrast to the tolerant attitude towards lapses in marital fidelity, is the uncompromising condemnation of clan incest. Sexual congress between members of the same clan, irrespective of their marital status, is considered a crime and my Sherpa informants were unanimous in the affirmation that a couple guilty of such incest would not be tolerated in the village. None of them remembered an actual instance, but they thought that in the event of a case occurring the offenders would be bound and delivered to the Government court for trial. In the absence of specific cases, I omitted to inquire whether incest is considered a sin as well as an offence against society, but none of my informants mentioned it when enumerating the various types of sinful behaviour.

Indeed there are some indications that transgressions of the moral code which incur retributions in the world beyond are not considered subject to social sanctions, whereas morally neutral but socially undesirable behaviour may have to be checked by secular punishments. Just as Evans-Pritchard found among the Nuer tribes that sins do not arouse indignation[1] the Sherpas are not indignant about adultery or the killing of animals, punished no doubt in the next world, but reserve their indignation for such acts as the flaunting of an order of the village assembly or a breach of the custom of clan exogamy.

We may then conclude that certain actions, such as incest, are prohibited, because they arouse social disapproval, while others are interdicted and considered 'sin' because they result in a loss of *sönam* and possibly punishment in the world beyond. The idea, so widely current in other religions, that violations of the moral code or tribal custom may entail immediate retribution in the form of sickness or other disaster is not a part of Sherpa belief.

Sickness and other misfortune is often attributed to ghosts, house-deities and evil spirits, who have been offended by the actions of the persons concerned, but the actions which cause offence are usually trivial and lacking in ethical aspects. In order to avert the spirits' unwanted attention and cure the sickness, it is necessary to placate them with offerings, but the question of avoiding morally negative acts is usually not involved.

The idea of contagious pollution, which occupies a position of cardinal importance in Hindu social ideology, is virtually absent among Sherpas. There is no suggestion that a grave sin or social offence could debase the ritual and social status of the perpetrator to such an extent that contact with him or her would spread the corruption to persons unconnected and innocent of the original offence.

The Sherpas, who believe that every human action will find its own reward in the world beyond, do not think of immoral behaviour in terms of change or loss of status. The locus of all sanctions imposed on those who sin lies outside the human sphere, and a man's kinsmen and co-villagers do not arrogate to themselves the right to forestall this transcendental judgement.

[1] *Nuer Religion*, Oxford, 1956, p. 189.

Values and Moral Concepts

Another vital feature of Sherpa ideology is the equation of knowledge and virtue. The greater a lama's learning, the greater is his claim to sanctity, for Sherpas believe that an intellectual grasp of the true doctrine will normally result in virtuous behaviour. They emphasize, however, that in relation to the eternal order a pure heart is more important that all knowledge of scriptures and the lavish performance of rites and ceremonies. The most elaborate and costly rites do not serve any purpose if performed for the benefit of those lacking purity of heart, the most essential of all qualifications for the gain of *sönam*. This purity of heart manifests itself in charity and kindliness towards all living beings, and it is the charitable, mild and tolerant person whom Sherpas admire. Even wealth is conducive to social prestige mainly when it is given away in charity or spent on religious works. Not the possession, but the generous disposal of riches is an object of admiration and social approval.

There is a certain analogy between the approved disposal of wealth and the ideal use of an accumulation of *sönam*. While a rich man is expected to distribute, on occasions such as a funeral feast for a deceased parent or wife, large portions of his wealth to lamas and the general population, a saintly lama possessing a store of *sönam* which would enable him to attain the paradise of Devachen may forgo the immediate attainment of bliss and place his *sönam*, wisdom and own personality at the disposal of humanity by consenting to be reincarnated. The free and joyous employment of resources, material in the one and spiritual in the other case, for the benefit of others, characterizes the ideal attitude to fellow human beings, and it is this model attitude which accounts for so many aspects of Sherpa social behaviour.

THE IDEA OF THE GOOD LIFE

The acquisition of wealth and its proper utilization are basic to the average Sherpa's idea of the good life. The instinct of traders is evident in most Sherpas, even in those villages not greatly engaged in trade, and men and women, no less than half-grown boys and girls, seldom miss a chance when there is the opportunity to engage in some petty transaction or to sell their services for wages. This eagerness for gain has made it possible to recruit large numbers of porters for mountaineering expeditions, and it accounts for the Sherpas' unceasing and strenuous efforts to keep moving the flow of goods along one of the world's highest trade-routes, namely the track running from Namche Bazar to Tingri over the Nangpa La. Not only the trader but equally the cattle-breeder is motivated by the incentive to make profits. He does not think of his yak mainly as a source of dairy produce and meat, but counts on a cash income resulting from the sale of calves. This attitude is far removed from that of the primitive subsistence farmer even though in fact many Sherpas do maintain themselves by subsistence farming. Most men aspire, however, to the acquisition of sufficient wealth to permit also some participation in trading operations.

What the Sherpa values is not so much the material comfort which riches can buy, but the prestige derived from the possession and expenditure of wealth. The rich, no doubt, possess better houses than people of modest means, and on many occasions they eat superior food and can afford more and better drink. Yet, many wealthy men spend weeks and months on high pastures with their yak-herds living as frugally and in as much discomfort as many a poor man. Similarly on trading journeys they cheerfully put up with many hardships, and when camping without shelter on the roadside rich and poor suffer in much the same way from the cold and other hazards of an inclement climate.

Where the rich man scores over his poorer neighbour is in the sphere of activities directed mainly towards the gain of prestige. Sherpas enjoy dispensing hospitality, and only the rich can afford to entertain many visitors with tea and alcoholic drink, and to ask their friends frequently to a substantial meal. By lavish hospitality and particularly the feeding of lamas on the occasion of rites and ceremonies, they build up a reputation of open-handed generosity. In the great memorial feasts for deceased relatives this trend to ostentatious expenditure of wealth reaches its climax, and a man may virtually impoverish himself in order to gain the honour of having dispensed extravagant hospitality.

Similar liberality is shown in gifts to lamas and monasteries. A wealthy man may take on the restoration or decoration of a temple, and spend a great part of his liquid resources on such an enterprise. Generosity in the service of religion outshines in Sherpa eyes most other virtues, and covers a multitude of sins. One of the most respected women of Khumbu was Ngawang Samde, the sister of the *pembu* Ang Chunbi of Kunde. This attractive and spirited lady, who at the time of my visit lived with her seventh husband in a small house high above Pangboche, had at one time been a nun in Devuche. Despite her eventful marital career and the fact that several of her husbands were ex-monks who had returned to secular life on her account, she enjoyed the reputation of great piety, and continued to be a frequent and welcome visitor in the house of the abbess of Devuche. This reputation was due to her great expenditure of wealth on religious works. Her talent as a trader had enabled her to pay for the construction of *mani*-walls, the decoration of the temple of Pangboche, extensive pilgrimages to holy places in Tibet, and innumerable other activities of religious merit. To the average Sherpa such a life seemed far more commendable than the monotonous existence of the average virtuous housewife, absorbed in domestic duties. The genuineness of Ngawang Samde's devotion can be judged by the fact that in 1957 she and her much younger ex-monk husband had embarked on a two-year period of retreat and spiritual exercises. While in the first year the husband did not leave their isolated residence, and she maintained connections with the outside world, in the next year the rôles were to be changed and Ngawang Samde then intended to observe a year's retreat, while her husband would provide for their material needs.

Second only to the prestige and admiration gained by generosity in the expenditure of wealth is the value placed on courtesy, gentleness and a spirit of compromise and peacefulness. The Sherpa does not admire the strong and ruthless man, though it cannot be denied that there are examples of strong men gaining considerable influence and of using the office of *pembu* or their position as *sirdar* of a big mountaineering expedition to exploit their fellow villagers. The whole system of village government with its insistence on the allotment of office in rotation is designed to curb such tendencies, and the annual selection of village officials by informal consultation assures that reasonable and considerate people rather than aggressive personalities are placed in positions of authority. More than anyone else it is the peace-maker who gains social esteem and approval as well as religious merit. In most villages there are one or two men known as *pharkimi* or mediators. They do not hold an official position, but when a quarrel arises and the persons involved are too angry or too proud to make up their differences by themselves, a *pharkimi* is likely to approach them and to work for a reconciliation. The usual way of achieving this is to invite the two opponents to the *pharkimi*'s house and to provide beer or liquor for a party. This, however, is done only after the mediator has succeeded in persuading them to adopt a somewhat conciliatory attitude. The person who is either much junior or was clearly in the wrong, has to offer *yangdzi*, i.e. a drink offered with an apology (cf. p. 82), to the person whom he has offended, and there is frequently also an exchange of presentation scarves. The *pharkimi* derives no profit from the proceedings except for social prestige and the good will of the parties concerned, and he usually bears some of the expense of the drinks.

Sometimes reconciliation parties are given with the intention of ending more than one quarrel. In Khumjung I once attended such a party held in the house of Pasang Sona, commonly known as Mendoa, as he was the leading member of the Mende clan. The purpose was to bring to an end three quarrels which were disturbing the harmony of the community, particularly as the men involved were all of some prominence. One of the senior lamas, Sharap Lama, had quarrelled in public with Ang Chiri, who some years previously had been engaged to the lama's daughter; the *pembu* Ang Chunbi of Kunde had had a minor brush with Kapa Kalden, the famous painter; and the latter had quarrelled with Lama Karma, when both had been drunk at the time of the Yer-chang celebrations.

Pasang Sona, though a popular and extremely wealthy man, had failed in his first attempt to reconcile the parties, and he therefore asked for the support of Dawa Tenzing, a famous mountaineering *sirdar*, and Ngawang Gombu, one of the more regular *pharkimi*. Together these three men provided beer and liquor, and finally induced the men involved in the recent quarrels to attend the party in Pasang Sona's house. Under the influence of the mediator's persuasion they finally agreed to make up their quarrels. Ang Chiri offered *yangdzi* and apologized to Sharap Lama for having kicked him in a tussle, though he privately maintained that Sharap Lama had gone out of his way to start the quarrel. But Ang Chiri was so much junior to the respected old lama that there was no question of the lama apologizing to him. The position of seniority was not as clear in the quarrel between Ang Chunbi and Kapa Kalden, as both were middle-aged and extremely respected men, but in the end the painter agreed to offer *yangdzi* to Ang Chunbi, while in turn Lama Karma offered *yangdzi* to Kapa Kalden.

As soon as these formalities were over, the atmosphere became relaxed and indeed extremely jolly. A great deal of liquor and beer was consumed and when supplies ran low Ngawang Gombu collected money from all those present for the purchase of more drink. At such a party, which is held for the public good, it is quite usual to collect contributions for the purchase of more drink. Even when everyone was fairly drunk, the women continued to press more drink on the guests, singing and dancing before each person as they offered cups of beer and liquor. Particularly Dawa Tenzing, who had recently lost his wife, was offered drink by all those present, everybody begging him to cheer up and forget his loss and sorrow. Finally scarves were offered to the three promoters of the function, and the party ended in an atmosphere of general jollity and good will. By that time Dawa Tenzing and Ngawang Gombu had already passed out and were lying unconscious on the window-bench.

The party was considered a great success and the villagers felt relieved that thanks to the mediators' initiative an end had been put to the open frictions between some of the community's leading men.

Pharkimi may act in the interest of peace and tranquillity even when a quarrel breaks out among people not normally resident in the village. Once a dispute arose between two Tibetan butchers, both of whom had come to Khumjung to sell meat. Jealousy over their customers was the root of their quarrel, but rather than let them fight it out, Dorje Ngungdu, who though not wealthy often acted as *pharkimi*, bought a bottle of liquor and inviting the two butchers for a drink settled their quarrel. Such a spirit of altruistic helpfulness is greatly valued and finds its intangible reward in the popularity of a successful *pharkimi*.

The sentiments of tolerance and consideration for the interests and feelings of others, which are central to Sherpa morality, find their outward expression in courtesy and good manners. Great emphasis is placed on the graces of conduct, and every visit to a Sherpa house is an occasion for the display of an elaborate etiquette. While Sherpas are very free in verbal expressions and a male visitor may joke with his hostess in a manner which in many other societies would be considered outrageous, both hostess and visitor will seldom fail to maintain the strictest etiquette in the serving and acceptance of drink. It is essential that the hostess should refill his cup at least twice, and the guest accepts this with only faint gestures of refusal.

But when she tries to fill his cup again, he has to protest vigorously and the game of pressing tea or liquor on an ostensibly reluctant guest, who seems to yield only under pressure, is continued for a long time.

Etiquette also determines the order of seating, and at any larger gathering in a private house, there is a continuous reshuffling, as people give up their seats to those of greater seniority. The place of honour is the one next to the host, who sits immediately next to the fireplace. Other prominent guests sit in strict order of precedence on the same bench along the window, while those more junior may sit on the floor, and women always sit on the floor near the hearth. An order of precedence is maintained also in the seating on the benches of the *gomba*, and this order which in each village seems to be well established is based on the factors of age, wealth, public office and family status. Except for lamas, who usually take precedence over laymen, men of Khamba origin seldom rank high in the order of precedence, and in Khumjung, for instance, the first places open to laymen are taken up by the members of a few well-established and wealthy Sherpa families. Among these age and personal prestige determine the precise rank of each individual.

Yet, the etiquette regulating personal relations works so smoothly and unobtrusively, that status differences are not unduly emphasized, and there prevails a general atmosphere of equality in which the powerful and the poor mix on easy terms. The overbearing behaviour of a high-caste Hindu landlord or merchant vis-à-vis his inferiors, would be unimaginable in Khumbu society, where the richest and most influential man speaks to a poor fellow villager as to a social equal. While lamas of high spiritual prestige are treated with deep respect, and even old men will prostrate themselves before a reincarnate lama, in ordinary conversation lamas do not adopt a tone of superiority and laymen will speak to them freely and jokingly without a display of excessive humbleness. Similarly men and women talk to each other freely and without any inhibitions. A Sherpa wife, however young and attractive, will unhesitatingly entertain male visitors in the absence of her husband, for the demands of hospitality and courtesy to guests impose on a woman the same obligations as on a man.

In a society where individuals follow a number of different callings, it is not easy to generalize about the ideal of a good life.

The yak-breeder spending months on end with his herds close to the eternal snows obviously has tastes and aspirations different from those of the trader familiar with the life in a number of Tibetan towns. Common to all Sherpa laymen would seem to be the ideal of occupying a respected and secure place within a closely knit community of fellow villagers, who co-operate in the control of natural resources and the manifold ritual activities designed to protect them against supernatural dangers. Sherpas are sociable and uninhibited people, who greatly enjoy the pleasures of conviviality and abandon themselves whole-heartedly to the thrills of dancing and choral singing. Even middle-aged men and women will dance until late into the night, and during the limited periods when all the villagers are collected in the main settlement, friends and neighbours frequently entertain each other in their houses, arrange open-air picnics known as *kiki-tongu*, or pool their resources to provide the drink for dance-parties held in the one or other of the bigger houses. All these social activities, which have no parallels in the Hindu villages of Nepal, reflect the intense pleasure the average Sherpa takes in the company of his fellow men. To be popular among them is hence of vital importance to a person's happiness, and social success is an essential aspect of the good life.

The warmth and cordiality which pervades the relations between friends and fellow villagers is intensified among close kinsmen, and the atmosphere in the average Sherpa home is one of relaxed and affectionate cheerfulness. Relations between husbands and wives are usually amicable and based on mutual tolerance, for those of incompatible temperaments have little incentive to stay together. The ideal of the good marriage is not a unique relationship emotionally so highly charged that its persistence stands and falls with the preservation of absolute exclusiveness, but rather a stable and secure union based on affection and common interests, in which both spouses are tolerant enough to overlook a casual lapse in the partner's fidelity. There is an emphasis on broad-mindedness and tolerance rather than on passionate possessiveness, and the disinterest in exclusiveness in sexual relations provides an explanation for the success of polyandrous marriages.

Tolerance and an innate respect for the individual determines also the attitude of parents to their children. Sherpa parents are seldom domineering and even half-grown children enjoy a high degree of independence. Their elders expect them to act responsibly and often entrust them with tasks demanding perseverance and initiative.

While harmonious relations with members of his family, kinsmen and fellow villagers are in Sherpa eyes the one main facet of the good life, the gaining of religious merit is the other. In the background of all worldly desires and aspirations which the average Sherpa pursues with zest and a remarkable *joie de vivre* there is the deep-seated conviction that ultimate happiness can be gained only by the acquisition of merit and the concentration on other worldly realities. Minor religious practices productive of merit are part of everyday life, and most Sherpas expect that with advancing age they will be able to devote more and more time to prayer, the turning of prayer-wheels and the circumambulation of *mani*-walls and *chörten*. Old men and women turning small silver or copper prayer-wheels and making their rounds of religious monuments are a common sight, and some retire for the last years of their life to the tranquil atmosphere of a monastery or nunnery even though they retain their status as laymen. To the Sherpas this is the ideal ending of a fulfilled life, and the best possible preparation for the next incarnation.

Basic to their world-view is the idea of the individual as a free moral agent, responsible for his actions and capable of moulding his fate in the next life. Unlike the Hindu, the Buddhist Sherpa does not consider himself primarily as the member of a kin- or caste-group, whose ritual status is insolubly linked up with that of the other members of the group. Just as a Sherpa's sins or breaches of rules do not affect the status of others, so he is not subject to pollution or other loss of status through the actions of his spouse, children or kinsmen. There is no group responsibility comparable with that of a Hindu family or caste-group, and every individual stands for himself in his quest for the perfection, however inadequately realized, which will assure his welfare in future existences. And among all the virtues which help a man or woman to gain this mental perfection there is in Sherpa eyes none greater than the virtue of compassion with all living-beings.

Appendix

*Kinship Terms of Reference
as used by the Sherpas of Khumbu*[1]

ava	father
ava gaka	father's father mother's father
ama	mother
ama gaka	mother's mother father's mother
au	father's brother (elder and younger) mother's sister's husband
ajang (ashang)	mother's brother (elder and younger)
ani	father's sister (elder and younger) mother's brother's wife husband's younger sister
uru	mother's sister mother's brother's daughter wife's younger sister (as term of address only)
ajo	elder brother father's brother's son (younger than speaker) husband's sister's husband
nu	younger brother father's brother's son (younger than speaker)

[1] The Sherpas of Solu use, for some relationships, slightly different terms; 'father', for instance, is *papha* and 'grandfather', *pagava*.

shangbu	mother's brother's son
tsabyuk	father's sister's son brother's son (man speaking) sister's son (woman speaking)
mau (mapu)	mother's sister's son
aji	elder sister father's brother's daughter (older than speaker) wife's brother's wife
num	younger sister father's brother's daughter (younger than speaker)
tsabyung	father's sister's daughter brother's daughter (woman speaking) sister's daughter (man speaking)
mawin (mapin)	mother's sister's daughter
phujung	son brother's son (man speaking) sister's son (woman speaking)
phum	daughter brother's daughter (man speaking) sister's daughter (woman speaking)
tsau	father's sister's husband sister's husband sister's daughter's husband collective term for daughter's husband's kinsmen
tsevgo (tseto)	wife's sister's husband
tsevgom	brother's wife
khye-gha	husband
chermo; jomo	wife
chirma	junior wife

mem	husband's father
	wife's father
	husband's elder brother
	wife's elder brother
iwi	husband's mother
	wife's mother
	wife's elder sister
	husband's elder sister
yaku	husband's younger brother
	collective term for husband's younger kinsmen
niermu	wife's younger sister
tsam	son's wife
	brother's wife
makba	daughter's husband
nati (Nepalese)[1]	son's son
	daughter's son
	son's daughter
	daughter's daughter
samdhi (Nepalese)[2]	son's wife's father
	daughter's husband's father

[1] There is no Sherpa term for 'grandchild' and Sherpas use the Nepalese word *nati* rather than the Tibetan *tsau* (grandson) and *tsamu* (granddaughter).

[2] There is no Sherpa term for this relationship and Sherpas use the Nepalese word *samdhi*: the Tibetan term is *nien*.

Bibliography

BAGOT, J. *Representations Théatrales dans les Monastères du Tibet*, Les Classiques de l'Orient. Paris. *1921*

EVANS-PRITCHARD, E. E. *Nuer Religion*. Oxford. Clarendon Press. *1956*

EVANS-WENTZ, W. Y. *The Tibetan Book of the Dead: or the After-death Experiences on the Bardo Plane, according to Lama Kazi Dawa-Samdup's English Rendering*. Oxford University Press. *1957*

FÜRER-HAIMENDORF, Christoph von. The After-Life in Indian Tribal Belief. *Journal of the Royal Anthropological Institute*. Vol. 83. pp. 37-49. *1953*
Pre-Buddhist Elements in Sherpa Belief and Ritual. *Man*. Vol. 55. No. 61. *1955*
Ethnographic Notes on the Tamangs of Nepal. *Eastern Anthropologist*. Vol. 9. pp. 166-77. *1955-1956*
The Economy of the Sherpas of Khumbu. *Die Wiener Schule der Völkerkunde. Festschrift anlässlich des 25-Jährigen Bestandes des Institutes für Völkerkunde der Universität Wien (1929-1954)*. Vienna. Institut für Völkerkunde, University of Vienna. pp. 261-280. *1956*
Moral Concepts in Three Himalayan Societies. *Indian Anthropology*. Edited by T. N. Madan and Gopala Sarana. London. Asia Publishing House. pp. 179-209. *1962*
The Sherpas of the Khumbu Region. *Mount Everest. Formation, Population and Exploration of the Everest Region*. By Toni Hagen, G. O. Dhyrenfurth, C. von Fürer-Haimendorf and E. Schneider. Oxford University Press. pp. 124-181. *1963*

HOOKER, Sir Joseph Dalton. *Himalayan Journals*. London, Ward, Lock & Co. *1905*

NEBESKY-WOJKOWITZ, René von. *Oracles and Demons of Tibet. The Cult and Iconography of the Tibetan Protective Deities.* The Hague. Mouton & Co. *1956*

RIBBACH, S. R. *Drogpa Namgyel. Ein Tibeterleben.* (With a Chapter on Death Customs by Josef Gergan.) Munich. Barth. *1940*

SNELLGROVE, David. *Buddhist Himalaya: Travels and Studies in Quest of the Origins and Nature of Tibetan Religion.* Oxford. Cassirer. *1957*
Himalayan Pilgrimage. Oxford. Cassirer. *1961*

STEIN, R. A. *La civilisation tibétaine.* (Collection Sigma dirigée par Henri Hierche 1.) Paris. Dunod. *1962*

WADDELL, L. A. *The Buddhism of Tibet or Lamaism.* London. W. H. Allen. *1895*

Index

Adultery, 55, 64, 68, 73, 82, 83, 276, 277, 287
Agriculture, 7–11, 85, 86, 105, 107, 108, 179
Amitābha (Opame), 237, 245, 251, 262, 271
Ancestor worship, 250
Animal husbandry, 11–13, 25, 84, 86, 105, 107, 108, 208, 277, 282
Artisans, 15–17, 29, 30, 32
Authority, 100, 101, 104, 106–8, 113, 114, 123, 125, 197, 199, 207, 283
Avalokiteśvara (Pawa Cheresi), 183, 209, 223, 236, 251, 271
Avoidance rules, 96

Bacot, J., 211
Betrothal, 41–58, 68, 75, 77, 85, 89, 95, 279
Bhotia, xix, 1, 2, 8, 13, 25, 34, 269
Blacksmith, 16
Bön religion, 211, 217, 218
Brahmans, 46, 126, 188
Buddhism, development in Khumbu, 10, 11, 126, 127, 173, 174

Caste society, 16, 26, 34, 36, 38
Celibacy, 129, 130, 132, 134, 138, 143, 149, 150, 170, 275, 278
Charity, 28, 243–5, 274, 281
Chetri, 27, 36, 37, 39, 46, 125
Children, 84–8, 97, 287
Chinese, 14, 27, 38, 61, 149
Chiwong monastery, 157–9, 174, 175
Chorpen, 22, 105, 113, 114, 188, 217, 221, 240

Chorumba, 105, 113, 114, 189, 196, 198, 204, 207
Clan (*ru*), 18–27, 47, 51, 62, 77, 79, 91, 92, 100, 101
Clan-gods, 21–3, 80, 209
Class differences, 16, 34–6, 44, 45, 125, 189, 249
Crafts, 15–17
Cremation, 111, 132, 227–34
Crops, 7–11, 107, 108, 180, 268
Cross-cousins, 47, 53

Dances, 40, 53, 62–4, 135, 202–4, 213–24, 287
Darjeeling, xv, 3, 4, 9, 21, 70
Death rites, 224–50
Dedication of animals, 209
Deities, 22, 23, 126, 151, 177, 195, 201, 203, 209, 220–3, 251, 260, 261, 269–71, 273
Devuche nunnery, 138, 139, 170, 278, 283
Diviner, *see* Soothsayer
Divorce, 67, 74–6, 283
Dolpo, 2, 5, 13
Dowry, 58–61, 66, 95, 97–9
Dress, 15, 16, 50, 61, 63
Dumje, 32, 33, 36, 82, 90, 114, 115, 152, 162, 165, 172, 185–208, 223

Economics, 7–17, 56, 67, 81, 138, 139, 146, 173, 174
Education, 84, 85, 137, 139
Eschatology, 156, 226, 228, 230, 233, 236, 238, 241, 245–9, 251, 252, 265, 271, 272, 281, 288
Etiquette, 96, 244, 285, 286

Evans-Pritchard, E. E., 280
Evans-Wentz, W. Y., 228, 245, 246
Exchange-marriage, 47, 48
Exogamy, 20, 21, 23, 40, 47, 91–3, 280
Exorcism, 178, 179, 252–4, 277

Family, 39, 40, 84
Female line, 20, 99
Fines, 64, 68, 82, 83, 104, 107–9, 111–14, 148
Forest, 111, 112
Forest guards, 105, 106, 110–12
Friendship ceremonial, 15, 48
Funerary rites, 80, 95, 98, 124, 224–50, 266

Gelugpa, 155
Ghosts, 265, 266, 269, 270
Gods, see Clan-gods and Deities
Gorkha, 1, 119
Government, 100, 104, 114, 117–23, 279, 283
Gurung, 13, 25, 26, 36, 37, 111, 118–20

Harvest, 8, 29, 107, 123, 152
Hay, 6, 210
Hermits, xvii, 126, 128, 130, 162, 163, 168, 182, 274
Hindus, xviii, 16, 78, 80, 86, 94, 96, 97, 99, 125, 126, 167, 272, 279, 280, 286–8
Hooker, Sir Joseph, 9
Hospitality, 53, 54, 60, 64, 242–5, 282

Illegitimacy, 41, 43, 52, 67, 75, 77, 88–94
Illness, 133, 165, 167, 225, 257–63, 268
Immigrants, 16, 18, 23, 27–38, 101, 102, 124, 187, 207
Incest, 20, 21, 279, 280
Inheritance, 20, 55, 60, 70, 78, 79, 86–8, 97–9, 138

Jealousy, 70, 73, 82, 263
Justice, 100, 104, 108, 111–13, 124, 149, 278, 279

Kangyur (Tibetan canon), 115, 116, 133, 170, 172, 184, 203, 225, 273
Khambas, 23–36, 44, 45, 66, 93, 101–4, 106, 124, 207
Khumbu, xiv, xvii, 2–16, 100
Khumbu-yülha, 22, 127, 129, 198, 209
King of the Dead (Shinje-chogyal), 195, 228, 246, 247
Kinship, 47, 77, 94–7, 137
Kinship terms, 289–91

Labour gang (*ngalok*), 8, 85
Lamas, 127–33, 145, 162–70
Law, 107
Levirate, 47, 55, 76
Lhachetu, 22, 23, 80, 186, 209
Limbu, 120
Lineage (*kalak*), 47, 77, 79, 80, 101–3, 124
Lo (Mustangbhot), 2, 13, 25
Lu, see Serpent spirits

Magic, 105, 127, 177, 180, 227
Mani-rimdu, 135, 210–24
Marriage, 32, 39–99, 162, 287
Mediator, 76, 90, 124, 274, 275, 283–5
Medicines, 261
Memorial rites, 150, 242–5, 248, 249, 266
Merit (*sönam, pei*), 83, 133, 139, 141, 156, 172, 173, 175, 182, 247, 272–81
Monasteries, 10, 11, 126–74
Monks, 69, 82, 93, 128–55, 162, 163, 169, 173, 212, 283
Morality, xviii, xix, 32, 40, 41, 82, 83, 271–88
Mortuary rites, *see* Funerary rites
Mourning, 230, 237, 238, 246
Murder, 121, 128, 143
Mystery plays, 211, 223

Name-card, 235, 236, 238
Name-giving, 93, 94
Nebesky-Wojkowitz, R. de, 202, 215, 217, 218, 220, 266, 269
Newar, 27, 34, 36, 37, 39, 94
Niungne, 150, 153, 180–5, 211, 224
Nuns, 72, 87, 134, 138, 139, 143, 150, 157–60, 170, 173, 174, 195, 204, 274, 278, 283
Nyingmapa, 135, 145, 175, 250, 269

Offerings, 142, 176, 178, 180, 184, 191, 198, 201, 209, 212, 215, 221, 222, 232–5, 246, 249
Osho rite, 105, 108, 179

Padmasambhava (Guru Rimpoche), 18, 171, 183, 209, 210, 216, 239, 251, 267, 270
Painting, 6, 16, 25, 152, 171, 172, 189
Patrilineal descent, 20, 26, 47, 80, 90
Pembu, 20, 21, 75, 77, 80, 87, 100, 107, 109, 117–25, 167, 199, 200, 207, 283
Pharak, 2, 3, 7, 14, 19, 20, 23, 46
Pilgrimage, 224, 283
Pollution, 16, 17, 34, 36, 91, 103, 125, 280, 288
Polyandry, 68–74, 180, 287
Polygyny, 68, 73
Possession, supernatural, 221, 224, 255, 259–61, 268, 269
Potatoes, 7–11, 28, 30, 108, 174
Prestige, 11, 14, 66, 108, 114, 116, 139, 140, 160, 223, 242, 248, 281–3, 286
Property, 39, 58–60, 67–9, 71, 74, 78–80, 86, 95, 97–9, 138, 139
Punishment, 111, 146, 148, 149, 197, 278, 280. *See also* Fines
Purification, 125, 180

Rai, 2, 13, 39
Rebirth, xviii, 235, 237, 249, 251, 252

Reciprocal obligations, 52, 59, 60, 64, 85, 94, 97
Refugees, Tibetan, 27, 28
Reincarnation, 127–9, 131–3, 145, 155–61, 249, 272, 281
Resa, 7, 84
Revenue, collection of, 100, 117–24
Ribbach, S. R., 42
Rotation of offices, 103, 109, 114, 115, 116, 178, 181, 186, 187, 204, 283

Sakyapa, 145
Scarves, ceremonial (*kata*), 51, 52, 55, 59, 62, 75, 77, 89, 94, 149, 204, 215, 284, 285
Serpent spirits (*lu*), 183, 194, 202, 203, 209, 235, 256, 264, 266–70
Sexual relations:
 extra-marital, 43, 73, 83, 92, 277, 279, 287
 pre-marital, 40, 41, 43, 44, 54, 71, 82, 83, 85, 279
Shamans, 256
Sin, 83, 180, 183, 223, 228, 235, 247, 252, 272–80, 288
Slaves, 35
Snellgrove, David, xiv, 129, 175, 215, 225, 269
Solu, xiii, 2, 3, 7, 11, 13, 14, 18–20, 23, 27, 126, 133, 135, 137, 155, 156, 174
Son-in-law, resident (*maksu*), 20, 78–80, 98, 99, 187
Soothsayer, 29, 254, 255, 262, 263
Spirit-medium (*lhawa*), 29, 33, 194, 224, 254–62
Spirits, malignant (*shrindi*), 105, 194, 195, 227, 237, 251–4, 256–260
Status differences, 31–6, 40, 44, 97, 103, 125, 189, 226, 249, 280, 286
Stein, R. A., 20

Tamang, 13, 36, 37, 39, 126
Taxes, 117–20
Teknonymy, 96

Temple (*gomba*), 108, 113–15, 127, 128, 130, 170–4, 182–4, 186, 192, 196–208
Tengboche monastery, xvii, 131–74, 182, 185, 200, 238, 240
Thak Khola, 2, 5, 13, 25
Thami monastery, 129, 130, 135, 145, 147, 211–22, 238
Thread-crosses, 253, 254
Tibet, Tibetans, xix, 1, 11, 13–16, 18, 23–34, 71, 92, 103, 104, 107, 121, 127–30, 143, 145, 147, 148, 154, 155, 211, 283
Torma (sacrificial cakes), 12, 114, 115, 151, 153, 175, 176, 180, 184, 189–92, 200, 201, 205, 239, 253
Trade, 13–15, 30, 31, 81, 104, 146, 152, 281, 282
Trakshindo monastery, 137, 145, 148, 149
Transport, 12–14, 81, 107
Travel, 13, 15, 28, 92, 147, 149

Underprivileged classes, 34–6, 45, 103, 125, 189, 248
Untouchability, 16, 103

Values, 271–88
Village, 5, 6, 100–25
Village meetings, 107, 123
Village officials, 105–13, 167, 179, 181, 207, 278
Vows, 40, 84, 130, 132, 133, 138, 140, 142, 143, 150

Waddell, L. A., 61, 211, 218, 220, 241, 248, 249
Wealth, 30, 45, 54, 59, 101, 103, 105, 123, 241, 281–3
Weaving, 15, 29, 30
Wedding, 44, 57–67, 75, 89, 95
Widows, 76, 77, 86–8, 109, 115, 186, 187, 196
Witches (*pem*), 256, 263–5
Women, position of, 58, 59, 80–4, 87, 98, 279, 287

Yak, 7, 8, 11–14, 22, 84, 86, 282, 287
Yelmu, 3
Yer-chang, 22, 23, 115, 162, 165, 208–10
Yersa, 6, 22, 185, 208, 210, 227
Yeti, 202